THE TURNING POINT

*Jefferson's Battle
for the Presidency*

THE TURNING POINT

Jefferson's Battle
for the Presidency

Frank van der Linden

Fulcrum Publishing
Golden, Colorado

Library of Congress Cataloging-in-Publication Data

Van der Linden, Frank.
    The turning point : Jefferson's battle for the Presidency / Frank van der Linden.
        p. cm.
    Originally published: Washington : R.B. Luce, [1962].
    Includes bibliographical references and index.
    ISBN 1-55591-015-7
        1. Presidents—United States—Election—1800. 2. Jefferson, Thomas, 1743–1826. 3. Burr, Aaron, 1756–1836. 4. United States—Politics and government—1797–1801. I. Title.
    E330.V3 2000
    324.973'044—dc21   00-034834

Printed in Canada
0 9 8 7 6 5 4 3 2 1

Cover design: Livers Lambert Design
Front cover portrait of Thomas Jefferson: The White House
    Collection, copyright © White House Historical Association
Front background image: Letter from Margaret Bayard to Samuel
    Harrison Smith, courtesy of the Library of
    Congress, Manuscript Division

Fulcrum Publishing
16100 Table Mountain Parkway, Suite 300
Golden, Colorado 80403
(800) 992-2908 • (303) 277-1623
www.fulcrum-books.com

To my wife, Lyn, and the memory
of my father and mother

PREFACE

Historians have delved into Thomas Jefferson's psyche, his private life, and his political record in great detail since *The Turning Point* first appeared in 1962, but they have not essentially changed the twin stories that are dramatically intertwined in this book.

The first is an account of the public battles and the secret intrigues that enabled Jefferson to win the presidency, but only after his enemies tried to steal it from him and hand the prize to his crafty running mate Aaron Burr. Before the House of Representatives finally broke the Jefferson–Burr deadlock on the thirty-sixth ballot in February 1801, the young Republic came dangerously close to civil war.

The second story is the true romance between Margaret Bayard, the daughter of a firm Federalist family, and Samuel Harrison Smith, a young Philadelphia newspaper editor and ardent friend of Jefferson. Margaret's cousin, James A. Bayard, a Federalist congressman from Delaware, cast the deciding vote for Jefferson.

I discovered the love letters of Margaret and Samuel in the Manuscript Division of the Library of Congress one October day in 1954. They are as fresh and new today as when they were written two centuries ago. In these sometimes passionate letters, the lovers tell, in their own words, the joys and sorrows of a courtship that led to their marriage in the fall of 1800.

Margaret grows from a frivolous teenager into a serious writer, with an inquiring mind that distinguishes her as an early and eloquent feminist. "Forget I am a woman," she orders her sweetheart in 1800. "Remember only that I have a mind. . . . I am every day less contented with the circumscribed and degraded situation to which our sex is condemned. ... I am for tearing away the veil of ignorance, which conceals from me the light of knowledge."

It has been a rewarding experience to read innumerable letters, diaries, journals, pamphlets, newspapers, and books in the Library of Congress, the Historical Society of Pennsylvania, the American Philosophical Society, and the public libraries of Washington, Philadelphia, New York, and New Brunswick, New Jersey. To the librarians who have been courteous and helpful, I express my thanks.

I am grateful to my dear wife, Lyn, who has encouraged me to complete the task of organizing the material into a readable narrative—and who has steadfastly inspired the completion of several other books that I have written in the ensuing years.

I appreciate the enthusiasm of Fulcrum publisher Robert Baron and his associate Mark Carroll, who agreed upon the idea of presenting a new edition of this classic, *The Turning Point.*

Some of the scenes may seem to be fiction, but they are not. All quotations are derived from authentic sources and identified in the notes at the end of the book. Wherever possible, I have let the actors in the drama speak for themselves. We hear their voices and see their faces, if only in our imaginations. Thus, in this book, these men and women who have made their exit from the stage of life return to us and live again.

CHAPTER ONE

D^AVID C. CLAYPOOLE, editor of the *American Daily Advertiser*, walked through Philadelphia's cobblestoned streets on Friday morning, September 16, 1796, to a square brick mansion at 190 Market Street, next door to a hairdresser's shop. Climbing the "neat but narrow staircase, carpeted in the middle," he entered a well-furnished drawing room, where he found a tall, broad-shouldered man sitting alone near the fireplace.

George Washington arose with an old soldier's stiffness, received the editor kindly, motioned him to a seat beside him, and began to talk. In a velvet suit with silver buckles, his hair powdered and carefully tied into a black silk bag, the President of the United States seemed as much a military chieftain as when he had worn the buff and blue as commander of the Continental Army. He had an air of dignified reserve, which many observers noted, some calling it "majesty." Yet so completely did he resemble the "great and good man," revered by most of his countrymen, that the visitor felt respect rather than awe in his presence.

George Washington, at sixty-four, was a tired man with only three years left to live. His face seemed grave; no trace of a smile softened the hard line of his mouth, which puffed out a bit because of his painful artificial teeth.

His hands—the hands of a farmer, a surveyor, a soldier—were still so large and strong that they could bend an iron horseshoe, and the General liked to sit at the dinner table cracking nuts between a thumb and forefinger. His huge hands had held thirteen quarreling

1

colonies together through years of revolution and war and had welded the states into a union, which already seemed in danger of splitting apart. Now in the same hands, George Washington held a sheaf of papers. He had summoned Claypoole to talk about these papers. He spoke slowly, choosing his words with precision and care.

For some time, the President confided, he had been thinking about retiring from public life. He had some thoughts and reflections, written down in the form of an address to the American people. He wanted Claypoole to print this in his paper as soon as possible. The President did not explain to the visiting printer why he had decided to retire. Could Claypoole have read some of Washington's confidential letters, the reasons would have been clear.

After eight years of the presidency, added to his earlier years of service in the army, the General longed to return to Mount Vernon and spend a few years on his beloved Virginia estate before being called forever to "the mansions of rest." "The troubles and perplexities" of the presidency, he had told John Jay, "added to the weight of years which have passed over me, have worn away my mind more than my body; and renders ease and retirement indispensably necessary to both during the short time I have to stay here."

Washington had planned to serve but a single term. He had drafted a farewell address in 1792 but had laid it aside when persuaded that he alone could steer the frail craft of the new government safely through the gales of domestic politics and the stormy seas of foreign conflict. The President, who deeply believed that all Americans should place their country above local and party loyalties, had watched with mounting alarm as the people split into two warring factions. The factions were generally styled the "Federalists," those who supported his administration, and the "Republicans," those who criticized it. He had seen this warfare rage in his own cabinet in the fierce rivalry between Thomas Jefferson, the Secretary of State, and Alexander Hamilton, the Secretary of the Treasury. While Hamilton had enacted his plans for centralizing the government, establishing its credit, and fostering commerce, Jefferson had denounced these policies as schemes favoring merchants, "paper men," and lovers of monarchy in the British style at the expense of the farmers and mechanics. Finally, both geniuses of the cabinet had quit—Hamilton retiring to his New York law office and Jefferson to his Virginia estate; but both kept their hands on the strings of party politics leading into the capital at Philadelphia.

The French Revolution and the ensuing war between Britain and France furnished the fuel for new partisan fires. At first, nearly all Americans had hailed the Revolution with joy as the fruit of their own victory over George III, won with the help of the French. But when the French sent their king and queen to the guillotine, and convulsed their country with the slaughter of the Reign of Terror, many Americans recoiled in horror from the "terrible republic."

The Federalists looked to conservative, steady England to check the mad career of the bloody "atheists" who were setting forth with their armies to conquer all of Europe. The Republicans believed the French must win their war against England, or republicanism would not be safe in America either. Besides, the United States was still technically an ally of France and had promised to help safeguard the independence of the French West Indies. But President Washington insisted upon maintaining strict American neutrality. He knew that the United States, with no navy and with an army barely able to guard its own frontiers against the Indians, could be ruined by a war. He stuck to neutrality even when the British—in line with their policy of trying to starve out France—seized hundreds of American ships under an Order in Council that made food supplies contraband. Washington knew that war with England would destroy the Anglo-American shipping trade upon which most of the government's revenues depended. Further, he felt that if this nation became a satellite of either side in the war, it would surely lose its independence.

To avoid war with England, Washington signed Jay's Treaty in 1795. The French denounced the pact as a shameful act of ingratitude towards a loyal ally, and French raiders began preying on American ships carrying supplies to the British. Jefferson's Republicans raised a great hue and cry against the treaty, charging that it allied the United States with Britain in the war on France and sacrificed American rights on the high seas. Only the President's great personal prestige saved the treaty from defeat in the Senate.

The Republicans poured the vials of their wrath upon his head and George Washington, once revered by all as "the father of his country," now found himself reviled by one faction as the dupe of English monarchists, in the vilest language of the gutter.

The President's wrath over the newspaper attacks reminded Jefferson of the day when Washington had seen a cartoon which depicted him as on the way to the guillotine. "The President was much inflamed," wrote Jefferson, "... got into one of those passions when he cannot command himself ... said he had never repented but once the having slipped the moment of resigning his office & that was every moment since, that *by god* he had rather be in his grave than in his present situation, that he would rather be on his farm than to be made *emperor of the world* and yet that they were charging him with wanting to be a king; that that *rascal Freneau* sent him 3 of his papers every day, as if he thought he would become the distributor of his papers, that he could see in this nothing but an impudent design to insult him."

Philip Freneau had been the first Republican editor to snipe at Washington, earlier in his administration. Now the chief offender was Benjamin Franklin Bache, Benjamin Franklin's passionate grandson, nicknamed "Lightning Rod, Junior," who shot his lightning bolts against the Federalists in the Republican scandal sheet, the Philadelphia *Aurora*. Washington had reason to believe the Republican leaders were working hand-in-glove with the French and planting pro-French propaganda in Bache's paper.

Until recent months, the President told Jefferson, he would not have believed it possible that "every act of my administration would be tortured and the grossest and most insidious misrepresentations of them be made, by giving one side *only* of a subject and that too in such exaggerated and indecent terms as could scarcely be applied to a Nero; a notorious defaulter; or even to a common pick-pocket."

Washington had had enough of such political billingsgate. "I desire to be buffeted no longer in the public prints," he told Hamilton, "by a set of infamous scribblers." So he had finally made up his mind to retire, and this time there would be no turning back. He

4

dusted off his four-year-old farewell message and sent it to Hamilton for revision. He wanted to remove "doubts from the mind of *all*," so that nobody would waste any votes on him in the next election, and he wanted to leave "the field clear for *all*" candidates who might aspire to the presidency. He would not hand-pick his successor.

Now, after much revision, the final draft of the farewell message was ready, and Washington had selected Claypoole to publish it first. He wanted the editor to "usher it to the world, and suffer it to work its way afterwards."

Delighted to have the first release of this historic story, Claypoole burst into effusions of gratitude, but the President simply nodded and asked him how soon he could print it. They agreed upon the following Monday. So, on September 19, 1796, the address appeared.

"Friends and Fellow Citizens," the old soldier began. "The period for a new election of a Citizen, to Administer the Executive government of the United States, not being far distant, and the time actually arrived, when your thoughts must be employed in designating the person, who is to be cloathed with that important trust, it seems to me proper . . . that I should now apprise you of the decision I have formed, to decline being considered."

Then he added "the disinterested warnings of a parting friend":

"The Unity of Government which constitutes you one people is a main pillar in the edifice of your real independence, the support of your tranquility at home, your peace abroad; of your safety; of your prosperity; of that very liberty which you so highly prize." It must be protected against "every attempt to alienate any portion of our Country from the rest." Whatever the special interest of North, South, East, or West, all must be bound together as *"one* nation."

He warned the people against parties, particularly those based on *"Geographical* discriminations." As if recalling the "Whiskey Boys" insurrection in western Pennsylvania only two years before, and recurring rumors of attempts to detach the trans-Appalachian settlers from the Union, the General went on: "The very idea of the power and the right of the People to establish Government presupposes the

5

duty ... of every individual to obey the established Government."

The "spirit of Party" should be restrained, lest the domination of one faction should lead to despotism, or even "usurpation." "Religion and morality," he added, are indispensable to "private and public felicity." Americans, he said, should "promote institutions for the general diffusion of knowledge ... cherish public credit ... observe good faith and justice towards all Nations."

"Against the insidious wiles of foreign influence (I conjure you to believe me, fellow citizens)," he warned, "the jealousy of a free people ought to be *constantly* awake.... There can be no greater error than to expect or calculate upon real favors from nation to nation." He had clung to steadfast neutrality in the war in Europe, he said, so as "to gain time to our country to settle and mature its yet recent institutions.

"The great rule of conduct for us, in regard to foreign nations is ... to have with them as little *political* connection as possible. So far as we have already formed engagements, let them be fulfilled with perfect good faith. Here let us stop. Europe has a set of primary interests which to us have none or a very remote relation. Hence she must be engaged in frequent controversies, the causes of which are essentially foreign to our concerns....

"Why quit our own to stand upon foreign ground? Why, by interweaving our destiny with that of any part of Europe, entangle our peace and prosperity in the toils of European Ambition, Rivalship, Interest, Humour or Caprice? 'Tis our true policy to steer clear of permanent alliances with any portion of the foreign world.... Taking care always to keep ourselves ... on a respectably defensive posture, we may safely trust to temporary alliances for extraordinary emergencies.

"Though in reviewing the incidents of my Administration, I am unconscious of intentional error, I am nevertheless too sensible of my defects not to think it probable I may have committed many errors," he concluded. He urged his countrymen to view his errors with indulgence, so that "after forty-five years of my life dedicated to its service with an upright zeal, the faults of incompetent abilities will be consigned to oblivion, as myself must soon be to the Mansions of rest."

* * * * *

By publishing his Farewell Address, George Washington not only signaled the end of his own political career, he also officially opened the race for his presidential chair. Representative Fisher Ames, a Massachusetts Federalist, correctly forecast that the message would "serve as a signal, like dropping a hat, for party racers to start."

Benjamin Franklin Bache had expected the President to retire and had already guessed who the two chief candidates would be: "It requires no talent at divination to decide who will be the candidates for the chair," the *Aurora* editor wrote. "THOMAS JEFFERSON & JOHN ADAMS will be the men, & whether we shall have at the head of our executive a steadfast friend to the Rights of the People, or an advocate for hereditary power and distinctions, the people of the United States are soon to decide."

The Republicans generally agreed that Jefferson was the only candidate having enough national appeal to carry them to victory. But he did not wish to run. He had spent years in the public service, at great financial sacrifice, and in 1794 he had quit as Secretary of State and retired to his Virginia mountain top, where he reveled in the life of Monticello's "ante-diluvian patriarch," surrounded by his family, his fields, and his books. He was busy remodeling Monticello. He had no desire to move into George Washington's rented house in Philadelphia or, as in his days of cabinet conflicts with Alexander Hamilton, to "descend daily into the arena like a gladiator."

Jefferson's own favorite for the presidency was his friend and junior partner, James Madison. "There is not another person in the U.S. who, being placed at the helm of affairs, my mind would be so completely at rest for the fortune of our political bark," he told his Virginia neighbor.

Madison steadfastly refused, however, and the Republicans ran Jefferson anyway, whether he liked it or not. At the end of September, Madison wrote James Monroe, "I have not seen Jefferson and have thought it best to present him no opportunity of protesting to his friends against being embarked in the contest."

No shrinking violet was Aaron Burr, the suave and seductive Senator from New York, who prevailed upon Republican politicians to sponsor him as their choice for Vice-President. Burr had aspired to the prize four years before when only 36, but leading men in both parties distrusted him because he had a foot in each camp and nobody seemed to know what his principles—if any—really were.

Thus did Alexander Hamilton at that time warn the Federalists against his rival: "Burr's integrity as an individual is not unimpeached. As a public man, he is one of the worst sort—a friend to nothing but as it suits his interest and ambition." Financially embarrassed, "bold, enterprising and intriguing," Burr would "play the game of confusion" to seize power, Hamilton predicted. "He is determined . . . to make his way to the head of the popular party, and to climb *per fas aut nefas* to the highest honors of the State," and ultimately to supreme power. "In a word," Hamilton concluded, "if we have an embryo Caesar in the United States, 'tis Burr."

At the same time, James Monroe cautioned the Republicans against voting for Burr for Vice-President. "Some person of more advanc'd life and longer standing in publick trust sho'd be selected for it, and particularly one who in consequence of such service had given unequivocal proofs of what his principles really were," Monroe told Madison.

So, in 1792, the Republicans supported Governor George Clinton of New York, who made a good showing while losing to Vice-President Adams, and Burr claimed it would be his turn next time.

Hence, in 1796, the Republicans gave Burr his deferred opportunity, on the theory that he might help the Jefferson ticket in the eastern states, where he supposedly had considerable strength and where the Republicans were weakest. Yet the New Yorker lacked united support, as Oliver Wolcott, the Federalist Secretary of the Treasury, remarked: "The Antis [Anti-Federalists] do not expect that Col. Burr will succeed, and they secretly wish that Mr. Adams may be elected to his present station"; that is, that Adams should

8

be kept as Vice-President for a third term, with Jefferson as President, in Washington's place.

Adams suspected some such maneuvers by the "trans-Chesapeakes" gentlemen. "I am heir apparent," he told his wife, Abigail, but "the French and the Demagogues intend, I presume, to set aside the descent." The stout, bald Vice-President from Massachusetts had good reason to consider himself the "heir apparent"; most of his sixty years had been devoted to the service of the Republic—in the Continental Congress, as a signer of the Declaration of Independence, on missions to France, Holland, and England, and for the past eight years as the second man in the government.

"The French and the Demagogues" favoring Jefferson were not Adams' only enemies. There were many inside his own Federalist party. They were led by Alexander Hamilton who, although retired from the cabinet, still greatly influenced the party and the administration through his advice to Washington and his colleagues. Most Federalists looked to Hamilton and not to Adams as their leader and considered Adams a far from perfect prospect for the presidency.

True, Adams despised the French radicals and made indiscreet remarks about the virtues of a monarchy, but he was not pro-British either, for he resented the aristocrats who had snubbed him when he was minister to the court of George III. Hamilton distrusted Adams (or so Madison told Jefferson) because of the Vice-President's enmity to "banks & funding systems," and because "he is too headstrong to be a fit puppet for the intriguers behind the skreen." Hamilton and his allies did not trust Adams to be firm enough against French intrigues to dominate the American government. They also disliked his towering temper, his vanity and his egotism. They even whispered among themselves that the old man was a little bit "crazy."

Yet because of Adams' popularity with the rank-and-file voters, especially those in New England, the Federalist "intriguers behind the skreen" did not dare oppose him openly. So, the fertile mind of Hamilton concocted a clever scheme. It called for Adams' running mate, Thomas Pinckney, of South Carolina, to be slipped into the presidency ahead of him. This seemed possible on paper, at least,

9

because of the clumsy electoral system. Each elector voted for *two* men for President, and the runner-up became Vice-President.

While Adams appealed to northerners, the Federalists needed a popular southerner on their ticket to pick up strength in the South. Pinckney perfectly filled the bill. A Charleston aristocrat, Revolutionary war hero, former governor, and minister to Great Britain, he had crowded quite a career into his 46 years. He was on his way home in triumph from a special mission to Spain, where he had negotiated a treaty highly favorable to the United States.

Pinckney had persuaded the Spaniards to open the Mississippi River in Spanish-owned Louisiana to the commerce of American settlers on the western waters, and to grant the Americans a free port in New Orleans for the next three years. This presumably would make him a hero among voters who normally would favor the Republicans in the South and the West. Hamilton's plan was deceptively simple: All the Federalists in the North would be urged to vote for Adams and Pinckney equally, to keep out Jefferson and Burr, while those in the South would be told to vote for Pinckney and toss a few votes away from Adams. The plan had an especially good chance of working in Pinckney's home state.

Congressman Robert Goodloe Harper, a South Carolinian who naturally would favor a Charlestonian over anyone else, said Pinckney surpassed both Jefferson and Adams in "prudence, moderation, sound judgment, great coolness and discretion, calm, steady firmness of character and uniformity of conduct."

As for Jefferson, the Congressman told his constituents, "he possesses much knowledge, chiefly, however, of the scientific kind, the least useful for a statesman, whose business it is to judge and act, not to write books. No one will deny him the praise of considerable literary genius. But, from his public conduct, I take him to be of a weak, wavering, indecisive character, always pursuing visionary theories. . . . Like most literary men, greatly liable to flattery, and so devoted to popular applause that he cannot be relied on for the performance of any duty which might require him to risk it by a manly, decisive conduct in difficult situations. . . .

"I might think him fit to be a professor in a college, president of a Philosophical Society, or even Secretary of State; but certainly not the first magistrate of a great nation."

So much for Thomas Jefferson, author of the Declaration of Independence, a visionary literary scribbler unfit to be President! So much for "Long Tom—the moonshine philosopher of Monticello!"

Harper, like other Federalists, also feared that Jefferson's "hatred" of Britain and "enthusiastic attachment" to France were so strong that he could not act impartially between the two nations waging "deadly war against each other." In this respect, Harper echoed the voice of Hamilton, who warned the voters in a pamphlet titled, *The Pretensions of Thomas Jefferson to the Presidency Examined*, that the election of this incompetent Deist would surely bring about "national disunion, insignificance, disorder and discredit." (This pamphlet appeared under the by-line of another South Carolina Congressman, William Smith.)

John Beckley, the Republican Clerk of the House of Representatives and party hatchet man *extraordinaire*, told Monroe confidentially: "Adams, if Hamilton can prevent it without danger, is *not* designed as Washington's successor—Pinckney from London is the man."

The Federalists widely circulated Washington's Farewell Address as a campaign document, claiming his warnings against political parties were actually aimed at the Republican "French faction" and its leader, Jefferson, whose attacks on the "government" were weakening the Union.

The Republicans denied they were inciting insurrections and endangering the Union. They merely wished, as Jefferson said, to save the nation from its perilous drift toward British monarchy, and to swing the Ship of State back on her "old republican tack."

Jefferson, the reluctant candidate, made no campaign speeches. Throughout the autumn campaign, he was not an hour's journey from home. The other three candidates did little more—except for Burr's travels about the eastern states—for the day of barnstorming had not yet arrived to wear out the nerves of the nominees and the ears of the electorate.

There was not much point in haranguing crowds, anyway, for

most of the people did not vote even indirectly for President in 1796. In ten of the sixteen states, the electors were chosen by the legislatures; in four others, by district vote; and in only two, Pennsylvania and Georgia, by a general-ticket popular vote. Usually only men with some property were legally adjudged to be "freemen" eligible to select the electors, so the election of the President in 1796 was not strictly an achievement of the people.

Congress had set the first Wednesday in December as the day for the electors to cast their ballots—the electors to have been named within the thirty-four days beforehand. Therefore, the campaign would extend through the autumn and into December. Congress would officially tabulate the result on the second Wednesday in February.

*　*　*　*　*

Thomas Jefferson and the cause of republican liberty had no more ardent advocate than the editor of an unusual newspaper which appeared in Philadelphia on the eve of the 1796 presidential campaign. The paper was the *New World,* or *Morning and Evening Gazette.* Its publisher was young Samuel Harrison Smith.

The *New World* was the first newspaper in America to appear both morning and evening on the same day, in two separate editions different in every respect except the advertisements. It was not strictly a Republican party paper, for its editor was determined to stay above the gutter level of some of his colleagues in the noble calling of Philadelphia journalism. The *New World* published arguments for both Adams and Jefferson, for the avowed purpose of letting the readers decide for themselves, but the editor could hardly be blamed if the pro-Republican articles became more numerous as the campaign in Pennsylvania waxed warm. He himself admired Jefferson as the greatest statesman of the age.

In the age of European wars and revolutions, when ne'er-do-well printers from the Old World were drifting into Philadelphia to sell their services as character assassins for one political faction or another, the editor of the *New World* was a rare specimen: a native of the city, a gentleman, and a scholar.

While some of his rivals, such as "Lightning Rod, Junior" Bache and Federalist John Fenno, won notoriety for attacking one another with swords, fists, pistols, cudgels, horsewhips, or any other weapon that might come conveniently to hand, Smith distinguished himself by his courtesy and culture. "His manners are uniformly mild, kind and cheerful," said one who knew him well. "The most perplexed, hurrying and fatiguing business neither irritates his temper nor ruffles his tranquillity."

Not party factionalism but "public spirit and personal independence" were his chief characteristics, another friend said, and Smith was never known to ask a favor of any man. "This," he once confided, "is the key to the grand secret of my heart: I am ambitious. I wish distinction." He did not yearn to be a military hero, nor to "rule the political tempest," but to "rise to literary pursuits" and make the world listen to his ideas for reforming mankind. "Never, while I live," the idealistic young editor vowed, "shall I cease to triumph in the diffusion of truth."

Smith felt completely at home amid the political tumult of Philadelphia. He had been born there, on January 29, 1772, and had spent his boyhood amid the exciting scenes of the war. His father, Jonathan Bayard Smith, had played an important role in the great drama of the American Revolution. When the boy was just a two-year-old, barely able to hold his father's hand and toddle around the streets, Jonathan had been a member of the Philadelphia Committee of Correspondence, and Secretary of the Committee of Safety.

When Samuel was four, a crowd in front of the State House had wildly hailed the Declaration of Independence. On July 9, 1776, his father had received a commission, signed in the great sprawling hand of John Hancock, reading:

"We, reposing especial Trust and Confidence in Your Patriotism, Valour, Conduct and Fidelity, Do, by these Presents, Constitute and Appoint you to be Deputy Muster Master General for the Flying Camp and Militia ordered to Renedzvous in New Jersey—in the Army of the United Colonies raised for the Defence of American Liberty and for repelling every hostile Invasion thereof."

In 1777, Jonathan Bayard Smith became a delegate to the Continental Congress, member of the Supreme Executive Council of the Commonwealth of Pennsylvania, Prothonotary of Philadelphia County, and Justice of the Peace. As a colonel, he commanded the First Battalion of Philadelphia's gentlemen troops in battles against the British, who occupied the city in September of that year and forced Washington's army into its retreat to Valley Forge.

During those times which tried men's souls, the colonel's son drank of the delicious wine of liberty and never lost his taste for it, although it soured in the mouths of some other Americans later. He forever remained, like his father and their hero, Jefferson, "a passionate republican of the school of 1776."

The events which began on the Fourth of July, 1776, and "the principles which have produced our independence, are those which must in a short time establish the independence and . . . happiness of all nations," Samuel once declared in a burst of enthusiasm on the anniversary of the great day.

In 1787, the year when Washington, Franklin, Hamilton, Madison and other statesmen met at the State House in Philadelphia and wrote the Constitution, fifteen-year-old Samuel H. Smith entered the University of Pennsylvania. He won his degree at nineteen, a year after the Federal capital had moved from New York to Philadelphia. Then, from the lofty eminence of the University, the scholar descended to the lowly level of printer's apprentice. He had determined to become a newspaper publisher, and to learn the business from the bottom up. After mastering the essentials of the trade, Samuel set up his own print shop. He wrote to his sister Mary on June 3, 1794:

"What with unpacking my types, searching the town for an office, and getting done a thousand little trifles. . . . I promise myself to commence my typographical career in a very few days." His "typographical career" prospered enough to enable him, two years later, to launch his unprecedented twice-a-day newspaper.

"The New World . . . was begun on Monday week, and tho' it does not move with all the velocity of the Old World, the rapidity of which, you know, almost eludes figures, yet I assure you it is by no means tardy in its revolutions," Samuel announced on August 26, 1796. On September 11, he issued another bulletin to his family, reporting the infant paper's progress:

"With respect to subscribers, and indeed in every other respect, the encouragement has surpassed my expectations. The number of subscribers recd. since the appearance of the first number is nearly equal to the number previously received, and this, too, during a period in which the city is almost depopulated. I do not pronounce this encouragement great; but I consider it as flattering. It has confirmed my resolution to persevere.

"It is true that, in the commencement of a paper, an indefatigable attention is requisite, and it is also true that in no line of business is there a more active rivalship than among Printers of Newspapers. But amidst the greatest pressure of present employment, the future gleams with encouraging hope. A paper once established requires attention, but little labor. This, then, is the point of time on which I must fix my eye, and so long as every week, month or year draws me nearer to it, I must neither yield to depression nor fruitless anxiety."

As if to reassure his relatives that he was not working himself to death in the blazing heat, Samuel wrote: "With respect to the time I chose (not from choice but from necessity) I am glad it is past. The weather has not been warm, at least not oppressive, and my health is not in the least impaired."

"N.B.," he added in a postscript to his sister Mary, who was visiting her Bayard cousins in New Brunswick, New Jersey: "I send you a dozen papers, supposing you may wish to see a specimen of the New World. If they go by post, you will be obliged to pay as many cents, as the postage cannot be paid here. They are directed to M. A. Smith, and it will be necessary to send for them to the post office."

Smith, at twenty-four, was probably the youngest editor of a Philadelphia newspaper, and certainly the busiest. His twice-a-day editions kept him and his staff working practically around the clock. He himself had to collect the news, write editorials, sell advertising, keep the books, supervise the printers, and even address some of the papers for mailing. Every letter of type in the five-column sheet had to be set by hand; the papers were printed one at a time, on a slow hand press not immune to breakdowns; and the *New World* had to appear on time each morning and afternoon for the enlightenment of a portion of Philadelphia's 60,000 citizens.

On many a night the editor could be found in the shop, where some of the printers of his "family" lived. The employees received free board and room along with their wages which, for a journeyman, averaged six dollars a week. An apprentice was usually bound for seven years or until he was twenty-one; then he became a journeyman, free to hire out or to set up his own business, if he could raise the money for it. Printers, then as now, had a reputation for dry throats and itchy feet.

Competition in the printing business, as Samuel told his sister, was extremely keen. "There are two morning and as many evening papers published in the city," said Benjamin Davies in a contemporary Philadelphia guidebook, "besides two which are published weekly and two others twice a week—one of the former in the German language, one of the latter in the French." No Philadelphia paper in 1796 exceeded two thousand in circulation. Supposedly the subscribers paid in advance, but many defaulted. To make ends meet, most printers relied upon extra income from printing pamphlets, handbills and books and selling these along with stationery, goose quills and ink.

New World subscribers paid eight dollars per year, while advertisements cost "forty cents a square" for the first insertion, and twenty cents for each one after that.

James Molan, "surgeon dentist, bleeder, and man-midwife," of No. 7 Prune Street or Shippen's Alley, advertised his return from the West Indies and the opening of his Philadelphia office, where "he cleans, scales and makes artificial teeth, performs every operation in the human mouth, extracts teeth and stumps with peculiar care."

W. A. Stokes announced that his store at the corner of Chestnut and Fourth streets would sell "a variety of capital surtouts, consisting of Bath beavers, mixt coatings, elastic cloths, & c.," and "the most elegant assortment of Morocco, fancy, silk and elastic cotton suspenders in the city," besides "satins, velvets, silk quiltings, swans downs, and Marseilles quiltings for waistcoats."

Charles Harford, corner of Fourth and Shippen's streets, offered ten dollars reward for the return of "two indented servants, a man and his wife, named JOHN and LILLY FINLEY, born in the north of Ireland," who had just landed in Philadelphia. "He is a gardener by profession, about 5 feet 10 inches high, rather slender made, has straight short brown hair, and a slow deliberate way of speech, about 50 years old," Harford advertised, and "his wife is about the same age."

John Hilton Phillips, "Taylor," of No. 21 Swanson Street, Southwark, would pay ten dollars, too, for the recapture of his Irish servant boy named Daniel McGee, "about sixteen or seventeen years of age, well set, not very tall, very fresh complexion, thick lips pouched out, dark brown hair," wearing "a pale blue mixt Irish made coat, white buttons with a sprig, blue cloth trowsers, and an old beaver hat."

Jonathan Suplee, a farmer living about five miles from the city, informed all and sundry that he had "taken up" on the road one September day,

TWO STRAY COWS

"one of which is a young red cow with some white spots, and a little brindled, horns like a steer; the other is an older one, brown, with some white spots." "They each of them give a little milk," Jonathan advertised. "The owner is desired to come and prove his property, pay charges and take them away."

Samuel's print shop at 118 Chestnut Street, between Third and Fourth, occupied the front house in a range of red brick buildings owned by the Carpenters Company, on the south side of Chestnut at the corner of Carpenter's Court. The rent was two hundred dollars a year. In the center of the court stood the Carpenters' Hall, famed as the place where the Continental Congress had first met in the early days of the Revolution.

Whalebone Alley ran parallel to the court; Dock Street—a covered-over sewer—meandered along behind it, wending its crooked way to the Delaware River, four blocks to the east. From the docks, which were always choked with rotting filth, and from Howell's Tan Yards near-by, a medley of nauseous aromas wafted through the open windows of the print shop, along with swarms of mosquitoes and flies. "The very fly that now creeps with solemn gait over my nose," the editor wrote to his sister one day, "passes a practical malediction on my present employment."

The *New World* chronicled the events of the day from a vantage point close to the center of the city which the editor called "the seat of turbulence and activity." Samuel could roam the cobblestoned streets in any direction in search of news, and could usually find some; for Philadelphia considered itself the first city of the new republic, besides its political capital, its principal port of commerce, and the center of much of its culture.

A two-block walk would take the editor to Congress Hall, also on the south side of Chestnut, at the corner of Sixth. Even closer was the old City Hall at Chestnut and Fifth, and in between the two was the State House, where the Declaration of Independence and the Constitution had been signed. If he had business with the State Department, it was only a short stroll to the house near Chestnut and Third. If he wished to call on the President, he must walk only to 190 Market Street at Sixth, a block north of Congress Hall, where George Washington lived in the red brick mansion leased from the banker, Robert Morris.

Vice-President John Adams occupied rented rooms in the home of a Frenchman named Francis, on Fourth Street, with several members of Congress for company. Other members shared similar boardinghouse "messes" conveniently close to their meeting place.

Editor Smith had to walk but a few blocks eastward from his shop to the docks where the shipping business dominated the commerce of the capital, just as the white sails of the ships at the Delaware River wharves dominated the skyline. The ships, their masts and rigging standing out like a forest against the blue sky, brought news as well as cargo from the Old World.

Along Front Street, Samuel could see the sailors unloading goods from Europe and Asia and the Seven Seas and taking on board the products of Pennsylvania: wheat, rye, Indian corn and buckwheat flour, produced by the German and Quaker farmers on their rich acres at Philadelphia's backdoor; lumber, shingles, ship masts, tanner's bark from Pennsylvania forests; salted pork and beef, dressed sheepskins, leather, pig iron, nails, anchors, hoops, and a host of other goods from beer to beeswax.

Along Front and Water streets, he could see the mansions of the merchants and shipowners, the most wealthy men in Philadelphia society; in the shops he could buy almost anything his fancy and his purse would allow, from a cask of wine to a bolt of calico.

Philadelphia lay on a level plain at the narrowest part of the isthmus between the Delaware River, on the east, and the Schuylkill, on the west, about five miles above the point where the two rivers came together. Business and government centered about the area fronting on the Delaware and spreading a few blocks to the west. The rest of the land in the direction of the Schuylkill remained in the same state of nature that William Penn had found there, a wilderness favored by Samuel H. Smith and other young romantics as a choice place for woodland walks.

Westward from the Delaware ran the main streets: Arch and the "High" street, named Market Street for the long shed of the farmers' market there; and the ones named for trees—Chestnut, Walnut, Locust, Spruce and Pine—names that sounded so "whimsical" to one British visitor's ear. Running north and south, parallel to the Delaware, lay Front, Water, Second, Third, Fourth, Fifth and Sixth streets, completing the principal square of the orderly town laid out by Penn. Beyond Sixth, the blocks of neat brick houses began to thin out; few people had built west of Tenth by 1796.

Visitors from abroad—and there were many in this era when the new American republic was a pawn in the war between England and France—thought Philadelphia looked much like an English town. Its streets, shaded by poplars, resembled many of those in London except that the foot-pavement on each side was of brick instead of stone. Between the brick and stone pavements were gutters paved with brick to carry off the water, and rows of posts, placed outside the gutters at ten-to-twelve-foot intervals, protected pedestrians from the wheels of the carriages and wagons which jammed the streets. The clerk of the mayor's court recorded 520 "chairs" and 33 sulkies, or a total of 553 two-wheeled carriages, plus 307 four-wheeled carriages, 233 drays and 454 carts, all competing for space in the crowded streets of Philadelphia in 1796.

Strolling down the brick sidewalks beneath the poplar trees, Editor Smith could rub elbows with a startling variety of people. There were Quakers who used the pronouns "thee" and "thou"; German farmers famed for their thrift and hard work; immigrants from Ireland, England and Scotland (some of whom ran away from their masters, as the *New World* advertisements show); several thousand Frenchmen, refugees from the Revolution in their homeland and from the bloody uprising of the blacks in Santo Domingo; buckskin-clad hunters and trappers from the frontier; Indians come to the capital to make treaties of peace with the paleface government; also a number of Negroes, and "streetwalkers of every color."

"The Philadelphians," said one observer, "are from the highest to the lowest, from the parson in his black gown to the *fille de joie* or girl of pleasure, a set of beggars. You cannot turn round without paying a dollar."

The French were so numerous that they formed a colony in the American capital, supporting themselves by teaching, hairdressing, shopkeeping, instructing in dancing and fencing, and by many other occupations. M. Collot, a creole from Santo Domingo, mixed the two dissimilar vocations of first violinist of the Philadelphia Theater and proprietor of an ice cream parlor. Médéric-Louis-Eli Moreau de Saint-Méry, a tall, cultured lawyer born in Martinique, ran a bookstore and print shop at Front and Walnut streets, which became the rendezvous for his countrymen. Among the émigrés who gathered there were Charles Maurice de Talleyrand, the de-frocked Bishop of Autun destined to be Napoleon's foreign minister; the Duc de la Rochefoucauld-Liancourt; and the Duc d'Orléans, the future King Louis Philippe. The proprietor would tell of the days when he had been president of the provisional government of France at the beginning of the Revolution. "I was once King of Paris," said Moreau, who had fled France to save his neck from the guillotine, "and today I am forced to earn my bread by selling ink and pens and paper at Philadelphia."

Foreigners accustomed to the distinctions of European society were often shocked at the carefree manners of the independent Americans, who showed none of the servility to be expected of laborers and mechanics. One Englishman lamented that "a republican shopkeeper should receive his customer without taking off his hat or saying more than yes or no; that the English language should be spoken more fluently than correctly."

The Viscount de Chateaubriand was scandalized by the "elegance of dress, the luxury of equipages, the frivolousness of conversations, the unequality of fortunes, the immorality of banking and gambling houses, the noise of ballrooms and theatres." The Duc de la Rochefoucauld-Liancourt said "the profusion and luxury" of the upper classes, and the gowns of their wives and daughters were "extreme." Isaac Weld, an Englishman, found among the uppermost social circles "pride, haughtiness and ostentation are conspicuous" and in their manners "a coldness and reserve which chills the heart."

Both the Frenchmen and the Englishman agreed upon one topic: the beauty of Philadelphia women. "Exceedingly pretty," remarked the Viscount. "Beauty is general" with them, declared the duke. "The women, while young," said Weld, "are very pretty." "American women are pretty and those of Philadelphia are prettiest of all," said Moreau de Saint-Méry. "Philadelphia has thousands of them between the ages of 14 and 18; proof of this is on any fine winter day on the north sidewalk of Market Street, between Third and Fifth streets. There you can see 400 young girls, each of whom would certainly be followed on any Paris promenade. This tempting state of affairs is one which no other city in the world could offer in like degree. But they soon grow pale. While adorable at 15, they are faded at 23, old at 35, decrepit at 40."

Visitors from Europe could not understand some of the natives' peculiar customs either. Every Wednesday and Saturday morning,

Philadelphians could be seen washing their doors, sidewalks and window ledges, even on the freezing days of winter. "This lunacy exposes the passers-by to the danger of breaking their necks," grumbled Moreau de Saint-Méry. "Falls on the sidewalk are not rare."

Wednesday and Saturday were also the days when Philadelphians crowded the High Street market which, even the foreigners agreed, supplied the best fresh vegetables, meat and fish to be found anywhere in America. The shed extended all the way from First and Front streets, on the Delaware docks, along the long ridge of Market Street to Fourth. Farmers' carts and covered wagons mingled with the customers' carriages in ample parking spaces at this eighteenth-century supermarket. Peddlers also paraded the city streets during weekdays; oysters were sold up to ten o'clock at night by vendors "uttering mournful cries." Watchmen patrolled the streets from ten P.M. to five A.M., crying out every hour on the hour and telling the time and the state of the weather. The watchmen also gave warnings of fires, checked door latches to see if they were locked properly, and chased would-be thieves away.

Philadelphians, of high and low degree, enjoyed a variety of amusements, day and night: dancing, drinking, picnicking in the public squares or at Gray's Gardens on the Schuylkill; watching boxing matches, plays and cock fights, and the dazzling acrobatics at John Bill Ricketts' Circus. Ricketts, an athletic Scotsman, amazed his customers with equestrian feats such as these: "leaping over ten horses, riding with a boy on his shoulder in the attitude of Mercury; going through the manual exercise with a firelock, dancing a horn-pipe in the saddle, the horse being in full speed." A *New World* advertisement for one Saturday night's entertainment at Ricketts' Circus promised not only "equestrian exercises" but also "the splendid pantomime of DON JUAN; or THE LIBERTINE DE-STROYED."

The New Theatre, at Chestnut and Sixth streets, just opposite Ricketts' Circus and diagonally across from Congress Hall, drew mixed crowds which varied from aristocrats in the reserved-seat boxes to common men and women who munched cakes and guzzled drinks in the pit, roaring with laughter at the often indecent performances on the stage. A drama critic for the *New World* complained one day in 1796 that the performance of Falstaff in *Henry IV*, featuring Shakespeare's "obsolete wit," showed "such a farrago of folly, vulgarity and indelicacy that it would seem unworthy of the approbation of an enlightened audience."

Much more modern was the double bill performed at the same theatre a few nights earlier, consisting of a tragedy titled *The Fair Penitent* and a farce in two acts, *Who's the Dupe?*

Philadelphians seeking more intellectual amusements might visit the library on Fifth Street, where a statue of Benjamin Franklin wearing a Roman robe looked down from a niche above the door; or they could visit Charles Willson Peale's museum, where stuffed animals and birds, paintings, fossils and wildlife specimens were jumbled together in wild profusion, all to be seen for an admission fee of only twenty-five cents. The American Philosophical Society allowed the artist Peale to house his museum in the ground floor of its handsome brick building on Fifth Street, just south of the Supreme Court building. In the Society's headquarters upstairs, men of science, literature and art could find congenial spirits; such men were surprisingly numerous in the cosmopolitan capital of Philadelphia in this era. Among its members were Colonel Jonathan Bayard Smith and his brilliant son, Samuel.

This, then, was the Philadelphia scene when Samuel launched the *New World* into the arena of city journalism and national politics in 1796.

*   *   *   *   *

The *New World* whirled around on its twice-a-day "revolutions," as the editor called them, for two hectic months. Then the issue of October 26 carried this front-page notice:

"The New World this day assumes a new form, and from a paper published twice a day is converted into a paper published daily.... This deviation from the original plan has the sanction of a large majority of the subscribers, and indeed of every one who has been consulted. . . .

"The advantages attending a more frequent publication are derived from an ability to communicate interesting intelligence with the greatest expedition. These have been found on experience to be more than outweighed by the important sacrifice of correctness, method and comprehensiveness of statement. . . . Every Newspaper should be as complete in itself as possible; otherwise the mind of the reader will be distracted without being informed.

"This alteration has not arisen from the difficulties connected with the execution of the original plan. They were all of them foreseen in their full force, and encountered with a zeal which has overcome them. The *practicability* of publishing a paper twice a day has been demonstrated, though at the expence of its *elegibility*.

"The patrons of the New World have a right to know that it now stands on a firm and liberal support; that its circulation is already extensive, and that every day continues to extend it. If the result of the past be permitted to throw any light on the prospect of the future, the Editor cannot indulge a hope which may not be realized. During the short period of two months, more subscriptions have been received than previous to the commencement of the publication.

"The sincerest acknowledgements are due by the Printer to his advertising friends. Their favours have been liberal; and their number is steadily increasing."

Referring to his coverage of the presidential campaign, Samuel said:

"It would be improper in the Editor to suffer this occasion to pass without announcing his determination, strengthened by the conviction of experience, to persevere in the line of duty which he originally prescribed. IMPARTIALITY, equally dictated by duty and interest, should exhibit the most inflexible character. Political discussion will be encouraged, and not repressed, so far as it is connected with principles and the general good. But it always will be rejected, when its object is personal resentment or party malevolence."

To prove his impartiality, the editor published in the same issue two articles "containing strictures on the talents and political virtues

24

of the candidates for the office of President of the United States," one for Adams, the other for Jefferson. Samuel added, however, this escape clause: "It must not be expected that *every* future paper will contain pieces on both sides, or that there will be the precise quantity allotted to each side."

Campaigning warmed up to fever pitch in Pennsylvania in late October, as both parties struggled to capture the fifteen electoral votes which might swing the close election either way. The electioneering centered in Pennsylvania because it was the only state except little Georgia where the people would choose all the electors by a general ticket. Either party, therefore, might take all fifteen electoral votes in a winner-take-all sweep by winning a bare majority of the ballots to be cast on Friday, November 4.

John Beckley, clerk of the U.S. House of Representatives, directed the Republican drive with the techniques of a modern political boss. He first selected a ticket of outstanding men as candidates for electors, headed by Thomas McKean, chief justice of the State Supreme Court and future governor. The Federalist nominees headed by Israel Whelan were not nearly so well known. Next, Beckley sent agents riding by "express" into every county, distributing handbills and sample ballots with instructions for writing in the names of the fifteen true-blue Republican candidates on November 4. In Philadelphia the propaganda was printed in French and German, as well as English.

Republican party workers were exhorted to bring every voter to the polls on election day. "Let every citizen be impressed with the belief that his single vote will decide the fate of his country," said a Republican appeal in the *New World* of Tuesday, November 1. "As the election is to be by the state at large, every vote will be of importance." In the lead story of the same day, the *New World* lost a good bit of its impartiality, and sounded "the tocsin of alarm" against the evil machinations of the deceitful Federalists:

"Attempts are at this moment making to place in the Presidential chair, a man who has proclaimed to the world his hostility to republican government: JOHN ADAMS. He who is the professed champion of the British constitution—the declared advocate of

25

ranks and orders in society—the enthusiastic friend of hereditary power. . . .

"Beware, fellow citizens, of the artifices made use of by the friends of Mr. Adams. They have framed a ticket correspondent with their wishes, and this ticket they have denominated the Jefferson ticket, and have *palmed* it upon numbers of republicans under that treacherous garb. . . . Such a cause, like the bird of the night, skulks from the light of the sun. Be not imposed upon—the ticket which they have promulgated is composed of characters that, they believe, will befriend the election of Mr. Adams.

"Friday, the 4th of November, will be the day of election. Let no consideration prevent you from asserting the most invaluable right of a freeman on that day. Neglect may make it the last day on which you will have the opportunity of exercising such a privilege.

"Thomas Jefferson is the man on whom the friends of a republican government cast their eyes—a man of such enlightened views, such pure patriotism, such unsullied integrity, and such zeal for human happiness, can alone make our country flourishing, tranquil and happy. He will be the cement of discordant interests, and of jarring passions—of no party but the great party of human benefactors, he will allay the heats of our country, heal its divisions, and calm the boisterous elements of political controversy.

"To promote the election of the great Jefferson ought to be the object of every friend to republicanism and his country."

On Thursday, election eve, the *New World* published a Republican appeal on even less lofty lines:

"Thomas Jefferson is a firm REPUBLICAN—John Adams is an avowed MONARCHIST.

"John Adams has already had for eight years the pay of thirty-three dollars per day, during the session of Congress, for acting as Speaker of the Senate; and three lucrative offices in the government have been given, two to his sons and one to his son-in-law. New England men are exclusively in possession of almost all the great offices of the Federal government. . . .

"Are you disposed to add to all this, Pennsylvanians, by giving

26

your votes to make a New England man president of the United States? . . .

"Thomas Jefferson first drew the Declaration of American Independence; he first framed the sacred political sentence, that all men are born equal. John Adams says this is all a farce and a falsehood—that some should be born kings, and some should be born nobles. . . . Will you, by your votes, contribute to make the avowed friend of monarchy President—or will you, by neglectfully staying at home, permit others to saddle you with political slavery?

"Adams has sons who might aim to succeed their father; Jefferson, like Washington, has no son.

"Put in your tickets for fifteen good republicans and let the watch words be LIBERTY and INDEPENDENCE!"

* * * * *

In the closing days of the campaign, the Republicans fired their biggest gun: the threat of war.

The French minister, Pierre Auguste Adet, openly threatened that, unless the American voters elected a President acceptable to Paris— to wit, Thomas Jefferson—they would suffer the displeasure of the terrible French Republic, which already had most of Europe at its feet and would not hesitate to punish the weak little United States.

Adet had earlier reported to his superiors in the French foreign office about his successful electioneering tour among "nos amis," the Republicans of New England. "They promised me," he said, "to act industriously in dropping John Adams and electing Jefferson." Believing the American merchants could only "be led by fear," the French minister then proceeded, with his government's approval, to attempt the tactics of fear.

On Monday, October 31, the *New World* and Bache's *Aurora* celebrated Hallowe'en in right jolly fashion by holding up a jack-o'-lantern made in Paris. They printed a letter which the French minister had sent Secretary of State Timothy Pickering, four days before, and had then conveniently released to the Republican gazettes. Adet announced that "the flag of the Republic will treat the flag of neutrals in the same manner as they shall suffer it to be treated by the English." In other words, the French would seize American ships carrying war supplies to Britain.

The letter complained that the English had seized American ships and "dragged from them Frenchmen and French property," and so the French could no longer keep their promise to consider as "American," any English cargo found aboard American ships. Instead of making the British respect their ships, Adet claimed, the United States had negotiated the Jay Treaty and the English had gone right ahead seizing ships and impressing seamen.

If the United States wanted respect for her neutrality, Adet went on, she should not let the English disregard it; nor could Americans complain if France, "to restore the balance of neutrality to its equilibrium, shall act in the same manner as the English."

Pickering, a violent anti-Gallican, exploded when he saw that this supposedly confidential letter had been released by Adet to the Republican newspapers in a flagrant attempt to frighten some voters into supporting Jefferson in the Pennsylvania election four days away. With President Washington's approval, the Secretary of State sent an angry reply. The 1778 treaty between the U.S. and France, he observed, clearly said, "Free ships make free goods." While Britain could seize war cargoes from U.S. vessels under the law of nations, the 1778 treaty specifically barred France from thus raiding the ships of her ally.

The Federalist *Gazette of the United States* tried to make the French threat boomerang on the Republicans. "The Aurora threatens us with war if we elect John Adams president," it said. "Will the real and independent Americans be so crouching as to have a President forced upon them by such daring maneuvers?"

Adet continued his "daring maneuvers" by issuing three more diplomatic notes as campaign documents, all duly published by Bache's *Aurora* and reprinted by the *New World* and other gazettes. The first ordered all French citizens in the U.S. to wear the tri-color cockade of the Revolution; the second suspended full diplomatic intercourse between Paris and Philadelphia; the third reviewed French policy toward America and lavishly praised Jefferson as a patriot who cherished true "republican" principles.

France, said Samuel H. Smith's paper, is resolved to be "terrible to its enemies, but generous to its allies."

Never has a foreign government more crudely and directly intervened in an American presidential election. Alexander Hamilton denounced the minister's interference, saying it was no wonder the Directory at Paris had intervened in behalf of Jefferson; he was their agent to assure the conquest of the United States, the chief of the "French faction" that had sold itself body and soul to France. George Cabot wrote Oliver Wolcott, Hamilton's successor in the Treasury: "Mr. J. B. Cutting tells us that French successes in Italy will entirely secure the election of Mr. Jefferson. France, he says, must be appeased, by our making the President she likes." "The election of Mr. Jefferson," Wolcott commented, "I consider as fatal to our independence, now that the interference of a foreign nation in our affairs is no longer disguised."

John Adams, facing possible defeat by the French intrigues, said Adet's proclamation would reconcile him to private life. "It will purify me from all envy of Mr. Jefferson, or Mr. Pinckney, or Mr. Burr, or Mr. Anybody who may be chosen president or vice president," he told Abigail. Facing up to the peril of war with France, he added: "I think the moment is a dangerous one," but "I am not scared."

Pennsylvania's election day November 4 provided scenes of intense excitement. In Philadelphia, the British minister Liston reported, Republican sailors paraded with clubs and threats and "a great number of peaceable voters were prevented by force from even approaching the place of election."

The next day Editor Samuel H. Smith displayed his journalistic enterprise by publishing in the *New World* the complete box score of votes for electors in all twelve Philadelphia boxes. His count indicated the Jefferson ticket had carried the city and county combined by about 2,000 votes. Later editions showed Adams taking a state-wide lead, until returns from the far western mountain counties—the stamping grounds of the "Whiskey Boys"—finally gave Jefferson a winning margin as thin as a razor's edge—about one half of one per cent. Republican candidates for electors led the

Federalists by an average margin of fewer than 100 votes. On Friday, November 25, the *New World* reported Governor Thomas Mifflin had "this day" proclaimed the choice of electors who would cast fourteen votes for Jefferson and one for Adams.

Naturally, the Federalists claimed force and fraud had defeated them. Oliver Wolcott was not surprised at the Republican votes in western Pennsylvania; but the Quakers of Philadelphia, he said, had been bullied by the charge "that the election of Mr. Jefferson was necessary to prevent a rupture with France." John Adams agreed that "Adet's note had some effect in Pennsylvania and proved a terror to some Quakers."

But Congressman Andrew Jackson of Tennessee, who hated the British with a passion, defended the French meddling in American politics. To John Sevier, back home on the frontier, the twenty-nine-year-old freshman wrote these words in his painfully original spelling:

"The Republik of france was slow in their Determination what line of Conduct to pursue with Respect to america, but when once they have Established that line of Conduct (which they have by a decree) if we Judge from their former Steadfastness they will strictly adhere to it, with firmness.

"Their Decree is thus Expressed 'She will Treat Nutral flags as Nutral flags suffer themselves to be treated by the English.' They have under the decree gave orders to their armed vessels to capture all vessels bound to or from ports of great Britain. Britain captures all vessels bound to or from French ports. therefore their Captures are similar, and this is the advantage our Commerce derived from the British Treaty. The Merchants . . . petitioned for the ratification of that Instrument, and now they are Enjoying the fruits of their Industry."

When Congress convened December 5, and young Jackson took his seat as the first representative from the new state of Tennessee, the final returns of the presidential election still were not in. Every report made the pendulum swing wildly to and fro. Members of Congress and newspapermen compared notes on the possible outcome. Samuel H. Smith, circulating among the Republicans, stuck to Jefferson to the end. As late as December 4, the *New World* editor said, "I still think Mr. Jefferson will win."

But Albert Gallatin, the Republican floor leader from Pennsylvania, insisted sadly in his French accent (a legacy of his birth in Switzerland): "Pinckney will be the man."

"This question hangs on a thread," Samuel commented, "and the final decision may depend on a single vote."

On Thursday, December 22, he announced in the *New World* that South Carolina's electors had completed the double-cross play devised by Alexander Hamilton. They had given eight votes each to the Republican, Jefferson, and to the Federalist, Pinckney. Had all Federalist electors elsewhere voted equally for Adams and Pinckney, the South Carolina diplomat would have become the second President, for he would have had all the Adams votes, plus eight from his own state. Returns trickling in from New England showed, however, that Adams' friends had been busily undermining Pinckney. Eighteen Adams electors, to make sure that Pinckney did not slip in ahead of him, threw away their second votes on men who were not even running; Chief Justice Oliver Ellsworth, a Connecticut favorite son, got most of them.

Aaron Burr suffered a similar fate. While Jefferson carried twenty of Virginia's twenty-one votes, his official running mate, Burr, received only one. Fifteen were tossed away on Governor Samuel Adams of Massachusetts, and several other Republican electors in Southern states likewise "cut" Burr. Two voted for George Washington! "Virginia has treated Burr scurvily in the election, and North Carolina not much better," Federalist Representative Chauncey Goodrich, of Connecticut, commented. John Langdon, a Republican Senator from New Hampshire, said Burr "might have known they would lurch him."

By December 22, as the *New World* indicated, "the certainty is ... that Adams will be President, and the probability that Jefferson will be Vice-President." Congressman Andrew Jackson told his home folk correctly: "Adams will be President and Jeferson vice. Adams has 71 votes and Jeferson 68."

Representative Robert G. Harper relayed the same news to his

South Carolina constituents, adding glumly that Pinckney had run third with 59 and Burr a poor fourth with 30. "The event," Hamilton commented, "will not a little mortify Burr."

The net result of the election was that nobody rejoiced. Adams resented his selection as President by a mere three votes; Jefferson did not really care to be Vice-President; Pinckney and Burr had good reason to feel they had been betrayed. Hamilton considered Adams' victory a "miracle." It did seem an accident. One elector in Virginia and one in North Carolina, states which gave heavy majorities to Jefferson, tossed a complimentary vote to the Massachusetts statesman in remembrance of his services in the fight for independence. Without those two windfalls, Adams would not have won by 71 to 68. He would have lost by 69 to 70.

Adams felt keen chagrin that Hamilton had nearly succeeded in sneaking Pinckney into the presidency ahead of him. "To see such a character as Jefferson, and much more such an unknown being as Pinckney, brought over my head, and trampling on the bellies of hundreds of other men infinitely his superiors in talents, services and reputation, filled me with apprehensions for the safety of us all," he exclaimed. Only a "sordid people," he said, "could submit to be governed by a Pinckney."

Jefferson said he did not mind playing second fiddle to Adams. He rejoiced at "escaping" from the presidency, an office where "it would be impossible to satisfy either friend or foe, and least of all at a moment when the storm is about to burst which has been conjuring up for four years past."

"The honeymoon would be short . . . and its moments of extasy would be ransomed by years of torment & hatred," he commented. "I have no ambition to govern men, no passion which would lead me to delight to ride in a storm. . . . This is certainly not a moment to covet the helm." Let John Adams worry about avoiding a war with France. While the Yankee skipper steered the ship, the Virginia philosopher would sleep quietly in his berth below.

As for the vice-presidency, Jefferson said, it is "the only office in the world about which I am unable to decide in my own mind whether I had rather have it or not." "A more tranquil & unoffend-

ing one could not have been found for me," he said. "It will give
me philosophical evenings in winter & rural days in summer."

The President-elect welcomed his chance to take command. "John
Adams must be an intrepid to encounter the open assaults of France
and the secret plots of England in concert with all his treacherous
friends and open enemies in his own country," he told Abigail.
"Yet I assure you he never felt more serene in his life."

*　*　*　*　*

On March 2, 1797, a stagecoach from the south lumbered into
Philadelphia, and a band of military men greeted it with salvos of
artillery beneath a banner, "JEFFERSON, THE FRIEND OF THE
PEOPLE." The Vice-President-elect had deliberately chosen to
travel by stage "to avoid any formal reception." Beneath the hard
plank seat he carried a bulky bundle: some fossil bones of "an
animal of the lion kind but of most exaggerated size." These he
would soon present as an interesting archaeological exhibit to the
American Philosophical Society. The Society had recently elected
him president, to succeed the late astronomer and passionate
Republican, Dr. David Rittenhouse; Jefferson considered that office
as great an honor as being Vice-President of the United States.

As Jefferson stepped down from the mail coach, Philadelphians
could see once more the tall, raw-boned, long-limbed Virginia
planter who had made his name immortal in their city twenty-one
years before, by writing the Declaration of Independence. Con-
temporaries described him as a giant, six feet, two-and-a-half inches
tall, with a very red freckled face, his skin so thin that it peeled
after the slightest exposure to wind or sun; his hair, once reddish
or auburn in color, now in his fifty-fourth year becoming a little
streaked with gray; his eyes hazel and usually bright; his carriage
erect; his step firm and elastic; his manners dignified and reserved
with strangers but frank and cheerful with his friends.

He is described on one occasion as wearing a blue coat, a thick
gray waistcoast with a red under-waistcoat lapped over it, green
velveteen breeches wtih pearl buttons, yarn stockings and shoes
down at the heel. He may very well have looked like that when he

came back to Philadelphia to become Vice-President in March, 1797.

Jefferson quickly walked over to the Frenchman Francis' rooming house on Fourth Street to shake hands with John Adams, congratulate him on winning a fair fight and pledge him hearty cooperation. Each man apparently planned to take the other into camp. Jefferson had confided to a Republican friend: "There is reason to believe he is detached from Hamilton, and there is a possibility he may swerve from his politics." To Madison, Jefferson had written: "If Mr. Adams can be induced to administer the government on its true principles, and to relinquish his bias to an English constitution, it is to be considered whether it would not be on the whole for the public good, to come to a good understanding with him as to his future elections. He is perhaps the only sure barrier against Hamilton's getting in."

Meanwhile, Adams having heard some nice things Jefferson had been saying about him, confided to a friend: "I have ever believed in his honor, integrity, his love of country." While alarmed by Jefferson's "entanglements" with bad "characters and politicks," Adams added: "I hope and believe that his advancement and his situation in the Senate, an excellent school, will correct him. He will have too many French friends about him to flatter him; but I hope we can keep him steady."

Supreme Court Justice William Paterson looked with pleasure upon the scene of apparent bi-partisan harmony displayed by Adams and Jefferson at Francis' boardinghouse. "The thing carries conciliation and healing with it, and may have a happy effect on parties," the firm Federalist told Justice James Iredell. "Indeed, my dear sir, it is high time we should be done with parties. I hope that, in a short time, we shall have no interest or views but what are purely American."

Alexander Hamilton, having little faith in either Jefferson or Adams, contented himself with this wry comment: "Mr. Adams is President, Mr. Jefferson Vice-President. Our Jacobins say they are well pleased, and that the lion and the lamb are to lie down together. Mr. Adams's personal friends talk a little in the same way: 'Mr. Jefferson is not half so ill a man as we have been accustomed to think him. There is to be a united and vigorous administration.' Skeptics like me quietly look forward to the event, willing to hope, but not prepared to believe."

* * * * *

Before noon on Saturday, March 4, 1797, a mob of Philadelphians jammed Congress Hall, filling the lobby and gallery of the House chamber to the suffocation point and spilling out the front door into Chestnut Street. Into the midst of the crowd stepped a tall, dignified, grave-faced man who wore a black suit and a military hat with a black cockade. George Washington, happy to become a private citizen at last, had walked over from his Market Street mansion to the two-story red-brick building where he would hand over the presidency to John Adams with the greatest feeling of pleasure and relief.

At the sight of the retiring President, the crowd burst into a wave of applause, which followed him as he quickly stepped inside and took his proper place for the ceremony. The hall was described by Thomas Pinckney (the disappointed Charlestonian Federalist candidate for the presidency and/or vice-presidency) as "a room without ventilators, more than sufficiently heated by fire, to which is super-added the oppressive atmosphere contaminated by the breathing and perspiration of a crowded audience."

The House members—106 in all—sat on a raised platform, three feet high, plainly carpeted. Their desks formed two semicircles facing the Sixth Street windows and the Speaker, Jonathan Dayton of New Jersey. At four narrow desks jammed between the windows sat the newspapermen who kept the records of the congressional debates. One of the shorthand stenographers was the *New World* editor, Samuel H. Smith.

The applause which had greeted the arrival of Washington swelled again as Thomas Jefferson entered, leading the thirty-two Senators in from their upstairs chamber, where he had taken the oath as Vice-President a few moments before. Jefferson, wearing a long blue frock coat, his hair lightly powdered and queued with black ribbon, escorted the Senators down the aisle to their reserved seats.

Then more cheering arose outside in Chestnut Street as John Adams arrived in his brand-new carriage, drawn by two "young but clever" horses, which (to the dismay of his thrifty Yankee soul) had cost him a thousand dollars. The new President, in his sixty-first year, was "rather short and thick, in his manner somewhat cold and reserved," and he usually dressed rather modestly, like "an English country gentleman." On this day of days, however, he was resplendent in a pearl-colored broadcloth suit. A cockade and a sword gave him almost a military air.

In his inaugural speech, the new Federalist President expressed some opinions pleasing to the Republicans. He voiced "a personal esteem for the French nation, formed in a residence of seven years" abroad as an ambassador, and "a sincere desire to preserve the friendship" between the United States and France. He spoke with an outwardly firm manner which concealed much agitation inside. "I was very unwell, had no sleep the night before, and really did not know but I should have fainted," he confided afterwards to Abigail. "I was in great doubt whether to say anything or not beside repeating the oath. . . . I did not know whether I should get through or not. I did, however. . . ."

Adams, who should have enjoyed his triumph, instead felt depressed and lonely. None of his family attended the ceremony which marked the peak of his political career. Abigail had to stay in Quincy to nurse his aged mother in her last illness, and two of their sons were in Europe on diplomatic missions. "I think of you, and dream of you, and long to be with you," he had written to Abigail.

Moreover, Adams could not restrain his morbid jealousy of the two tall Virginians who towered over him and dominated the scene in which he should have starred. He knew he could never have the reverence which the people accorded to Washington or even the popularity of Jefferson, whom he had defeated by a mere three electoral votes.

"A solemn scene it was, indeed," Adams told his wife, "and it was made affecting to me by the presence of the General, whose countenance was as serene and unclouded as the day. He seemed to enjoy a triumph over me. Methought I heard him say, 'Ay! I am fairly out and you fairly in! See which of us will be happiest!'

"In the Chamber of the House of Representatives was a Multitude as great as the Space could contain and I believe scarcely a dry Eye but Washington's. The Sight of the Sun setting half orbed, and another rising, though less splendid, was a novelty. It is the general report that there was more weeping than there has ever been at the representation of a tragedy. But whether it was from grief or joy, whether from the loss of their beloved president, or from the accession of an unbeloved one, or from the pleasure of exchanging presidents without tumult . . . I know not. One thing I know, I am a being of too much sensibility to act any part well in such an exhibition."

After the ritual ended, Adams sat for a moment in his chair; then bowed to the audience and walked out amid applause. Jefferson arose to follow him, then stepped back to give precedence to Washington; but the General, now a private citizen and glad of it, insisted upon following the new Vice-President. As the three walked out, another roar burst from the multitude. They were the Big Three of the Revolutionary Era—Washington, Adams, and Jefferson. They would never be together on a state occasion again.

"This day JOHN ADAMS was inaugurated into the Office of PRESIDENT of the United States and THOMAS JEFFERSON was inaugurated into that of Vice-President of the United States, with the forms and comformably to the directions of the Constitution," the *New World* duly announced in its edition on Inaugural Day. That night, as the paper reported in its next issue, the merchants of Philadelphia honored George Washington at a public dinner at Ricketts' Circus as "testimony of their approbation of his conduct as President." The 240 guests, including all the foreign ministers, many members of Congress, and Governor Thomas Mifflin of Pennsylvania, met at Oeller's Hotel next door and entered the rotunda to the sound of "Washington's March." When they were all seated, a curtain rose and "discovered a splendid emblematic painting" by Charles Willson Peale—a full-length picture of Washington with "Fame" holding a laurel wreath over his head.

The "sumptuous" menu (followed by sixteen toasts) consisted

of no less than four hundred dishes, served by Samuel Richardet, master of the City Tavern and Merchants' Coffee House, "in a manner which did him the highest credit." "We are happy to learn," Editor Smith commented, "that the remains of this festival were given to the prisoners in the gaol and to the sick in the hospital, that the unfortunate and afflicted might also rejoice upon the occasion."

On the surface, at least, there seemed to be almost unanimous acclaim for the retiring commander. But Jefferson privately confided to Madison, "The President is fortunate to get off just as the bubble is bursting, leaving others to hold the bag.... He will have his usual good fortune of reaping credit for the good acts of others, and leaving to them that of his errors."

Jefferson's fellow-Republican, Benjamin Franklin Bache, voiced similar sentiments openly in the *Aurora,* on the day of Washington's departure from the presidency. "If ever a nation was debauched by a man, the American Nation has been debauched by Washington," old Franklin's grandson shrieked. "If ever a nation was deceived by a man, the American Nation has been deceived by Washington.... This day ought to be a JUBILEE in the United States."

*   *   *   *   *

But there were no cheers that day for Aaron Burr, and he had no part in the ceremony. Not only had he run a poor fourth in the election; he had even lost his seat in the United States Senate which, six years before, he had taken away from Hamilton's father-in-law, General Philip Schuyler. The New York legislature, now firmly in Federalist hands, booted out Burr in 1797, and gave the Senate seat back to General Schuyler, who began his term on Inauguration Day. At forty-one, ex-Senator Burr seemed to have come to the end of the road in his aspirations to national power. But the dream had not died. It lived on in the mind of the man whom Hamilton feared as an "embryo Caesar." As he left Philadelphia and returned to New York, Burr's ever-active mind was already planning the first step on the trail which would lead him to the threshold of the presidency four years hence.

CHAPTER TWO

SAMUEL HARRISON SMITH did not devote all his time and his youthful energies to covering the debates in Congress Hall and supervising the daily publication of the *New World* at his newspaper office on Chestnut Street. On many evenings in the winter of 1796–97, he would wend his way eastward to Water Street near the docks and call at the home of his cousin, Andrew Bayard. The attraction there was not Andrew, who was a merchant and banker, but his sister Margaret.

Margaret, a vivacious, intelligent and beautiful girl of eighteen, was spending the winter with her Philadelphia cousin and his family. Samuel had met her the previous July when he and his sisters, Mary and Susan, had visited Margaret's home in New Brunswick, sixty miles from Philadelphia on the cool green banks of the Raritan River in New Jersey. That day, as Peggy liked to express it, was a day of "destiny." In their very "first interview," without making the slightest attempt at flirtation, she had won the young editor's heart.

As he confessed, a little later in his courtship: "When I saw Margaret, I was instantaneously delighted. Her countenance, her manner, her voice convinced me that she was amiable in the highest degree. Her heart seemed to be the most prominent feature in her character. It seemed to me to take its greatest delight from the happiness of those around her."

Margaret's mind, also, impressed her suitor as being remarkably mature for a girl of eighteen in an age when fashion decreed that women should have no concern with matters of the intellect. At

39

eleven, she had read Goldsmith's *Greece,* and in her sixteenth summer, she had read fifty volumes, ranging from *Newton on the Prophecies* to the plays of Sophocles. Her mind could "succeed in any intellectual acquirements," Samuel believed. "It united all the loveliness and grace of sentiment with the dignity and energy of truth."

Editor Smith was seeking a girl who could combine "the virtues of the heart with the endowments of the understanding," and in Cousin Peggy he had found the perfect combination, all he could ever desire. "Here and here only," he told himself, "is my happiness."

Unfortunately for Samuel, though, she did not consider him the answer to a maiden's prayer.

He was not handsome (he had a long face and a big nose like his father's), nor was he a gay and witty beau who could charm a girl with compliments or sweep her off her feet. She found him "quite unprepossessing in his appearance and manners," entirely too solemn for her taste.

"Our dispositions are in every point opposed to each other," she told him in a letter some time later. "You are very grave. You never can or will be gay."

"It is true that I am so serious," he admitted. "Tell me whether you would be better pleased with my exhibiting more gaiety."

"No," she replied, "I do not wish you to be gay; it is not natural and therefore would not be becoming to your physiognomy."

Even worse than his "physiognomy," he was "prone to disputation," which of all things she most heartily disliked. He would argue about politics, religion, philosophy, literature, and always with an air of superior wisdom; and, since she disagreed with him on many cardinal points, she tried to avoid arguments. If ever there were an unlikely partner for a love affair, she realized, he was the one.

True, Peggy and Samuel were second cousins and presumably "kissing kin." In other respects, however, they might as well have been a Montagu and a Capulet.

She was a gay girl, fond of dancing, games and laughter, calling herself once "a downright trifler and romp," and on another occasion, "one of the veriest little fools you ever beheld"; he was a solemn owl, mooning about philosophy and the future of mankind.

She was an affectionate, outgoing creature, whose heart overflowed with concern for everyone, especially the poor and needy; he was a scholar, forever studying or scribbling, for he aspired to become a man of letters as well as a newspaper editor and a power in politics.

She was a fervent Presbyterian, following her father's faith; Samuel was a skeptic, an "unbeliever," as she called him, an acolyte of the French Philosophers who ruled the Age of Reason and rejected Christianity as a "fable."

She was a firm Federalist, like her father and brothers, devoted to the party of Washington, Hamilton, and Adams; he was a "passionate Republican," devoted to Thomas Jefferson and the Rights of Man.

Like Jefferson, his idol, Samuel insisted upon the freedom of the mind. "Let the mind forever remain distinct and independent," he once told Margaret when they argued about religion. "I feel that this topic is my hobby horse."

Samuel would go to church sometimes, but he disliked the oratorical style of most ministers as well as their theological sermons. "Mr. Linn uttered a torrent of froth," he reported in disgust one Sunday afternoon, "a succession of swollen sentences, apostrophes, partial quotations. . . . His eloquence is said to be unrivalled, and yet he could scarcely keep me awake."

The young editor admired the astronomer, David Rittenhouse, who had been a leader in the Democratic Societies that had hailed the French Revolution and had frightened the Federalists with fears of "Jacobin plots" to overthrow the government. Upon the scientist's death at Philadelphia in 1796, Samuel had commented: "Rittenhouse, above all other men, possessed that firmness of mind, that dignity of soul, which no temptation and no fear could tempt or prevent from asserting the independence which it felt. He felt more homage for merit in obscurity than for depravity on stilts. With regard to religious sentiments, he did not affect to conceal what he sincerely believed. He dared to speak out. Dr. Rush told me at the funeral that he fully believed in the divinity of the Christian system, but disbelieved the divinity of Christ."

Margaret, who deplored such philosophy, found Samuel's "disputation" obnoxious; and during the first days of his summertime visit, she tried to avoid conversation with him. But as the days went by, her naturally warm heart began to soften, and she wrote in her journal afterwards:

"He passed a week here and every day the unfavorable impression made by first sight grew less. I even met, instead of retiring from, occasions of conversation. One morning, I was upstairs and I heard him enter the parlor below. I knew he was alone, and before I had thought about the matter, I was with him and he had hold of my hand.

"I felt my face glow. This, perhaps, arose from a perception of his emotion, the cause of which I had already guessed.

" 'Will you not write to me, cousin Margaret?' " asked he.

" 'Write to you? Why, what could I possibly have to write about?' I treated it quite in a jesting manner. He, however, was in earnest and gained his end.

"He left me, and on bidding the family farewell, shook hands with all. When he took mine, his trembled, and that, I suppose, was the reason that mine trembled, too."

* * * * *

Samuel, although he had no way of knowing it, was the latest in a long line of young men who had been bewitched by the brilliant and beauteous Miss Bayard without winning her wayward heart. She had been attracting men ever since she had left boarding school at thirteen to run around Philadelphia with a set of boys and girls who were equally gay and aristocratic. Margaret's father, Colonel John B. Bayard, was a rich Philadelphia merchant, descended from Huguenots who traced their blue-blooded line all the way back to the famous Pierre du Terrail Bayard, "Chevalier sans peur et sans reproche."

For a century, the Bayards had owned large estates on the Eastern Shore of Maryland, and the "Great House" of their Bohemia

Manor commanded a breath-taking view of the green fields of Cecil County and the blue Bohemia River. At the manor house, on August 11, 1738, twin sons were born to James and Mary Asheton Bayard, and named John Bubenheim and James Asheton. The twins were unusually close, and devoted to one another. After their school days, they both went to Philadelphia, where John became a merchant and James a doctor. John married Margaret Hodge, daughter of merchant Andrew Hodge; James married her sister, Agnes. Within a few years, both James and Agnes Bayard died; John adopted their three orphaned children and reared them with his own.

Colonel John Bayard was a man of amazing vigor, who fathered fourteen children, eight of whom lived to maturity. It is easy to imagine how his huge house in Philadelphia must have echoed to the laughter of boys and girls of all ages ranging from teen-agers down to babes-in-arms.

Colonel Bayard commanded a regiment of Philadelphia gentlemen in the battles of Brandywine, Germantown, Monmouth and Princeton. Just before Philadelphia fell to the British in September, 1777, Colonel Bayard moved his large family to a farm at Plymouth Meeting on the Schuylkill River about eighteen miles from the city. It was at Plymouth, in a house near the Swedes' Ford, that Margaret Bayard was born on February 20, 1778. During a part of that winter her father was with George Washington at Valley Forge.

Shortly thereafter, according to family tradition, Mrs. Bayard heard that her son, James, on his way home from Princeton College, had been imprisoned at Philadelphia as a "rebel spy" and sentenced to hang. Her husband was at Lancaster with the State Assembly, so she hastened alone through the British lines and saved her son from the hangman's noose. Mrs. Bayard, in delicate health, endured still another trial when the enemy came through the Swedes' Ford and ransacked her house. She escaped, taking the baby Margaret and the other children to a neighbor's home.

Worn out from the strains and shocks of war and childbirth, the once beautiful Margaret Hodge Bayard died on April 13, 1780. She was only thirty-nine. "Oh, what a loss!" exclaimed her daughter,

Jane, in later years. "I feel as if I should have been another creature, had she been spared to me, for then I should have believed that I was truly beloved." Margaret, too, did not fully recover from this great loss, and her older sister became, for her, a substitute mother, guide, and "guardian angel."

A year after his wife's death, the Colonel married Mary Hodgden; she died in 1785, and in 1787 he took a third wife, Johanna White, sister of General Anthony White, of New Brunswick. In the post-war financial debacle, the Colonel's prosperous mercantile business floundered dangerously near the rocks. He wrote to a creditor in 1786: "My confidence in my country—and my zeal to promote her best interests—has led me to put the greatest part of my estate in her funds at a time when such loans were absolutely necessary. I have, by this conduct, incapacitated myself from fulfilling my engagements with that punctuality I could wish, and also been prevented from assisting my children, who have grown up and have a just claim on me. But my consolation is, I did it with a single eye to the good of my country."

Then, in 1788, after the deaths of two wives and six infant children, the Colonel suffered another crushing blow. His son, James—the one saved from hanging as a spy—died on a mercantile voyage to South Carolina. In despair, Colonel Bayard gave up his business, sold his beloved Bohemia Manor lands in Maryland to pay his debts, and moved to New Brunswick to start a new life.

It is not hard to imagine how the confusion of her family's affairs must have affected Margaret. The little girl had three mothers and a series of homes but no true security. She was sent off to a boarding school conducted by the Moravian Church at Bethlehem, Pennsylvania. The school is thus described by Theophile Cazenove, agent of Dutch bankers speculating in U.S. bonds and land, who visited the Lehigh Valley settlement in the 1790's:

"The boarders are divided among six rooms, not large, and over-heated by large German stoves. They sleep in two rooms, with low ceilings; thus there are forty beds in each room and not a fire-place, only a small air hole in the middle of the ceiling—nothing could be more unhealthful.... The food is good, but not extra. I doubt if the education given by the Moravian teachers, who do not know life, is very useful to form character, but they teach needle-work, painting, music, reading, writing and arithmetic . . . I shall never put in the Bethlehem School any girl for whom I am responsible."

The other girls at the school thought Margaret Bayard a strange creature. On her first night there, she ran away from the rest of the children, wrapped herself in a filmy white gown, and sat down beneath a tree to gaze at the moon. She forgot all about the time of night until aroused by the screams of some of the girls. "A ghost! a ghost!" they cried. It was no ghost; it was merely their new schoolmate, Margaret.

When a teacher demanded what on earth caused her to give the girls such a fright, the moon-gazer in the ghostly white gown replied: "I had promised a friend always to look at the moon at a certain hour." Secretly, Peggy was in love with "an ideal being" and dreaming of "hours of joy" with her imaginary lover.

A "devotee of nature in all her forms," she would often ramble alone along the river banks, scrambling up and down the rocks, gathering wild flowers to be pressed between the pages of her "commonplace book." She could not tell whether she delighted most in "the loud tempest of roaring winds and dashing waves" or the silvery beams of the moon. The wildness of a storm aroused some answering wildness in her heart.

In calmer moments Peggy filled her mind with romantic notions gleaned from reading forbidden novels. At thirteen, she was keenly interested in the subject of love and eager to learn about it from personal experience. On leaving school that year, she wrote:

"There first my youthful bosom learnt to know
"What raised soft sighs and taught warm tears to flow."

"My mind and heart had arrived at greater maturity than is usual for that age," she later wrote in her journal. "With quick and ardent affections, with a lively imagination, a susceptible heart, a candid, unsuspicious and communicative disposition, and with the extravagant and false view of life drawn from novels," she went to Philadelphia to live with her older brother, Samuel, a lawyer rising to prominence in the capital. Samuel's wife had just given birth to a baby and of course she had no time for mothering little Lewis' precocious Aunt Margaret. So pretty Peggy was left free to roam around the city with the inevitable result.

She quickly fell in with a fast set of "ignorant and frivolous young men and women," as she later described them, who devoted their time entirely to the pursuit of happiness. Determined to be a "heroine," and to have all sorts of thrilling adventures like those in her clandestine novels, she determined, "I must have a bosom friend and a lover." In the first role, she cast a beautiful girl (identified only as "Frances ———") she shared her unlimited "vanity and desire of conquest." In choosing her lover, she could not quickly make up her mind, for her notions were so exalted that only a titled nobleman could win her heart.

Fortunately for her purposes, French aristocrats had come to Philadelphia by the boatload, some as refugees from the Paris mobs of the Revolution, others fleeing the slaves who were murdering the whites in Santo Domingo. A handsome young Frenchman, identified in her memoirs as "the Viscount Albert D — — — —," found his attentions well received. For six months, he and Peggy shared "all the romantic extravagancies" which her age and situation would allow. "Yet, wild and romantic as I was," she wrote, "my heart was not destitute of true affection and sensibility." She read the *Tales of the Castle* and resolved to copy the heroine Pamela, who went about doing good. She would spend whole mornings with a seamstress in her brother's home, making clothes for poor children. But most of her time, when not cavorting with viscounts and idlers, she spent reading novels.

The following summer, at home in New Brunswick, the romantic maiden met another young man who made her forget her French nobleman. In all the novels she read, she pictured him as the hero. Every attention he showed her, she construed as "proofs of love," and any appearance of neglect would cost her a flood of tears. If he entered the room, she would tremble; if she heard his name, tears and blushes would betray her love. "I committed a thousand improprieties," she later confessed. "Every evening was passed from home and my friends became sincerely distressed for the levity and impropriety of my conduct."

Eventually, her family determined that something must be done to save the fourteen-year-old madcap from ruin. The solution came in November, 1792, when her sister Jane married the able New Brunswick lawyer, Andrew Kirkpatrick. Sensing that her little sister needed a mother, Jane invited her to come and live with them. Andrew (presumably with a little less enthusiasm) consented to let Peggy share the honeymoon home.

Margaret soon learned that Jane and Andrew Kirkpatrick were determined to make her a lady. Jane banished the romantic novels and insisted that her sister stay home at night and read more edifying books. Andrew, whose biting wit could make learned lawyers quail in the courtroom, never let any of Peggy's many faults escape his sharp tongue. Andrew was a man of great personal dignity who, within a few years, would become Chief Justice of the Supreme Court of New Jersey. A firm believer in capital punishment and the whipping post for criminals, he often said: "There are but three ways of punishing—by the *neck, back,* and *pocket.*" To his family, he was fond of preaching this maxim: "Whatsoever thy hand findeth to do, *do it with all thy might.*"

Andrew's bride was a match for him. "Graceful, tall, dignified, commanding, with countenance grave and intelligent, yet cheerful and benevolent," Jane had a quick mind and her manners "would have graced a court." Dr. Benjamin Rush had met Jane while attending her sister-in-law, Mrs. Samuel Bayard, and her baby in Philadelphia in July, 1791. "A most charming girl," the physician had observed. "I have seldom been more delighted with a first interview with anyone."

The Kirkpatricks' first year together—traditionally supposed to be the hardest—passed so pleasantly that they could easily qualify for the prize awarded under an old custom still in effect then in New Brunswick. If a man and wife could testify that, at no time during the first year of marriage, either had wished to be single again, the bride's father must give them a flitch of bacon.

In keeping with his duty under the custom, Colonel Bayard

wrote to his daughter in 1793: "My dear Jane: As you intend keeping to-morrow as the anniversary of your marriage, we ought to have held a court to have examined both you and Mr. Kirkpatrick, whether you are entitled to receive the flitch of bacon. As I presume you might pass trial, I have sent you a ham (not having a flitch) and a tongue, which please to accept from

"Your affectionate father, John Bayard."

Such were the substitute father and mother who were to rear the wayward Margaret. They succeeded to a considerable degree, for she gradually realized that, though her former antics had "amused many," she was "loved by few and respected by none." She began to read the Gospels and sermons at the rate of one a day. Bruce's Travels and Ossian's Poems and other treasures from Andrew's library improved her taste so that she could relish real life instead of fictional romances. Still did she taste forbidden fruit: *Eloisa,* for instance, had been banned as "highly pernicious," but she read it anyway. "I am ashamed to say," Peggy later confessed in her journal, "that is the very reason I read it. I wanted to find out what it could contain which everyone disapproved of. But it was in vain I sought for the bad parts, for all I understood, I approved."

In September of her seventeenth year, a yellow fever epidemic in New York drove many families to New Brunswick for safety. Among the refugees was a well-to-do lawyer and amateur poet, Anthony Bleecker.

Anthony, twenty-five, was "a gentleman of classical acquisitions and refined belles-lettres taste," and he and Peggy naturally discovered a common love of literature. Thereafter, for the next six weeks, he rarely let a day go by without spending part of it with her. She found in him "more taste, more improvement of mind" than in any other suitor she had known. But he was an "unbeliever." She prayed fervently that he might be led to the Christian religion, but he would only reply, "If ever I am converted, it will be by you, Margaret."

When the Bleeckers returned to New York, after the frosts had killed the yellow fever, Margaret followed them. She spent the winter with the family of the Reverend John Rodgers, a Presbyterian minister whose daughter, Eliza, was the widow of Peggy's brother, James. Margaret spent much time with young Bleecker, but she also paid attention to a "little parson," the Reverend Samuel Miller. "When I came here I made a firm determination not to allow my peace to be wounded by this little enemy," she said—referring to Cupid. "I know not how far this determination might have shielded me, while in company with Anthony, had not Mr. M.———— stopped in now and then. . . . I see both very frequently and esteem both alike. . . . My heart enjoys the most perfect tranquillity."

In the spring of 1796, Peggy returned to New Brunswick, without having lost her heart to any of her New York beaux, and it was in this state of "perfect tranquillity" that she met her cousin, Samuel H. Smith. She did not love anyone in Philadelphia, New York, or New Brunswick. "My heart," she commented, "requires too much for its own happiness. Where I do love, I love so entirely that I cannot be contented without a like return. Yet I fear that I shall never meet with a heart which concentrates its affections as I do."

When Samuel left New Brunswick that summer, urging her to write to him, he gave her an eagle's quill. But she refused to use it as he had hoped. She resolved to use the gift only for love letters, and she was not in love with Samuel H. Smith. She addressed him strictly as "my cousin," using no words of affection, not even "Dear Sir."

Through the autumn, while Samuel was busily publishing his *New World* and encouraging the Republicans in the presidential campaign of Thomas Jefferson, letters from his Federalist cousin came more frequently to the print shop at 118 Chestnut Street. They told of a Bayard family excursion to the falls of the Passaic; of the excitements of Princeton commencement (then an event of the fall instead of the spring), where the "belles & beause" displayed their finest feathers in the ballroom; of a weeklong visit in New York with "friends."

Margaret was still on guard against the "little enemy," Love, when she came to Philadelphia to spend the winter of 1796-97 with her brother Andrew and his wife, to serve as baby-sitter, nurse and playmate for their children. She did not come primarily to make it more convenient for "Cousin Samuel" to pursue her. She would see him, but only as an occasional incident in a round of social activities. Since her father was a personal friend and old wartime comrade of General Washington, Peggy easily attained the peak of social success, an invitation to Martha Washington's drawing room. There she found "a large circle of ladies and a crowd of gentlemen," and her closest companions were the hostess' granddaughter, Miss Custis, and Mrs. Oliver Wolcott, wife of the Secretary of the Treasury.

Late hours and company defeated Peggy's plans for a winter of study. "I have so little time for drawing that I am almost tempted to give it up, and not to attempt French," she wrote her sister Jane. Taking Jane's advice, she stayed away from the Dancing Assembly. She began to spend more quiet evenings at home, where she and "Sister Sally" would work and talk over their sewing or read to one another; and for a little while she "wished for nothing more."

Peggy saw Samuel and his sisters, Mary and Susan Smith, only once or twice a week at first. As the winter wore on, however, she began to mention "S." more frequently in her letters to Jane.

"Cousin S." came one evening and "staid till past 10."

"Cousin S." came the next evening to keep her company while her sister-in-law went dancing.

"Cousin S." and Margaret, a few days later, heard Dr. Rush deliver his "eulogicism" on the character of the late astronomer and ardent Republican, Dr. Rittenhouse.

"Cousin S." began increasing his visits to three or four a week, and finally he came every night. A little after sunset, Margaret would light the candles in the company parlor, stir up the fire on the hearth, set the tea table for two, and then settle down in her chair to listen for a knock on the door.

Soon she found herself listening anxiously for his knock; and if, by nine o'clock, it was not heard, for the rest of the evening she felt depressed. Although she dared not admit it, even to herself, Samuel's company had become essential to her happiness. To converse with him was the greatest satisfaction she knew. "While others ridiculed me for my fondness of reading, he applauded it; while others censured my withdrawing from fashionable amusements, he thought it indicated a rational and well-regulated mind and prized me the more on that account," she later recalled.

"My constant attendance on religious societies, my absolute refusal to attend the theatres and assemblies exposed me to reproof and ridicule. The avidity with which I sought for books, and the eagerness with which I devoured them, exposed me to all those commonplace reproaches of pedantry and uselessness with which our sex are branded when they discover a taste for literature."

Samuel—far ahead of the opinion of his time—did not think it silly for a woman to read. He constantly supplied her with books and encouraged her to develop her mind, which he considered remarkably superior, for a girl yet in her teens.

For several days in December, Peggy's sister-in-law was confined to her room by a severe toothache. Peggy attended her throughout the day and passed the evenings alone with "Cousin S." From Samuel's viewpoint, this proved a providential toothache, for in the long winter evenings together he and his lovely cousin attained a perfect harmony of mind and heart.

As Margaret herself recaptured that magic time, "unreserved and copious conversations beguiled these long evenings. Every subject relative to taste, literature, moral principles and reigning manners was discussed. I discovered a similarity of taste, a coincidence of opinion, an ardor in the pursuit of knowledge, and a value for intellectual attainments, which I had met with in no one else."

What did it matter now, that their personalities were so different? Who cared if he could never be anything but serious, while she still loved to be gay? She was trying her best to change from a dancing madcap, anyway; she had given up the dancing assemblies and the theatre (at least for this winter); and she was striving to live up to her father's ideal of a good Presbyterian girl, who devoted her time to the Bible and other uplifting books. Margaret could not bring herself to embrace Samuel's Deism, nor could she agree with his scorn of Federalism, his love of Republicanism, or his inordinate admiration of Thomas Jefferson. But she could forget their differences over religion and politics while they delighted in finding they agreed upon philosophy and literature.

* * * * *

Anthony Bleecker, who had fallen deeply in love with Margaret, continued to court her in ardent letters from New York. She called him "the brother of my soul," and encouraged the correspondence, hoping it would preserve "the pure and inextinguishable flame of friendship." But Anthony's was a warmer flame than that, and he contended that "friendship could not exist between the two sexes" without ripening into love. Hoping to convince both her suitors that she wished only "friendship," Peggy drafted a letter to Anthony and promised to show it to Samuel before mailing it. This, she reasoned, "would discover my sentiments of friendship and the existence of it for another object." She suddenly changed her mind, however, and refused to let Samuel see the letter. This turn-about provoked a stormy scene one night in Andrew Bayard's parlor. For nearly two hours, Samuel persisted in his demands to see "the letter." Peggy refused and then lapsed into silence. Finally, she "coldly bade him good night."

Very early the next morning, a messenger brought her a long letter in which Samuel apologized for his conduct and insisted she had "treated him unkindly." Receiving no answer, he sent her a book. Still, she continued her silence, though realizing that it "must inflict pain" on Editor Smith, who had "such quick, such lively feelings."

The next night, the determined young editor called again, and by an hour and a half of argument with "a seriousness and tenderness that was irresistible," finally obtained the letter. "I am surprised, I am astonished, to find under so unpromising an appearance as Mr. Smith's person, such strength of argument, such energy of thought, such irresistible persuasion," Peggy confided to Sister Jane. "They have conquered, and never before did I yield with more satisfaction and pleasure. . . .

"Yesterday I gave him a great deal of pain, tonight I have made him happy. Ah, my sister, how delightful to possess such a power! How cruel not to use it!"

This time, when he left her, Samuel pressed Peggy's hand in a way that expressed his thanks far better than all his previous assurances.

"This is an interesting period to me, my sister," Margaret wrote Jane. "I cannot describe to you altogether the situation of my heart. Its affections are in part divided, and the next letter will decide them altogether."

* * * * *

On Saturday night, March 11, 1797, Margaret Bayard and Samuel Harrison Smith sat together before the flickering fire in a candlelit parlor, closed away from the other rooms in Andrew Bayard's house. Now the time had come for Samuel to say the words he had been rehearsing to himself for days. But the bright young editor, who could write reams about political affairs and crises with France, and solve the problems of mankind in *New World* editorials, found himself at a loss for words.

"I had nothing to say, words would not aid me," he later recorded. "A scene which gave to my feelings all the romance of the liveliest imagination seemed to petrify me. I should have poured out my very soul. Every word that I uttered should have been a word of fire."

But his words were far from fiery. As the clock struck eleven, somehow he managed to find his tongue and stammer out the most important sentence: "I love you—Margaret, I love you."

He had loved her for months, he told her, ever since that summer day when he had first seen her in New Brunswick. She personified everything he had dreamed about as his ideal; a lovely girl with a brilliant mind and an understanding heart. Would she—could she possibly consider—would she consent to be his wife?

His proposal overwhelmed her for a moment. She trembled, and wept, and found a refuge in his arms. Yes, she confessed, she knew he sincerely loved her, and she had found in him alone a "congenial mind." She felt grateful to him for appreciating her as a woman with a mind of her own.

Although their dispositions were quite different and their opinions varied, also, their tastes were the same, and she had always believed that was "absolutely necessary" to happiness in marriage. Yet she could not tell him truthfully that she loved him. She did not feel the ecstasy which she had expected to enjoy in her lover's arms. "You must expect nothing," she warned him, "but friendship, dictated by understanding." That was enough for him, he said; he would be happy if only she would consent to marry him.

Peggy gave him leave to "hope," and he embraced her with boundless gratitude. He went away so excited that he stayed awake all night.

Margaret, however, could not share his joy.

After he had left, her sister-in-law came into the parlor and found her in tears. "It was impossible to conceal my agitation, she knew of every incident that had occurred thro' the winter, she could not be ignorant of this," Peggy reported to Jane. "She look'd inquiry, I could not answer but by tears, which I endeavor'd to conceal by hiding my face in her lap. She did not take my hand, she only laugh'd and said, 'For shame, for shame.'... I recovered my firmness, I answered her questions and we sat till one o'clock talking."

After a night of weeping, Margaret began to have doubts about the wisdom of her choice. Samuel's rapturous expressions of happiness only filled her with gloom. She told herself that since she had made him happy, she should be happy herself. Then she realized the awesome importance of marriage. She felt sure that her father, despising Samuel's beliefs on religion and politics, would not approve of him.

"I feel as if I had done wrong, as if I had deceived you," she wrote Samuel. "But I have not. I told you that I felt not the sentiment of love, that you must expect nothing but friendship dictated by understanding. You were contented, but I am not. No, no, you deserve more and I cannot be content, I cannot but doubt. I cannot approve what I have done while this doubt remains."

54

Peggy longed to see her sister Jane and ask for her motherly advice. "I feel forlorn, destitute, alone; nobody here can comprehend my feelings," she said. "If I had but her approbation I should feel a thousand times more content; for hers and Papa's are always the same. Yet I cannot write, at least alone." Samuel must write to Jane and tell her about his proposal, and ask for her consent. "Write to her as if you had known her for years," Peggy begged him. "Write by tomorrow's post. The sooner her answer arrives, the happier I shall be."

But Samuel objected to letting her sister in New Brunswick pass judgment on their love affair. How could anyone at such a distance, and "knowing but little of me, form a just opinion?" he asked. "No one knows anything of my heart but you. Think how mad it would be to make anyone the arbiter of my happiness! No, before God and man I am ready to declare that my happiness is complete. Nothing can deprive me of it!"

Samuel wept at the idea of letting his happiness depend upon the whims of Sister Jane. He feared that, since Jane did not know him well, and since she must disapprove of his religious and political beliefs, she would disapprove of the match. Margaret was so unhappy, however, and so determined to have Jane's advice, that he finally consented. Accordingly, both wrote to Mrs. Kirkpatrick, telling her everything.

"The happiness of two beings depends upon you," Peggy wrote. *"My only Mother,* my darling sister, my dearest friend upon earth, it is you, you alone that can decide. . . . Alas, how destitute am I without you! I sit all day in my room, I cannot weep, I cannot feel, but my head burns and aches, and my heart trembles. . . . I feel a great deal, but nothing in comparison with my friend. . . . He could scarcely bear the idea of being in this uncertainty for 2 days; he bids me, he repeatedly urged me, to request you to answer his letter the same day you receive it. . . . Yet one line, one simple line, would diminish the burden of my heart."

Samuel's letter ran more than a thousand words long. "In submitting to your judgment all that I hold dear in life," he wrote Jane, "I know that your heart and your understanding will pronounce the language of tenderness and truth. Margaret considers you as her guardian angel, as her mother and her friend. Let me appeal to you in these endearing characters. . . ."

He begged Mrs. Kirkpatrick to grant her approval immediately. "Suspense is scarcely to be endured," he wrote. "You only have the power to dissipate every fear, and to create ecstasy in their place. . . . To you my heart addresses all its feelings. Do with them as you please, I shall submit."

After days of suspense, the mail coach finally came from New Brunswick, bringing Jane's reply to the Bayard residence in Philadelphia. Peggy rushed the letter by messenger to Samuel at his print shop on Chestnut Street, along with a little note of triumph. Jane had advised her little sister to "try the effects of Brunswick air and absence," before becoming finally engaged; otherwise, she made no objection to the match.

Joyfully, Samuel dropped his work at the *New World* office and joined his sweetheart for a gay celebration. "Oh, with what ecstasy did I read your note and cousin Jane's letter!" he exclaimed, in a little note afterwards. "What a glow of joy was mine!" They walked together all the way across Philadelphia to the Schuylkill River, hardly noticing the countryside, and his heart found more words than ever before to express the emotions that seemed to make it almost burst. The next evening they were together again, and this time the strain of courtship was beginning to show. The following day he received a sharp little note of reproof.

Peggy warned him that her future happiness would depend upon "tenderness," not alone upon "esteem and respect." "I *might* be happy without either of those," she wrote, "but not without *that*."

"I could not resist the impetuous energy of my feelings," he apologized in an answering note. "Hereafter they *shall* be subdued."

"Are my visits too frequent, too importunate, too long?" he asked anxiously. "If they are tell me so. Does my conversation fix on improper subjects? Should I say nothing of my feelings? All this I will do if you direct it."

"No, my friend," she smoothed his ruffled feathers, "your visits are neither too long nor too frequent, your conversation neither improper nor unpleasing. Last evening was the happiest I ever spent with you."

Relieved by this reassurance, he asked her for some word of endearment which he could use in addressing her. "I look back upon the calm period when I called you 'cousin,' " he said, "and now my feelings are not satisfied with this. I would call you 'my love.' " But that would never do; it would be disrespectful. So, he concluded, "I will call you 'lovely Margaret.' " She agreed, with all her heart. "Call me," she said, *"your* Margaret."

When April came, Peggy determined to go home to New Brunswick. Samuel longed to go with her, but he know this would tell everyone of their engagement, and she wished to keep it a family secret for a while. Besides, her father still had not given *his* consent to the marriage, and there was a strong possibility that he might object. The Colonel could hardly be expected to cheer over the prospect of acquiring a Republican "unbeliever" as a son-in-law.

On the eve of parting, Margaret expressed to Samuel her deepest concern over the one great doubt in her heart: their differences over religion. "You know how entirely my happiness rests on religion," wrote the once wayward but now devout young daughter of the Presbyterian elder, Colonel Bayard. "With regard to your pure morality I have not the least fear. On this we shall never differ, but with regard to Faith I feel more anxious. It is an impossibility to force belief, but there are one or two sentiments that I should rejoice could you feel their force.

"The first is to lay aside a philosophizing spirit, give up the pride of reason. Secondly is a belief of the providence of God, of his individual care of every part of Creation. . . . And now, my friend, I come to what I think a duty: I mean prayer. To these prayers, let me direct you; believe me, they will give you more knowledge than all the controversies of the learned or all the works that human reason has produced."

Touched on a tender spot, the youthful philosopher took his quill in hand and replied, a bit stiffly: "I can never embrace as true what I do not believe. *My mind* will not yield a partial assent to truth. It will, when discovered, seize it entirely. . . . With respect to your tender solicitude, I feel, I acknowledge, all its force. I wish you the highest happiness. . . . Peace and happiness attend you, wherever you go."

When her coach drew near the next morning, and she prepared to say good-bye, Samuel slipped a little box into her hand, and she slipped one into his. Inside, she found a portrait of him; and he found in his package a miniature of her. With his gift he enclosed a note:

"Whenever I think of this portrait, I shall reflect that it is yours —yours *alone*—that it is placed in a repository sacred to secrecy— that it will revive the recollection of scenes in which my heart took an active part, and in which your heart benevolently sympathized.

"Go, then, my little representation—whisper into the gentle ear of my Margaret that she has made a human being happy—inspire her mind with whatever is pleasing, and protect her from whatever can wound or oppress. Tell her that your reign will be transient, and that the time will soon arrive when you will be only valued as the remembrance of past pleasures."

It was a "charming little miniature," she assured him. She carried his portrait next to her heart through the long and tiresome journey home to New Brunswick. She could remember the final words of his farewell note:

"Adieu . . . my heart is yours."

*   *   *   *   *

As the stagecoach carried Margaret through the New Jersey countryside, Samuel strolled across Philadelphia to Gray's Ferry on the Schuylkill River, enjoying the "delightful fancy" that they were both being charmed by the "fairness and serenity" of the same radiant April day. While she was admiring the beauties of spring through the open windows of the coach, jolting northward to New Brunswick, he was "plucking here a hyacinth and there a daffy." Filled with new hopes of happiness, she found the "expanding bud and full-blown blossom promised future blessings" for herself and the man she loved.

Peggy felt so cheerful that she did not mind the discomfort of the crude horse-drawn carriage, a long, high, narrow, springless wagon. It had three hard benches, without backs, holding three passengers each. Travelers entered in front, and those occupying the rear seats had to crawl over those in front; everyone had to stow his luggage wherever he could find a little space beneath his feet. There was nothing at the side openings but leather curtains to keep out the rain.

The coach, which was a mail wagon as well, was called the "Flying Machine" because the drivers—often slightly drunk from frequent stops at wayside taverns—drove so recklessly that accidents were common. For the privilege of risking life and limb while being bounced and jounced along a rocky, rut-filled road, the passengers paid four pence per mile. "Women on stages are not obliged to share in the expenses for wine, liquors or other spirituous drinks served with a meal," observed the French émigré, Moreau de Saint-Méry. "I will whisper this: That this courtesy is sometimes extended to courtesans who figure that a stage can be made to serve purposes quite foreign to modesty."

Peggy could tell she was nearing the end of her tedious sixty-mile journey when she could see the spires of the churches two miles from her home town. When the coach came a little nearer, she could view the beautiful Raritan River as it flowed from the hills, curved through the tangled woodlands, and encircled the town before going down to Perth Amboy and the Bay. Sometimes the roads leading into New Brunswick were crowded with Conestoga wagons. The wagons, drawn by four or six horses apiece, hauled grain from the neighboring counties. Sloops would sail up to the local docks and take on cargoes of grain and flour for delivery in New York, Newport, Charleston, Savannah, the Bermudas and the Bahamas. The war between France and England had greatly stimulated the American grain trade.

New Brunswick "has more than two hundred houses, mostly of wood and only one story high, and more than fifteen hundred inhabitants," one traveler observed. "It has increased so rapidly that a third of its houses weren't in existence ten years ago, particularly the best-looking ones; and in that time rents have doubled."

One of the most imposing homes was the "Mansion House" of

Margaret's father, which dominated the town from the heights of Albany Street. Colonel Bayard—who had served as mayor and now was judge of the Somerset Court of Common Pleas—was an important figure in the town. Close by, on Livingston Avenue, stood the new house of his daughter, Jane, and Judge Andrew Kirkpatrick. Margaret usually stayed with the Kirkpatricks (when she was not gadding about to New York or Philadelphia), while her younger sister, Maria, lived with the Colonel and his third wife.

The house on Albany Street was a haven of hospitality, not only for the prolific Bayards and their kin, but for the select society of Federalist First Families in New Brunswick. It was also a favorite half-way house for the Colonel's friends on their travels between New York and Philadelphia. Around his festive board, by candlelight, the leading men of the government would enjoy elaborate dinners, washed down with glass after glass of rare old madeira, claret and burgundy. Colonel Bayard, "one of the most liberal of men, not only lived up to, but beyond his income," Peggy once said, and he never would retrench.

The names of the guests at his table could serve as a roll call of Federalist chieftains: President Washington, Vice-President Adams, Alexander Hamilton, Chief Justice John Jay, Justice William Paterson (the Colonel's brother-in-law), Elias Boudinot, former President of the Continental Congress, and many more. Regarding Boudinot's visits, one of the Bayard granddaughters recalled in later years:

"Still I hear the rumble of the old coach up the hill. I see the gouty old gentleman descend, then Madame followed by her trunks and boxes. Then the finery she condescended to show us. Then the dinner in Mammy Sally's best style. Then the long wearing through the day of ceremony, the breakfast, the farewell, and the coach, coachman, footmen and agreeable visitors departed."

At other times would come old Dr. John Rodgers, pastor of the Wall Street Presbyterian Church in New York, with his buzz-wig, his well-polished, silver-buckled shoes, and his knee-breeches; the patroon, Van Rensselaer, who came in his own coach-and-four from his Albany manor house on the Hudson; and Colonel Bayard's old comrades-in-arms of the Revolution—General Anthony Wayne, the Polish hero Kosciusko, and General Washington.

Going home from New York to Mount Vernon for the first time as President, Washington dined with the Colonel. Often they recalled the bitter night in 1776 when they had crossed the Delaware, and the desperate winter of 1778 when Bayard had brought food and clothing to the starving, ragged rebels at Valley Forge. Margaret and her sister Maria, coming home from school one day, saw their father and the tall Virginian pledging each other's health from a huge punch bowl. The two little girls never forgot the golden moment when the great Washington spoke to them "in a kindly manner."

On her return to New Brunswick from Philadelphia in April, 1797, Margaret paid her respects to "Papa and Mama" at the mansion and then went to her customary quarters in the Kirkpatrick residence. The two-story frame Colonial house had a simple front porch, hip roof and double chimneys at each end; there were six shuttered windows across the front of the upper story and three dormer windows above. Except in winter, when it was too cold to stay there, Peggy occupied her own private room in the attic. Through the dormer windows she could see the secret retreat she called "my valley," where she loved to wander amid the wild scenery of the Raritan banks, just as she had roamed along the Lehigh River as a schoolgirl at Bethlehem.

Now in the early days of April it was good to be back again in the little room which, she imagined, greeted her like an "old friend." "It seems as if *it* sympathized and partook of all my feelings," she once told Samuel. On her writing table near a window, she kept her "commonplace" book, her book of Biblical Extracts, writing case, pen and ink. Nearby, she arranged her small library which—thanks to the Kirkpatricks' schooling—no longer included trashy novels.

Peggy arose the next morning with a light and joyful heart. She surprised her little niece, Mary, who did not recognize her aunt who had been away in Philadelphia all winter. Then, Peggy reported to Samuel, "she flew to my bosom and entwined her little arms around my neck while she bestowed a thousand kisses." In the afternoon,

Margaret dined with "Mama and Papa," made calls on several young friends, who welcomed her home again, and had tea. Not once in the entire day did anyone mention the name of Samuel Harrison Smith.

Peggy did not dare to tell her "kind, dear," Federalist Presbyterian papa that she was secretly engaged to marry her cousin, a Republican newspaper editor and an "unbeliever" to boot. She and Papa loved each other, but they had been separated so much that she did not feel able to confide in him—not yet. Instead, after everyone else had left the supper table and gone to bed, she and Jane had a confidential talk. In two hours of the most personal revelations, Margaret told her older sister everything. "Oh, my friend," she wrote to Samuel afterwards, "never, never was there a more affectionate mother. She has opened all my heart, she has seen its inmost recesses and the discovery has been without pain. I am perfectly happy."

The next day, for the first time, Peggy wrote with the eagle's quill —the one she had determined never to use except for love letters. She told her sweetheart that she had not dreamed, when he had given it to her last summer, "they would have been directed to you." "How unsearchable," she exclaimed, "are the ways of Providence!"

"I feel very gay today and my heart is so light," she wrote, "that I am inclined to fly." But she came down to earth long enough to tell him this: "Write to Papa. I feel more guilty than ever, in acting without the knowledge of this kind parent."

Samuel followed her bidding, and on April 18 she told him: "This morning Mr. Kirkpatrick, with Papa, went to Somerset court, and Papa got out of the carriage to tell me he had received a letter from you." But Papa did not reveal what his answer would be.

"To tell you the truth, I dread my next meeting with Papa," she confided. "He is good, kind and affectionate, but he knows not my heart, and constant separation has produced a diffidence in disclosing its feelings. . . . But it must be done. I know he will not write to you till he has conversed with me. Oh, my dear friend, must anxiety and doubt constantly embitter the cup of delight? Must uncertainty always cloud the bright colorings of hope? A thousand fears assail my heart. . . . I can scarce restrain from weeping. This is foolish, but, alas, I am sometimes very, very weak."

By Thursday, two days later, Samuel was beginning to worry because her father's answer had not come. "I need not beg you to give me the earliest possible information," he told Peggy. "He *may not* write. *You* will then be my only refuge. Express to me every word, every look. Let nothing be untold nor a moment lost in communicating it to me."

On Friday, April 21, the Colonel ended the suspense and sent for Margaret. It was with fear and trembling that she met him alone in his Albany Street mansion, for he was indeed a formidable figure who inspired respect as well as affection.

He was "above all a gentleman," said one who knew him well. "Medium size, with hazel eyes, and light brunette complexion, with a half-playful, half-melancholy smile, but ever kind and courteous; always dressed in the gentleman's costume, and wore his hair powdered, as represented in Peale's portrait." The Colonel had been born too soon to relish the freedom of democracy, another acquaintance once said, "and there hung about him a little of the formality and stateliness pertaining to that period. He and his friends looked upon themselves less as the representatives of the people than as their guardians and protectors, who endeavored to preserve what they deemed the necessary distinctions of society."

Colonel Bayard's stateliness could vanish in the presence of his family and friends; and in his gayer moments, when his face was lighted with his engaging smile, he could entertain his guests with anecdotes and sallies of wit. Essentially, however, he was a serious man, a Presbyterian of the stern old school who believed that life was a pilgrimage and not a gay frolic down the easy road of pleasure. His own life had been filled with vicissitudes, and only his Christian faith could have sustained him through the losses of so many loved ones.

What a list those lost ones made: His twin brother James, for whom he still grieved after more than twenty years; six of his children who died in childhood and another, the eldest, in young manhood; his first wife, Margaret Hodge; and his second, Mary Hodgden, and an infant son.

Now his little Margaret proposed to marry her cousin, Samuel Harrison Smith, a young editor he knew only by reputation, a man he considered far too radical in his views and uncertain in his prospects for the future. Colonel Bayard, a Presbyterian elder and a trustee of Princeton College, could not heartily approve of anyone who doubted the divinity of Christ. Nor could he accept Samuel's glib assertion that he respected the Deity, a rather abstract Deity and not a personal God. Margaret knew how Samuel had refused her pleas for him to pray. Only with the greatest pain could Bayard think of his daughter marrying a man whom she herself had described as an "unbeliever."

Almost as important, in the Colonel's view, was the difference of opinion over politics. In this field, too, Peggy's father viewed the Philadelphia editor as a theoretical philosopher with little common sense. Samuel, following that other airy philosopher, Thomas Jefferson, believed in the ideals of the French Revolution long after the mob rule in Paris and the deaths of the aristocrats on the guillotine had made other Americans see clearly that the "terrible Republic" was really a tyranny.

Margaret thus reported the interview to Samuel:

"He was alone. He told me he had received a letter from you. I perceived a hesitation in his manner that pain'd me. He told me he knew you not; that he had no ambition as to my situation in life and even thought a retired one more favorable than an elevated one; that his first and only consideration was my happiness and that he was willing to do everything that would promote it.

"I answer'd sincerely to all these points, but still I perceived not that perfect approbation I wished for. I told him, and I told him sincerely, that my happiness was deeply interested, but that I had determined never to act without his most cheerful concurrence.

"He again repeated that my happiness was his only wish, and that if it was necessary to it, I should have his consent and that he would write you that he had no objection. Thus ended this conference. Alas, it was not all I wished; but how should I expect more? He does not know you. . . . I cannot help feeling a thousand anxieties."

Colonel Bayard still must have more information on two points: first, Samuel's "pecuniary circumstances"; second, his religion. His letter to that effect reached his prospective son-in-law on April 26.

The young editor, whose newspaper was struggling through its first difficult year, had to reply that his means were only "moderate." They would insure the comforts of life, but could not free him from work for many years to come. As to his faith, he felt much hesitation about writing. "No one can entertain higher conceptions of the Supreme Being or feel a purer and a warmer love for Him than I do," he declared, though he could not believe in a personal God. But, he insisted, this should be no barrier. "No man's religion precisely corresponds with the religion of another," he argued. "Others have not the right to impose upon me any particular system of belief, nor have I the right to coerce them into the adoption of my particular tenets."

Margaret did not appreciate the careless way her suitor tossed off the vital question of his faith. Nothing could injure her hopes of future happiness so much as the fear of his "prejudice and carelessness" about religion. She begged him to read the Bible and learn the Gospel in which he did not believe. "The simple sentiment of Deity has always existed in the world," she wrote, and that was not enough for salvation. "A revelation has been made and, I firmly believe, made by God. Therefore, it must be necessary to Man. Such are my convictions and while they remain I can never enjoy perfect satisfaction till you receive them, too."

"You have reasoned yourself into a belief that virtue, principle, duty and even happiness originate from the understanding," she argued. "But, believe me, it is the heart that governs; passions are the moving principles. It is their impulses that impel to action. It is religion only that can triumph over them." (How well she knew this, from her own experience with a wayward heart!)

In regard to Samuel's financial situation, she said, "Papa meant to tell you that *in giving you his daughter, he had nothing more to give.*" The Colonel had lost heavily in investments since he left his mercantile business. He had invested in the stock of the Society for Useful Manufactures, promoted by Alexander Hamilton and several other Federalist friends, to establish American industries. They had founded a town near the Falls of the Passaic, named it Paterson for Justice Paterson, then the governor of New Jersey, and started textile mills there. The war between Britain and France had disrupted trade and credit, skyrocketed costs, and forced the company into bankruptcy. It was a wonder that Bayard could rear and educate his large family, plus the three children of his twin brother, and yet live as well as he did in the Mansion House.

Thanks to his generosity, Margaret said, from earliest infancy she had always enjoyed luxury and ease. But, she insisted, she did not need these to be happy. She asked only "the peace flowing from reciprocated affection, the devotion of a whole life ... a mind, pursuing what you pursue. If these are the most valuable riches," she assured Samuel, "I will promise you the possession of *these*." If his newspaper business should fail and "leave us destitute," she promised, even then "I will never regret the loss," for she would still have her Christian faith. "It is the influence of religion on my heart which has made my happiness and ambition independent of the wealth, the honor and the power of the world. May the first wish of my heart be realized in seeing you a happy Christian!"

But her Jeffersonian philosopher stood his ground with a stubborn pen. "Yes, my Margaret," he told her, "I know the value *your* mind sets on religion. You, too, know the value which *my* mind sets on truth. . . . I have *resolved* to think for myself."

Stubborn, willful, proud of his independence, Samuel refused to yield his convictions, even at the risk of losing the prize he desired above all else in the world.

Equally stubborn, willful and proud, John Bayard would not agree with the young philosopher. Yet, when Margaret told him, tearfully, that only Samuel could make her happy, her father cast aside his authority to forbid the marriage and let her have her own way.

"I hope you will be happy, my dear daughter," he said in a voice of loving kindness, "and as far as I possibly can, I will exert myself to assist you."

66

No wedding date could yet be set, for Samuel's finances were uncertain, and Peggy did not wish to rush into marriage immediately. After deciding upon the most important step of her life, she now began to hesitate a little before breaking the ties that bound her to her loved ones.

One evening, at the Kirkpatricks' supper table, the conversation turned upon the vicissitudes of "Papa's" life. Margaret remarked that she had had no such ups and downs of fortune as those which had given her father riches and debts, joys and sorrows, and yet not shaken his faith. "My life has passed smoothly away, I have now gained the summit of the hill of happiness," she said. "But how little, how very little, do we know of the future!"

Then Jane and Andrew spoke of their plans for retiring to a house in the country. "Where shall we be, five years from now?" she asked. Peggy looked around the table and thought, "Ah, I shall be far from you, dear, kind, beloved friends. I shall be separated from you, and God only knows how different, how very different, may be my lot."

Judge Kirkpatrick tried to reassure her by saying, "We shall be here in this room, at this very table." But tears came into her eyes and the affectionate glances of her loved ones only drew forth more. "Oh, Mr. Smith!" she burst out, writing to Samuel that night, "I do not know you! You scarcely know me! Will increase of years and increase of knowledge be likewise increase of happiness? They say that on the stream of life, every one must meet with storms. Mine are yet to come, then." She was only nineteen, and her life had hardly brought her to maturity. "But there is one anchor that will withstand the rudest storm. Humble faith can say, 'Father, Thy Will be done.' "

*   *   *   *   *

In May, the Colonel came to Philadelphia and met his future son-in-law in Andrew Bayard's home in Water Street. Margaret had been ill, he told the editor, but was beginning to recover and "in a day or two would be quite well."

"Is this the real state of the case?" Samuel demanded of her in a frantic letter. "Or is it stated in this favorable way to avoid giving me pain? Your not writing to me, of itself, speaks loud, and while this silence continues, I cannot be easy."

He "flew" to New Brunswick as fast as the "Flying Machine" mail coach would go, and found his sweetheart almost well again. He pressed her to agree upon a wedding day, preferably no later than December. But she firmly replied, "No, it is an impossibility." He persisted in his pleas, thought he had won the argument, and told Jane to expect the December wedding as a fairly likely date.

But Peggy sharply corrected him. "You are deceived, or at least you have deceived Sister," she wrote. "How, my strange friend, could you tell her that I had acquiesced in your wish of my leaving Brunswick in December? I know that you would be happier were we united, to separate no more. Pardon me, then, if I say to you, my resolution is unalterable. Ten months more will I devote to friendship and then the rest of my life I will devote to you."

"From November till April will be spent under the roof of my beloved sister," she informed him. (Delicately, she did not say why. If he had any perception at all, however, he should guess that Jane was expecting another baby.)

Furthermore, "there are a thousand little preparations, impossible to mention, which are necessary previous to such a change in life" as marriage, Peggy explained. "On your side," she told the editor, the delay would prevent all "hurry" in his business and perhaps would give greater certainty to the prospects of his paper.

He was crushed, but he had to consent: "If *my Margaret* is decided," he replied, "I will not attempt to shake her resolution." He closed his letter on a lighter note: "I have often been rallied, since my return, about the visit I paid to Brunswick. I found everybody knew it, though I disguised it under the name of a jaunt to New York. This, however, would not do, and I have been the subject of many a sportive remark.

"My vanity, at any rate, has been flattered."

CHAPTER THREE

THE GREAT THEME of every man's inquiries is, 'Are we going to war with France?'. . . France is feared as if her cut-throats could fraternize us, and loved by the multitude as if they were not cut-throats."

Fisher Ames, a Federalist who had just retired from Congress to his home in Massachusetts, thus summed up the crisis as Congress met at Philadelphia on May 15, 1797, called into special session to cope with the danger of war with France.

French privateers were stepping up their seizures of American merchant ships carrying food and war supplies for the British. "Picaroons" manned by cut-throat crews were cruising off the Capes of the Delaware and capturing unarmed United States vessels. Nearly every ship from Europe brought news of further aggressions by the armies of the French, who had first gone to war against the kings of Europe but were now gobbling up little republics right and left, in the name of "liberation." Only Britain stood as a barrier to complete conquest; if she fell, the next victim might be the United States.

The rulers of France were determined to make the United States regret having signed the Jay Treaty with England.

The French rulers, said Alexander Hamilton, intend to "punish and humble us." Their conduct, George Washington fumed, was "outrageous." They are acting, George Cabot said, "as I have seen a cunning knave . . . first commit the most insufferable injuries, and then take the high ground of complaint." "They are vext at our refusing to join them in the war," said Representative Robert G. Harper, of South Carolina, "and having found that coaxing and flattery would not do, they are now resolved to try blustering and ill-treatment."

When James Monroe, an ardent friend of the French Republic, was recalled as the United States minister to Paris, the French Directory bade an affectionate farewell to him personally, but with threats and insults against his government. The Directory rudely refused to receive the Federalist Charles Cotesworth Pinckney (brother of Thomas Pinckney) as his successor until France received some balm for her "grievances"; i.e., the United States might redeem itself by scrapping the Jay Treaty and giving up its trade with Britain.

President Adams recited the Directory's insults in his address to the 106 Representatives and 32 Senators who assembled in Congress Hall on May 15. By refusing to receive General Pinckney, he said, the French had treated us "neither as allies nor as friends, nor as a sovereign state." Barras, President of the Directory, had made an open appeal to the American people to repudiate their own government. This, said Adams, "discloses sentiments more alarming than the refusal of a minister, because more dangerous to our independence and union. . . . Such attempts ought to be repelled with a decision which shall convince France and the world that we are not a degraded people, humiliated under a colonial spirit of fear and sense of inferiority, fitted to be the miserable instruments of foreign influence, and regardless of national honor, character and interest."

Since the previous October, the President said in a later report to Congress, French privateers had captured more than three hundred American ships. Some vessels had been "wantonly burnt," their masters tortured and the crews confined with prisoners of war and "subjected to the most dreadful sufferings." This was, in fact, as Hamilton commented, "war of the worst kind, *war on one side.*"

Yet the little American Republic was in no condition to fight a war. It had a regular army of only thirty-five hundred men and virtually no navy (three frigates were being built), and its fortifications were old and weak. Adams recommended a provisional army, a reorganization of the militia, and the arming of the merchant ships to enable them to protect themselves against the privateers. In one last attempt to prevent hostilities, the President proposed a special mission to Paris.

Adams had first thought of sending Jefferson, as a gesture of bi-partisan unity on foreign policy, but the Vice-President declined, saying, "I am so sick of residing in Europe, that I believe I shall never go there again!" Then Adams, on second thought, concluded that the Vice-President, being the "heir apparent" to the presidency, should not be sent abroad as an errand boy anyway. He next proposed Madison, who declined, and that was just as well, for the Federalist cabinet members felt he was far too friendly to France. "He has been a frequenter of Mr. Adet's political meetings," protested Oliver Wolcott, the Secretary of the Treasury. At last Adams selected John Marshall, a Virginia Federalist lawyer and Francis Dana, Chief Justice of the Massachusetts Supreme Court, and they were confirmed. Dana declined, however, and against the unanimous opposition of his cabinet, Adams chose Elbridge Gerry, of Massachusetts, a nominal Federalist with Republican leanings and a personal friend.

Jefferson hailed the selection of his "dear friend," Gerry, with "infinite joy," as assuring a Republican counterweight to the firm Federalists, Marshall and General Pinckney. Since Jefferson hoped France would bring the British to their knees by the end of the year, "it would certainly be better for us to rub thro' this year," without being dragged into the war on either side, he advised Gerry. "Our countrymen have divided themselves by such strong affections, to the French & the English, that nothing will secure us internally but a divorce from both nations; and this must be the object of every real American."

With artful flattery, Jefferson thus persisted in his attempts to form a coalition between his Republicans and the moderate Federalists and to pull the Adams administration away from Hamilton's control. While Jefferson and Adams differed on many points, they agreed upon at least one: They mortally hated and feared the domineering Hamilton. In his New York law office, Hamilton remained the mentor of the cabinet members whom Adams had held over from the Washington regime: Wolcott, the Treasury Secretary; Timothy Pickering, the Secretary of State; and James McHenry, the Secretary of War. These three looked to Hamilton, not to Adams, and constantly begged him for advice, and even for drafts of cabinet papers which they submitted to the President as their own.

Fully realizing Adams' weaknesses of vanity, jealousy, capriciousness, and terrible temper, the Secretaries considered themselves his wardens, or guardians, tactfully trying to keep him on the path of true Federalist principles. They have been likened to "conspirators," untrue to their chief, but in their own eyes *they* were the faithful sentinels and *he* was the weak, wavering one who, in the end, went over to Jefferson's policies of peace at any price.

Adams sounded firm enough, however, in his first message to Congress, as he defied France and called for congressional action to strengthen American defenses. The Federalists in Congress Hall were even firmer. They drafted such a harsh reply to the President's message that even Hamilton considered it too warm. "Hard words are very rarely useful," he told Wolcott. *"Real firmness* is good for every thing. *Strut* is good for nothing."

The debates in Congress were filled with "hard words." The Ultra Federalists fought for a greater army and navy, and the Republicans resisted it as being secretly designed to lead the country into war with France. Young, hot-blooded speakers on both sides of the aisle rose to prominence during the House debates.

Among the newcomers in the Federalist ranks, none won more immediate attention than James A. Bayard. Only 29 years old, the freshman occupying Delaware's only seat in the House promptly became a major spokesman for his party. Tall, erect and impressive in face and figure, with light hair, florid complexion, an "intelligent and manly expression, and courteous and dignified manners," Bayard closely resembled his distinguished uncle, Colonel John B. Bayard. James was one of the three children orphaned by the deaths of James and Agnes Hodge Bayard. All three had been adopted by the Colonel and reared as his own. Thus, James had grown up in the Philadelphia household as a "brother" of his cousin, Margaret Bayard, and the numerous other young Bayards.

Young James had the aristocrat's love of fine feathers. He dressed so fastidiously that some of his colleagues dubbed him "the Chevalier," in reference to his reputed ancestor. One Senator described the Delaware congressman as "a fine, personable man of strong mental powers, vast resources . . . a lawyer of high repute and a man of integrity and honor." "His eloquence was lofty and commanding," said another admirer, "and he stood second to no man in either the House or the Senate." His "polished elocution and lofty scorn for all things Republican," said another, "marked him as the equal of Gouverneur Morris in oratorical finish and Federalist distrust of the people."

President Adams' son, John Quincy, who later served with Bayard in the Senate, said: "His fluency is inexhaustible. He speaks with so much ease, that he is never for an instant embarrassed. . . . His reasoning is clear, forcible, and overflowing with illustration." Truly, he was a terror in debate.

Yet Bayard was so amiable, so jovial, so affectionate, so addicted to wine and to whist, that he was constantly surrounded by a host of boon companions. "He is very fond of pleasure . . . a married man but fond of wine, women and cards," Senator William Plumer, of New Hampshire, noted. "He drinks more than a bottle of wine each day. . . . He lives too fast to live long." Benjamin H. B. Latrobe, the Capitol architect, said Bayard had "every qualification of head and heart" but, unfortunately, "a bottle and a pack of cards during many a night were habitual and almost necessary amusements for him." Bayard's letters to his cousin Andrew, the Philadelphia merchant, are peppered with sentences like these:

"My dear Andrew: The two cases of wine you sent me arrived safely and I am much obliged. . . . If any good madeira occurs for sale, not out of the way in price, will you let me know of it? . . . I want a cask of common wine, of any kind so that it is sound and dry."

Bayard, in brief, lived like an aristocrat, in the manner to which he had been born, reared and educated, in the same manner in which his cousins, Margaret, Samuel, Andrew and all the others lived in the home of Colonel John B. Bayard—members of one of the First

Families of Federalism. His cousins considered him a brother rather than a cousin, and to Andrew he once wrote, "I have no relation for whom I have equal affection, an affection which has never changed."

James attended Princeton with Samuel, both preparing for the law. At commencement in September, 1784, Colonel Bayard had the great satisfaction of seeing James open the ceremonies with the salutatory oration and Samuel close them with the English valedictory. Moving to Delaware three years later to begin his law practice, James entered the best society of Wilmington and the little capital, Dover. He became a protégé of the wealthy, powerful lawyer Richard Bassett, soon to be governor and Senator, and married the Great Man's daughter, Ann. This alliance brought him not only a lovely wife, but eventually a part of Bohemia Manor, the Bayards' ancestral home in Maryland. Governor Bassett inherited a large tract of the Cecil County estate and passed it on to his daughter.

"I go there with a pleasure that I scarcely go any where else," James once told Andrew. "I should like to spend a week there with you in the summer, where we could occasionally amuse ourselves in fishing and crabbing."

James' ties with the Bassetts, coupled with his keen intellect, his political ability and his family connections, enabled him to make a smooth, swift rise to the top in law and politics. Hence it was that, at twenty-nine, he found himself in Philadelphia as Delaware's Representative—one of the youngest and ablest members of the House engaged in the furious fights over defense against the aggressions of France.

From Massachusetts came another tall and handsome young Federalist who also marched straight into the front line of the fray. Harrison Gray Otis, of Boston, thirty-two, with bright blue eyes, black hair, rosy face and thin patrician nose—a Beau Brummell, affable, and devoted to pleasure, dinners, dances, and women.

Robert Goodloe Harper, the fiery South Carolinian, also thirty-two, with only a year's seniority in the House, nevertheless held a commanding post in the Federalist firing line. Of medium height, and with a handsome head and a barrel chest, Harper was a picture of force and drive. Albert Gallatin, the Republican floor leader who had no particular reason to admire him, said Harper was "good-hearted and not deficient in talents," but "as great a bungler as ever I knew."

Unrivalled captain of the "Jacobins," as the Federalists styled their Republican foes, was Gallatin—Abraham Albert Alphonse Gallatin—the clever Congressman from western Pennsylvania. A visitor to the House at this time could not fail to notice Gallatin's profile, "the thin, sharp outline of a Frenchman's face . . . the slow perpendicular movement of his right arm sawing the air" as he spoke with "a slow and rather embarrassed delivery" as well as his "peculiarity of accent."

A roaring Republican bull in debate was William Branch Giles, of Virginia. In his thirty-fifth year, he was already a veteran of seven years of combat in the House. A typical Virginia gentleman, the stocky, broad-beamed member from Amelia Courthouse loved to talk, eat and drink, and never tired of Virginia canvasback ducks, Virginia hams, Virginia chickens, and non-Virginia madeira. Also prominent among the "Jacobins" were John Nicholas, of Virginia, Nathaniel Macon, of North Carolina, and the patrician Edward Livingston, of New York.

Even more rough and ready in debate than the Virginia "bull," Giles, was the "lion" of Vermont—Matthew Lyon, a rude, coarse vulgarian born in Ireland, who roared his radical opinions in a thick Irish brogue. William Cobbett, the editor of *Porcupine's Gazette,* a native of England and scornful of all things French and Irish, thus hailed the arrival of Lyon in the capital: "To-morrow morning at eleven o'clock will be exposed to public view the Lyon of Vermont. This singular animal is said to have been caught on the bog of Hibernia and, when a whelp, transported to America."

Bayard, in his maiden speech, attacked Gallatin as the chief of a faction which, he charged, favored the French over the Americans. Bayard contended that the French, "the most intriguing people in the world," had insulted America by refusing to receive Ambassador Pinckney and by threatening him with arrest. "We owed the French

75

no gratitude" for their help in winning our independence from Britain, he said, and "if we did, we could pay them in powder and ball." It was their good sovereign, the murdered King Louis XVI, who had aided us, not Carnot, Barras, Brissot or Robespierre.

The Federalists accused the Republicans of selling out to their mistress, the "harlot" France. The Republicans with equal fervor charged that the Federalists meant to use the crisis as an excuse to build up an engine of "monarchical" executive power to deprive the American people of their liberty and to provoke a needless war with the French. When the special session began in May, Jefferson feared the Federalists would pass all their measures intended to "shew our teeth to France." But the war fever cooled down in June when Congress heard the news that the French had won a series of smashing victories and that Britain apparently was on the brink of ruin.

Napoleon Bonaparte had beaten the Austrians in northern Italy, and Venice and Genoa had been overrun. The Corsican was reportedly gathering a fleet on the French Channel coast to invade England and "liberate" the British Isles. The Bank of England had failed; there was a mutiny in the British fleet; the United Irishmen were in rebellion. No one could predict whether or not the English could keep up the war. Britain "is gone beyond recovery," Gallatin exulted. "Adams says that England is done over and I am told that France will not make peace with that country but mean to land there." Jefferson hailed Napoleon's triumphs as "splendid... miraculous," and eagerly awaited the downfall of the British throne.

Chiefly because of the Republican opposition and the chilling news from Europe, Congress enacted only bits and pieces of Adams' ambitious defense program. Finally adopted, after weeks of bickering, were some additional funds for fortifications, an increase in taxes, a defense loan, and an act to finish three frigates—the *Constitution*, the *President* and the *United States*. The Republicans congratulated themselves that they had kept their foes from dragging the nation into war with France on the eve of a final French triumph.

Yet Jefferson saw, with dismay, that the French aggressions against American commerce were driving many moderates into the camp of the Ultra Federalists, which he despised as the "British faction," led by Hamilton; and he feared a war with France would ruin the Republicans. Somehow, the party must be strengthened in the East, where the Federalists had swept the electoral votes in 1796; and one possible instrument to this end, in Jefferson's view, was Aaron Burr. So, on June 17, Jefferson sent a letter to the former United States Senator from New York—apparently their first contact since Burr had gone home in defeat.

Jefferson volunteered "some general view of our situation & prospects, since you left us," and said the letter would "give me an opportunity of recalling myself to your memory & of evidencing my esteem for you." Recent local elections had indicated "a dawn of change" in Federalist New York state; but with the "English influence" in the lower part—Manhattan—and the "Patroon influence" in the upper part, he said, "I presume little is to be hoped." Then Jefferson hinted at a plan to set up more Republican newspapers in the East, to give the voters the true republican doctrine: "If a prospect could be once opened . . . of the penetration of truth into the Eastern States; if the people there, who are unquestionably republican, could discover that they have been duped into the support of measures calculated to sap the very foundations of republicanism, we might still hope for salvation and that it would come, as of old, from the East. But will that region ever awake to the true state of things? Can the Middle, Southern & Western States hold till they awake?

"These are painful & doubtful questions; and if, in assuring me of your health, you can give me a comfortable solution of them, it will relieve a mind devoted to the preservation of our republican government in the true form & spirit in which it was established, but almost oppressed with apprehensions that fraud will at length effect what force could not, & that what with currents & counter-currents we shall, in the end, be driven back to the land from which we launched 20 years ago. Indeed, my dear Sir, we have been but a sturdy fish on the hook of a dexterous angler, who, letting us flounce till we have spent our force, brings us up at last."

"I consider the future character of our republic is in the air," the

Vice-President sighed; "indeed, its future fortune will be in the air, if war is made on us by France & if Louisiana becomes a Gallo-American colony."

Burr, who had by no means abandoned his dream of attaining national power, replied immediately: "I thank you, my Dear Sir, I thank you sincerely for your letter. The moment requires free communication among those who adhere to the principles of our Revolution. The conduct of some individuals of the Treaty majority has disappointed me a good deal. That of the executive something also, but much less." Then, apparently referring to President Adams' overtures for a bi-partisan foreign policy pact with Jefferson, Burr went on:

"From the insidious professions which were made in Feby. and March I had been led to hope that a more temperate System would have been adopted. All such expectations are now abandoned. The gauntlet, I see, is thrown and the fruit of our War with Britain is again in Jeopardy. The prospect is afflicting, but we must not dispond."

Burr, ever resourceful, had some ideas for building the Republicans' strength in the benighted East, but, like Jefferson, he feared that the treacherous Federalist postal clerks would tamper with his mail. "It would not be easy, neither would it be discreet, to answer your inquiries or to communicate to you my ideas with satisfaction to either of us, in the compass of a letter," he wrote. "I will endeavor to do it in person. Let me hope to meet you in Philadelphia on Sunday." He closed his letter with assurances of "my entire attachment and esteem."

The tête-à-tête took place, and it would be interesting to know exactly what the Republican "team" of 1796 talked about. If Burr complained about the Republicans in Virginia and elsewhere in the South who had "lurched" him and caused him to run a poor fourth, there is no record of it. Better that he swallow that humiliation and attempt to get iron-clad pledges from the Southerners that they would guarantee him absolutely equal support next time. Then if Burr should happen to pick up an extra vote or two in the North, *he,* and not Jefferson, would become the next President.

Jefferson fully realized that he had polled his maximum strength in the South and the Middle States in 1796, when he had still fallen three electoral votes short of Adams. Even if Jefferson held all that strength, and it was unlikely that he could win another fourteen-to-one victory in Pennsylvania next time, he could not become President without some aid from the eastern states. Burr, being a native of New Jersey and a resident of New York with family ties in New England, might supply that necessary help, in return for southern support for second place.

Burr had already taken the first step back up the ladder. In the spring election of 1797, he had been elected a member of the New York State Assembly. This would seem a lowly office, indeed, for a man who had been a United States Senator and who aspired to be President. But Burr considered it useful in advancing some financial schemes which would clear up some of his enormous debts, and the proper connections in the legislature would be useful links in the power machine he hoped to build in New York state.

His enemies realized his Assembly post could be a threat to them; General Schuyler, who had regained his seat in the Senate, voiced concern about Burr's future plans: "His views . . . alarm me and if he prevails, I apprehend a total change of politics in the next Assembly—attended with other disagreeable consequences."

Burr visited Philadelphia in time to join other Republican bigwigs in giving a hero's welcome to James Monroe, the deposed envoy, who had finally returned from Paris. They gave a "splendid dinner" for the Virginia diplomat at Oeller's Hotel with Jefferson, Burr, Gallatin, Judge McKean, Governor Mifflin, and about fifty members of Congress among the exhilarated guests, and old General Horatio Gates in the chair. They drank toasts to Monroe, to the Freedom of Ireland, to Liberty, etc., etc. "I expect," Gallatin predicted to his wife, "Porcupine & Co. will roundly denounce us."

Gallatin guessed right. "At some tavern in the city," *Porcupine's Gazette* reported, "a most ludicrous farce called 'The Welcome of Citizen Monroe' was performed. The principal characters were the Virginia Philosopher, Mrs. McKean's husband, and Monsieur

Citizen Tazewell of the Ancient Dominion commonly called the Land of Debts."

That was just a sample of the scurrility heaped upon Jefferson and his friends by the British-born Editor Cobbett, who was more than a match for the chief Republican poison-pen artist, Editor Bache of the *Aurora*. Jefferson, who deplored party violence, found himself assailed in the Federalist press all over the country in 1797 for a letter he had written the previous year to his Italian friend, Philip Mazzei, who had lived near Monticello for about ten years before returning to Florence.

Incensed because George Washington had carried the Jay Treaty into effect, Jefferson wrote his former neighbor, now in Italy: "The aspect of our politics has wonderfully changed since you left us. In place of that noble love of liberty & republican government which carried us triumphantly thro' the war, an Anglican, monarchical, & aristocratical party has sprung up, whose avowed object is to draw over us the substance as they have already done the forms of the British government. ... It would give you a fever were I to name to you the apostates who have gone over to these heresies, men who were Samsons in the field and Solomons in the council, but who have had their heads shorn by the harlot England."

Published in an Italian paper, reprinted in a Paris journal, the letter at length appeared in the New York *Minerva* and touched off a political explosion. The Federalists charged that in attacking "Samsons ... who have had their heads shorn by the harlot England," Jefferson meant George Washington; and they denounced him for "libelling" the Father of His Country. Jefferson refused to say whether he had written the notorious letter or not; Monroe urged him to admit it, since it was true, but the cautious Madison advised him to lie low and let the storm blow over.

Sitting silently in the Senate, where the Federalist majority hated him, the Vice-President longed to flee from the political passions of Philadelphia to the peaceful refuge of Monticello. "Men who have been intimate all their lives, cross the streets to avoid meeting, & turn their heads another way, lest they should be obliged to touch their hats," Jefferson lamented to his friend, Edward Rutledge, of Charleston. "This may do for young men with whom passion is enjoyment, but it is afflicting to peaceable minds. Tranquillity is the old man's milk. I go to enjoy it in a few days & to exchange the roar & tumult of bulls & bears for the prattle of my grand-children."

*   *   *   *   *

In the first weeks of the special session of Congress, one of the busiest scribblers in the congressional halls and lobbies was the *New World's* editor, Samuel H. Smith. He was not only publishing his daily paper; he was preparing to launch a weekly, intended for national circulation, to be called *The Universal Gazette*. It is quite likely that this is one of several papers which Jefferson encouraged the Republicans to set up as an antidote to the Federalist "poison," in hopes that the voters might be cured of their war fever before the election of 1800. Jefferson wrote a political ally one day in June: "Bache has begun to publish his Aurora for his country customers on 3 sheets a week instead of six.... Smith begins in July to publish a weekly paper without advertisements, which will probably be a good one."

The Vice-President, apparently serving as a volunteer solicitor of subscriptions, also wrote Madison: "Smith proposes to issue a paper once a week, of news only, and an additional sheet while Congress shall be in session, price 4 dollars." A prospectus in the *New World* read:

THE UNIVERSAL GAZETTE.

On the first day of July next,

SAMUEL H. SMITH

Will commence printing a Paper, designed
for national circulation, on the following plan:
I. The Paper shall be published once a week, at the price of three dollars per annum. One year's subscription to be paid in advance.

II. It shall be printed on paper equal in size to the largest newspaper at present printed in the United States.

III. It shall be printed on an elegant small distinct type, so as to admit all the interesting intelligence of the week.

IV. As it is designed for extensive circulation, local advertisements shall be altogether excluded and those of a general nature shall never occupy more than two columns.

IT SHALL CONTAIN

Foreign intelligence, in detail, domestic information, including the debates of Congress, information connected with the advancement of agriculture, trade and manufactures; concise notices of subjects of science, literature and taste. From the compact nature of the printing and the size of the paper, the editor will be able to admit every article which is found in a daily paper; presenting at the same time in a connected manner the whole occurrences of a week.

As the Editor has been for some time, and is at present, engaged in the superintendence of a daily paper, he may be presumed to possess the means of accurate and extensive information. Of any qualifications he may possess, it becomes him to be silent, trusting entirely in the opinion of the public, and to the favorable sentiment of those gentlemen who have offered their services toward the promotion of this publication.

"Those gentlemen," were, of course, Jefferson, Madison, and the other leading Republicans who hoped to educate the public in true political principles, and by 1800 to place the ship of state, as the Vice-President liked to say, back on "her republican tack."

In June, however, the familiar figure of Editor Smith was missing from Congress Hall, and his letters to Margaret Bayard in New Brunswick suddenly stopped. His sisters informed her that he was indisposed, but that she would hear from him soon.

Alarmed, she wrote to him: "This warm weather makes me tremble with anxiety. Do, my dear friend, hasten from the city." She realized that he had to work hard to make his paper succeed, for her sake as much as his own, but she assured him: "I would gladly suffer many inconveniences rather than you should be exposed to the heat of a city and the fatigue of business. Ah, what is any earthly possession, compared to health and peace of mind?"

Samuel did not answer her letter, nor any of the others she sent to his father's house at 71 North Third Street in Philadelphia. He could not write a letter or even read one. On a bed in the house on Third Street, he lay unconscious with a fever, fighting for his life.

Apparently, the young editor was one of the first victims in a new epidemic of yellow fever. The mysterious disease had killed four thousand people in Philadelphia only four years before. It had turned the busy capital into a ghost town and the scene of such loathsomeness—corpses lying in the empty streets, decaying in deserted homes, corrupting the air with sickening stench—that everyone felt horrified at the thought of another like calamity. The arrival of warm weather brought instinctive fears to their minds, and Peggy Bayard shared that feeling of dread when she learned that Samuel was ill.

His symptoms were alarming: he had a fever and a violent pain in the head, and he was extremely weak. He was in the care of an uncle, Dr. Hugh Hodge, one of the best physicians in Philadelphia, and his sisters, Mary and Susan, were nursing him day and night. Yet no one knew exactly what to do to save a fever victim from death.

The doctors did not know what caused the fever, let alone how to cure it. They were as mystified as their patients. Did the fever arise from rotten filth inside the city, or from foreign ships in the harbor? Samuel, who had lived through the '93 fever, said then, "The cause of this malady is enveloped in darkness." He supposed it was "imported from the West Indies by infected sailors, or animal or vegetable substances." "It is a disease of contagion and not of infection," he speculated, "for the air destroys it by decomposing its poisonous qualities. Little, if any, danger can be rationally entertained except where a person unnecessarily exposes himself by entering sick-rooms, attending funerals, and touching or very nearly approaching the infected body. The yellow fever is taken, and only taken, by actual contact."

His friend, Thomas Jefferson, wrote Madison that summer: "A malignant fever has been generated in the filth of Water Street. It comes on with a pain in the head, sick stomach, then a little chill, black vomiting and stools, and death from the 2nd to the 8th day." The victim first complained of a languid feeling, a headache, an upset stomach, and then a chill and fever. His eyes turned yellow and then the entire skin became yellow. Near the end, the poor victim became delirious and the awful black vomit signified his certain death.

Smith and Jefferson were correct geographically—though not in their medical theories—in pinpointing the source of the disease as Water Street. This was a filthy thoroughfare on the Delaware River docks at dead sea level, where great areas of swampland provided plenty of puddles for mosquitoes to breed. Here, also, to the docks came many ships from the West Indies and Latin America. One infected sailor lodged in an unscreened house on the waterfront, and bitten by mosquitoes, could easily start an epidemic.

No one knew the mosquitoes were the carriers. The learned Dr. Benjamin Rush observed that "moschetoes were uncommonly numerous" in the summer of '93, but he did not know he had stumbled upon the villain that would be exposed a century later as the carrier of yellow jack. Nor did anyone pay much attention to a notice in the *American Daily Advertiser* of Philadelphia, telling how to kill mosquitoes, "those poisonous insects so distressing to the sick and troublesome to those who are well." A little oil poured into their breeding places in cisterns and rain barrels would kill the "whole brood," Claypoole's paper advised; but not many took the advice.

Dr. Rush blamed the fever on some damaged coffee which had putrefied on the wharves. Other doctors speculated that the disease spread by personal contact, or by some "miasmata" or "noxious vapours" in the air. The physicians differed, also, over how to treat it. Dr. Rush first purged with calomel and jalap and called it a "cure," but the College of Physicians disagreed. Then he turned to "phlebotomy," bleeding the poor patient unmercifully, sometimes to the point of exhaustion. No one will ever know whether more of these patients died from the fever or from the bleeding.

"Those who are taken sick die either by the disease or the doctor —or both," commented the caustic Secretary of the Treasury, Oliver Wolcott. From his safe refuge at Gray's Gardens on the Schuylkill, Wolcott reported: "The Jacobinical affection in my bowels has been cured by small doses of rhubarb and drinking camomile tea. I should have had the honour, if I had been in the city, of having been cured of the yellow fever at an expense of 150 ounces of blood and a salivation." Walking in the gardens, Wolcott told his wife, he felt like Adam strolling alone in Eden "before he lost a rib." At night, however, he added, "we have Eves in plenty, of all nations, tongues and colours—but do not be jealous; I have not seen one yet, whom I have thought pretty."

Many people, assuming correctly that they knew almost as much about the fever as the doctors did, dosed themselves with "Duffy's Elixir" and vinegar in a sponge. They chewed garlic, built bonfires in the streets, and shot off guns. More than once, a panicky Philadelphian would shun the sidewalk, run down the middle of the street, or duck into the nearest alley when he heard a carriage coming. He would think nothing of going six blocks out of the way to avoid passing a house where a dead body had been. If he met a friend, they would not shake hands but each, bowing and scraping, would seek to get to the windward of the other. Inside his home, the nervous citizen would carefully hold a piece of tarred rope in each hand, put a sponge wet with camphor to his nose, and tuck in his pocket a handkerchief well soaked with the latest quack preventive his friends had told him to try.

Dr. Hugh Hodge, no disciple of Rush and his bleeding theories, had his own ideas about treating yellow fever victims. He had an opportunity to try them all on Samuel H. Smith during those steaming summer days of 1797, but nothing seemed to do any good. Samuel sank into a coma, and the end of his life seemed near.

Sixty miles away in New Brunswick, Margaret Bayard paced the floor of her room, weeping in anguish and torment. She would have gone to Philadelphia long before this, to see for herself if her lover really was recovering, as her relatives had led her to think, but her family strictly forbade her to go. A nice girl had no business traveling alone to a city to see a young man, even though they were secretly engaged; besides, Peggy should not endanger her own life by going to the scene of the fever.

Unable to see him, she poured out her heart in letters which he was too sick to read. She avowed her love in the most passionate terms she had ever used. She declared that if only her family would allow it, she would be at his bedside, holding his head to her bosom, loving him back to health. The fear of losing him forever drove away all reserve. The restraints of custom which forbade an aristocratic young maiden to reveal her passion for her fiancé, seemed to her like vanity. What difference could such silly rules make now, when he might be "on the verge of another world"? "The distinctions of sex" and the edicts of society were brushed aside in her mind as she told him of her eternal love and devotion.

To his sister Mary she wrote begging for all the news of his condition. "If you knew how terrible it was to be at this distance and in such painful incertitude you would not only excuse, but you would seek to banish, all my apprehensions," she wrote. "Yet do it not at the expense of truth. No, no, I can bear all. . . . Hasten, hasten, dear Mary, to tell me that you are again without anxiety."

On the morning of the Fourth of July, the holiday which her "passionate republican" sweetheart liked to celebrate as the beginning of a new era of freedom for all the world, Peggy awoke with an awful feeling of dread. "I feel this morning a degree of gloom and depression which I in vain endeavor to overcome," she wrote. "Oh, my dear Mary, do not be displeased at my confiding my weakness to you. I cannot, dare not indulge my feelings . . . which I cannot communicate to another. You know not how cheerless and melancholy I feel, yet how happy are you. Yes, Mary, you are with him, you can excite his tenderness, you can alleviate his sufferings, you can hear him speak. You know all you have to fear or hope, while I—but, my dear Mary, I am doing wrong. You likewise suffer and I shall perhaps increase your sufferings only for the selfish gratification of weeping with you."

Margaret's tears fell upon the page, blotting the next lines, as she scribbled on: "But it is selfish, my heart is wrung with anguish. Yes, it is indeed anguish, for what pain can equal that of ignorance and uncertainty? Dear Mary, why cannot I be there, too? But no, you will not approve of it, you will tell me it is improper, impossible. It is your prudence, joined to your affection, that has made you so good a nurse. Yes, I will remain here, remain alone, and suffer in silence. Never before did I know what suffering was."

When she learned he could not read her letters, she exclaimed, in alarm, "He must indeed be ill, for if I were dying I could read his letters." Then she realized that her passionate love letters to him might be opened and seen by strangers' eyes. "If *he* is not able" to read them, she ordered Mary, "lay them aside. There are feelings of the heart too sacred for the eye of anyone else."

Mary told her no more, but asked her to pray.

"Pray for you, Mary?" Peggy replied. "Yes, from the bottom of my heart, with all the powers of my soul, with all the confidence of faith will I pray for you. But I will only pray that the will of Heaven may be done and that we may be resigned to that!" Surely the God she loved would not take away her only hope of future happiness. Yet this might be His inscrutable will, and somehow she must strengthen herself to accept it.

The horrible thought weighed heavily on her mind, and she could not shake it off. Her fears increased until one day, the darkest day of her life, she felt sure in her heart that Samuel was dead.

She wandered blindly out of the house and down to the river, to the woods by the Raritan where she and her sweetheart had had a secret meeting place. Whenever he came to visit her, they would ramble together through the wilderness and share their dreams of future happiness. She liked to call this place "my valley," and now, in her dark despair, it seemed to be the Valley of Death.

Alone beneath the trees, Peggy fell to her knees and prayed to God. Spare his life, she begged, if it be Thy will. But if she must give up all she valued in life, all her hopes of future joy, then she vould be resigned to accept her fate. She would never renounce her belief in the mercy of God. She would still believe that "whatever was, was right, and that even affliction might terminate in my future good."

But it would be hard, hard to bear that cross. With tears in her eyes, she lifted her face to Heaven and cried, "Thy will be done!"

CHAPTER FOUR

O N MONDAY, July 17, 1797, the mail coach from Philadelphia brought a letter addressed to "Miss Margaret Bayard, New Brunswick."

When she saw the handwriting on the cover, Margaret breathed a silent prayer of thanksgiving to an all-merciful God. Her name and address were written in the sprawling script so familiar to her now. Clearly, Samuel must be better or he could not have written a line.

She ripped open the letter, and found that he had, indeed, recovered from the fever. He was well enough to move to Abington, the country home of a Reverend Mr. and Mrs. Tennent a few miles from Philadelphia. The Tennents were old Presbyterian friends of the Bayard family. "It would give me great pleasure to see my Margaret there," he wrote, "but I find that the unoccupied part of the mansion is confined to a single room; I know not, therefore, where my Margaret could be placed."

"I have a thousand things to say, but which I feel that I should express awkwardly, perhaps unintelligibly," he told her. "But I put a period to my letter by imploring a continuance of that cheerfulness which is the greatest happiness. Farewell. S. H. Smith."

"I forgot to mention," he added in a hasty P.S., "that I have rode for 2 days past a considerable distance."

"Oh, my dear friend," she replied, "to receive again a letter dictated by your heart, traced by your hand, yes indeed, it made me happy. A few months ago, my happiness would have been unaffected by your existence, but now it is entirely dependent upon it.

"But it is a dependence I wish not to shake off. No, tho' it should bind me to wretchedness, yet while it binds me to you I will be contented. My heart feels the most lively gratitude to my Heavenly Father. His hand directs all things, and I realize His power and adore His mercy."

"There were moments of torturing suspense in which I wrote to Mary, which I now sincerely regret," she went on. "Bid her not love me less. I often regret that my feelings, whether excited by tenderness, joy or grief, are always too strong. It is my daily endeavor to regulate and restrain my affections which, as they are the most copious sources of the richest pleasure, so are they, if not governed, the source of the most bitter wretchedness." At nineteen, Peggy realized, "this is the first severe trial I have ever met with and these irresistible feelings of mine had too great influence. But how is the scene now changed, how differently do those feelings now operate! Last night, I could hardly sleep for joy. . . . Good morning, dear friend, think often of your gay, your happy Margaret."

From Abington, in late July, she received another letter in the familiar scrawl, even less legible than usual, he explained, because he was writing with "a parson's pen" and couldn't find a pen knife. For the first time, he realized how close a brush he had had with death. He had to admit, with a perverse sort of pride, that he felt "a degree of pleasure at the danger I had escaped."

"Judge of the savagery of the fever," he told her, "when I tell you that all feeling was suspended, so that I would not be able to affirm that for the first weeks I had any existence." When he was finally allowed to read the love letters in which she had poured out the agony of her heart, he wept "tears of joy."

He gave Peggy part of the credit for saving his life. If she had not accepted him when he had proposed, he said, he might have quit fighting, for he would have lacked that incentive to live. "The strong motives I had to live," he said, "may have decided my fate."

Near the end of August their months of separation were over.

and he arrived at New Brunswick by stagecoach, to be greeted as one returned from the dead. As soon as they could break away from the family, Peggy led him down to "her valley" near the Raritan, the "little spot, remote from view, unknown and unvisited except by ourselves." "It was in that spot, that, yielding up the most valued hope of my life, realizing that you were no more, I spent the most gloomy hours of my life," she confided to him in a letter afterwards. She told him of the awful day in July when she had thought he was dead and had knelt in prayer to God that His will be done. Now it was in the same place, under the shade of the same tree, that he was restored to her in perfect health. So the shadow of death was lifted from her valley, and there in their trysting place she could give him her love again and share his dreams of their wedding day.

The wedding day depended in part, however, upon the success of his business, and how had that fared in his long illness? "Has not your long confinement very much deranged your business, and will it not require much application to restore it to order?" she had asked in a letter written during his convalescence. "Be not alarmed," he had reassured her. "My affairs have been thrown out of their usual channel. But they are in a state of restoration and but little ultimate injury will be produced."

He had spoken too soon. The yellow fever, which had come within an ace of taking his life, became in August a raging epidemic. Twenty thousand people fled Philadelphia, the government offices moved to surrounding towns, and a general panic depopulated the infected city. While Samuel was regaining his health at Abington, his printers quit. His *New World* issued its last edition on August 16, 1797. It was killed by the yellow fever.

Thus ended the *New World,* which had begun with such promise just the summer before as the nation's only twice-a-day paper, and later had prospered as a daily, giving Philadelphia a high standard of intelligent, objective journalism. Samuel's ambitious plans for his new national weekly had, of course, been dropped during his illness. He had hoped his papers would make him financially independent. Yet now he had no business and very little money and was casting about for some new way to earn a living. How, under these circumstances, could he hope to marry Margaret?

Their debate about a December wedding date now seemed absurd. They would have to wait not until spring, as she had insisted, but even longer; how long, only time would tell.

Samuel had fully intended to tell Peggy all of this when they were reunited at New Brunswick. He reasoned that it was the only fair and manly thing to do. But when they met, he could not bring himself to mar her joy. Why should he tell her then? he rationalized. They had no plans to marry before next spring, and by that time he might be in business again. So he kept the truth to himself and disguised the true extent of his losses.

Peggy spent the fall and winter in New Brunswick where she felt she was needed. Her sister Jane gave birth to her third baby October 19—a boy, named Littleton Kirkpatrick. (He was destined to become a New Jersey congressman, 18.3-45, and, of all things for this son and grandson of fiery Federalists, a Democrat!) "It was my arms which first received the dear little being; mine was the first heart he was pressed to," Margaret told Samuel in a first-hand report of Littleton's birth. "If I were allowed, I would have him continually. I cannot describe to you the new and sweet sensations I have proved." A short time later she informed her fiancé: "Littleton seems to grow by the hour. He reminds us of you by winking his eyes in the same manner."

Now Aunt Margaret, who loved her duties as nurse, teacher and playmate for the Kirkpatrick children, had three to love and cherish. The eldest, Mary Ann, celebrated her fourth birthday September 29, and John Bayard, named for his grandfather, turned two on August 18. Peggy loved the "sweet little beings" as if they were her own, and never tired of them, even when they interfered with her letter writing. Here, for example, is a typical scene in her room at the Kirkpatrick house on Sunday, November 5, 1797:

"I just now lent Mary my pencil; Bayard snatched it from her, which made her cry. I first silenced her by representing Bayard as a child whom she ought to indulge and as a brother whom she should love. In a moment she was silent, and I then asked Bayard in the most affectionate way for the pencil, trying to explain to him that it was her right. After a moment's hesitation he, in very good humor, gave his sister the pencil, which she returned to him, because he had been a good boy, and he wrote with it for a few minutes and then gave it to Mary."

On another day, Aunt Margaret gave Mary a slate and began to teach her arithmetic. "How much, Mary," she asked, "did the cherries come to this morning? There were four quarts and each quart was three pence."

"How can I find out, Aunt?" Mary piped, holding out her slate. "I wish you would tell me."

"Willingly, my dear. Make four strokes, under each stroke put three dots. Now count the dots, which are pence, and you will know."

"Twelve pence—that's a shilling, Aunt! Now I'll see how much raspberries come to, and currants, too, and strawberries, too."

"Now, Mary, if I were to take one quart away, how many would remain? How much is three times three?"

"I can't tell, Aunt."

"Put three dots there, three further off, three a little further. There, now, are three threes. Count and tell me how many that makes." Little Mary succeeded and asked for one sum after another until Aunt Margaret went downstairs.

One Sunday morning, before the whole family went to the Presbyterian church, Mary read one of her own little sermons. The text was, "He shall feed His flock like a a shepherd, He shall gather the lambs in His arms and carry them in His bosom." Mary could not comprehend how she was guarded by an invisible Being. "How, Aunt, does He carry me in His arms? What green pastures does He lead me to?" Peggy found it as hard to explain as it was to convert Samuel to her Presbyterian doctrine.

*   *   *   *   *

By November the frosts of autumn had killed off the mosquitoes and Philadelphia once more was free of yellow fever. Returning to the capital, President and Mrs. Adams paused in New Brunswick on November 8, at the Indian Queen Hotel, and fifty guests sat down to dinner with them at the White Hall Tavern. Colonel John Bayard served on the reception committee. His daughters, Margaret and Maria, spent the afternoon at the home of General and Mrs. Anthony White, with the presidential couple, General Kosciusko, and "a number of other great folks."

Home again in Philadelphia for the first time since his illness, Samuel searched at once for his miniature of Margaret and pressed it to his heart. "There it is lodged in safety," he assured her, "where the dear original is and ever will be."

After three months' absence, he viewed the "animated scene" of the bustling capital city as if with the eyes of a stranger. "It seems to me something like enchantment," he told Peggy. "Every object appears new, everything appears interesting. Who can be indifferent to the theatre of his various pursuits and the residence of many friends? I have many friends yet to see, many to thank for their attentions, many to felicitate on their being still alive and in health." It was like greeting the survivors of a war, an earthquake, or some other catastrophe; they could hardly believe they had been so fortunate, for 1,292 had died of yellow fever.

The *New World* also was dead, so Samuel must seek another paper to continue his career as an editor. Fortunately, his good friend Joseph Gales, Sr., a fellow laborer in the Republican vineyard, planned to move to Raleigh, North Carolina, and set up a new paper to help convert the Federalists in that benighted part of the country, as part of Jefferson's plans for the New Enlightenment of Voters. Gales sold Samuel the good will and the subscription list of his Philadelphia weekly, *The Independent Gazetteer, or the Chronicle of Freedom,* and the new editor changed its name to *The Universal Gazette.*

Exactly how Samuel raised the money is not clear, but Jefferson's earlier letters to leading Republicans, urging them to subscribe to the *Gazette,* indicate the party chieftains intended the national weekly to do much good for their cause in future elections. An associate of Gales has recalled: "Another paper began to be called for by the party then growing into consequence in Congress and in the country under the lead of Mr. Jefferson." This paper was "to be published weekly, so as to fit it for diffusive circulation through the country by the mails." Samuel's "character and known political sentiments had secured him the confidence of the Republicans," so they helped him to launch the new *Gazette* which first appeared November 16, 1797.

The Republican leaders privately patronized other, less scholarly scriveners than Samuel H. Smith. When the Federalists fired John Beckley as Clerk of the House of Representatives in 1797 because of his blatant electioneering for the Jefferson-Burr ticket, he sought revenge by publishing some well-kept secrets about the private life of Alexander Hamilton. The scandal story appeared in a book entitled, *The History of the United States for the Year 1796;* the author was James T. Callender, a Scottish radical hack writer who had been forced to flee to America for his attacks upon the British government.

Callender, who was once thrown out of Congress Hall because he was covered with lice and filth, was described by "Porcupine" Cobbett as "a scald-headed, lousy Scotch candidate for Botany Bay...a dirty little toper with shaved head and greasy jacket, nankeen pantaloons and woolen stockings."

Callender charged Hamilton with corruption, bribery, and illegal speculation in government securities while Secretary of the Treasury, in cahoots with a confidence man named James Reynolds. Hamilton had confided the true story to three Republicans in Congress— Muhlenberg, Venable, and Monroe—when they had inquired about it four years before, and the tale also was known by Jefferson and Oliver Wolcott. When Monroe refused to vouch publicly for Hamilton's integrity, after the Callender book came out, Hamilton determined to clear himself by telling the whole sordid story in a pamphlet in the fall of 1797.

In this sensational pamphlet, Hamilton admitted that, for months, he had carried on an illicit love affair with Reynolds' wife, Maria, who had come to him asking for money as a lady in distress. Later, Hamilton said, Reynolds blackmailed him for more than a thousand dollars in hush money, before being sent to jail on other charges. Hamilton accused Monroe of having instigated the Callender attack, and a duel between the two statesmen was averted only by the intervention of Aaron Burr. Later the ineffable Mrs. Reynolds divorced her swindling husband—with Aaron Burr acting as her lawyer—and married Jacob Clingman, Reynolds' former companion in crime.

Hamilton's pamphlet may have saved his reputation for financial integrity, but only at the cost of embarrassing his wife, who stood by him faithfully, and he ruined any possibility of his ever being elected President. Jefferson managed to restrain his grief over this prospect, commenting that Hamilton's "willingness to plead guilty as to the adultery seems rather to have strengthened than weakened the suspicions that he was in truth guilty of the speculations."

Jefferson bought Callender's books and pamphlets, and gave him several donations of fifty dollars each, the recipient usually requesting that the payments be made through a dummy third party, "to keep his name out of sight." "If I could find any fourth person to do what Mr. Dallas or one half what Leiper or Mr. Jefferson have already done, I would make myself heard very distinctly, for a considerable distance," the "scald-headed" Scot declared. Jefferson claimed his gifts were merely acts of charity for a poor scribbler oppressed by the British faction for championing the cause of republican liberty, but it is clear that the Vice-President was willing to use any weapon, even one covered with lice and filth, to beat down the hated Hamilton.

The "Reynolds affair" shared the limelight, in late 1797, with the vituperative battle between "Porcupine" Cobbett and Dr. Benjamin Rush. The Federalist editor, who would stoop to any gutter in his fight against "French principles," despised the doctor who was an ardent Republican as well as a signer of the Declaration of Independence. Like the deadly mosquitoes that had spread the yellow fever, the "Porcupine" blistered the physician with a series of biting attacks on Dr. Rush's attempts to cure the fever by bleeding. Cobbett likened the "Philadelphia phlebotomist" to "Dr. Sangrado," the quack teacher of Gil Blas, a "tall, pale, hungry-looking fellow" who, after drawing six porringers of blood from a patient, says, "It is a gross error to suppose that blood is necessary to the conservation of life."

A fanciful "advertisement" in *Porcupine's Gazette* read: "Rush and his Patients: Wanted, by a physician, an entire new set of patients, his old ones having given him the slip; also a slower method of dispatching them than that of phlebotomy, the celerity of which does not give time *for making out bills.*"

When told that Dr. Rush was "useful to society," the English-born editor jeered: "So is a mosquito, a horse-leech, a ferret, a pole cat, a weasel; for these are all bleeders and understand their business fully as well as Doctor Rush does his." Maddened by these incessant stings, Dr. Rush sued Cobbett for libel, and all Philadelphia wondered whether the State Supreme Court would rule in favor of the Porcupine or the victim of his quills. The eager citizens would have to wait two years for the answer, though, while the battle raged on.

*   *   *   *   *

Samuel H. Smith tried to rise above the level where such scandalmongers as Callender, Cobbett, Bache and John Fenno bit and scratched. He sought to be a philosopher rather than a politician, an essayist instead of a character assassin. In the previous winter, the American Philosophical Society, of which he was a secretary and Jefferson president, had started a contest for the best essay on a system of education for the nation. It is reasonable to conjecture that Jefferson himself suggested the idea, for he constantly promoted public education.

A hundred-dollar prize was offered for "the best system of liberal education and literary instruction, adapted to the genius of the Government of the United States; comprehending also a plan for instituting and conducting public schools in this country." The judges considered two essays of equal merit—one by the Reverend Samuel Knox, of Bladensburg, Maryland, the other by Samuel H. Smith. Both essays would be published the following year.

Triumphantly, in the week before Christmas, 1797, Samuel rushed the good news to Margaret. He would soon appear "before the dread tribunal of the public" as an author. "Have I not reason to be alarmed?" he asked. "Would you be surprised if restless nights and anxious days should disturb my peace until its reception is known? But this is not the case. My expectations are moderate. I did not write the piece under any sanguine hope of acquiring fame. I shall be content if it shall draw the attention of talents to a subject more interesting than any that can occupy the mind of the public."

Sending her a copy, he said: "It has nothing to do with politics, it neither extols the Federalists nor anathematizes the Anti-Federalists. It attempts simply to express those truths which, however weak they now may be, will, before many years revolve, universally prevail." Leafing through it, Peggy discovered anew that her fiancé was a man with a mind of his own, ranging far ahead of his age in advocating the education of the common people as the surest foundation stone for democracy.

He began with a radical idea: That the twelve-hour work day be reduced to ten. He thought the time saved would be devoted by the working men to "reflection" and make them thereby better informed and more independent. "Society must establish the right and duty to educate all children," Samuel declared—a novel idea, indeed, in 1797. It is the duty of the nation even to "coerce" the education of every boy from five to eighteen, he said, and to punish all parents refusing to send their sons to school. He would finance the schools from taxes "raised from the citizens in the ratio of their property."

Samuel admitted some truth to the main argument against public schools: "Wherever there are numbers of children assembled together, there will be mischief and immorality." But more mischief and immorality, he claimed, have resulted from "adoption of parental error or vice." Competition with other children would excite study, he said, and "with children there is certainly no danger of too much thought."

Since "discord and strife" arose from "ignorance and passion," he reasoned, education would promote peace and harmony at home and respect abroad for the infant United States. "The era is at hand when America may hold the tables of justice in her hand, and proclaim them to the world," the editor said, in a flash of prophetic vision. "Scarcely a century can elapse before the population of America will be equal, and her power superior, to that of Europe. We may expect to see America too enlightened and virtuous to spread the horrors of war over the face of any country, and too magnanimous and powerful to suffer its existence where she can prevent it."

Margaret was amazed at the maturity of Samuel's essay. "I own to you I did not expect this little production would have gained the preference," she told him frankly, "as your sentiments and opinions must have been all drawn from imagination or the theories of others." But she discovered that Samuel, at 25, had won the favorable attention of many older men, including the learned members of the American Philosophical Society, and the essay brought him the lasting respect of Thomas Jefferson.

So the year 1797—filled with the ecstasies of love, the excitements of courtship, the dangers of death and the loss of everything deemed dear in life—came to a close on a note of triumph. On New Year's Eve, when she "scarcely ever wished for him more," Peggy eased her loneliness by having tea with her sisters and Judge Kirkpatrick. Jane, her husband, and sisters Margaret and Maria sat together, holding hands, and the Judge said:

"We are all very happy, and are now drawing to the close of a happy year. This day next year, where shall we all be? Separated, perhaps by many miles, we shall perhaps be in the country. You, Margaret, will have left us and poor Maria will be alone. Your Papa will really be to be pitied if you, too, leave him, Maria."

"I shall very seldom leave him," Maria answered. "If you and Margaret are away, I will always stay at home. Heaven only knows what the lapse of another year will effect!"

After all the others had retired, Peggy sat up and wrote to her lover by the flickering candlelight.

" 'Tis almost midnight! Everyone has retired to rest, and silent and alone I stand upon the imaginary line which bounds the last and opens the coming year. At this still moment, the soft accents of departed moments awaken memory and speak to my inmost heart.

"How eventful has this year proved to us! The important moment which united our existence, and determined the future felicity or misery of life, has flown. . . . Oh, my dearest, my best, my most valued friend, would that you were here, that at this moment I could pour out my whole heart into your bosom, that we might together reflect on the past and anticipate the future."

In that silent hour, as her quill scratched over the paper, the flickering candle suddenly guttered out. Terrified, she fumbled in the dark to re-light it, but her fingers, numb with cold, could not. The symbol of the snuffed-out candle seemed a reminder of the dying year when his life had almost flickered out, and an evil omen for the future.

Mercurial Margaret's mood soon changed to its natural gaiety a few nights later, however, when a group of friends took her "a-frolicking" on a sleigh ride over the snowy hills around New Brunswick. Later they danced half the night away. Someone suggested it would be fun to have a make-believe wedding, in the new style of the "matrimonial shackles forged in France," which were "worn only while agreeable"; and an "Ensign Boot" was chosen as the bridegroom, and Margaret as the bride.

"Your old friend Margaret enlisted as a volunteer," she confessed to Samuel, asking him to forgive her for thus "deserting" him.

"After a ride—or, rather, flight—of six or seven miles, we arrived at the destined rendezvous. The animating sounds of the violin inspired all our spirits and put in motion all our feet. I was introduced as 'Mrs. Boot' and received the accustomed congratulations. 'Mrs. Bride' and 'My dear wife,' 'My love,' grew quite familiar, and you would have been quite surprised to see how well I played my part. How I wish you could have seen me . . . one of the veriest little fools you ever beheld. As for how charming, I can't tell . . . Mrs. Boggs . . . says I never looked so well before and that I danced with the lightness of an aerial being. . . .

"I tried once or twice to check myself, for to tell the truth I fear I was a little too high, but, thank fortune, I got no fall. I danced

11 dances with 3 agreeable partners, I laughed 4 hours and rattled 3 more. Everyone was as gay as they could be. And even our grave sister Maria laughed and talked almost as much as any of us. You may believe we were pretty well pleased with our amusement when I tell you it was past 2 when we got home.

"Well, now, don't you wish you had been with us, that you might have seen your sentimental Margaret transformed into a 'charming fool'?"

Sobered down the next morning, she added this P.S.: "What a silly letter is this. I am really afraid you will think my wits are turned. . . . Pray burn this the moment you read this and do not read it a second time."

He need not worry lest she desert him for Ensign Boot or any other suitor, she reassured him. "To tell you the truth, you have contrived to fasten so strong a chain around me that no human art, I fear, can free me."

Samuel did not resent her sudden "marriage" to Ensign Boot, either, since it was only in make-believe. "To be the mad-cap now and then is to be happy," said the solemn editor, who seldom played that role himself.

Her letter made her "seem to fly," and he wished he could fly to her arms in New Brunswick. But he had to stay on duty in Philadelphia, for Congress was in session again, and the Federalists and the Republicans were at each other's throats.

* * * * *

The Hall of the House of Representatives displayed less decorum than usual on the morning of January 30, 1798. On that day the unkempt, wild Irishman from Vermont, the Honorable Matthew Lyon, strolled over to the solidly Federalist delegation from Connecticut and struck up a conversation, not intended to be friendly.

Chewing a quid of tobacco as he spoke, Lyon denounced the right honorable gentlemen as a pack of office-hungry rogues who ought to be thrown out of Congress. If he could bring his democratic printing press across the hills into Connecticut, he bragged, he could change the political complexion of the ignorant old Nutmeg State in jig time.

The Connecticut members knocked the chip off his shoulder. They told him, in effect, to bring his lying, Jacobinical printing press into their state; and, Roger Griswold threw in for good measure, be sure to bring along your "wooden sword."

Everyone knew what Griswold meant: Lyon—unjustly, he always insisted—had been cashiered out of the army during the Revolutionary War, on charges of cowardice. The story that General Horatio Gates had ordered him drummed out of camp to the tune of the Rogue's March and made him wear a wooden sword, was "utterly false," he asserted.

Stung by Griswold's insult, Lyon spat a stream of tobacco juice straight into Griswold's face. Moreover (or so said *Porcupine's Gazette*) the crude, bog-trotting Hibernian also uttered three coarse words meaning "the posterior, or hinder parts, of him, the said Lyon." Immediately the outraged Federalists moved to toss Lyon out of the House for his "violent attack and gross indecency."

"There is no doubt but a majority will vote for the expulsion," Representative James A. Bayard said February 7, but, lacking the required two-thirds majority, "we have little hopes of expelling the Beast." Sure enough, there were 52 votes for expulsion and 44 against it. "Both parties are in a state of high irritation," Margaret Bayard's adopted brother observed. "I think the session will not go over without some blood-letting."

On Valentine's Day, President Adams' good wife Abigail commented: "Congress has been fitting (fighting) not the French, but Lyon; not the Noble British Lyon, but the beastly transported Lyon. The Brute has not been in the house for several days, but he is unfealing enough to go again, and if he does, I have my apprehensions of something still more unpleasant."

Abigail proved a good prophet. The next day, just after the chaplain's prayer but before Speaker Dayton had called the House to order, Griswold strode into the chamber armed with a hickory stick.

This was the scene, as described by Editor Cobbett in his satire, *House of Wisdom in a Bustle:*

> When the parson retired, some members sat musing
> While others were letters and papers perusing,
> Some, apples were munching; some laughing and joking;
> Some snuffing, some chewing, but none were a-smoking;
> Some warming their faces, others back s - - - s indulging;
> Whilst they to their colleagues were secrets divulging . . .

Finding Lyon at his desk, Griswold whacked him over the head with the hickory stick, getting in several good licks before Lyon, caught between the desk and his chair, could struggle to his feet and defend himself. Lyon seized the fire tongs beside the stove and repaid Griswold thump for thump. Then the two honorable gentlemen rolled to the floor, kicking, punching and clawing.

"Everything was confusion and uproar and the gallery and lobby were on the point of breaking in upon us," Bayard reported. But "the blood of the old soldier boiled in the veins" of General Daniel Morgan, a Federalist Representative from Virginia. "He forgot his years and infirmities and would not suffer any interference till he thought Lyon well flogged."

Two members tried to take Griswold off by pulling his legs, but Speaker Dayton objected: "He should be taken off by the shoulders."

Out in the lobby, an unidentified Democrat from the region "over the mountains" tried to rush in to help Lyon. But Allen McLane, another old soldier, now customs collector in Delaware, stopped him, saying, "The members should settle their own business." When the mountaineer threatened to spit in McLane's face, then, the Delaware veteran retorted: "Well, sir, I tell you, if you spit in my face you will never go over the mountains again."

"If the fellow had spit on me," McLane told his friend Bayard, "I would have killed him on the spot."

Once again, after Lyon and Griswold had been separated, the House voted on their conduct. "I do not think that either of them will be expelled," Bayard predicted. He was right again; a resolution of reprimand lost, 48-47. "The House of Congress," said a disgusted observer, "is becoming a boxing school."

* * * * *

Late in the evening of March 4, 1798, dispatches from the long-absent American commissioners finally arrived from Paris. They came in a single packet to the Secretary of State, Timothy Pickering, who rushed them to President Adams. Some were in code, others not. All told a story so scandalous that Adams did not dare to release the text. Solemnly he reported to Congress that the mission had failed. A new French decree ordered the capture of all neutral ships bound with goods for England or her colonies.

"This is, in effect, a general declaration of war against our whole trade," Representative Robert Goodloe Harper exclaimed. "Are we to submit? Or shall we rouse once more the spirit of '75? At only fifteen years old, I took up arms to resist the English, and I then resolved *to live free or die*. At thirty-three my resolution is not altered and I have no doubt that all my constituents will join me in declaring that the blood which flowed at Kings Mountain did not flow in vain."

Adams called for warlike measures of defense, a large army, a separate navy, higher taxes, arms for merchant ships, all suggested by Hamilton in private advices to the cabinet.

The Federalists rushed in to pass the necessary bills, but the Republicans hung back. They proposed, instead, a resolution limited strictly to defensive measures and asserting that "under existing conditions it is not expedient for the United States to resort to war against the French Republic." Adams' "insane message," Jefferson protested to Madison, gave the Federalists "exultation and a certainty of victory," while the Republicans were "petrified with astonishment." The Vice-President proposed that Congress adjourn to "consult their constituents," a move really intended to stall for time until the French could invade England. "The best anchor of our hope is an invasion of England," Jefferson believed. "If they republicanize that country, all will be safe with us." He feared the Federalists would rush the United States into war against the French "conquerors of the universe" just at the time the British were going down and the country would be left to face the French alone.

Jefferson's disciples demanded that Adams release the full text of the dispatches from Paris. They believed the papers would prove the Federalists had exaggerated the need for war preparations merely to entrench themselves in power. For four days, in secret session, the House debated the issue. Then the doors were thrown open and the crowd in the galleries could hear the wrangling over how many copies should be printed. "One thousand, two hundred," said Bayard. "Three thousand," said Harper. "Seven thousand," roared the "spitting" Lyon, "for the papers are so trifling and unimportant that no printer would risk the printing of them in a pamphlet."

Harper prevailed, and the three thousand copies rolled from the printing press. They struck the Republicans like so many cannon balls, and none felt more shattered than Samuel H. Smith. The young editor had been following the Jefferson "party line," charging the Federalists had merely concocted a scare story to frighten Congress into war.

But the papers from Paris told a fantastic story of insult and intrigue. The three American commissioners had first been refused an audience with Talleyrand, the unscrupulous Minister for Foreign Affairs. Then they had been approached by three blackmailers, whose names Adams discreetly disguised as Messieurs "X," "Y," and "Z."

"Monsieur X" confided that the men of the Directory ruling France were incensed at the United States but could be mollified by a softener of, say, fifty thousand pounds sterling (about a quarter of a million dollars) to be paid to Talleyrand to line the pockets of the politicians, plus a substantial loan to the government of France. "Monsieur X" and his companions, "Y" and "Z," also demanded that the American envoys disavow, in writing, all the obnoxious statements about France in Adams' speeches to Congress and pay "reparations"; then France would enter into a new treaty with a secret clause arranging for the so-called loan. "You must pay money," "Monsieur Y" reiterated, "you must pay a great deal of money."

Politely, the blackmailers reminded the Americans that the young military genius Napoleon Bonaparte had knocked all the Italian states out of the war, had forced a treaty on defeated Austria, and even now was mounting his armies for a victorious invasion of England. The Americans could look to tottering Britain for no help now; they must make a deal with all-conquering France. "It is money, it is expected that you will offer money," "Monsieur X" insisted. "What is your answer?"

"It is no, no," Charles Cotesworth Pinckney exclaimed. "Not a sixpence!"

Pinckney's reply, broadcast in the papers from Congress, became a national rallying cry overnight as Americans united in a wave of patriotic resentment against the bullying French; and his words echoed later in the toast to John Marshall upon his return from France: "Millions for defense, but not one cent for tribute!"

The Federalists, favoring war with France, rode high. The Republicans were cast down into a pit of deepest gloom. Here, in the printed dispatches, day by day, word by word, was apparent proof of the Federalists' claims of French hostility to America, and the existence of a "French party" in America, the Republicans, who would be a willing tool of the Directory even in a contest between their own country and France.

The "X Y Z" dispatches "produced such a shock on the republican mind as has never been since our independence," Jefferson mourned. He realized, with dismay, that the "base propositions" by Talleyrand and his agents would "excite disgust and indignations in Americans generally, and alienation in the republicans particularly. . . . These papers do not offer one motive the more for our going to war. Yet such is their effect on the minds of wavering characters that I fear that, to wipe off the imputation of being French partisans, they will go over to the war measures so furiously pushed by the other party."

Madison considered Talleyrand's conduct "incredible," not because of its "depravity" but because of its "unparalled stupidity." George Washington hoped the revelation of the "profligacy and corruption" of the Directory would "open the eyes of the blindest"

Republican still dazzled by the illusion of liberty-loving France, but he feared it would not change "the leaders of the opposition unless there should appear a manifest desertion of the followers."

While the Republicans were "thunder-stricken," the old General said, their chieftains tried to resolve the damning dispatches into "harmless chit-chat—mere trifles." That, indeed, was Jefferson's propaganda line and his loyal editor, Samuel H. Smith of the *Universal Gazette,* faithfully echoed it.

Samuel realized, with acute embarrassment, that the dispatches had proved "his Margaret" and the rest of the Bayards right in distrusting the tricky French; and his faith in the chastity of the Republican goddess, La Belle France, was sadly shaken. He resented nevertheless, the Federalists' "extravagant attempts to implicate one half of our citizens," that is, the Republicans, including himself, in the corruption of Talleyrand. "Talleyrand is a corrupt man," he had to admit to Peggy. "This is undoubted. He charges the Directory with being also corrupt. Of this, there is no other proof than his assertion. Talleyrand wanted money. He unblushingly tells our Commissioners, 'You must give money.' To whom? To the Directory. But does it follow from his assertion that it was *actually* to go to the Directory? Is it not most probable that this is only a *cloak for himself?*"

Samuel held no brief for the "immaculate virtue" of the Directory. "I have long thought they possessed too much power," he admitted, "and this unavoidably produces corruption. But will it follow from this that the whole system is corrupt? That the whole nation is depraved?" Swallowing his pride, the "passionate Republican" had to concede: "The French government are really, or appear to be, hostile to our government. The duty of self-defense becomes the first of duties. To this, I do not believe there is a dissenting voice. It is probable that all the measures of defense will be agreed upon without dispute, except that of arming merchant vessels. If it is not opposed, then indeed I shall dread war."

Samuel, who boldly accepted the Federalists' epithet of "Democrat," though they meant it as an insult, then gave Margaret

107

a concise summary of the difference between his party and the "Aristocrats."

"In all doubtful cases, where the Constitution is obscure, the Democrat is in favor of the people or the House of Representatives and the Senate; while the Aristocrat is in favor of the President. The Democrat believes that the Legislature possesses most integrity and intelligence. . . . Nothing to him is more degrading than the submission of great events to the will of one man."

Despite all the "calumny cast upon them," he said, the Democrats "never wished for war in favor of France, or against England. All that they desired was that our government should avoid injuring France by any act of partiality to England." They favored the principles of the French System, he said, "not because they were French but because they were principles of truth" while the Federalists espoused "English principles" which would lead to monarchy. Samuel insisted the English people were "the most miserable" in all of Europe, while in France "the poorer classes were infinitely happier since the Revolution than they ever were before." From the charges of the Federalists against France, he wrote, "you would believe the whole nation was one great mob; that all morality was prostrated; that robberies, murders and assassinations formed the leading features in the actions of the citizens." Actually, he declared, the reverse was true.

Samuel could not convince his Margaret. Although she was only nineteen years old and admitted she knew "very little" about international politics, still even a teen-age girl with her eyes open could see the tyranny of the French aggressors as it actually was, and not be blinded by the rosy mists of "Democratic theory."

Facing the facts about France, she asked her fiancé, "Where is the freedom which she boasts? Where is that power in France which preserves the rights and liberties of man? His most sacred rights & dearest liberties have been crushed under the foot of a power more inhuman & unjust than any that was ever crowned! Corruption of manners, falsehood & flattery have been called the offspring of Monarchy, but what court or reign discovers more complete corruption, more abject flattery or more entire destruction of truth?

"To call the proud conqueror of Italy (Napoleon) the friend of liberty, to call that ensanguined warrior the Pacificator of Europe! He who broke the legitimate bonds of nations but to impose the chains which his ambition and power had forged!"

"You cannot be blind to the terrible effects of democracy in France," she told Samuel. "The first revolutionists were, I doubt not, actuated by the most pure & sublime patriotism & philanthropy. They wished only to break the disgraceful chains which bound the people and to restore Man to his native dignity, which had been degraded by tyranny. But *these* authors of Revolution, in wresting the power from the supreme executive and giving it to the people, gave it to a power as uncontrollable as the tempestuous ocean. . . . Now behold the fatal effects of misguided liberty."

Peggy regretted that she must disagree so radically with her sweetheart on this most critical issue as well as on the still-unsettled question of his religious faith. She wished she could agree, but she had to affirm that the leaders of the "aristocratic party," as he called them, were right. So she stood firmly with her father, her brothers, and her cousin, Congressman Bayard, in opposing the French even though that opinion placed her in opposition to her fiancé.

Ironically, her friends who knew of her engagement to the "Democratic" newspaper editor assumed that she had become a Democrat, too. "I am often rallied on being a Democrat," she told Samuel, "but my friends little mean or think of the pain they inflict."

* * * * *

There was talk of war in Philadelphia in the spring days of 1798, even around the President's dinner table where Congressman Bayard was among the guests. "Dinner was over and the wine had been some time on the table" (and Bayard, no doubt, was making his usual inroads into the bottles), when the conversation turned to the possibility that Elbridge Gerry might yet get a treaty with France. Gerry, the Marblehead fish merchant and the personal choice of Adams for the mission to Paris, had stayed behind to dicker with Talleyrand on his own, while Pinckney and Marshall had left in disgust.

General Samuel Smith, a Maryland congressman who was no relative of Editor Smith, said, half in jest, that the French demand of a bribe "ought not to stand in the way, but that Gerry ought to pay it." Adams exploded in one of the outbursts of temper for which he was famous. "No American, republican, or virtuous man could entertain such a sentiment," he snapped. Not a shilling would be given! General Smith insisted it might be wise to pay fifty thousand dollars for a peace treaty that would "save us millions."

"Sir," the red-faced President turned on him angrily, "if that be your serious opinion, you cannot be an American, a republican, or a virtuous man."

There was talk of war in the streets of Philadelphia, too, and Republican editors like Bache and Samuel H. Smith found their property unsafe from the wrath of patriotic mobs.

Down cobblestoned Market Street on May 7, 1798, marched twelve hundred young bucks of the local militia, wearing the Federalist black cockade and keeping step to military music. "Every female in the city whose face is worth looking at," commented "Porcupine" Cobbett, brightened the way with her smiles. At the President's house, the marchers cheered, and John Adams' chubby figure appeared on the steps in full military regalia, complete with cockade and sword. He denounced the French in violent terms, which one Republican called "abominable."

Inspired by the speech—and even more so by wining and dining in the taverns till ten o'clock at night—the militia reeled down to the house on Chestnut Street where Bache printed the pro-French *Aurora*. They banged on the windows and doors and threatened to wreck the place until some of the neighbors chased them away.

Two nights later (after a day of prayer and fasting) a crowd cheering for the Republican cause milled about the streets. John Adams claimed "ten thousand people were parading the streets" and filling Market Street, shoulder-to-shoulder, "even before my door." The President became so alarmed that he had "chests of arms from the war office, brought through by lanes and back doors" to his house, when some of the domestic servants, "in frenzy," determined to sacrifice their lives in his defense. The militia swooped down on the crowd and broke it up, while a different gang, of Federalist persuasions, smashed the windows in Bache's house and smeared mud on the statue of his grandfather outside.

The mob spared Samuel Smith's printing plant nearby at 118 Chestnut Street, but he had no assurance of being so fortunate again. He could not be sure, either, that some Federalist hothead would not strike him on the street. Fenno, a Federalist editor, and Bache came to blows one day after Fenno charged Bache with being in the pay of France, and Bache said Fenno had sold out to Britain. Fenno called Bache a "villain," and Bache called him a mercenary scoundrel, which made it just about even. When they met on Fourth Street, the Federalist struck at Bache, and "Lightning Rod, Jr." rapped his cane over his rival's skull.

Federalists, sporting the black cockade, and Republicans, flaunting the tri-color of France, fought in the streets and ripped off each other's badges. At the New Theater, hisses, boos, rotten eggs and overripe fruit greeted the actors who sang the once-popular "Marseillaise" and other French revolutionary airs, and the crowds cried for "Yankee Doodle." One spring night the orchestra obliged the throng by swinging into "The President's March," and an actor named Gilbert Fox sang some new lyrics written by young Joseph Hopkinson:

> Hail, Columbia! Happy land!
> Hail, ye heroes! Heaven-born band
> Who fought and bled in Freedom's cause!

The crowd joined in the choruses so lustily that Abigail Adams said "you might have heard a mile—my head aches in consequence of it."

"Hail, Columbia!" swept the nation amid the applause of all but the most ardent Francophiles. Bache, naturally a critic, called it "the most ridiculous bombast and the vilest adulation to the Anglomonarchical party and the two Presidents." Jefferson derided it as a "poor song" written by a youth noted only for his "extreme toryism."

Jefferson was sickened by the "war spirit worked up in the town." He thought war "almost inevitable." Threatening letters came to him

111

and he suspected that spies kept guard outside his door and eaves-dropped at his dinner table. On many a night, he heard the insulting "Rogue's March" played beneath his windows. "All the passions are boiling over, and one who keeps himself cool and clear of the contagion is so far below the point of ordinary conversation that he finds himself insulted in every society," he lamented to a friend. For a little peace and rest, he sometimes slipped into the library of the American Philosophical Society, where, as like as not, he might find his friend the secretary, Samuel H. Smith, seeking to ease the strain of party passions with soothing reflections about poets and philosophers.

Dr. George Logan, a visionary apostle of the French Revolution, often a gracious host to Jefferson and other Republican leaders at his home near Philadelphia, conceived the idea of going to France and persuading its rulers to stop threatening the United States. Jefferson and Justice McKean gave him letters as credentials to the Directory, and the good doctor sailed secretly June 12, 1798, but the secret soon leaked out amid a loud uproar of Federalist outrage. Brown's *Philadelphia Gazette* said Logan was carrying dangerous information to the French and would return with a Gallican army to destroy American lives, property, liberty, and "holy religion."

In this atmosphere of war fever, John Marshall, author of the "X Y Z" dispatches, came home from his mission to France. When he entered Philadelphia on June 18, the capital gave him the greatest welcome accorded any American except George Washington.

Out into the suburbs north of the city streamed an immense throng of citizens. Secretary of State Pickering and many other dignitaries went in carriages, others on horseback, and plain people on foot. Three companies of cavalry gave the parade a martial air. Even in the Northern Liberties, a fiercely Republican suburb, repeated shouts of applause greeted the cavalcade. Jefferson could not deny his hated rival's overwhelming popularity. "M. was received here with the utmost éclat," the Vice-President wrote to Madison. "On his arrival here in the evening, the bells rung till late in the night and immense crowds were collected to see and make part of the shew, which was circuitously paraded through the streets before he was set down at the City Tavern." A dinner in his honor at Oeller's Tavern produced the famous toast which gave the nation its battle-cry: "Millions for defense, but not one cent for tribute!"

President Adams breathed a like spirit of defiance when he told Congress on June 21: "I congratulate you on the arrival of General Marshall. . . . The negotiation may be considered at an end. I will never send another Minister to France without assurances that he will be received, respected, and honored as the representative of a great, free, powerful, and independent nation."

Congress responded by passing a series of acts which placed the United States actually at war with France without precisely saying so. It repealed all treaties with the French; voted to raise an army of ten thousand men; created a separate navy, with a marine corps; empowered the little navy to seize the warships of any foreign nation "found hovering on the coasts of the United States for the purpose of committing depredations on the vessels belonging to the citizens thereof"; armed merchant ships for self-defense against search and seizure; authorized United States vessels to seize French warships or privateers on the high seas; and levied a direct tax on houses, land and slaves to pay the costs of defense.

A declaration of war would have been rammed through, too, "if a majority could have been found to favor it," Senator Henry Taze-well, of Virginia, told Andrew Jackson, now a Senator from Tennes-see. Jefferson believed the "Tory leaders" had planned to make a formal declaration of war on France on the Fourth of July, but some of the "timid" ones held back from taking the final step.

George Washington was called out of retirement at Mount Vernon to be commander-in-chief of the army, and Alexander Hamilton acted as day-by-day director of the new military force. Washington believed that the French, if they really planned an invasion, would first attack the southern states, which lay closest to their West Indies bases, and that they might stir up a slave revolt and create a puppet republic west of the mountains. "They had been led to believe by their agents and partisans amongst us," he told Adams in a dig at the Republicans, "that we are a divided people," but the French

113

had calculated incorrectly in thinking Americans would not support independence "at every hazard."

Riding high on the crest of popular enthusiasm, the Federalists found themselves in a delightful position. They could look forward cheerfully to continued victories at the polls, picturing themselves to the voters as the only party favoring a strong defense and the Republicans as apologists for the French. The Federalists, however, were not content with necessary measures to defend the country against foreign enemies; they passed other bills intended to cope with enemies at home. These were the Alien and Sedition acts.

The first of the four bills was the Naturalization Act of June 18, 1798. This required an alien to reside in the United States for fourteen years, instead of five, before becoming a citizen. It was aimed at the rebellious Irishmen who were pouring into this country by the boatload to escape British persecution, and they almost invariably voted Republican. The bill would make the sons of Erin wait a bit longer and not rush directly from the boats into the arms of the Republicans. The ultra-Federalist Senator Uriah Tracy, of Connecticut, said that in a long journey through Pennsylvania he had seen "very many Irishmen, and with very few exceptions they are United Irishmen, Free Masons, and the most God-provoking Democrats on this side of Hell."

Second came the Act Concerning Aliens, enacted June 25, 1798. This empowered the President to deport "such aliens as he shall judge dangerous to the peace and safety of the United States, or shall have reasonable grounds to suspect are concerned in any treasonable or secret machinations against the government itself." This measure let the President deport any alien suspected of subversive activities, whether French, Irish, English, or any other. If an alien ordered out of the country was found at large, he could be jailed for as much as three years; if he returned, after being deported, he could be sent to prison for as long as the President decided the "public safety" required.

Third came the Act Respecting Alien Enemies, enacted July 6, 1798. In case of war or threatened invasion, the President could seize, secure or remove all resident aliens who were citizens of the enemy nation. Although the enemy was not named, everyone knew it was France. Representative Harrison Gray Otis, the Massachusetts Federalist and chief sponsor of the bill, demanded action to "take up that crowd of spies and inflammatory agents which overspread the country like the locusts of Egypt" and to "strike these people with terror."

Fourth and last came the Sedition Act of July 14, 1798, by unhappy coincidence, Bastille Day in France. The Sedition Act, limited in its duration to March 3, 1801, imposed fines and prison terms upon persons "conspiring" to oppose or impede the government; for "insurrections, riots or unlawful combinations" or for "false, scandalous and malicious" writings against the government, Congress or the President, with intent to bring them into contempt or to "excite the hatred of the good people" against them; to "resist, oppose or defeat" any law; or to aid "any hostile designs of any foreign nation against the United States, their people or government."

Almost any criticism of the government could be called "false, scandalous or malicious" or intended to bring officials into contempt; and Federal judges could, with a clear conscience, sentence fellow-Americans to prison for their political beliefs. The Republicans considered this a far cry from the ideals of the Revolution and the guarantees of the First Amendment.

The Federalists justified the laws on the ground that the United States was actually, if not formally, at war with France. No one knew how many spies and secret agents were swarming over the land. Thousands of Frenchmen were here; some were refugees from the waves of tyranny that washed up in the wake of the Revolution, others had fled from the chaos of Santo Domingo; there were thousands of Irishmen in this country, too, many of them radicals and rebels fleeing from agents of the crown.

As the Sedition Act came from the Senate, written by General James Lloyd, of Maryland, it was harsher than in its final version. In the House, Bayard, Harper and Otis, the three young aristocrats of the Federalist phalanx, toned it down a bit. Bayard added an amendment allowing evidence of the truth to be offered in defense against libel charges. This gave the defendant more rights than he had had in libel suits under the old common law.

Even with its amendments, however, the Sedition Act had plenty of teeth, and every newspaper editor in America knew its purpose was to stop criticism of the government, or, as Jefferson said, to stop the "Whig presses" of his party. Federalist Representative John Allen, of Connecticut, made the motive clear in debate. Waving aloft several New York and Philadelphia Republican sheets, Representative Allen asked his colleagues whether a "dangerous combination does not exist to overturn and ruin the government by publishing the most shameless falsehoods against the representatives of the people."

Albert Gallatin, the Republican minority leader, admitted some of the articles recklessly attacked the President and the Federalists, but, he asked, was the administration afraid that error could not be successfully opposed by truth? Did the bill mean that anyone who disliked the measures of the present administration or the "temporary majority in Congress" is "an enemy, not of the administration, but of the Constitution, and is liable to punishment?" In that case, no Jeffersonian editor could feel safe from prosecution, certainly not the wildly partisan Benjamin Franklin Bache, and possibly not even the mild, scholarly Samuel Harrison Smith. Anyone who criticized officials must be deemed a foe of the government.

Even such Federalists as the men in Margaret Bayard's family, men of learning and integrity, fell into that fallacious line of thinking. In the eyes of Colonel Bayard and his sons and his nephew in Congress, their kinsman Samuel Smith was not merely a critic but an "enemy of the government."

They so branded him in angry accusations that wounded Peggy's heart. "Why are there enemies to a government which consults only the happiness of its subjects?" she asked Samuel. "Why, ah, why is the friend of my heart numbered among those enemies? Ah, my friend, how much anxiety does this give, how do my feelings rise, when I hear the epithet of 'party' applied to you! While I listen to a father whom I respect as equally as I love, and to the nearest friends I have, and discover all their sentiments and political principles directly opposed to you, my heart sickens within me. . . . How dare I to hope that *you* alone are capable of rising superior to the prejudices of *family interest,* of education and party? . . . Though I am a woman, I cannot be indifferent to what involves the welfare of my country and my family."

To his sister, Mary Smith, she would be "fearful" of revealing this unladylike concern with party politics, but she felt no fear in confiding in her fiancé, she told him, for "you respect our sex and believe their minds capable of embracing the most important truths. I am convinced that you act from principle, that you wish only to promote the welfare of your country and that you would never be the slave of party." But her Federalist relatives and friends were not so charitable; after all, they were not in love with him.

"I have never been an enemy of the government," Samuel hotly retorted. "Nor have I raised the voice of hostility against measures or men that were wafted on the wings of popular favor." Why, then, he asked, should "loud and false condemnation" be poured upon "all those who do not rush with madness into measures prescribed by the violence of party?"

Samuel's passionate protests were not enough to convince his Federalist relatives that he was not a "slave" of the Republican party, or the "French faction," as they called it, and their suspicions presented Margaret with a difficult choice: To marry Samuel, whom they considered an "enemy of the government," she might have to break with her own family. She could not bring herself to give up either her family or her fiancé, and so the date of the wedding receded further and further into the future, as the fever of the undeclared war with France grew warmer all across the land in the summer of 1798, the summer of the "XYZ hysteria."

CHAPTER FIVE

I N EARLY August, 1798, Supreme Court Justice William Paterson came home to New Brunswick from Philadelphia, bringing news that chilled Margaret Bayard's heart: Another yellow fever epidemic gripped the capital.

Peggy seized her quill and wrote in haste to the "dear partner" of her heart: "Will you immediately leave the city? You can secure agreeable lodgings here. Come prepared to spend two or three months with your dearest friends. We shall be united and you will find a happy asylum in the abode of health and the bosom of your Margaret."

His sister Mary, paying her usual summertime visit to the Bayards in New Brunswick, added this practical postscript: "Do not forget to furnish yourself with warm clothing in case of a change of weather; give the same caution to Brother John. The accounts of this day are so alarming that we shall be in daily or hourly expectation of seeing you both. My dear brother, send to Mr. Fenton, shoemaker in Race street, and request him to make for Miss Mary Smith a pair of dark blue Morocco shoes as he made the last for me. Should the shoes be finished in time you can bring them."

Much to Margaret's dismay, however, Samuel refused to flee from the pestilence. He agreed that it did exist but claimed it was "local." "The infected part of the city is from Front street to the river, between Walnut and Spruce streets," he said. "A number of persons have been seized with it in this place, the greater part of whom have died." He insisted that "no risque is run by those who avoid the infected quarter."

Samuel determined to stay and keep on printing his *Universal Gazette*. To suspend it would be "in the highest degree injurious if not destructive." Well did he remember how his proud *New World* had been destroyed by the yellow fever the summer before, and he could not let the enemy kill his second paper. He would even risk his life to save it, because all of his hopes of marrying Margaret depended on its financial success. "Nothing but the dictate of duty" and their future together, he assured his sweetheart, made him stay and work in the stricken city instead of "flying· to Brunswick" to enjoy a carefree holiday with her.

Reluctantly, she accepted his plan to remain for a little while, but she demanded a daily report of his health, even if it were no more than a single line assuring her, "I am well." "When 24 hours prove fatal," she told him, "you cannot wonder that 24 hours' silence will make me unhappy."

She painfully regretted that she had not married him already, so that they could be together now in this time of trial, no matter how poor they might be. "We might have lived obscure and unnoticed, but should we not have been the world to each other?" she asked. "How much more willingly would I participate in your danger than live here in safety while you suffer alone. And if — — but oh, my God, Thou art everywhere present and Thy will is everywhere sovereign and unchangeable! How vain, how trifling does every provision for the future seem, for that future which may never come! It is our future comfort and happiness you seek but think you not that you endanger it? Oh, think if your conduct should be fatal, what a shipwreck you would make of my peace!"

Moved by her pleas, and by the growing death toll of the epidemic, Samuel finally fled from the fever August 21. He removed his printing plant, his workmen and his newspaper office to a house he had leased on the Common, about nine miles from the city. "I am out of danger," he assured his fiancée. "It is true, I have the city full in my view, but it is so distant that I contemplate it more from

119

curiosity than from fear. I have an open square in front and in rear and so much air that I can scarcely write."

His "Nine-Mile Cottage" was far from elaborate, but its naked walls and unfurnished rooms did not dismay the young editor. "All my workmen are under my roof," he told Peggy, and he had a house-keeper to take care of them—the wife of "a journeyman of the most decent manners." He would not be bored, himself, because "I have brought with me about thirty volumes, serious and comic, and I propose taking lessons on the flute."

Books also distracted Margaret's mind from her fears for his safety. She read the life of Madame Roland, and determined to imitate this heroine who sacrificed her life in resisting the Terror in France. "For instance, the other night, I heard Littleton cry," she wrote, referring to sister Jane's little son. "I trembled at the idea of going upstairs alone and in the dark. But I reasoned that if Madame Roland had yielded to such a weakness, she could never have been tranquil in a dungeon, surrounded with murderers and villains." Summoning up her courage, she went to the little boy who was crying in the dark, comforted him and enjoyed sound repose until morning.

"My disposition is opposite to Madame Roland's," she told Samuel. "I am gay, thoughtless, inconstant and trifling, while she was reflective, serious and persevering. I have not the ardor, the energy or discrimination of Madame Roland though I have her sus-ceptibility, tenderness and benevolence. Her faults were those of a great and strong mind; mine are those of a trifling and light one. She is pure and unadulterated wine; I am wine mingled with water."

Samuel expressed surprise at this "very whimsical" self-portrait. He could not recognize the Margaret he knew. He could see these resemblances, he wrote, between the "two modern females of dis-tinction":

"1. In expression of face.
"2. In an ardent desire of intellectual improvement.
"3. In an enthusiastic, tho' rational, attachment to Nature.
"4. In a spirit of universal philanthropy."

The traits of difference, in Samuel's view, were these:

"1. In intellectual, as well as active pursuits, M. Roland had less discrimination than M. Bayard.

"2. M. Bayard was more fitted for love than M. Roland.

"3. M. Roland, tho' a republican, was aristocratic in all her personal feelings, while M. Bayard, tho' an *aristocrat,* was democratic in hers! ! !

"4. It *would seem* that M. Roland had a mind more likely to pursue with inflexible adherence one particular object, while M. Bayard delighted in a change of objects. But this may be because M. Roland was more than forty when her character was drawn and M. Bayard only 20."

"Indeed, my dear friend," Peggy told Samuel, "I have a great, great many faults and I fear when you know me better you will esteem me less. . . ." Dreaming of their marriage, she related to him the experience of Jane and Andrew Kirkpatrick: "Sister has said that the first year after a connection is, take it all together, the least happy of any that succeed. There are so many little disappointments and embarrassments arising from previous ignorance of each other that it disturbs all that delight which the heart feels. This first year is one of hard apprenticeship, in which you must learn to bear with faults which you before never suspected. You must learn to sacrifice your own feelings and wishes when they are in opposition and acquire a conformity of disposition, at least to a certain degree.

"This picture is drawn from experience and I have every reason to believe it is true, tho' my heart cannot understand its possibility. Amidst the enthusiasm of feeling, we feel none of the imperfections of humanity and we forget that they exist. But when this glow shall fade away, when we enter realities, 'tis then that we discover that we are frail and imperfect. But we are all apt to make ourselves exceptions and feel tempted to exclaim, 'I shall escape without any of these predicted sufferings.' There are moments when the interesting importance of my situation fills my soul with apprehension. At such moments how do I wish for the presence of my beloved friend, for when you are with me, I feel no doubts or alarm."

As much as he wished to be with her, however, he could not. He stubbornly continued to publish his paper in the Philadelphia suburbs, although his loved ones worried about his health. His father wrote from Bristol, Pa., the refuge of many Philadelphians, to his daughter, "Miss Polly Smith, care of Colonel Bayard, Brunswick, N.J.": "Your brother Samuel's situation distresses me and he knows it from every letter I have written, nor shall I cease. He was well last morning and your brother John two days ago."

While the death toll rose, the editor strove to maintain an outward show of nonchalance. "He who is near a scene of danger," he wrote, "must soon become a philosopher or a coward." By the end of September, the fever had reached its peak. Thousands of Philadelphians had fled to the Common, camping in tents for lack of houses, and hardly anyone remained in the capital which once more resembled a ghost town. Taverns, dance halls, gambling dens closed and business was suspended; only the doctors and the coffin-makers were working amid the scenes of unspeakable horror.

The fever killed two of Samuel's rivals in journalism: John Fenno of the Federalist *Gazette of the United States* and Benjamin Franklin Bache of the Republican *Aurora*. Fenno and "Lightning Rod, Jr.," heroes of so many battles in their newspapers and in the city streets, would fight no more. Some Federalists, while mourning for Fenno, could hardly restrain their glee over the demise of the "scoundrel" Bache. Russell's *Gazette* of Boston exulted: "The Jacobins are all whining at the exit of the vile Benjamin Franklin Bache; so they would do if one of their gang was hung for stealing."

"Where, where will this terror end?" Margaret Bayard exclaimed in September. "Is there nothing to arrest its progress? My mind ... is an April sky. One hour it is clear and serene, the next it is dark with clouds. ... I am safe, but I have friends who are not. With what impatience do I await the winter, the only conqueror of this terrible enemy."

"I have sometimes dreaded your being too much of a philosopher," she confided to Samuel, "but as your philosophy has the power to calm the agitations of fear, and invigorate the mind and to elevate

122

it above the influence of danger, I rejoice that you are blessed with its influence."

* * * * *

Samuel returned to Philadelphia in October, 1798, his health and his *Gazette* intact. He soon found, however, that Republican editors faced new terrors besides those of the fever. He or any other editor criticizing the government stood in danger of being arrested for "sedition." He never could know when some political foe might consider an article disrespectful of the President or the administration, and have him haled before some fanatical Federal judge for prosecution. Some Republican editors already were bowing before the black-robed majesty of the Federal courts under the new wartime law.

One of the first victims was a member of Congress, Matthew Lyon, of Vermont. Already notorious for spitting in Roger Griswold's face, and wielding the fire tongs to repel his rival's hickory stick, Lyon had gone home from Congress as one of the most despised "Jacobins" in all the land. At Trenton and New Brunswick he had found tavern crowds hissing and booing and serenading him with "The Rogue's March." Home again, he struck back at his critics—this time not with spit but with ink.

In the *Vermont Journal,* he charged that under President Adams, "every consideration of the public welfare was swallowed up in a continual grasp for power, in an unbounded thirst for ridiculous pomp, foolish adulation, and selfish avarice." Furthermore, Lyon printed a letter from Joel Barlow, the expatriate poet in Paris, who said the whole trouble between France and the United States had arisen from "the bullying speech of your President and the stupid answer of your Senate." Instead of sending Adams to "a mad house," where he belonged, Barlow wrote, the Senate had echoed the anti-French speech with "more servility than ever George III had experienced from either House of Parliament."

For printing these two articles, Congressman Lyon was indicted for sedition and brought into Federal court. He found himself before Supreme Court Justice Paterson, Colonel Bayard's brother-in-law.

(Before the creation of separate Federal circuit courts, the Supreme Court justices had to "ride circuit" through the states.) Lyon conducted his own defense, basing it on his claim that the Sedition Act was clearly unconstitutional, a violation of the First Amendment which assured freedom of speech and of the press. Audaciously, the "spitting Lyon" sought to make Judge Paterson a witness in his own defense.

"Have you not frequently dined with the President and observed his ridiculous pomp and parade?" the Congressman asked. Paterson replied that he had, indeed, dined with Adams, but "had never seen any pomp or parade" but "on the contrary, a great deal of plainness and simplicity." A jury of free Vermonters brought in a verdict of guilty as charged. Justice Paterson sentenced Lyon to four months in jail and a thousand-dollar fine.

The Honorable M. C. was hustled off to a jail at Vergennes, Vermont, with an armed guard and tossed into a cell usually occupied by "horse-thieves, counterfeiters . . . and felons." In one corner he found a toilet emitting "a stench about equal to the Philadelphia docks in the month of August." From this malodorous cell, Lyon sent out a stream of letters protesting his innocence, and incidentally campaigning for reelection. He won another term—in Congress, not in jail—by a lead of two thousand votes over his nearest rival.

Meanwhile his Republican friends had transformed him, in the public eye, from a vulgar brawling politician into a saintly martyr, suffering durance vile for the sake of the sacred freedom of speech and press. His Vermont friends ran a lottery, and Republicans throughout the country collected funds to pay his thousand-dollar fine. On the day of Lyon's release, Senator Stevens T. Mason of Virginia rode up to the jail, carrying a thousand dollars in gold in his saddlebags, and the Vermonters graciously let the Jeffersonian Solon pay half the fine.

"I am on my way to Philadelphia!" Lyon shouted as he stepped from his smelly cell, thus claiming a Congressman's immunity from arrest while traveling to the capital. He knew the Vermont authorities were waiting to pounce on him with new warrants for his arrest on charges of violating the state libel and sedition laws. For that reason, the "spitting" Lyon moved, the next year, to Kentucky.

When he resumed his seat in Congress, a Federalist uncharitably observed that he looked "remarkably well for a gentleman just out of jail." Congressman Bayard tried, but failed, to have him barred from his seat as a convicted felon. Some Philadelphians gave a party in honor of the martyr's return and, growled "Porcupine" Cobbett, they got "as drunk as democrats generally do whenever they get a chance to swig."

Friends of Lyon paid a price for their loyalty. The Reverend John C. Ogden, on his way to Philadelphia to ask a pardon from President Adams, was jailed in Litchfield, Connecticut, for "debt." On his release a group of soldiers, calling him a "damn democrat," would have beaten him if a crowd of civilians had not chased them away.

Anthony Haswell, editor of the *Vermont Gazette,* appealed in his paper for funds to pay Lyon's fine. Haswell also charged that the Adams administration favored Tories "who had shared in the desolation of our homes and the abuse of our wives and daughters." Justice Paterson convicted him of sedition and sent him to jail for two months.

Charles Holt, of Connecticut, editor of the *New London Bee,* stung the Federalists with a series of attacks on the army and its de facto commander, General Alexander Hamilton. "Are our young officers and soldiers," he asked, in a jibe at the Reynolds affair, "to learn virtue from General Hamilton? Or, like their generals, are they to be found in the bed of adultery?" Holt was convicted not only for sedition but for discouraging recruiting, and sentenced to six months in jail plus a two-hundred-dollar fine.

James T. Callender, who won such notoriety with his account of the Reynolds affair, fled Philadelphia to escape prosecution for his scurrilous scrivenings, seeking refuge in Jefferson's Virginia, where he was arrested near a distillery outside of Leesburg as a vagrant. Senator Mason, who had hurried to Vermont to pay Lyon's fine, hastened to Leesburg this time to free Callender. From Mason's home, "Rasberry Plain," the Scottish malcontent wrote Jefferson that he was happy to be out of "that sink of destruction," that "porch of perdition," Philadelphia, where two Federalist newspapers were bad enough to have brought on the yellow fever. "I hope that this pestilence, so justly deserved by all the male adults, will prove a happy check to a much worse one, the black Cockade fever," he told his benefactor, the Vice-President.

Callender continued his labors in the Republican cause by working on the Richmond *Examiner,* but he could not escape jail forever. Eventually, he was indicted for sedition because of many attacks upon President Adams in a book, *The Prospect Before Us,* which Jefferson had approved in manuscript. Adams, said the author, "is not only a repulsive pedant, a gross hypocrite, and an unprincipled oppressor, but in private life, one of the most egregious fools upon the continent." On the basis of these and similar samples of his slashing style, Supreme Court Justice Samuel Chase had no difficulty in deciding to sentence the bibulous bibliophile to nine months in jail and a two-hundred-dollar fine.

John D. Burk, an Irishman who edited the Republican *Time Piece* in New York City, fell afoul of the law by charging that someone in authority had tampered with a letter from Elbridge Gerry to Adams, concerning Gerry's mission to France in the "XYZ affair." The prosecution of Burk was dropped on condition that he would leave the country; instead, he, too, went into hiding in Virginia.

Most ludicrous of the sedition cases was the one involving Luther Baldwin, a tavern lounger in a New Jersey town, convicted of voicing a fervent wish for the early demise of President Adams. When the President drove through Newark in the summer of 1798, and was greeted with the cheers of the citizens and the roar of cannon, Baldwin was drinking as usual with some of his friends in the nearby tavern.

"There goes the President," one roisterer exclaimed when they heard the cannon boom, "and they are firing at his — — —."

"I don't care," Baldwin shouted, "if they fire *through* his — — —!"

"That's sedition!" cried the bartender, and Baldwin was arrested and fined a hundred dollars.

There was no wave of arrests under the Alien Law, chiefly because many aliens fled the country. Among the French who departed hastily were Moreau de Saint-Méry, the Philadelphia book-shop proprietor, and Count Volney, the radical French philosopher, who was a friend of Jefferson and Samuel H. Smith. The Federalists thought the Count must surely be a spy. Upon Volney's departure, Jefferson commented bitterly: "It suffices for a man to be a philosopher and to believe that human affairs are susceptible of improvement & to look forward, rather than back to the Gothic ages, for perfection, to mark him as anarchist, disorganizer, atheist & enemy of the government." The Vice-President well knew that a certain Virginia "philosopher" also was being branded with those same epithets, in this nationwide "reign of witches." He even hinted in one letter that he would not be surprised if he, although Vice-President of the United States, might be prosecuted as an "enemy of the government."

"There is no event, therefore, however atrocious, which may not be expected," he wrote. "I have contemplated every event which the Maratists of the day can perpetrate and am prepared to meet every one in such a way as shall not be derogatory either to the public liberty or my own personal honor." He consoled himself with the thought that in his own state, the "deep-rooted disgust produced by the Alien and Sedition acts is beyond any thing ever seen since the days of the Stamp Act."

To strike back, Jefferson secretly drafted a series of resolutions which were adopted by the legislatures of Kentucky and Virginia late in 1798. These were the famous "Kentucky and Virginia Resolutions." They branded the Alien and Sedition Laws unconstitutional, and therefore null and void. They called upon the legislatures of the other states to protest, also, and urged Congress to repeal the hated statutes. Both resolutions were interpreted as claiming that a state could nullify a Federal act which it considered a violation of the compact of states that created the Union. Extreme Federalists interpreted the Kentucky and Virginia acts as a sign of future secession or rebellion, and Alexander Hamilton proposed stern measures to put the "rebels" down.

General Hamilton suggested dividing the "great states," such as Virginia, into several smaller ones more easily controlled, and he would have a Federal justice of the peace in every county of the land, plus a permanent army on a wartime basis, to protect the national government from the rebellious men whom he considered its internal enemies. Indeed, John Taylor of Caroline, an extreme Virginia Republican, actually proposed that Virginia and North Carolina should secede, but Jefferson vetoed the idea.

Jefferson hoped that New York, Pennsylvania and New Jersey at least would endorse the Kentucky and Virginia resolutions, but he was sadly disappointed. Not a single one of the fourteen other states joined Virginia and Kentucky in the protest, and several denounced it in strong language. The Delaware legislature, in the first reply, called it "a very unjustifiable interference with the general government . . . and of dangerous tendencies." Rhode Island, Massachusetts, New York, Connecticut, New Hampshire, Vermont, Maryland, New Jersey and Pennsylvania, one by one, joined the chorus of rejection.

Several Southern states, normally considered Republican, maintained a very discreet silence. This hostile reaction hardly justifies the claim that the Alien and Sedition Laws stirred the American people to a great wave of protest, which swung the 1800 election to the Republicans. The Federalists, on the contrary, made striking gains in the elections of 1798 and early 1799 when they were riding high on the wave of patriotic fervor whipped up by the French war scare. Even in Virginia, Jefferson glumly observed in late 1798, "a most respectable part" of the citizens were "enveloped in the XYZ delusion," which kept the Old Dominion from being solidly Republican. "This disease of the imagination will pass over, because the patients are essentially republican," he predicted. "Indeed, the Doctor is now on his way to cure it, in the guise of a tax gatherer."

In November, Generals George Washington, Alexander Hamilton and Charles Cotesworth Pinckney assembled in Philadelphia and began selecting officers to command the additional regular army of 10,000 men and the provisional army of 50,000. The Triumvirate (as John Adams called them) spent nearly five weeks at the task of selecting the best possible Federalists for commissions; Republicans need not apply. "You would as soon scrub the blackamore white," General Washington said, "as to change the principles of a profest Democrat."

High on the blacklist of those thus barred from command was Aaron Burr. The New York Republican chieftain eagerly sought a commission as a brigadier general, and even his old enemy, Hamilton, had considered finding a place for him as a "useful co-operator" in the war effort. Adams also said, in later years, that he recommended Colonel Burr to be a brigadier general, but General Washington turned him down.

Washington, according to Adams, said, "By all that I have known and heard, Colonel Burr is a brave and able officer; but the question is, whether he has not equal talents at intrigue." So, Adams said, "I was not permitted to nominate Burr." Yet General Washington had already forced his successor to make Hamilton second in command, much against Adams' own wishes. "He had compelled me to promote, over the heads of Lincoln, Gates, Clinton, Knox, and others, and even over Pinckney, one of his own triumvirate, the most restless, impatient, artful, indefatigable and unprincipled intriguer in the United States, if not in the world, to be second in command under himself, and now dreaded an intriguer in a poor brigadier!" Adams always resented the way Hamilton had been crammed down his throat, and, with increasing jealousy he saw "the Creole" assuming the dominant role in mobilizing the nation for possible war.

When Washington retired again to Mount Vernon, retaining only the formal title of commander-in-chief, Hamilton moved into actual command of the army. The new major general gave up his New York law practice to devote all his time to whipping the troops into shape to repel a potential invasion. He took over the duties of President Adams, War Secretary McHenry, and the War Department clerks in his untiring efforts to manage the war effort single-handedly. Adams, however, showed little enthusiasm for building up the army after he was forced to take the hated Hamilton as its chief. "This damned army will be the ruin of the country" by raising debts and taxes, the President grumbled in words paraphrasing Jefferson and the Republicans. Cooling off considerably from his war fever of the springtime, Adams concluded by autumn that there was "no more prospect of seeing a French army here, than there is in heaven."

Whether the French ever landed on these shores or not, General Hamilton had ambitious plans for using his new army. He dreamed great dreams of leading it into Louisiana, the Floridas, and even into Central and South America, in a crusade to place the American flag on the ruins of the Spanish Empire. Spain having become an ally of France, the United States could feel free to attack any part of the Spanish possessions as soon as war with France could be officially declared. Unless Louisiana and the Floridas could be annexed by the United States, Hamilton feared the area between the Mississippi River and the Appalachian mountains might become a collection of confederacies, hostile to this country and mere satellites of European powers.

Already, some American settlers across the mountains were dickering with the Spanish on possible alliances to keep open the port of New Orleans. Senator William Blount of Tennessee had been expelled from Congress for planning a military enterprise in that area in 1797, and before many more years would pass, Aaron Burr would stand trial for treason on charges of plotting a fantastic scheme to make himself emperor of that inland empire.

In 1798, General Hamilton was already discussing his dream of taking over the Spanish possessions, in conversations with a Latin American soldier of fortune, Francisco Miranda, of Venezuela. Miranda had told Hamilton of his plans for liberating the colonies from the yoke of Madrid, and had even persuaded the British prime minister, William Pitt, to consider using the British fleet to carry out the scheme. England would furnish the ships and the money, and the United States would supply several thousand troops, easily recruited from the ambitious woodsmen of the frontier.

To Rufus King, the American minister in London, Hamilton reported he was ready to lead the great enterprise, in which King promised "precisely such a cooperation as we wish, the moment we are ready." "The command in that case would very naturally fall upon me, and I hope I should disappoint no favorable anticipations," Hamilton told King, a close friend and former New York senator. The General considered the American people not quite ripe for the expedition but added, "we ripen fast and it may, I think, be rapidly brought to maturity."

To Miranda, General Hamilton wrote that an army was being recruited, with General Washington at the head, and "I am second in command." To Senator James Gunn of Georgia, Hamilton wrote in the fall of 1798 about the need of heavy cannon and mortars for defense in case of a siege by the French. "If we engage in war, our game will be to attack where we can," the General wrote. "France is not to be considered as separated from her ally. Tempting objects will be within our grasp."

To Representative Harrison Gray Otis of Massachusetts, Hamilton proposed a little later that if the United States and France should not have a peace negotiation actually under way by August 1, 1799, the United States should declare war and use its land and naval forces "for preventing and frustrating hostile designs of France, either directly or indirectly through any of her allies."

Since France might at any time try to take Louisiana and the Floridas, Hamilton told Otis, the United States should seize them herself, "to obviate the mischief of their falling into the hands of an active foreign power" and to secure the advantage of "keeping the key of the Western country," which he considered essential to "the permanency of the union."

"If universal empire is still to be the pursuit of France," he asked, "what can tend to defeat the purpose better than to detach South America from Spain, which is the only channel through which the riches of Mexico and Peru are conveyed to France?"

In late 1798, there seemed little prospect of peace with France, and yet no signs of formally declared war. Dr. George Logan returned from his volunteer mission to Paris, bringing a report that the wily Talleyrand had given him an audience and had indicated a willingness to receive a minister from the United States. "Yes," President Adams retorted in a chilly interview, "I suppose if I were to send Mr. Madison or Mr. Giles or Dr. Logan they would receive either of them. But I'll do no such thing; I'll send whom I please."

Timothy Pickering, the Secretary of State who yearned for war with atheist France, considered Logan's tale a mere Jacobin trick to gull the Americans into the clutches of the French. "Sir," he rasped, looking down his long, thin nose at the Philadelphia Quaker, "it is my duty to inform you that the government does not thank you for what you have done."

Referring to the Logan mission, Adams told Congress in late 1798: "I have seen no real evidence of any change of system or disposition in the French Republic towards the United States. Although the officious interference of individuals, without public character or authority, is not entitled to any credit, yet it deserves to be considered whether that temerity and impertinence of individuals affecting to interfere in public affairs between France and the United States, ... ought not to be ... corrected."

Congress thereupon passed the Logan Act which declared that any United States citizen who "shall, without the permission or authority of the government of the United States, directly or indirectly commence, or carry on, any verbal or written correspondence with any foreign government, or any officer or agent thereof, with an intent to influence the measures or conduct of any foreign government, or of any officer or agent thereof, in relation to any disputes or controversies with the United States, or to defeat the measures of the United States, shall be guilty of a high misdemeanor."

* * * * *

The shadows of the Sedition Act prosecutions and the threat of open war with France, together with the deepening bitterness of partisan conflict in Congress, darkened the winter of 1798-99 for Samuel H. Smith. But the Republican editor could find one bright ray amid the gloom: "His Margaret" had come to spend the winter in Philadelphia.

Samuel would leave his office at 118 Chestnut Street in the late afternoon nearly every day, and hurry over to the home of the Widow Hodge, on Arch Street above Fourth, where her niece Margaret would give him a cheery greeting at the door. Then, seated by a crackling fire on the open hearth, with candlelight glinting on tea cups and silver, the lovers would spend many joyous hours together in the widow's parlor, just as they had done in Cousin Andrew Bayard's house two winters before.

On the day after New Year's in 1799, Mrs. Hodge gave a tea party for the Hodge and Bayard children and grandchildren, and thirteen of them made the house echo with their shouts and laughter. Peggy threw aside her cap, and with her hair combed back and a pink sash around her waist, she played the part of a little child herself. About teatime, Samuel came in from the newspaper office, and Peggy introduced him as "Judge Paterson," since everyone in the parlor game was assuming a make-believe name. Sally Bayard played "Miss Paterson," and Ann Hodge impersonated "Mary Ann Kirkpatrick" and recited, "How Doth the Little Busy Bee."

When the tea table was taken away, everyone rose to dance. The sedate Mrs. Hodge and the solemn Mr. Smith joined in the romping and, Margaret later affirmed to Sister Jane in New Brunswick, "I never saw Mrs. H. or Mr. S. to greater advantage."

Peggy welcomed the rare occasions when Samuel relaxed in this way, for she feared his health would otherwise be ruined by overwork. "He goes to the office before the rest of the family are up, devotes but a few minutes to dinner and does not leave his office until dark, and on Wednesday night not till 12 or one o'clock," she reported to her family. Wednesday was make-up day, when his weekly *Universal Gazette* went to press, and he had to work late making sure the papers were printed correctly and mailed to the subscribers across the country. "He allows himself no time either for the pleasure of society or reading," Margaret wrote. "Such a life ought to be rewarded by success but as yet he has met with nothing but disappointment."

Little by little, in early 1799, she began to realize the truth: Although Samuel drove himself to labor, day and night, his paper was not a financial success. It might be a triumph of literary polish, and filled with brilliant articles on politics, but it was not making money. His subscribers were scattered all over the land, and he had no way of making them pay on time; so, no matter how hard he worked, he could not make the revenues large enough to support a wife.

Peggy thus found herself in an impossible situation. The more she knew him, the more she loved him, and the more she wanted to become his wife; and yet, assuming she would defy her Federalist relatives' objections to a Republican editor, how could they afford to marry? Samuel finally told her, that winter, what he had meant to say more than a year before, after the daily *New World* had collapsed.

"In the summer of 1797," he said in a letter which repeated a poignant face-to-face conversation, "I determined that the first words I addressed to you should be these: 'Margaret, I still love you . . . But my affairs have been suspended; nothing is absolutely to be relied upon . . . There must be delay, where before I hoped there would have been none.'" He had planned then to offer to release her from their engagement.

"But when I saw you at Brunswick, the superstructure fell at the first touch of feeling. I thought such a declaration might be construed into unkindness." Since then he had often determined to admit his poverty and his uncertain prospects but could not muster the nerve to do it. Now at last he made a full confession, and as she comprehended it, tears came into her eyes, tears of "indignation mingled with tenderness." She accused him of lacking affection for her, of being indifferent to her feelings and her happiness. Sadly, he reassured her of his love but offered to free her so that she could seek her happiness "elsewhere."

But she could not "seek happiness elsewhere." She loved no other man; after their winter together, she loved Samuel more than ever. There must be some way to conquer the barrier to all their hopes! But she could not find it, and neither could he. She believed she could not honorably remain in Philadelphia now, and there was nothing left for her to do but go back to New Brunswick to wait, and hope.

With a heavy heart, she returned to the home of Sister Jane and resumed her occupation as the companion, nurse and teacher of the Kirkpatrick children; she had good reason to wonder whether or not she might forever remain the old maid "Aunt Peggy," who could never become "Mrs. Samuel Harrison Smith."

"I cannot help thinking of times to come," she wrote in her diary, "and exclaiming, 'Where shall I be this time next yr.? What, then, will be my situation?' My Faith replies, 'Whatever is thy lot, it will be the will of thine Heavenly Father.' Thy Will be done, Gracious Creator!"

O N FEBRUARY 18, 1799, John Adams gave his High Federalist critics good reason to believe their theory that, at times, he was just a little bit crazy.

On that day, without consulting his cabinet, the Senate, or any other leaders of his own party, he sent to the Senate the nomination of William Vans Murray as Minister to France.

Only a few months before, the temperamental President had solemnly declared to Congress that he would never send another minister to Paris without assurances that he would be "received, respected, and honored as the representative of a great, free, powerfull and independent nation." Yet, in an apparently sudden change of mind, he had decided to send Murray, who was already in Europe as the Minister to The Hague. Why? the Federalists wondered. The reason was that the Directory had given Murray indirect intimations that an American envoy would be received in exact accord with Adams' requirements, and there was a chance of ending the undeclared war.

If Adams had put on a French uniform and run down the middle of Market Street foaming at the mouth, the High Federalists would not have been more convinced of his "insanity." Timothy Pickering, the Secretary of State, told a confidante that on the day of Murray's nomination "one of Mr. A.'s special friends, a member of the House of Representatives, stepped over to my office and with an air of alarm asked me, ... 'Is the man mad?' "

"We have all been shocked and grieved at the nomination of a minister to negotiate with France," Pickering told Alexander Hamilton. Already convinced that Adams was a man of "freakish humors," Hamilton believed the old man had made a terrible mistake in this sudden move for peace with the treacherous French. George Cabot, a former Massachusetts Senator who still held a high place in the Essex Junto in Adams' home state, ascribed the President's sudden turnabout to jealousy of Washington and Hamilton. "Surprise, indignation, grief and disgust followed each other in quick succession in the breasts of the true friends of the country," Cabot reported, when the startling news got out.

Federalist Representative Robert G. Harper of South Carolina was so disgusted with Adams' about-face that he "prayed to God" the President's horses would run away with him and "break his neck."

Fisher Ames considered that Adams had surrendered to the Republicans, with an eye cocked for votes he might pick up from them in the election the following year. Pickering speculated that the wily Jefferson, "who knew the superlative vanity" of Adams, had flattered him with "visions of everlasting fame" as a peacemaker, thus laying "a sure foundation" for Adams' re-election.

Jefferson was as pleasantly surprised as the Federalists were dismayed by Adams' impulsive turn to the Republican position for peace. "The event of events was announced to the Senate yesterday," he exulted on February 19. "The President nominated . . . William Vans Murray, minister plenipotentiary to the French republic and added that he shall be instructed not to go to France without direct and unequivocal assurances from the French government that he shall be received in character. . . . The Senate have passed over this day without taking it up. It is said they are gravelled and divided; some are for opposing, others do not know what to do. . . . It silences all arguments against the sincerity of France, and renders desperate every further effort towards war."

To the Federalists it simply did not make sense for their own President to throw away the weapon with which they had expected to consolidate their control of the country, and possibly even stamp out Republicanism for good. The fervor for war with France over the "X Y Z" insults had propelled the "friends of government" into

137

the greatest height of popularity in their entire history and had sunk Jefferson's Republicans into the thankless role of carping critics who, in the Federalists' eyes, formed a "French faction" of conspirators favoring the enemy over their own country.

If the undeclared war with France should be maintained for another year, with a continuing series of spine-tingling triumphs at sea and possibly widened into a general war, then Hamilton could realize his dream of leading American troops to the conquest of Louisiana, the Floridas and other parts of the American empire of France's ally, Spain. All Adams had to do was to keep the patriotic fever at high pitch, strengthen the army and navy, and show the damned frog-eaters that Americans would not take their insults without a fight, and the United States would win peace with dignity and honor—and empire.

Furthermore, if the voters could associate the word "Federalist" with "patriot" and the word "Republican" with "traitor," then indeed Thomas Jefferson and all his French faction might be sunk without a trace in the election of 1800.

Now, however, by accepting the indirect offer of a deal with the crafty Talleyrand, Adams proposed to kiss the hands of the bloody French who had slapped America's face; now Americans, after standing up manfully and declaring "Millions for defense, but not one cent for tribute," would become "soothers and suppliants for peace with a gang of robbers"—so the Federalist fire-eaters claimed.

The Republicans had been charging that the "X Y Z" stories of threats and attempted blackmail were only a pack of Federalist lies, and Hamilton's army was a needless engine of tyranny imposed on the poor taxpayers for the purpose of setting up a British-style monarchy. Now, the followers of Jefferson could say that Adams had swung over to their side and proved that they had been correct in holding out to the bitter end for peace. Jefferson instantly seized the issue with glee and began making exactly that claim. Editor Samuel H. Smith, of the *Universal Gazette,* picked up the party line from his friend, the Vice-President, and so did the other Republican newspapers already gearing up a publicity campaign to elect Jefferson President the next year.

Desperately, the "war" Federalists fought back against Adams. Their Senate chieftains threatened to reject confirmation of Murray, so the President consented to send two more emissaries to make a three-man mission, more heavily weighted on the side of firmness and presumably unlikely to sell out to Talleyrand. The nominations of Chief Justice Oliver Ellsworth, a Connecticut Federalist, and Governor William R. Davie, of North Carolina, along with Murray, were confirmed by the Senate.

Even after the Senate's action, the Federalist leaders did their best to delay the departure of Ellsworth and Davie, on one excuse or another, in hopes they might never sail at all. The three cabinet members who secretly looked to Hamilton for guidance, Pickering, McHenry and Wolcott, threw every possible wrench into the wheels of the peace mission. Pickering, the Secretary of State, stalled in sending Murray the news of his nomination, and insisted that the other two must not go until the French explicitly promised to receive the envoys with all the courtesy and respect which Adams had demanded. Hamilton came to Philadelphia to confer with his cabinet agents, and other Federalists. Seeing the handsome, gallant General in cahoots with Gouverneur Morris (who shared his weakness for women), the *Aurora* drily announced that they had "kept the fast in Philadelphia" and "a pair more pious, more chaste, more moral perhaps never mortified the flesh and the spirit since the days of David and the fair Shunammite."

Representative James A. Bayard of Delaware and other Federalists in Congress, echoing Hamilton's views, sought to persuade Adams to delay the mission. Several years later, Adams recalled a "sombre dinner" he had given soon after announcing the peace maneuver, "a measure which produced a real anarchy in the government and infinite vexation to me." Bayard, one of the guests, began a "whining harangue" (as the President described it) against sending the envoys to Paris. This is Adams' version of the conversation:

Bayard: "Ah! It is an unfortunate measure. We know not the consequences of it. England will certainly be offended at it, they cannot fail to take umbrage and they might declare war on us."

Adams: "Mr. Bayard, I am surprised to hear you express yourself in this manner; would you prefer a war with France to a war with England, in the present state of the world; would you wish for an alliance with Great Britain and a war with France? If you would, your opinions are totally different from mine."

Bayard: "Great Britain is very powerful, her navy is very terrible."

Adams (losing his temper): "I know the power of Great Britain. I have measured its omnipotence without treasure, without arms, without ammunition, and without soldiers or ships; I have braved and set at defiance all her power. In the negotiation with France we have done no more than we had a perfect right to do; England has no right, or color of right, to take offense at it, and if she did I would not regard it as a farthing. For in a just and righteous cause I shall hold all her policy and power in total contempt."

Adams' acquiescence to the French overtures for peace seemed all the more galling to the Federalist war hawks because it came at a time when the American Navy was winning brilliant victories over the French, and curbing their piratical outrages upon American merchant ships. The little fleet of four squadrons was busy convoying the United States vessels, cruising the Caribbean, forcing pirate ships to stay in port or seizing them if they ventured out. On February 9, 1799, the *Constellation,* flagship of Commodore Thomas Truxtun, cruising off the island of Nevis, sighted the French frigate *L'Insurgente.* Truxtun attacked, and after a short but furious fight, *L'Insurgente* surrendered. When the good news reached Philadelphia, after Adams' decision to send the new mission to Paris, Pickering said: "The only negotiation compatible with our honor or safety is that begun by Truxtun in the capture of *L'Insurgente.*"

Adams boasted that he was the man who had created this fleet—the "Father of the American Navy." "I humbled the French Directory, as much as all Europe has humbled Bonaparte," he claimed in his old age. "I built frigates, manned a navy, and selected officers with great anxiety and care, who perfectly protected our commerce, and gained virgin victories against the French."

While the new navy was writing its glorious record on the pages of history, the United States army was very slowly growing in the early days of 1799. George Washington lamented that recruiting

140

dragged so badly that the army would be lucky to enlist anyone but "the riff-raff of the country and the scape-gallowses of the city." Adams, so proud of the navy which he claimed as his own, exulted in later years that Hamilton and Washington, of whom he was so morbidly jealous, could not raise their army to its authorized strength. "With all the influence of Hamilton, reenforced by the magical name of Washington," he said, the recruiting officers could not "raise one half of their . . . little army."

Adams, like the Republicans, could see little need for an army, anyway, now that the danger of invasion seemed past. What would the troops do, except idle away their time and harass the peaceful taxpayers? General Hamilton, however, had his private plans for marching into Spain's possessions when the right time came; he also considered the army most useful in keeping down riots and insurrections at home. He would like nothing better than to use his troops to whip Jefferson's discontented Virginians into line and make them show proper respect for the central government.

Hamilton finally found an insurrection to justify his army. It arose, not among the Jacobin states rights secessionists below the Potomac, but among the steady, sober, industrious, frugal Germans in eastern Pennsylvania. The Pennsylvania "Dutch," heretofore generally Federalist in their politics, resented the direct tax levied on houses and land to pay for the army and navy. As Jefferson had correctly prophesied, the "Doctor" to cure the "X Y Z fever" had arrived in the person of the tax collector.

The Germans especially disliked the Federal inspectors, nosy fellows who came and listed the number and size of every window in every house for the purpose of figuring out the tax. The Republicans also spread the word that all the real property in the country would be mortgaged and that Adams would marry his son to a daughter of King George III.

Farmers in Northampton, Montgomery and Bucks counties refused to pay the taxes to the unpopular window-counting collectors. When some of the farmers were jailed, a Bucks County auctioneer named John Fries led a band of armed men who forced the marshal

141

at Bethlehem to free them. Hamilton feared the Germans were leading a "Jacobin" revolt to overthrow the government. Adams proclaimed the Pennsylvania riots were a "war" upon the United States and sent a large part of the regular army to the battle front, calling out two Philadelphia volunteer companies under the command of Brigadier General William MacPherson. MacPherson's "Blues" had already distinguished themselves by fighting the "Jacobins" in the "cockade riots" on the capital streets; the militant young Federalists, famous for their blue uniforms and close-order drill, marched out to administer a lesson to the German rebels.

Arriving at Bethlehem, they found no insurrection anywhere. The houses were closed, the farmers were working in the fields as usual. John Fries was busy at his old trade of auctioneering at a farmhouse sale, standing on a barrel with his bell in hand about to sell a fire shovel. Waving bare sabers, the troops charged on the crowd as constituting a "sedition" gathering. Spectators scattered in all directions and the slowest ones were captured. Fries hid in a marsh but was dragged out and arrested, too.

Fifteen prisoners were carried off to the Philadelphia jail on treason charges, and twenty more were accused of lesser crimes. Samuel H. Smith's *Universal Gazette* carried this news in its April 25 issue:

INSURRECTION

Our last account left the troops at Allen Town. From this place they proceeded to Greenmeyers, from thence to Karacker's Town, and from that to Reading, where the troops arrived at one o'clock on Saturday.

Writs had been issued for apprehending 16 persons in Greenmeyer township, but when the troops arrived there, 14 of them surrendered themselves; a detachment of horse was sent after the other two, but they were not found. A report was in circulation that a large meeting of armed insurgents was to be held at a blacksmith's shop about 14 miles beyond Karacker's, on Monday last, but on examination it proved unfounded.

On Tuesday afternoon, Brigadier General MacPherson,

commander-in-chief of the troops employed in the expedition against the insurgents of Northampton & C., arrived in town from Reading . . . .

The Grand Jury of the Circuit Court of the United States, now sitting in this city, have found Bills against three of the Northampton Insurgents for high treason; of this number, *Fries* is one.

About thirty of the "insurgents" were imprisoned or fined. Fries and two others—identified in Samuel's paper as John Gettman and Frederick Hainy—were convicted of high treason and sentenced to death. But President Adams, against the advice of the ultra Federalists, pardoned all three. In charging the grand jury in this case, Supreme Court Justice James Iredell asserted that if traitors went unpunished, "anarchy will ride triumphant and all lovers of order, decency, truth & justice will be tramped under foot." Adams, by pardoning the three rebels, weakened the whole foundation of respect for federal authority—or so the ultras said. His motive, they asserted, was to gain popularity among the Pennsylvania voters, hoping they would gratefully give him more than the single electoral vote he had received in that state in 1796.

Justice Iredell, while presiding at Fries' trial, related to his wife some news about another "extraordinary event" which might interest her even more. It concerned the young daughter of Mrs. William Bingham, wife of a Pennsylvania Senator, and Queen Bee of the capital's high-toned Federalist society: "Count Tilly, an eminent French nobleman, about forty or forty-five, a very dissipated man and immensely in debt, but distinguished for being remarkably handsome, eloped with Maria Bingham and was married to her at half after one in the morning, at a Universalist Minister's of the name of Jones; and at five in the morning they were found in bed at a milliner's, the corner of Market and South streets," the learned Justice reported on April 18, 1799.

"She was taken to her father's house where she has ever since remained, but it is generally believed the marriage is a valid one. Her mother for a long time was in a state of distraction, and could only be composed by laudanum." (The legislature later annulled the nuptials.)

* * * * *

Again, for the third straight summer, the yellow fever menaced Philadelphia in 1799, and again the government had to flee with most of the population to presumably safer regions in the suburbs. This time Samuel H. Smith did not linger in the city. He moved his printing plant across the Schuylkill River to a rural area several miles from the infected capital. Knowing the river separated him from the fever, Margaret Bayard felt more at ease about his security. But she begged him to "jump in the stage and leave business for a day or two," to join her in New Brunswick, where they could "follow the windings of the river, admire its beauties, sit beneath the shade of the trees together" in the secret valley where they had spent so many happy hours before.

Margaret had come home in time to assist the Kirkpatricks in greeting their fourth baby, Jane Eudora, who had arrived on May 26. "Sister is very well indeed," Peggy reported to her fiancé. "Her little ladyship is very good and we, her attendants, are very happy."

One night Peggy dreamed that she and Samuel were seated together on the sofa, as they had been many nights in the Widow Hodge's house on Arch Street the previous winter. "I was seated by you on the sofa; your arms were around me, my head was supported on your shoulder, your cheek pressed mine, I felt your heart beat against my bosom and the warmth of your breath upon my face. . . . I awoke, and it was but a vision! A vision, I fondly trust, which will *one day* be realized."

He finally arrived in New Brunswick in late September and spent four golden days with her. Every evening found them "contemplating the moon beside the soft-flowing Raritan." There, she assured him, "I never could feel more sacredly yours."

The day after he left she wrote to him: "Last night, I but whispered, I but sighed, and you could hear, understand and answer me. Words were unnecessary to inform you of what was passing in my heart; it beat against your bosom and spoke more forcibly than

144

any words. . . . I never before found it so difficult to leave you as I did last night. . . . Oh, when we can be so happy together, why are we torn asunder?"

A week later, on a cold and cheerless October day, when an easterly wind brought wintry weather ahead of the season, Peggy sat before a blazing fire and wrote to Samuel while her little nephew, Littleton Kirkpatrick, slept in her arms. "When I close my letter," she wrote, "I am going to read your paper of last week. The idea of reading what you have before read gives it a greater charm. I shall then sit down to the tea table, with Littleton on one side and Bayard on the other; put them to bed, and then, seated at the stand, pass the evening in sewing. Maria perhaps will join me. Do you not wish you could? Yes, and so do I."

One evening when she put the youngsters to bed, she spent more than an hour with them, telling stories and singing nursery rhymes. "Do sing another song," begged little Mary, and so did her brother Bayard until he fell asleep. Then Aunt Peggy said to Mary, "You must not talk any more, as I want to think."

"Very well, Aunt, I will think, too," Mary piped. "I can think very pretty on my wedding cake."

"Now do you guess, my friend," Peggy asked Samuel, "what do you suppose *I* thought of?"

By eleven o'clock in the evening Peggy usually was so sleepy that she could not keep her eyes open. "But then," she explained, "I am awake with the sun, for I sleep in the nursery where there are three heralds of the dawn."

* * * * *

In late October Samuel sent her reassuring news: "My office is moving, and I am on the wing, once more to mix in the turbulent scenes of a town where life and bustle are almost synonymous terms."

Returning to Philadelphia, the Republican editor learned that the peace commissioners, Ellsworth and Davie, had finally left for France, and the High-Federalists, who had opposed their departure to the very last, were filled with gloom. Hamilton's followers realized there would be no further justification for keeping up an army large enough to carry out his dreams of the conquest of Louisiana and the Floridas, or anything else in the Spanish empire in America. Naturally, the Republicans cheered the defeat of the war hawks and the growing split between Adams and the Hamiltonians as an omen of a possible Jefferson victory in the presidential election of 1800.

The Republicans delighted in a foretaste of triumph when they elected Chief Justice Thomas McKean governor of Pennsylvania in the fall of 1799, and they celebrated in lusty style. At Zeigler's Plains, Spring Garden, "a fine fat steer was immolated on the altar of Liberty beneath the flag of America, surmounted by the classic emblems of Liberty and Peace"—the French Liberty Cap and a wreath of laurel and palm. "Libations of red and white wine were poured upon the altar," and doubtless many more libations rolled down the happy Republicans' throats.

William Cobbett had sworn he would leave the state if McKean won the election, so now it was time for "Peter Porcupine" to go. But before he could bid a sad adieu to the rascally Pennsylvanians, the British scrivener had to stand trial in the libel suit which Dr. Benjamin Rush had filed against him in their dispute over the good doctor's bleeding "cure" for yellow fever.

Judge Shippen, in charging the jury, said the editor had repeatedly called the plaintiff "a quack, styling him the Samson of Medicine, slaying his thousands and ten thousands," and sundry other epithets in a similar vein. The jury brought in a verdict of five thousand dollars in damages, and Cobbett's property was seized to pay the fine. "Nothing provokes me," Cobbett remarked, "but the thought of such a whining Republican rascal putting the 5,000 dollars in his pocket."

Cobbett went to New York, where he edited a paper called *The Rush Light,* and finally he sailed for his homeland. The Jeffersonian poet Philip Freneau bade him godspeed with these touching lines:

> O, may the sharks enjoy their bait;
> He came such mischief to create
> We wish him not a better fate.

146

The final tragedy in this year of tragedies befell the Federalists on December 14, 1799. "As the stage passed through Philadelphia," said John Marshall, a new Congressman from Virginia, "some passenger mentioned to a friend he saw in the street, the death of General Washington. The report flew to the hall of Congress, and I was asked to move an adjournment. I did so." The next day, Marshall officially announced the "lamentable event" and proposed resolutions of mourning, prepared by his Virginia colleague, Henry Lee. These expressed "profound sorrow . . . on the loss of a citizen, first in war, first in peace, and first in the hearts of his countrymen."

The whole nation plunged into mourning. To Federalists, such as the family of Margaret Bayard, the death of the general who had won the colonies' independence and had established the new nation was a calamity to cause the deepest grief. Even moderate Republicans like Samuel H. Smith, who had criticized the late President in milder terms than those of the party hacks, were shocked and saddened.

Margaret, who was in New York visiting friends at the time, found the whole city draped in black, the men with crepe arm bands on their coats, the women wearing black ribbons and black gloves. She attended the memorial services in St. Paul's church on December 31, and heard the oration by Gouverneur Morris, but confessed she grew weary of the rites which were seven hours long. This is her pen picture of the scene:

"It was eleven o'clock when we entered and six o'clock when we left it. These tedious hours were passed in the cold, without any kind of refreshment . . .

"The church was *dreadfully* crowded; pews, window seats, all were filled. Never before had I seen such a multitude! The confusion, contention and noise at first alarmed me, but when once assured of safety, I felt nothing but astonishment at seeing so many human beings together.

"The windows being filled, the light was dim. The music began and I felt inclined to solemnity and devotion. But the discordant sounds and unharmonious voices soon changed my feelings. At last silence was proclaimed and the Orator arose. I was all attention, but the hum of voices, the opening and shutting of doors, together with coughing, drowned almost every word.

"The darkness increased, his figure was no longer seen, he stopped to look at his notes, his manner was cold and unimpressive. He could see no longer. He stopped, and several voices cried, 'A candle! A candle!'

"After some minutes, one arrived. The discourse was resumed, all the pathos seemed reserved for one point, but it was so violent and so artificial that it produced no effect . . . not a single tear!

"This music again began. Some of it was tolerable, some execrable, and some ludicrous. 'And is it possible you did not like it?' cried a young gentleman. 'Why, it is one of Handel's best pieces!'

" 'Alas,' said I, 'the name of Handel cannot put my ear in tune.' "

*   *   *   *   *

Margaret spent the winter of 1799-1800 in New York as the guest of Mrs. Julia Martin Scott, whose wedding she had attended as a bridesmaid the previous year—with Anthony Bleecker, incidentally, as one of the groomsmen. Although he fully realized that Margaret's heart belonged to Samuel H. Smith, Anthony remained as much in love with her as ever. "His manners towards me were unaltered, attentive and affectionate," Peggy recorded in her diary. "I was to him, as I had long been, the first object of regard and attention. No day passed without some hours spent together."

On the night of March 11, Margaret sat down at her writing desk before a cheerful fire and heard the wind whistling around the eaves of Julia's house. "My friend, my friend," she wrote to Samuel, "this is the eleventh of March. This night three years ago, at this hour, seated by each other, what new, delightful, strange emotions swelled our hearts! Freed from the most cruel and tormenting suspense, we exulted in the convictions of reciprocated love. . . . What a perturbed and restless night did I pass, how was my pillow moistened with my tears. Yet I would not have exchanged it for the most profound repose."

She could scarcely believe that three years had passed since the

148

night when he had asked her to become his wife. How greatly she had matured since then, from a gay and frivolous girl of nineteen to a serious grown woman of twenty-two! Then she had not really loved him, but, after suffering the agony of fear that he would die of the fever the following summer, she had loved him with all her heart.

Remembering the miniatures they had exchanged one April day, she drew his picture from her bosom and gazed lovingly at his face. Then she read again his last letter, imagining she could hear his voice. "Thank you for your sweet letter," she wrote. "Shall I not do more than thank you? Certainly I will. I will pay you: X X X X X Oh, that I could hear you say, 'Thank you, my Margaret.'"

While drinking a cup of tea alone by the fire, she thought, "How much more pleasant it would be, if you could be beside me, and while I poured out our cups, I could talk to you. Then I would hand it to you and say, 'Is it strong enough? Let me give you some more sugar. This is a very nice toast; do eat another bit. Come, do take another cup.' At last we are done—I leave the table, I fix my eyes on your face, and while I read there the tenderness of your heart, I chatter away; tell you all that passed through the day, how I employed myself while you were absent; how I listened at evening to every footstep and how my heart leapt for you when you came *home*.

"You kiss your little girl and sweetly chide her for prattling away so much time. Then I . . . snuff the candles and listen to the instructive voice of love . . . My God! Shall this imaginary happiness be ever realized? . . . Oh, my love, my love!"

* * * * *

While she hoped her wedding day would become reality sometime in 1800, Peggy made the most of her last opportunity to mingle with her friends in New York who shared her love of literature, music and art. She associated with a remarkable circle of gay young people who, as she said, were "closely united by congeniality of taste, and never disturbed by the ranklings of jealousy or the agitations of love."

Among them were Margaret's favorite feminine confidantes, Maria Nicholson and Maria Templeton, and several men who had formed the "New York Friendly Club" for the "pleasures of unshackled intellectual intercourse." Peggy's faithful former suitor, Anthony Bleecker, contributed poetry, while literature came from the pen of Charles Brockden Brown, America's first professional novelist; and their sessions were also enlivened by the brilliant minds of James Kent, who was destined to become Chancellor of the New York State Supreme Court and author of the renowned *Commentaries on American Law;* William Johnson, reporter to the Supreme Court; William Dunlap, poet, painter, and dramatist, manager of the New York Theater; the incredibly versatile Dr. Samuel Latham Mitchill; and "the two Doctors Miller," Edward Miller, M.D., and his younger brother, the Reverend Samuel Miller.

In Miss Templeton's "little, plain, neat, snug parlor, destitute of all ornament but abounding in comfort," they passed many happy hours in conversation over the teacups. Miss Nicholson, who had "a strong, masculine, highly cultivated mind," dominated many of the sessions by expressing her firm opinions. "Dr. Mitchill, full of playful wit, mirth and frolic, with all his learning and philosophy, was sportive as a boy," while Anthony Bleecker was equally gay, Margaret recorded in her journal. "I attached myself most to these laughing philosophers."

A physician at New York Hospital, a lawyer, and a professor of chemistry at Columbia College, Dr. Mitchill was also editor of the *New York Medical Repository* magazine; he was a student of Indian lore, a pioneer investigator of geological science, and a politician. He would be elected to Congress in 1800, at 36, reelected and then sent to the United States Senate, in each case as a firm adherent of his fellow philosopher and lover of science, Thomas Jefferson.

Charles Brockden Brown reminded Margaret very much of Samuel H. Smith in the way he "speculated about principles" while she tried to base her philosophy on experience. If the novelist and the editor would stop moralizing about the perfectability of man and realize that he needed the restraints of orderly society, said the Federalist Miss Bayard, she would join them in their hopes that some day such restraints would no longer be necessary.

But not now—not in the light of the French Revolution, which had plunged through the last stage of its convulsions and cast forth the militarist, Napoleon Bonaparte, as the dictator of France and the would-be conqueror of all Europe.

"Is not the premature birth of liberty in France the cause of all the disorders it has brought with it?" Peggy asked. "Had those philosophers who wished the regeneration of their nation, awaited the slow but certain progress of Truth, how many calamities would have been avoided."

Margaret could not stand to read the Gothic horrors of Brown's novels, either. After sampling a few pages of the latest epic, *Arthur Myrven,* she dreamed of "nothing else but scenes of death." The author urged her to read his equally blood-curdling *Edgar Huntley,* but she positively refused. "He condemned the weakness of my mind and advised me to strengthen it by inuring it to such scenes," she commented. "But my constitution will not allow me to follow his advice."

To strengthen their minds, Margaret and Maria Templeton began studying mathematics. "Thomas Smith began at the highest branch and repeated a most unintelligible jargon about the doctrine of fluxions," Peggy reported to Samuel. "Mr. Brown told us something of conic sections and Mr. Bleecker of circles, angles, etc. But I have to blush at my ignorance when in company with our scientific friends. The other afternoon at Dr. Mitchill's I could scarcely comprehend a sentence, and lost some fine strokes of wit because I knew nothing of chemistry."

Miss Templeton also placed in her hand the writings of Mary Wollstonecraft, the English high priestess of female freedom, who practiced what she preached. These ideas, Peggy admitted, "put strange notions" into her head, and she resolved to continue cultivating her intelligence despite "the ridicule of my own sex."

Her friends might laugh at her ignorance of chemistry and mathematics, but they began to respect Miss Bayard's skill as a writer. One day, at the urging of Miss Templeton, she read aloud to them some of the reflections she had written in her commonplace book.

"It is very excellent," said Johnson, the playwright. "I had no idea that your style was so correct, your sentiments so just."

"If that were in print—" said Brown, the novelist—

"—why, if it were in print," Johnson broke in, "It would be admired!"

Glowing with pride, Peggy showed several articles from her private journal and Brown asked permission to publish them in his *New York Magazine*. At first she refused, but when he promised not to reveal her name as the author, she consented.

With a new air of authority, derived from her forthcoming debut as a magazine writer, Margaret directed Samuel, "Let our correspondence assume a different form. Treat me, not only as the object of love, but the object of esteem, not as your mistress but as your friend. Forget I am a woman; remember only that I have a mind. . . .

"I am every day less contented with the circumscribed and degraded situation to which our sex is condemned. My restless and inquiring mind will not keep in the beaten track, but is perpetually wandering into paths untrod before.

"I am for tearing away the dark veil of ignorance, which conceals from me the light of knowledge! I cannot believe things because others say they are true but am perpetually asking, 'Why?' and 'How are they so?' Oh, my friend, will you not feed a mind, hungering and thirsting after knowledge?"

Samuel agreed to her request with great pleasure. He was delighted to find his Federalist fiancée expressing the same openminded thirst for truth which he, himself, shared with Thomas Jefferson. "It did appear to me that *intellectual* letters were unpleasant to you," he replied. "If this be your wish, no one will more cheerfully comply with it than I—and permit me to say, my profit will be equal to yours."

However, her new interests in the freedom of the mind did not free her completely from her natural femininity. To her sister Jane she wrote one day from New York: "Do not the children want clothes? I send you a pattern of some calico I have purchased for a gown and which makes up beautifully. The muslins do not wear well and as there are chintzes of more beautiful patterns and nearly the same price, I suspect you would be best pleased with one. I am looking for a lead or dove-colored nankeen or jean or plaid gingham for a riding dress; something of the same kind would be pretty for Bayard. Let me know if there is anything which I can get for you."

CHAPTER SEVEN

A s THE presidential year of 1800 began, Thomas Jefferson surveyed the political scene from his vice-presidential chair in Philadelphia, and lo! for the first time he found it good.

Only a year before the Federalists had been riding high on the tidal wave of national fervor against the infernal French and their high-handed attempt to blackmail the United States in the "X Y Z" affair. Jefferson and his fellow Republicans, striving to save the nation from drifting into war with France, had been degraded into a mere "French faction," accused of favoring a foreign country over their own, even suspected of being conspirators plotting to overthrow the government.

In the past twelve months, however, the war scare had fizzled out. The new United States navy had whipped several proud French warships and cut down piratical attacks upon American merchant shipping. John Adams' new peace mission had left for Paris, and the army, raised to combat a possible invasion of the United States, had nothing to do. The Republicans, taking their cue from Jefferson, called the soldiers a bunch of lazy loafers preying upon the citizens, while the recruiting officers were "lounging at every courthouse and decoying the laborer from his plough." The taxpayers were urged to rebel against the direct tax, the standing army, and "the usurious loan to set these follies on foot."

Jefferson, being a shrewd politician, knew the average American hated two nuisances, a standing army and high taxes. Both issues had led to the rebellion against George III, and they could be exploited again in a rebellion against the "British faction," the monarchy-loving Federalists. The Vice-President also excoriated the Alien and Sedition Laws, but these—contrary to some accounts—were not the deepest roots of the "Revolution of 1800." The Alien and Sedition Laws affected a comparatively few foreigners and newspaper writers, while the high taxes hurt the pocketbook nerves of everyone. Even some Federalists were starting to doubt the need for a large army and navy, and nobody liked the high taxes. A Pennsylvania Federalist said the tax on real property, which led to the Fries Rebellion there in 1799, "was the fatal blow to Federalism in Pennsylvania." A farmer in Northumberland County might not care if some ink-stained Republican scribbler was beaten up by the soldiers in Lancaster or Reading or Philadelphia, but the same land-owner would scream in protest when he had to pay his taxes.

So the Republicans who, only a year before, had been lying low as suspected conspirators against the government, now in early 1800 could raise their heads high and even contemplate an event that had seemed impossible: the election of Jefferson as President! The Federalists, who had been cocks-o'-the-walk, now seemed crestfallen, and they were quarreling among themselves as the followers of Hamilton bitterly resented Adams' sudden peace mission to France. "The Feds. begin to be very seriously alarmed about their election next fall," Jefferson wrote to James Madison, March 4, 1800—exactly one year before the next presidential inauguration day. "Their speeches in private, as well as their public and private demeanor to me, indicate it strongly."

Unknown to Jefferson, the Federalists were confirming his remarks in bitter exchanges of views about the political scene. "There is a *decided and deep rooted disgust* with Mr. Adams on the part of his *best old friends,*" Hamilton's lieutenant, Robert Troup, wrote from New York to Rufus King, the minister to London. "The Eastern delegations in Congress almost entirely ... believe that the preservation of the Federal cause essentially depends on removing Mr. Adams and appointing a more discreet man to the presidency."

"Nothing but a great hazard of losing the election" to the despised

155

Jefferson would stop the High Federalists from dumping Adams and offering Chief Justice Oliver Ellsworth, head of the new peace mission, for President with General Charles Cotesworth Pinckney, hero of the old Paris mission, for Vice-President. King, however, warned the "wise men of the East" not to do "so indiscreet a thing," which would surely lead to their defeat.

Theodore Sedgwick of Massachusetts, new Speaker of the House of Representatives, lamented that "the Federal nerve seems to have become palsied by the mission to France." Despite the "gloominess of the prospect," Sedgwick saw a ray of hope for the Federalists: They could defeat Jefferson, "the one we all dread," by voting equally for both candidates on their own ticket and then trusting the House to break the tie by choosing—not Adams, but his running mate, Pinckney.

As his own prospects brightened, Jefferson stopped playing the role of the shy philosopher who longed only to read his books, raise his tobacco, remodel his house and gaze at the beautiful Blue Ridge mountains from the porch of Monticello. No longer did he protest that he would rather run second, or even third, and content himself with the few innocuous duties of the vice-presidency. No longer did he declare that he had no desire to defeat his old friend, John Adams; no desire to take the helm of the ship of state amid the storm. After tossing about on that ship for nearly four years as first mate, and being ignored by the capricious skipper who zig-zagged left and right with each prevailing breeze, the tall Virginian actively desired to seize the wheel and turn the ship back onto her old "republican tack."

So Jefferson came down from his mountain-top and grappled with the practical realities of collecting enough votes to win the presidency. To his neighbor, Madison, the Vice-President summarized the facts with the precision of a campaign manager and the coolness of a professional politician.

Generally speaking, Jefferson's figures showed that he would win most of the South, and the Federalists would carry New England, as in 1796, when Adams had won the presidency with 71 electoral votes and Jefferson had come in second with 68. Assuming

156

the same total of electoral votes, Jefferson would need only to hold his own and add two more to make the necessary majority, 70. This, however, could be calculated more easily on paper than in fact.

The election, Jefferson figured, would be determined chiefly by the three "middle states," Pennsylvania, New Jersey and New York.

Pennsylvania, which had given Jefferson a 14-1 edge over Adams in 1796 electoral votes, might not cast any votes at all this year. The legislature, "obstinately divided," had failed to pass a bill providing for the selection of the presidential electors. The Republican House had insisted upon a general ticket vote, hoping for another state-wide sweep, while the Federalist Senate had refused to go along. Thomas McKean, the new Republican governor, "intends to call the legislature to meet immediately after the new election, to appoint electors themselves," Jefferson told Madison. "Still . . . there may arise a difficulty between the two houses about voting by heads or by houses," so he could not count on fourteen Pennsylvania votes this time.

New Jersey, which had given all seven of its votes to Adams in '96, now seemed to be leaning slightly Republican. "The Republican members here from Jersey are entirely confident that their two houses joined together have a majority of Republicans," the Vice-President assured Madison.

In New York, which had awarded all 12 of its votes to Adams last time, the Federalists controlled the present legislature. But a new one, to be chosen late in April, would name the presidential electors. Since the Federalists expected to keep a slight edge upstate, the Republicans' only chance of victory lay in New York City. "All depends on the success of the city election," Jefferson told Madison. "If the city election of New York is in favor of the Republican ticket, the issue will be Republican; if the Federal ticket for the city of New York prevails, the probabilities will be in favor of a Federal issue, because it would then require a Republican vote from both New Jersey and Pennsylvania to preponderate against New York, on which we could not count with any confidence."

The Federalists in Congress fully realized the grave danger of their defeat. Senator William Bingham of Pennsylvania observed: "Unfortunately, by unremitting industry and perseverance, aided by the most skilful address to the passions and low interests of the people, the anti-Federal party in some of the states is gaining ground. It will not be determined on any national calculation until the result of the state elections of New York and Jersey is known."

James Ross, the other Pennsylvania Senator, and the recently defeated Federalist candidate for governor, introduced a bill intended to assure his party a chance to count its candidates in should the presidential election be close. This bill provided that a "Grand Committee," consisting of six Senators and six Representatives and the Chief Justice of the Supreme Court, should take over all the electoral votes, after the ballots had been opened in Congress. This committee would have absolute authority to throw out votes it considered illegal, whether because of bribery, intimidation, or force in the balloting; and its report would be final. Obviously, a "Grand Committee" bold and daring enough could decide the presidential election.

Before the Senate passed the bill in secret session, a Republican member "leaked" a copy to the *Aurora,* which published the text in full and denounced it as a plot to steal the election. In the House, John Marshall opposed the provision giving the committee the final authority, and persuaded the House to substitute his version which merely allowed the joint committee to investigate alleged election frauds. The Senate, by a strict party-line vote, rejected the House bill, and the whole measure died—amid the cheers of the Republicans and the groans of the High Federalists.

For publishing the bill and denouncing it, the Senate resolved that Editor William Duane of the *Aurora* had committed "a high breach of the privileges of the Senate," and his "false, defamatory, scandalous, and malicious" charges tended to bring the Senators into "contempt and disrepute." Duane was summoned to appear at the bar of the Senate, but he refused. The Senate voted him guilty of contempt and ordered the sergeant-at-arms to arrest him, but the editor adroitly stayed out of his clutches.

To win the New York City election, which he considered the

turning point in the entire presidential contest, Jefferson had to depend upon Aaron Burr. The smooth, unscrupulous little "magician," who had a well-deserved reputation as a master of intrigue as well as an insatiable ambition for power, had suffered several reverses of fortune since he had sought the vice-presidency as Jefferson's running mate in 1796. When the Federalist legislature had voted him out of the U.S. Senate and given his seat back to General Schuyler, the father-in-law of his implacable enemy, Hamilton, Burr had won a place in the state assembly. But he lost even his assembly seat in the Federalist sweep of 1799, amid a loud outcry over a bill he had slipped through, ostensibly creating a company to provide a water supply for Manhattan. The Manhattan Company eventually did supply the water, all right, but through an unnoticed provision in its charter, also created a new bank—a "perfect monster," Hamilton called it—which provided convenient credit for leading Republicans, none of whom needed money more desperately and constantly than Colonel Burr.

From the very bottom of the political ladder, the undaunted little Colonel now intended to vault back to the top. He still aspired to be President of the United States, and, in Hamilton's opinion, to seize complete power just as Napoleon had established himself as the First Consul of France. If the little Corsican could rise from obscurity to the pinnacle of empire, so could the little Colonel. Burr, who wanted another chance at the vice-presidency—and even, if possible, to supplant Jefferson as President—knew that his price of admission to the national ticket must be a victory in his own city elections.

So the alert, erect, imperious Burr, with the ingratiating smile and the glittering black eyes, strode boldly into the middle of the tangled Republican factions in New York and declared himself their leader. He drew up the strongest possible ticket of candidates for the legislature, carefully including spokesmen for the Clinton, Livingston and other warring clans, and topped the list with two famous "old Revolutionary characters," as Jefferson called them: former Governor George Clinton and General Horatio Gates.

Hamilton, leading a desperate Federalist effort to save the state, could muster only a mediocre ticket of candidates including a ship-chandler, a baker, a potter, a bookseller, two grocers, a shoemaker, a mason, three lawyers, and a bankrupt. His aide, Robert Troup, lamented: "It is next to an impossibility to get men of weight and influence to serve." Troup, "full of anxiety about the election," warned the Federalists: "We must bring into action all our energies; if we do not, the election is lost—and if our legislature should give us anti-Federal electors, Jefferson will be in."

Hamilton threw himself into the task of electioneering with all his energies. At rallies of the Federalists, a Republican paper reported, "Hamilton harangues the astonished group; every day he is seen in the street hurrying this way and darting that; he here buttons a heavy hearted Fed, and preaches up courage, there he meets a group, and he simpers in unanimity, again to the heavy headed and hearted, he talks of perseverance and (God bless the mark) of virtue!"

Burr matched his enemy, though, in energy, skill, and tireless campaigning, and in attention to the most minute details of machine politics. He made lists of voters; sent solicitors to well-to-do Republicans, collecting money; organized precinct and ward meetings; raced from one to another, preaching the gospel of party unity. Burr "travels every night from one meeting of Republicans to another, haranguing and spiriting them to the most zealous exertions," a Federalist sheet reported. "Many people wonder that the ex-Senator and the would-be Vice President can stoop so low as to visit every low tavern that may happen to be crowded with his dear fellow-citizens. But the prize of *success to him* is well worth all this dirty work."

"The prize," as Burr well knew, was a place on the Republican national ticket, and it would be awarded by the party's members of Congress soon after the New York election results would be known, the first of May. Burr made sure those gentlemen appreciated his labor; to their floor leader, Representative Albert Gallatin of Pennsylvania, came a series of glowing letters from the pen of Matthew L. Davis, one of the most zealous of the clique of young men who were attracted to the brilliant, intriguing Colonel.

160

"If we carry this election, it may be ascribed principally to Colonel Burr's management and perseverance," Davis told Gallatin. "Hamilton fears his influence; their party seem in a state of consternation, while ours possess more than usual spirits. . . . We shall open the campaign under the most favorable impressions, and headed by a man whose intrigue and management is most astonishing, and who is more dreaded by his enemy than any other. . . ."

The balloting ran through three days, April 29 and 30, and May 1, and New York seethed with excitement. Hamilton rode on a white horse from one polling place to another, making frantic appeals for the Federalist ticket. Burr, with equal energy, led the Republican legions, reinforced by the brawny mechanics from the "Pig Pen" of Tammany Hall. Burr "has remained at the polls of the Seventh ward ten hours without intermission," Matthew Davis reported in a note to Congressman Gallatin. "Pardon this hasty scrawl. I have not ate for fifteen hours."

Davis headlined his news bulletin on midnight of May 1, in the best modern newspaper style:

REPUBLICANISM TRIUMPHANT.

"It affords me the highest gratification," he wrote Gallatin, "to assure you of the complete success of the Republican Assembly ticket in this city." The entire slate of candidates for the legislature had won, though by margins of only about 400 votes, and Burr himself had been elected from Orange county. Gallatin's father-in-law, old Commodore James Nicholson, said the victory was so "miraculous" that it must be credited to the "Supreme Power and our friend Burr the agent." Matthew L. Davis, however, would not share any credit with the Deity; he claimed, "To Colonel Burr we are indebted for everything."

However small the margin, and whether due to the Deity or the Devil, the Republicans had won control of the New York legislature, and twelve all-important electoral votes, formerly Federalist, would swing to Jefferson.

"The republic is safe!" Virginia Congressman John Dawson exulted in a note to James Madison. "Our ticket has succeeded in the city of N. York by a majority of about four hundred. . . . We may count on a majority of thirty in their legislature and there is good ground to believe that N. Jersey will exhibit the same spirit. . . ." The Federalists, said Congressman Dawson, "are in rage and despair and will endeavour to move heaven and hell, rather than give us the loaves and fishes!"

Truer words were never spoken. In desperation, Hamilton urged Governor John Jay to call the Federalist legislature into special session, and transfer the selection of the presidential electors from the legislature directly to a popular vote, by districts. That would, at least, give the Federalists a chance to name several electors from safe Federalist districts, rather than lose them all.

"In times like these in which we live, it will not do to be over-scrupulous," Hamilton told Jay. "It is easy to sacrifice the substantial interests of Society to a strict adherence to ordinary rules." Certainly, in "the great cause of social order," the friends of government should be able to take "a *legal* and constitutional step to prevent an atheist in religion and a fanatic in politics from getting possession of the helm of state." Jay merely wrote on the back of the letter, "Proposing a measure for party purposes, which I think it would not become me to adopt."

* * * * *

Immediately after his stunning victory in New York, Burr's little band of myrmidons began bombarding the Republican party leaders with demands that he be rewarded with second place on the Jefferson ticket. The Congressmen, who would soon recommend a nominee, had been considering former Governor George Clinton of New York, their choice in 1792. John Dawson had asked Madison: "What say you to old Governor Clinton? He is in pretty good health, and I have good reason to believe that he would be more acceptable to New York and New Jersey than any one else."

Shortly before the caucus, Matthew Davis sent Gallatin a letter strongly recommending Burr. "It is generally expected" that the nominee must come from New York, the young newspaperman wrote, and "three characters only can be contemplated": Governor

162

Clinton, Chancellor Robert Livingston, and Burr. Then Davis proceeded to knife the first two with deft stiletto strokes: Clinton "grows old and infirm," and yearns to retire from the "cares and toils" of public life; there was a prejudice against Livingston and his family, besides "doubts . . . of his firmness and decision." "Col. Burr is therefore the most eligible character, and on him the eyes of our friends in this State are fixed."

Although he was one of Burr's most intimate associates, Davis claimed he was "totally ignorant" of whether his chief would even accept the nomination, but "if he is not nominated many of us will experience much chagrin and disappointment."

Confused by these conflicting reports, the Republicans in Congress delegated Gallatin to find out which man the New Yorkers actually wanted. He relayed the question to his wife, who was visiting her father, Commodore James Nicholson, in New York. "Who is to be our Vice President, Clinton or Burr?" Gallatin asked. "This is a serious question which I am delegated to make, and to which I must have an answer by Friday next. Remember this is important, and I have engaged to procure correct information on the wishes of the New York Republicans."

Ruling out Livingston, whose deafness would have handicapped him severely as the Senate's presiding officer, the Commodore interviewed Clinton and Burr, and quickly reported back to Gallatin. The old Governor was quoted as saying his age and infirmities ruled him out and "he thinks Colonel Burr is the most suitable person and perhaps the only man. Such is also the opinion of all the Republicans in this quarter that I have conversed with; their confidence in A.B. is universal and unbounded. Mr. Burr, however, appeared averse to be the candidate. He seemed to think that no arrangement could be made which would be observed to the southward; alluding, as I understood, to the last election, in which he was certainly ill used by Virginia and North Carolina.

"I believe he may be induced to stand if assurances can be given that the Southern States will act fairly . . . but his name must not be played the fool with."

To these remarks, the Commodore's daughter, Mrs. Gallatin,

added: "Burr says he has no confidence in the Virginians; they once deceived him, and they are not to be trusted."

Burr had good reason for playing hard to get. He knew the vice-presidential nomination would be worthless unless the Southern Republicans would promise to support him equally with Jefferson, and not throw away their second votes, as many Virginia and North Carolina electors had done in 1796, humiliating him with a poor fourth place in the race. To make sure he would not be "lurched" again, he insisted upon blood-oath pledges of absolutely equal support.

If Burr had "no confidence in the Virginians," they, too, had their doubts about him. James Monroe had cautioned them against backing Burr for Vice-President in 1792, and they had then supported Governor Clinton. This same distrust of Burr, who had appeared to attract the corrupt portions of both the parties, may have been one cause of his meager southern support.

Burr's enemies later claimed that he tricked Clinton out of the nomination at the time Commodore Nicholson was sounding out the New York Republicans about the ticket in 1800. Clinton claimed in 1803 that the Congressmen really favored him and that Nicholson "importuned me very earnestly" to accept. "I finally agreed that in answering Mr. Gallatin's letter he might mention that I was averse to engage in public life, yet rather than that any danger should occur in the Election of President . . . I would so far consent as that my name might be used without any Contradiction on my part. It being understood, however, that if elected I would be at liberty to resign. . . . He agreed to draft a Letter to Mr. Gallatin & shew it to me."

Clinton claimed Nicholson drafted the letter in that fashion but, "on reading of it, Mr. Burr was much agitated, declared he would have nothing more to do with the Business, that he could be Governor of the State whenever he pleased to be. This conduct alarmed Mr. Nicholson and to appeaze Mr. Burr and his Party he consented to alter the Letter to Mr. Gallatin to an unqualified declension on my part and by this means Mr. Burr's nomination was effected."

However it may have been edited to please Burr and his little band, the letter to Gallatin achieved the desired result. "We had last night a very large meeting of Republicans," Gallatin wrote his wife from Philadelphia on May 12, "in which it was unanimously agreed to support Burr for Vice-President."

If any of Jefferson's friends had reservations about the character or integrity of his running mate, these were subdued in the common desire to unite the Republican party and win the election. Jefferson himself later called Burr "a crooked gun," but he did not hesitate to fire that "crooked gun" at the Federalists in the battle of 1800.

*   *   *   *   *

Depressed by their disastrous defeat in New York, the Federalists in Congress caucused May 3 at Philadelphia and decided upon "some hocus-pocus maneuvres" (as Jefferson called them) to win the presidential election. Their plan called for a repetition of the 1796 maneuver whereby Hamilton had hoped that Thomas Pinckney, the ostensible nominee for Vice-President, might be slipped in ahead of Adams into the presidency. This time, Thomas' brother, General Charles Cotesworth Pinckney, the "X Y Z" hero, was chosen as second man on the ticket; and again, General Hamilton's battle strategy called for the same tactics: The Federalists in the North must cast equal votes for Adams and Pinckney, while South Carolina would vote for Pinckney, its native son, and *not* for Adams. South Carolina had kept its part of the bargain in '96; the plan had miscarried only because 18 New England electors, voting for Adams, had refused to support Pinckney. Now Hamilton was determined to hold the Eastern states in line by the Federalist Congressmen's pledge to support both candidates equally. "If this agreement be faithfully executed we shall succeed," Theodore Sedgwick commented, "but otherwise we cannot escape the fangs of Jefferson."

The "dump-Adams" scheme quickly leaked out. On May 6 Gallatin, the Republican House leader, told his wife that the Federalists had "agreed that there was no chance of carrying Mr. Adams, but that he must still be supported ostensibly in order to carry still the votes in New England, but that the only chance was to take up ostensibly as Vice-President, but really as President," General Pinckney, of South Carolina. "I think they will succeed neither in S. Carolina in getting the votes for him, nor New England in making the people jilt Adams," Gallatin predicted.

Furious over this new scheme to trick him out of re-election, Adams at last decided to make a complete break with the Hamilton wing, even at the cost of splitting the party and blowing up the administration. He determined to get rid of two cabinet members whom he considered disloyal to him, and mere tools of the hated Hamilton. Two days after the Federalist caucus, the President sent a note to the Secretary of War: "The President requests Mr. McHenry's company for one minute."

Then, for considerably more than "one minute," the red-faced President berated the dumfounded Secretary with a torrent of abuse, so outrageous that poor McHenry thought Adams had gone completely mad. Out of the jealous President's heart poured all the resentments he had treasured up against the cabinet members he had inherited from George Washington. Adams charged McHenry with influencing Washington to make Hamilton actual commander of the army; with refusing an army commission to the only North Carolina elector who had voted for Adams; with joining the other secretaries in an attempt to halt the peace mission to France.

Raving with fury, Adams cried that he would rather serve as Vice-President under Jefferson than be indebted for his re-election to "such a being as Hamilton . . . a bastard and as much alien as Gallatin."

"No one could have imagined Mr. Adams capable of such billingsgate language," Timothy Pickering commented afterwards, "but a man so entirely under the dominion of violent passions is capable of anything."

McHenry quickly resigned. A few days later Adams called for Pickering, the Secretary of State, to get out, too. Pickering demurred; he could not afford, he said, to give up his salary, the sole support of his large family. Adams sent him an icy note that ended

166

with these words: "You are hereby discharged." John Marshall became Secretary of State; Samuel Dexter, Secretary of War.

"Oh, mad! Mad! Mad!" Hamilton exclaimed, when he heard that his allies in the cabinet had been kicked out. Senator Benjamin Goodhue, of Adams' own state of Massachusetts, gathered a similar impression from a stormy interview with the explosive President. Adams, he reported, cried that a "damned faction" composed of "Hamilton, Pickering and some others" were constantly trying to "ruin" him; they had "crammed Hamilton down his throat" as head of the army; the Federalist Senate had "wounded his feelings" by refusing to confirm his son-in-law, Colonel William Smith, for an army commission because he was a bankrupt; and only the deciding vote of Vice-President Jefferson had averted a similar fate for Joshua Johnson, head of the Stamp Office, whose daughter had married the President's son, John Quincy Adams.

Adams, according to Goodhue, said he probably would not be re-elected, and that "after forty years' service for the public, he would be obliged to return to Quincy and follow the plow for a living"; but he was proud he had sent the envoys to France, to prevent war, "it was one of the most glorious deeds he ever did; he would order it to be engraved on his coffin."

Hamilton's lieutenants believed there was method in Adams' "madness." They charged that when he realized his own party planned to replace him with General Pinckney, he could save himself only by seeking a coalition with Jefferson. Pickering claimed Adams had made a "corrupt bargain with the Democrats to secure his second election"; and that explained the new "negotiation with France." George Cabot said "there is a good understanding" between Jefferson and Adams that they would "make a joint-stock of their influence in the next election." When Adams denied the reports of the coalition, Pickering contented himself with this wry comment: "I will only say that the President is not always consistent or accurate in his remembrance."

General Pinckney was astonished by the reports that Adams was "endeavoring to coalesce with Jefferson, that he stigmatizes the Federalists with the odious appellation of a British party, and that he declares that he and Jefferson will convince the Federal Junto of their joint power." If the Federalists would act with "decision, energy and union," the General wrote to McHenry from his Southern Army headquarters in Virginia, they could still defeat the "Jacobinical party," despite their setback in New York and the "tergiversation" of Adams.

Speaker Sedgwick admitted that the President's "late conduct" in seeking peace with France had "endeared him to the great body of the Federalists," but it had also "created an entire separation between him and those whom he heretofore deemed his best friends," and they would have nothing more to do with him.

"Most of the *influential men"* of the Federalist party, Hamilton commented, "consider him as a very *unfit* and *incapable* character. My mind is made up. I will never more be responsible for him by any direct support, even though the consequence should be the election of *Jefferson*. If the cause is to be sacrificed to a weak and perverse man, I withdraw from the party."

Federalists who had seen Adams' temper tantrums, and therefore were convinced of his emotional and mental instability, agreed with Hamilton that the President must go. Speaker Sedgwick called Adams a "semi-maniac." Oliver Wolcott, the Secretary of the Treasury, told Hamilton: "The people believe their President is crazy. That is the honest truth." Secretary McHenry, shaken by the blast that had blown him out of the cabinet, gave Hamilton this pen-portrait of the President: "Whether sportful, playful, witty, kind, cold, drunk, sober, angry, easy, stiff, jealous, careless, cautious, confident, close or open, is so, almost always in the *wrong place* and to the *wrong persons*."

Representative James A. Bayard of Delaware, who had seen Adams' after-dinner eruptions over the wine bottles, commented: "The escape we have had under his administration is miraculous. He is liable to gusts of passion little short of frenzy, which drive him beyond the control of any rational reflection. I speak of what I have seen. At such moments the interest of those who support him, or the interest of the nation, would be outweighed by a single impulse of rage. . . . We may thank the guardian Genius of this country, which has watched over its destinies for the last 4 years."

* * * * *

Margaret Bayard witnessed the exciting three-day drama starring Hamilton versus Burr at the polls of New York, and was astonished by the Republican victory and the ensuing split in Adams' cabinet.

"There is no late occurrence which has excited so much surprise as the dismission of Pickering," she commented. "This man had always appeared to me to be distinguished by uncommon firmness and integrity, united with a republican simplicity and independence. Indeed, I have heard it suggested that his unyielding character, his plain, blunt manner which often led him to openly disapprove the conduct of the President, has been the chief cause."

When she voiced these views to Charles Brockden Brown, the novelist asked, in surprise, "Is it possible that you feel any concern in these political events?"

"Yes, I do," she replied, "I feel the greatest curiosity about this particular change."

"Why," he said, "a thousand conjectures have been formed, and some have gone so far as to say that a coalition has taken place between Adams and Jefferson, and that the first is making interest with the latter to be vice president. But what are your principles?"

Margaret laughed and said she was "too ignorant to have formed any," but Brown led her into a discussion of the leading differences between the two parties, and expressed amazement at her grasp of the subject. "Though I often converse with you, at each interview I discover something new," he exclaimed. "I thought I knew your character, yet the more I know the more I have to learn. But why never talk on this subject? Why conceal the interest you take in it?"

"I am afraid of becoming a partisan," she explained. "I have strong feelings, and when I allow them to fix on any object, they become exclusive and partial. . . . The warmth I should be too apt to discover would be unbecoming my sex. Few periods, certainly, can be more interesting than the present, as the peace and welfare of this country are in a great degree dependent on the next election."

Her fiancé naturally hailed the Republican triumph in New York with unbounded joy. "The elections in New York have been perfectly decisive," Samuel told Peggy. "They insure to Mr. J. 12 votes wch. last election were given to Mr. A. Besides they give that impulse to your state [New Jersey] wch. will make it Republican. Mr. J. will, therefore, be President, if supported by the undivided strength of the Republicans."

The Republican editor had a ready explanation for Adams' ouster of Pickering and McHenry:

"Desirous of securing his re-election, Mr. A. hoped, by his recent conduct, to divide and conquer. He knew that Mr. P. possessed neither the respect of his political friends or enemies, and that there was . . . a difference of opinion as to his incompetency to the place. He sacrificed him. This sacrifice proceeded either from policy . . . or from *impulse,* Mr. P. and he never having been cordial, and it is known that passion often, very often, sways where reason ought to rule."

Adams need not imagine, though, that he had thereby curried any favor with Jefferson and the Republicans. "Mr. A. can never possess their confidence. Mr. J. does possess it in a higher degree than any man in the nation. He can have made no coalition, for he knows that were he to part with his principles, he would forfeit all his friends. . . . The most intelligent Federalists consider Mr. J. our future P [president], and the small portion of doubt I entertain is too trifling to impair the pleasure wch. such a prospect affords."

Samuel added this concise summary of his party's philosophy:

"The republican party entertain this great principle: Be jealous of executive power. Instead of increasing it, guard its exercise by efficient restraints. War is almost always the offspring of executive ambition, and always tends to increase executive power and it rarely, if ever, is beneficial to nations themselves. Avoid war, therefore, as the greatest of all curses. Let the sword never be drawn but in defense of invaded rights, and especially let no *imaginary* alarm,

170

managed by executive agents, hurry one nation into hostility with another.

"... This principle has been opposed in all the important measures of the present administration, and the only refuge of the Republicans has been remonstrance and a free expression of their sentiments, for wch. many of them have suffered, or are now suffering imprisonment. . . .

"The tide, however, has been seen to be turning and is in my opinion now completely turned."

Peggy agreed with Samuel's analysis of Adams' actions and their effect on the election. "It indeed seems to me," she commented, "that, had he been trying to throw himself out of office, he could not have pursued a surer way." Her friend, the Reverend Samuel Miller, observed: "I regret most sincerely the infidelity of Mr. J., but am convinced his administration will be firm and dignified. When I reflect on the strength and power which but a little while ago was possessed by the Federalists and when I now behold it crumbling into nothing, and its destruction not the work of opposition but the effect of *their own conduct,* I own I am astonished."

Margaret, too, was amazed at the spectacle of the Federalists fighting among themselves, in the way the vulgar, unwashed Republicans were supposed to do. She had been taught, all her life, to believe that the Federalists alone were the wise and good people who would preserve society from atheism and mob rule, but she began to agree with Samuel that they had no monopoly on wisdom, or even common sense.

Then, as if to complete her disillusionment with the manners of Federalist gentlemen, came another shocking event: Her own cousin and adopted brother, James, had fought a duel with another Congressman; both men were wounded and hiding out from the police like a pair of thieves.

Bayard, a hot-blooded 33, had got into an argument with Rhode Island Representative Christopher G. Champlin, 32. They quarreled when Champlin proposed to reduce the pay of collectors at the ports of Wilmington, Delaware, and New London, Connecticut. Bayard, a boon companion of the Wilmington collector, Allen Mc-

Lane, took offense, and hot words were quickly followed by the challenge.

It was raining at the time, so the two honorable gentlemen repaired to the shelter of a saw-pit shed at the corner where the road led over the stone bridge from Philadelphia to Kensington. General L. R. Morris, a Vermont Congressman, and John Rutledge, Jr., of South Carolina, served as seconds. Champlin was wounded in the cheek, Bayard in the thigh.

"A prosecution is set on foot," Speaker Sedgwick informed a friend, May 11. "They have fled, except poor Champlin who, I fear, is unable to get off."

Three days later, Rutledge sent a bulletin to Bayard, who was hiding out in Delaware: "We are all in safety and our enemies and pursuers have been put to shame and confusion. Morris left town about the same time I did, and Mrs. Champlin, claiming to have exclusive property in the body of her husband, at a dead hour of the night when men of quiet consciences were wrapped in sweet sleep, wrapped up her husband and stole him unheeded from the city.

"I have a letter from Champlin, the morning after getting into the Jerseys. He mentions that his wound had been that morning dressed and for the first time he had seen it in the glass. He bids me tell you (in badinage) that he shall hold you in remembrance."

From his refuge at Wilmington, Bayard wrote to his cousin Andrew, the Philadelphia merchant-financier: "The escape I made from the city was quite lucky, but I do not like the idea of perpetual banishment which the affair is likely to occasion." Could Andrew find out whether Governor McKean—although a Jacobin Republican—would call off the prosecuting officers? "I do not mean to ask any favor of him, but if he has the feelings of a gentleman, he certainly has it in his power to put a stop to the business," James declared. Without some assurance of safety from arrest, he added, "I shall certainly not expose myself to the fury of the Jacobins. I shall never ask nor expect mercy from them."

Later James wrote to Andrew again: "I should have probably paid a visit to the city before this time if I had been entirely exempt from personal apprehensions. But as I have a great aversion from hard labor, I have preferred renouncing the pleasure to running any risks. If the Governor would say that at all events a *nolle prosequi* should be granted, I should feel myself restored to my ancient privilege of locomotion."

CHAPTER EIGHT

WHEN CONGRESS adjourned on May 14, 1800, its members paid a last farewell to the two-story red brick hall on Chestnut Street at Sixth, in Philadelphia, where for the past decade they had been meeting, and occasionally feuding, fussing and fighting with hickory sticks, fire tongs, fists, and dueling pistols. The entire Federal government, consisting of about a hundred clerks, with their records, furniture, families and assorted impedimenta, moved to the Maryland shore of the Potomac River, where the capital city was all too slowly emerging from the virgin forest.

John Adams went along to see the half-finished presidential "palace" and to make some "official" speeches that might help to assure him a four-year lease on the new mansion. He was the first President to make public stump speeches for re-election, and the Republican newspapers backing Jefferson, who had retired in dignified silence to Monticello, detected a little politicking in Adams' oratory. Duane's Philadelphia *Aurora* wondered why Adams rode fifty miles out of his way to Washington via Lancaster, Pennsylvania and Frederick, Maryland, and then traveled back northward by Annapolis and Baltimore. Surely, the Chief Executive knew that both Pennsylvania and Maryland were doubtful states which probably would split their votes in the election.

When the people of Alexandria, Virginia, celebrated the arrival of the government only a few miles away, Adams ventured into Jefferson's home territory and wooed the Virginians with oratory which lent substance to the recurring rumors that he and Jefferson were secretly united against Hamilton's "British faction."

Driving home to Quincy, Massachusetts, the peppery President paused to refresh himself at various places along the way, and to make more speeches against the leaders of his own Federalist party, never saying an unkind word against Jefferson. At a dinner in Faneuil Hall in Boston, Adams raised his glass in a volunteer toast to "the proscribed patriots," John Hancock and Samuel Adams, old radicals of the Revolution, a gesture interpreted widely as a bid for support from the "Jacobins." Such speeches, "queer toasts," and whispered "anecdotes" corroborated the rumors of the Adams-Jefferson coalition in the mind of an Essex Junto leader, Fisher Ames, who observed: "His language is bitter even to outrage and swearing and calling names. . . . He inveighs against the British faction and the Essex Junto like one possessed." Ames found Adams' supporters offering "to fraternize with Jacobins whom they denominate old friends, and openly rail against 'exclusive Federalists,' 'Hamiltonians,' 'Essex Junto,' 'Royalists,' 'British Partisans,' as they affect to call the men who stick to the good old principles and old cause."

Speaker Sedgwick correctly observed that the Federalist Congressmen's decision to recommend Adams and General Pinckney as "joint and equal candidates" for President had "excited the most furious indignation" in Adams' mind. "He everywhere denounces the men, . . . in whom he confided at the beginning of his administration, as an oligarchish faction, who are combined to drive him from office, because they cannot govern him, and to appoint Pinckney, by whose agency, under the control of this faction & particularly of Hamilton its head, this country is to be driven into a war with France and a more intimate, if not an indissoluble, union with Great Britain."

Representative John Rutledge, Jr., of South Carolina, reported to Hamilton from Newport, Rhode Island, that "Adams has begun a hot canvass and by civility & condescension is trying to have the Jacobins support him with Jefferson, but his countrymen are too cunning to be duped by him." Oliver Wolcott found that Adams' personal friends were talking of forming a new party, the "Constitutionalists," to draw moderate votes from both parties to Adams, and leave Pinckney in the lurch.

To counteract such alarming schemes, Hamilton made a personal tour of New England in June. Officially, the dapper little general went to bid adieu to his soldiers who were being disbanded, since Congress had decided a further build-up of the army was unnecessary to make the French sign a reasonable treaty with the new American mission to Paris. Unofficially, Hamilton used his travels as a convenient way of advising the Federalist chieftains to hold their electors strictly to the caucus pledge of equal support for both Adams and Pinckney. They must not, he warned, let anyone drop a vote from Pinckney, as some had "cut" his brother Thomas four years before, for the result would be the election of the dreaded Jefferson.

Hamilton candidly admitted that he would be delighted if General Pinckney should happen to pick up a few extra votes from his home state of South Carolina and thus finish first in the race. Hamilton found his lieutenants in the New England aristocracy, such as the Essex Junto, seemingly willing to sacrifice Adams.

Unfortunately, however, "the mass of the people," were still "attached to Adams," and so were the "leaders of the second class." They would not believe the reports of the President's instability, his volcanic eruptions of temper, his reversal of Federalist foreign policy. It was obviously too late in the day to change the opinions of these Adamsites overnight, for as George Cabot of the Essex Junto observed, "many will shut their eyes against the light because it would show them what they do not wish to see."

Fisher Ames knew the game that Adams was playing. Adams, he discovered, wanted the Massachusetts legislature to choose electors who would vote for himself and "throw away the votes for the other candidate." "This game will be played in Connecticut, New Hampshire and Rhode Island," Ames reported, to make sure Pinckney could not come in first.

But where would those wasted electoral votes go? Would they go, as in 1796, to such a Federalist as Chief Justice Oliver Ellsworth?

176

Or could they be diverted to the Republican candidate for Vice-President, Aaron Burr? As wild as it may have seemed at first glance, there actually was some basis for the possibility of Federalist New Englanders voting for Burr. "Col. B. of New York also is at market and may give his influence to the highest bidder," Ames reported.

On the strength of his New York triumph, Burr had obtained iron-clad pledges from the Republicans to support him equally with Jefferson in the presidential race. Everyone understood that Jefferson was the candidate for President, Burr for Vice-President. However, if the Republican electors should each cast one vote for Jefferson and one vote for Burr, and if Burr should somehow pick up a few Federalist votes in New England, then the wily colonel would become the next President of the United States!

Burr "is intriguing with all his might in New Jersey, Rhode Island, and Vermont; and there is a possibility of some success in his intrigues," Hamilton told Representative James A. Bayard. "He counts positively on the universal support of the anti-Federalists, and that, by some adventitious aid from other quarters, he will overtop his friend Jefferson." If he should win the presidency, "Burr will certainly attempt to reform the government à la Buonaparte," Hamilton warned his loyal friend in Delaware. "He is as unprincipled and dangerous a man as any country can boast—as true a Catiline as ever met in midnight conclave."

Burr apparently was paying his rival Hamilton the supreme compliment of imitation. If Hamilton could scheme to run General Pinckney ahead of President Adams by juggling the electors' second votes, then Burr could likewise scheme to slip in ahead of Jefferson by intriguing for some Federalist electors' votes. Burr further imitated Hamilton by making a New England tour, ostensibly to help Jefferson as well as himself but actually to bargain with the Federalists.

James Cheetham, a newspaper editor unfriendly to Burr, later charged that the Republican vice-presidential candidate "undoubtedly had a higher object in view" all along. "He had fixed his basilisk eyes on the presidency; and, in the fullness of his sanguine disposition, he entertained a hope that by able management he might fill that office before Mr. Jefferson. . . . Hence, the moment he was nominated he put into operation a most extensive, complicated, and wicked system of intrigue to place himself in the presidential chair." Cheetham claimed that Burr, loaded down with debts he could never pay except by seizing the United States Treasury, had hired agents to advance his presidential ambitions in many states. "The expresses kept on foot, the men he employed, and the expenses of their various agencies must have cost him a sum little less than one year's salary in his office," Cheetham charged.

Burr had influential friends and relatives with entree to the Federalist camp: Jonathan Dayton, New Jersey Senator and former Speaker of the House, once dubbed a "double-faced weathercock" because he vacillated between the two parties, favored Burr's cause in doubtful New Jersey; Burr also kept in close touch with his uncle, Judge Pierpont Edwards, in Rhode Island; and his brother-in-law, Tapping Reeve, in Connecticut. On his New England tour, Burr visited Governor Fenner in Rhode Island and learned that Rhode Island probably would "cut" at least one electoral vote from Pinckney.

Hamilton's friend, Robert Troup, kept tab on Burr's travels that summer: "Burr . . . our Chief Consul, is in very high glee. . . . He seems from his manners to be very sanguine of success." And later: "Burr has just returned from the Eastward where he has been for the purpose of effecting a division in the New England vote. . . . I recollect no period in Burr's life in which he has been more complacent." George Cabot, chief of the Essex Junto, told Hamilton: "The question has been asked, whether, if the Federalists cannot carry their first points, they would not do as well to turn the election from Jefferson to Burr? They conceive Burr to be less likely to look to France for support than Jefferson, provided he would be supported at home. They consider Burr as actuated by ordinary ambition, Jefferson by that and the pride of the Jacobinic philosophy. The former may be satisfied by power and property, the latter must see the roots of our society pulled up and a new course of cultivation substituted."

Charles Carroll of Carrollton relayed a similar hint from Maryland. "Burr will probably act with more decision than Jefferson, if elected President," the old Federalist told Hamilton. If the Virginia electors "should suspect that Burr might outvote their favorite, Jefferson, they will leave out Burr, or only leave him a few votes," as they did in 1796.

But Burr had taken great pains to keep the Virginians from "lurching" him again. That was why he had insisted that the Republicans, at their congressional nominating caucus, promise equal support for both himself and Jefferson. To make sure the Southerners honored their pledge, Burr sent their leaders confidential assurances that Jefferson would run ahead of him in the North by at least one or two electoral votes—in Rhode Island and Vermont, for example.

Therefore, the Southern Republicans must vote equally for Burr and Jefferson, so the argument ran, for otherwise either Adams or Pinckney would be elected Vice-President and Burr would be left out in the cold again.

* * * * *

The Republicans' brightening prospects of victory in the election —which they liked to call "the Revolution of 1800"—also brought about a revolution in the personal life of their most loyal and erudite Philadelphia newspaper editor, Samuel Harrison Smith.

After nearly four years of day-and-night labors Samuel had established himself as one of the most widely respected journalists in the city. He had two offers, almost at the same time, to buy other papers, one in Philadelphia, the other in New York. One, at least, was a Federalist sheet—yet Samuel was invited to take it over. This "uncommon coincidence . . . seems to mark the present period of your life as an important and momentous one," Margaret Bayard told him. "The offers you have received are decided proofs of the estimation in which your character is held; had they been made by one party, I might have believed that political considerations produced them; but when I behold those, absolutely opposed in opinion, thus distinguishing you, I certainly consider it as a most decided testimony of the independence and integrity of your character."

Margaret hoped he would buy the New York paper, since that would enable them to be married and live in the city where she had so many congenial friends. But he turned down both offers, primarily because he shrank from borrowing the necessary money. He had a horror of debts, realizing they restricted a man's independence, and he prized his independence highly.

Margaret's brother Samuel, although as staunch a Federalist as his father and brothers, indicated he would advance enough money to buy the New York paper if it would make her happy. However, Editor Smith's answers to his inquiries were so vague, revealing little of either his "present situation or future hopes," that Bayard felt his Good Samaritan offers were unappreciated, and he told Margaret so.

"I am certain the offer was made with the truest affection and most perfect sincerity," she assured her fiancé. "Provided the paper is still attainable, and on the same terms, *can you accept it?*"

"I can," he replied. But he dreaded to go into debt. Now, as to the misunderstanding with her brother: "I had a conversation with your brother. I am surprised that he should call it vague. He called at our house respecting some books of his. In the presence of others, he alluded to the New York scheme, offered any services in his power, and appealed to my ideas on the subject. . . . I conversed with him with more freedom than I recollect to have done with any third person. He repeated his solicitude for our welfare. Your brother then withdrew, saying that on his arrival at New York he would make inquiries respecting the papers and let me know the result. I replied that such a step would be perfectly satisfactory to me."

He would like to move to New York, he told her, but "you pass over too lightly a possible disastrous issue, involving dependence or poverty. . . . God knows that there is not a day of my life in which this is not the subject of long—of painful—reflection, as those thoughts often must be which dwell on obstacles without being able to surmount them."

After the Republican victory in New York, Thomas Jefferson had a private conversation with Editor Smith, and Samuel hastened to New York to tell Peggy all about it in strictest secrecy. This was the news: The Vice-President planned to have the Republicans set up a newspaper in Washington as the official voice of their party. If he won the presidency, as now seemed quite likely, this paper would become the journal of the new administration.

Its editor would be a man of power in the government. He would stand close to the inner circle of the President and his advisers; he could even leave his stamp upon history. Who should be the editor? William Duane, the slashing partisan who had succeeded the late Benjamin Franklin Bache as editor of the *Aurora,* craved the post as a reward for all the dirty work he had done in assassinating the characters of the Federalists, often at the risk of his life. Once a band of Federalist cavalry officers had marched on the *Aurora* offices, beaten up the editor, and kicked him down the stairs.

Yes, the wild Irishman Duane, and the lousy-headed Scot, James Callender, and others of their breed had done yeoman service for Jefferson. No doubt they felt entitled to promotion whenever Jefferson should come into his kingdom. But they did not fit his mental picture of a Republican editor for the new "court journal," a man of erudition, good taste, breeding, scholarship, philosophy. The man who did fit the picture precisely was the Vice-President's fellow-philosopher, Samuel Harrison Smith.

Margaret could hardly believe this good news. She had known her fiancé was a brilliant young man, respected for his integrity and independence, and his skill as a writer, as he had proved in winning the Philosophical Society's contest for the "Essay on Education." But she had never dreamed he would rise as high as this. To edit the official newspaper of the government at the age of twenty-eight!

It was truly a remarkable offer, and a providential solution to their financial problems. For, obviously, with the support of Jefferson and the other Republican party leaders, the new Washington paper would produce enough revenue for its editor to support a wife in the style her aristocratic Federalist father expected her to enjoy.

But there were arguments against accepting the Washington offer. First of all, Washington was not really a city. It was little more than a clearing in the woods on the Maryland side of the Potomac. Its spacious boulevards, imposing marble buildings, and elegant homes existed almost exclusively on maps drawn by the dreamers who were planning the metropolis. For ten years, the promoters had been gambling away huge sums of money in patchwork attempts to make the capital something more than a mudhole. Aside from the society of nearby Georgetown, however, Washington still had no circle of cultured individuals such as those with whom Peggy Bayard was accustomed to associate; indeed, it had few inhabitants except the poor mechanics erecting the government buildings, and the clerks who were just moving in. Only one wing of the Capitol would be ready for Congress in November; Congressmen, Senators, Federal officials, and nearly everybody else would have to live in boardinghouses.

If she and Samuel were to live in Philadelphia or New York, they would be within a drive of no more than a day or two from her home at New Brunswick, and the stagecoaches made regular runs several times daily along the New York-Philadelphia axis. But Washington lay many miles to the south, away from all the amenities of eastern civilization and far from Peggy's own family and friends. Samuel feared that her love for her family would not let her move so far away from New Brunswick. While he had long realized that she had an independent mind as well as "warmth and energy of feeling," still he could not be sure that "the heart would not control the judgment" in her decision.

To his surprise, she discussed the pro's and con's of the project in a calm and dispassionate manner. She conceded the certain discomfort of roughing it in the new capital and she dreaded to move so far away from her family; but she also weighed the advantages of his position of influence as the editor of the administration's paper, which would make him one of the foremost journalists in America. She could not bar him from this opportunity of a lifetime. So, after thoughtful deliberation, the once-impulsive Peggy agreed he must accept.

Her decision, he told her, "extended my admiration, increased my love, and made you more than ever mine." She loved him all the more for having taken her into his confidence as an equal partner in his enterprise. This act convinced her that he sincerely believed her mind was the equal of his, and that she was no longer a silly girl but a grown woman worthy to be his wife. "I feel I deserved this confidence," she told him, "and it made me more worthy of being, indeed, your *friend.*" While her "affectionate heart" must regret giving up her family, she assured him, "in your love I shall find a balm for every sorrow."

So it was settled. They would go to Washington, to launch the new paper, and they would go there as man and wife.

When Samuel returned to Philadelphia, he began immediately soliciting the support of the nation's most prominent Republicans to send the new paper off to a flying start. To James Madison, one of Jefferson's closest friends, he wrote:

"Sir:

"Mr. Gallatin some time since had the goodness to apprise you of my intention to conduct at the seat of the General Govt. a newspaper on a plan calculated, in my opinion, to advance the best interests of the Country. Having since matured my ideas, I now do myself the pleasure of addressing you, enclosing the within sketch of my plan.

"It is my wish, and will be my effort, to collect into a focus those talents, whose ascendency, generally speaking, only requires concentration and a correct adaptation to existing circumstances. And if, to the number of those who have offered the assistance of their talents, I be permitted to add yourself, you will confer not only an obligation on me, but one also on your Country.

"The dignified and moderate principles by which I design to regulate my professional deportment induce me with the less hesitation to invite your co-operation."

When Samuel told his family of his plans for marrying Margaret and taking her to the new capital, he was astonished to find they were strongly against it. His sister Mary thought it "a step of the utmost imprudence." His brother John even hinted he might block the credit which the editor must have to finance the new paper. John did not oppose the paper so much as the idea of taking Peggy to the unfinished village on the Potomac. It would be impossible for a married couple to find a decent place to live, he argued; their prestige would suffer great injury from living in a boardinghouse; and the editor must impress the public with some better station in life.

"If he chooses to exert this influence in extension of credit I may be seriously embarrassed," Samuel told his fiancée. "Write to me immediately, and tell me all you think. . . . On Friday, I start for Washington—direct mail to me there to 'Washington City.' "

Margaret was shocked by Samuel's indecision in the face of his family's opposition. She wept bitter tears of disappointment. How could he think of any further impediments to their marriage? She had given her heart to him more than three years before; she had defied all the objections of her own father and brothers who distrusted both his religion and his politics; she had waited for him through one delay after another. She could not think of waiting any longer.

Fearful that her emotions might be swaying her better judgment, she showed Samuel's letter to Jane, and asked her counsel. Jane agreed that more suffering of every kind would result from postponing the wedding.

Armed with Jane's advice, Margaret determined to send Samuel an irresistible appeal that would give him the courage to defy all the counsels of timidity and assert his rights as a man to claim the woman he loved. On August 14, 1800, in an agitated scrawl, Margaret wrote to her "best love" the most powerful letter that ever came from her pen.

She began with a very practical appeal to the dollars-and-cents economy of marriage: Whether married or single, the editor of the Washington paper "must have a house" in which to board his printers; and to take charge of this house and "family," he must have a woman. "Now, however faithful this woman might be, she must necessarily expend more in the provision of a family than I should. I should, with delight, enter into all the details and cares of a family; it has never been my expectation to sit down in a study, but to employ myself in active and personal cares. You will be at much less expense if I go *immediately* with you than if our union was deferred.

184

"In regard to the expense of furnishing the house, you will be at none. My father has already advanced some, and will in a month or two give me more than a sufficient sum to furnish it comfortably and genteelly. So that you need not expend a farthing, and will be at less expense than if you went alone." That answered his brother's first objection, the extra expense and inconvenience. Then she turned her guns on the second objection, that residence in a boardinghouse would deprive the editor of public respect.

"How can a sensible man say such a thing?" she asked. "Pride, and not reason, urged that argument. It would not injure your business for, although persons might not respect you, yet as a good printer they would employ you. But there is no truth in this remark. No one who removes to Washington will be exempt from the same difficulties; people of fortune and fashion, if there are no homes, must go to lodgings, and must live in unfinished buildings. This will not be the result of poverty but of local circumstances which must affect the rich and the poor.

"On the contrary, as a married man, you will be more known and more respected. We may not indeed associate with the rich and the fashionable; but is it their society we should select? It is not vanity but experience which convinces me that both you and I shall always be able to command that society we most esteem."

Margaret could not believe that Samuel's bachelor brother would refuse his financial aid, but suppose he did? "The influence of my father and brother would remove this obstacle. It would be a false and cruel pride, indeed, were you to refuse assistance from persons because they were not your relations."

Then she gave a very feminine reason for going ahead with their marriage now: "Papa, in order to give me the money I wanted, had to apply to his agent, who is my brother Andrew; he, therefore, informed him and brother Samuel, and through them, all my friends in Philadelphia will know it. The necessary household linen and furniture require a great deal of sewing, more than enough to occupy me constantly all the time from the present to the period we fixed on. I, therefore, immediately commenced my work and the purchases which this made necessary could not be concealed from the family;

indeed, Papa, who disapproves of all mystery, made no secret of it to any of my friends. Any delay would now give rise to the most painful and mortifying surmises.

"In short, my friend, all irresolution must now be given up. We must go on, and whatever difficulties we encounter, we must either conquer or submit to. I feel no hesitation; I am convinced that in a pecuniary light it will be advantageous to you, and that, to our peace of mind, it is indispensable. It is not my own happiness now, it is yours also that I have in charge; no feminine weakness, no false delicacy, shall induce me to give up that foundation on which it rests."

Finally, from the practical aspects of the matter, she turned to an emotional appeal that must have touched his heart:

"Rather than live any longer separated from you, I would eat bread and water, submit to the most menial and hardest labor. This is not romance, nor are my ideas of happiness romantic. My happiness must ever be derived from the discharge of my duty, and my duty is now inseparably connected with your interest. I no longer speak to you as a lover. The timidities, the reserves of a mistress are lost in the concern of a wife. In the eye of God I am yours. I consider myself as your wife. I shall act accordingly. And do you, my best beloved friend, in all you do, act as the husband. It is your duty to do so; from this time forward I shall look to you for all that is expected in that character.

"We have already calculated too long; too long have we been influenced by the opinions of others and that of the public. We must now act for ourselves. Our happiness must be the work of our own hands; do not let it depend on others. We have youth and health, and, my love, we have a motive for exertion, and we shall carry with us a constant balm for every care and an unfailing source of contentment.

"Oh, my dear, dear friend, listen to your own heart, and it will convince you that the conveniences of fortune, or the pleasures of society, are not essential ingredients in the cup of happiness.... If it is my happiness which you most desire, consent, then, to that on which it entirely depends."

For ten anxious days, Peggy heard nothing from Samuel in far-away Washington. At last, however, came a message in the familiar scrawl. "My dearest love," he began, she knew how nothing on earth was so "distressingly painful" to him as debts, which would rob him of his freedom. He, therefore, had hesitated when his brother had threatened to cut off his credit if he married Margaret before moving to Washington. He agreed with her, however, that some risk must be run.

Then came the words she was longing to read: He would stand up to his brother; he would go forward with the plans for a wedding in September.

"When the inflexibility of my purpose is known," he wrote, "my brother, I think" (he inked out "think" and scribbled in "hope") "will pose no obstacle. Why should he? If he regards my happiness (and I have no doubt of it) he will acquiesce."

As if to prove his own determination, Samuel had leased two houses in Washington—one for a home, the other next door for the printing plant. They were in a row called "The Ten Buildings," on New Jersey Avenue, on the south side of Capitol Hill. "A man who has lived on the spot for six years assured me the situation was very healthy, and that the water was equal to any in the world," he said. "There are not a great many houses near, but such as are erected are good ones, and will probably be filled with respectable characters."

The row was "not yet fully erected, but the owners have contracted to finish it entirely by Nov. 1 and the printing office part by Oct. 1." Apparently, Mr. and Mrs. Smith would have to spend their first month of married life in some Washington boardinghouse. But that was the best he could do, so the editor closed the deal and started for Philadelphia to settle his business there and bring Margaret to the capital as his bride.

At Chester, Pennsylvania, about nine o'clock at night, the coach suddenly lurched to a halt.

Through the open window, a paper was shoved into his hand.

Samuel read the message with dismay. It was an official proclamation barring from Philadelphia everyone who had been in Baltimore at any time within the past fifteen days.

There was pestilence in Baltimore; and Philadelphia was taking no chances on having the yellow fever for a fourth summer in a row.

Thus did Samuel's old Nemesis still pursue him. It seemed to him as if "the malevolence of fortune" was heaping upon him "its cruelest injuries." Fuming with frustration, he protested to the Board of Health that he should be considered as "not coming within the meaning of the proclamation." He had merely passed through Baltimore on his trip, he argued. If he could not be exempted from the ban, he told Peggy in a note from Chester, "here to my poignant mortification I must stay fifteen days, to the almost total derangement of my business during that period."

Two days later, the ban was lifted. Samuel's brother came and escorted him into Philadelphia, and assured him that he need worry no more about finances. John would not withhold his credit. In a "most confidential conversation" along the way, Samuel found John now positively willing to help with the plans for the wedding in late September. By August 28 the editor could report to his fiancée:

"I have just made arrangements with my paper maker. He has promised to supply me with paper on the 23rd Sept. My types are in rapid progress as well as other articles. In truth, I have been dashing about at such a rate that my mind has not been sufficiently at ease to write."

All the materials for the new Washington newspaper—types, paper, forms, ink, press, and other supplies—would be sent by the sailing ship *Harmony,* and the office of the printing plant would be officially moved by September 25. Should that also be the day, he asked Peggy, "on which I start for Brunswick?"

She knew what he meant: He was coming, this time, to marry her, and would she name the day? "Tell me, my love, all that you wish," he urged her. "Let us rise superior to those little delicacies of feeling that would obstruct a complete understanding."

She left the date for him to fix, so he suggested Monday, September 29.

"I consent, my dear friend," she replied in triumph. "Let Monday, the 29th, be the day which shall inseparably unite us."

She trembled with joy and yet with fear lest some "unforeseen barrier" might yet raise one more obstacle to their plans. "Where there is so much to lose, must we not fear?" she asked. "We are many miles apart and still must be many days separated. In that interval how many accidents may occur!" But, she consoled herself by thinking, "I know my life is designed by my Creator and that, without His permission no occurrence can take place."

As the time grew short, Peggy rushed through her final preparations for the wedding. "My sisters, desirous of doing everything to add to my comfort, and wishing to avoid the expense of hiring people, have undertaken to assist me in all the preparations," she wrote to Samuel's sister Mary. "In making up all the house linen, bedding, curtains, etc., you know there must be a vast deal of sewing; and, as the time is short, we have been constantly and busily employed. Maria spends every day here and works as if it were for herself. Sister Jane, who seems to consider me as her daughter, superintends everything. She says, as the things are to last for life, she is determined that they shall be of the best and that I shall have an abundance of everything that is necessary." Even her stepmother, Peggy said, "gives evidences of kindness" and "has taken a set of curtains to make."

Although Colonel Bayard had long ago opposed her marriage, he had determined to help her now, as she explained to Mary Smith, because "I told him that this only could make me happy." In fact, "Papa, who has been dissatisfied and displeased at the delays that have taken place, participates in that satisfaction which my friends seem to feel."

When the mountain of needlework was finished, "Papa" sent the load to Trenton, whence it would go by water to Philadelphia and then to Washington. "The articles I send consist of 2 chests, one large black trunk & 2 large sacks," Peggy told Samuel. "They are directed to you & to the care of Pettit & Bayard, as the boat they are sent in always lies at their Wharf. Papa sent them this morning to Trenton, where they are to be put on board a boat, which sails tomorrow & which probably will reach Phila. by Monday morning.

"Sister suggested to me the probability of your insuring the goods you send to Washington & said I had best let you know the value of what I send you. The amount of the whole is six hundred dollars." (She scratched out "six" and substituted "seven.")

"As feathers are so difficult to procure, I have purchased them here, and packed them in bags," Peggy informed Mary Smith. "What do you think, Mary, about taking any standing furniture from Philadelphia? Common tables and chairs may be procured at Washington. Mrs. Hodge had two high post bedsteads she wished to dispose of. Do you not think I had better take them—one, at least, for immediate use?

"I wrote to sister Sally [Mrs. Andrew Bayard of Philadelphia] about a carpet which Brother had purchased at a very low price. Will you ask her about it, and, if she can part with it, have it packed up with your brother's things? Mrs. Hodge has two pieces of my painting. Will you bring them on with you? They must be very carefully packed in my trunk and this I cannot do in Philadelphia as I do not expect to spend more than one evening there. . . .

"P.S. Maria Templeton and myself have just determined to begin a patchwork quilt, which is to consist solely of the pieces of our friends' gowns. She begs me to add, by way of postscript, a request that you will bring us some pieces of yours and Susan's. If the pieces are only two inches large, no matter; it is only as a memento that we make them."

Evidently Sister Mary relayed the requests, for the bridegroom wrote: "Mrs. Bayard has parted with the carpet, and Mrs. Hodge has also parted with the bedsteads." Now what should he do? Should he have a wedding bed made in Philadelphia or take a chance on finding one in Washington? The beds which Theodore Pettit had taken with him to the capital had proved too high for the ceiling, and Samuel could not remember how high the ceilings would be in his Washington house.

"Anyway," the bed "seems to me a matter of but little moment," he remarked. "If not taken, it can be made immediately at Washington."

Whether or not the bride agreed that the bed was "a matter of but little moment," she was much too modest to say. She was already agitated enough over the thought of leaving her home forever. While writing to her fiancé, she heard the wagon carrying her baggage away, and for the first time she realized the separation that would soon take place. "Until this moment," she wrote, "I did not *feel* that I was to leave my friends, leave this little room, the retirement of so many happy and so many wretched hours; here where I have sat to think of you with tenderness and delight; here where I have wept whole days and passed so many wakeful nights, tormented with doubt and uncertainty, surrounded by images of disease and death."

She rejoiced that his sisters, Mary and Susan, were coming to the wedding and she urged that his father and brother must come, too. "It will gratify me very much if they will," she assured him. "With what delight shall I embrace *your* father and *your* brother and call them *my* father and *my* brother! A thousand tender emotions circle round the name of 'father' and I cannot describe to you the affection I have ever cherished towards yours. When I was last in Philadelphia he often embraced me, even with fondness, and I remember one day he put his arms around me and pressed his lips to mine."

Now she realized that she must give up her family and go to "the land of strangers," but, she told Samuel, "where you are must be a home to me. You will be all to me. And to fulfill my duties to my God and my duties to you will henceforth be the objects of my life." Thus she closed her last letter to him as his fiancée.

"One letter more, and my pen, too, will be at rest," he replied. "Peace to its labors. It has striven to be faithful to affection, but it has poorly painted the feelings of my heart. . . . On Saturday at 8 in the morning I shall leave the city and reach Brunswick at night. Margaret, I shall meet you with new emotions—emotions which would speak the undisguised language of Nature if they dared. But, situated as you are, surrounded by friends, I shall be obliged to assume an air foreign to my heart! Be it so. A few hours shall break the chains of form, and then the soul *will* speak."

On her wedding eve, Sunday, September 28, 1800, Margaret penned this entry in her commonplace book: "After the lapse of more than three years, during which my heart was agitated by alternate hopes and fears, corroded by anxiety and soothed by tenderness, the period has now arrived which is to unite me to the chosen friend of my heart. The visions of imagination are to be exchanged for realities, and my fondest hopes to be realized.

"I am entering a new and untrodden path; let me not expect it strewn only with flowers, but rather prepare to encounter difficulties and disappointments. The change I am about to make is an important and momentous one. New cares and new duties, as well as new pleasures, lie before me. To perform these duties, various in their objects and important in their nature, is to be the future object of my life. I am no longer to live for myself; the happiness and the virtue of others is committed to my charge.

"Gracious God! At this moment do I realize Thy superintending Power, and acknowledge my entire dependence on Thee. I pray not for riches or for length of days. But I pray for a cheerful resignation to Thy will and Thy grace to enable me to devote that life which Thou hast given me to Thy glory and to the good of my fellow creatures."

* * * * *

And so, on Monday, September 29, 1800, more than four years after their first meeting in New Brunswick, Margaret Bayard and Samuel Harrison Smith became man and wife. All around them at the wedding were their loved ones of both the Bayard and the Smith families and their friends from three communities, Philadelphia, New Brunswick and New York. One of the groomsmen was Anthony Bleecker, Peggy's unsuccessful suitor, who would remain a bachelor, and her faithful friend and correspondent all the rest of his life.

With an ache in her heart, Margaret said farewell to her family and to the charming friends of her gay New York circle: now she must go south to a life of possible hardship as a Washington editor's wife, in a "land of strangers." But she gave up everything gladly, for, as she wrote in her diary, "I went with the husband I loved."

The hour of final parting with the past came in Philadelphia, where the couple had been overnight guests in the home of the bridegroom's family at 71 North Third Street.

Samuel's sisters and his brother John entered the dining room while the bride was finishing a hasty breakfast before starting out on the road to Washington. When she rose to leave and realized she might never see them again, she almost fainted. She would have fallen if John had not caught her in his arms.

With a great effort, Margaret composed her emotions. She told herself the journey would be arduous enough to harm her health, but if she yielded to this agitation, it would totally wreck her. She resolved to conquer her fears, forget the loss of her loved ones, and think only of the future with the man she loved.

Bravely, then, she said her last good-byes. She stepped outside into the cool autumn morning, drew aside her veil, and drank deeply of the bracing air, which soon cleared away her feeling of faintness. Then she and Samuel entered the stagecoach, and it carried them away from Philadelphia—away from the past—southward to Washington and the unknown future.

CHAPTER NINE

T HE STAGECOACH was only a wooden box on wheels, but Margaret and Samuel Harrison Smith paid no attention to the discomforts of travel—or, indeed, to anything else except each other—as they made their wedding journey to Washington.

They hardly noticed their fellow passengers, a carpenter and his wife, and an old "market woman" who did not talk or look at anyone. Peggy was so completely occupied with gazing at the bridegroom that she took little notice of the scenery in southern Pennsylvania, which she was passing through for the first time. She talked of her schooldays at Bethlehem on the Lehigh, of her family and friends; and he told historical anecdotes of the great men he had met. Together they recited poetry.

At sunset, on the first day of their journey, the coach reached Elkton, Maryland, where the road to the Susquehanna River ran through a wood. The road was quite straight, and through this long vista they could see the rich glow of the autumnal evening, which deepened as the harvest moon rose above the trees. It was a perfect scene to delight the bride's romantic heart—a moonlit honeymoon.

After many miles, the road became more hilly. Sometimes the travelers ascended a hill whose crest was gilded by the moonbeams and then descended into a dark and shadowy valley. Occasionally, they caught a distant view of the Chesapeake Bay, glittering like silver in the moonlight.

At ten o'clock at night, they reached the Susquehanna, a majestic dark-blue river a mile and a quarter wide. The tide was full, the breeze fresh, the sky unclouded, and the moon was at its zenith, its white rays scattered over the high river banks and dancing on the surface of the water. Not a sound broke the silence of the night until the boatman blew his horn to announce that the coach had come.

Then the ferryboat came and carried the travelers safely over the river. On the other shore, they entered an inn, ate a hearty supper, and without pausing for sleep, resumed their journey. The moon made the night almost as light as day, and the air was so mild that Margaret needed no extra coat until daybreak. Held close and warm in the arms of her husband, she did not feel the least fatigue, and not until almost morning did she find it a little hard to stay awake.

As the sun rose, Baltimore came into view. To avoid the city, which remained in the grip of the fever, they bumped along a wretched road through the backwoods and arrived, cold, hungry and sleepy, at a tavern which the bride could only describe as "miserable."

In the grimy kitchen, which had only the ground for a floor, they tried to warm themselves at an open fire. They drank weak, thick coffee out of ugly cups; the spoons were rusty and the tablecloth dirty. In the barroom their host was mingling his morning potion of mint-sling and sliced onions.

The beds in the tavern were too filthy for the bridal pair even to think of sleeping there; so after swallowing their breakfast, they walked along the road until the stage was ready. For the rest of the journey through Maryland, the road led through a thick forest, winding up and down a succession of hills, in "very uncultivated country." "We seldom met with a cottage or a field of grain, and but twice or thrice in the whole way with a gentleman's seat," Peggy reported to her family in New Brunswick, "and as for the comfortable farm houses and orchards so common in Jersey, I did not meet with a single one."

The Smiths dined at a "neat and excellent" wayside inn, where the dishes of ham and chicken cooked in the Maryland style were among the best on the table. In the afternoon, they passed through Bladensburg, a village consisting of a few dwellings and two or three inns. The crowds of rude men lounging about the taverns and the "dreadful and constant" swearing of the stage drivers were the most peculiar things that Peggy observed in her first foray below the Mason-Dixon Line.

Margaret thus described to her family the way she and Samuel entered Washington, late in the afternoon of October 3, 1800:

"At last we drew near this, our future abode. We left the woods, among which a boundary stone marked the beginning of the city. We entered a long and unshaded road, which rises a hill and crosses a vast common, covered with shrub oak and blackberries in abundance. I look in vain for the city. I see no houses, although among the bushes I see the different stones which here and there mark the avenues, foot paths and roads. The extensive plain is exactly like the common the other side of the Raritan, only more extensive and more productive of blackberry and sweet briars.

"At last I perceive the Capitol, a large, square ungraceful white building. Approaching nearer I see three large brick houses and a few hovels scattered over the plain. One of the brick houses is the one where we lodge. We drive to it. It is surrounded with mud, shavings, bricks, planks, and all the rubbish of building. Here then I am. I alight, am introduced to Mr. Stelle [Pontius Stelle, the proprietor], and led into a large handsome parlor. I seat myself at the window and while Mr. Smith is busied with the baggage, survey the scene before me.

"Immediately before the door is the place from whence the clay for the bricks has been dug, and which is now a pond of dirty water. All the materials for building—bricks, planks, stone, etc.,—are scattered over the space which lies between this and the Capitol, and which is thickly overgrown with briars and blackberries and intersected with footpaths. Some brick kilns and small wooden houses and sheds diversify the scene. About half a dozen brick houses are seen at a small distance.

"The Capitol stands on a hill, which slopes down towards the Potomac. From the bottom of this hill to the river extends a thick and noble wood. Beyond this you see the river, and the scene is then closed by a range of hills, which extend north and south, far as the eye can reach."

After enjoying this view, the bride was led into the tavern chamber which would be her home until the houses on New Jersey Avenue could be finished. Her host, Pontius Stelle, was "pleasant, genteel and well-behaved," and he had the virtue of being a man of Huguenot descent, from her own state of New Jersey. His guests were "people of decent deportment," including three ladies from Charleston, South Carolina, who had "the most pleasing manners."

Entering her bedroom alone, Margaret found a scene of surprising beauty. Through the windows facing the blue Virginia hills, the rays of the setting sun were reddening the white walls of the chamber. Opposite the cheerful fireplace she found a neat bed with a white counterpane; between the two windows, which had red copperplate print curtains, there was a dressing table; beside the hearth were a tea table and white Windsor chairs.

By the time she had changed her dress and sat down by the window, the October sun had set, and the horizon glowed with the richest crimson of the dying day. As she gazed on the strange new scene, Peggy was overwhelmed by the realization that she was a stranger in a strange land, and a few tears of homesickness started to her eyes.

Then Samuel came in, sat beside her and pressed her tenderly to his heart. "My Margaret," he said softly, "now you are *only* mine, henceforward it is to be the business of my life to make you happy. ... Teach me how to make you happy."

They called for tea, and a "fine little black girl" named Charlotte brought it in with toast, biscuit and ham to make an excellent supper. When the candles were brought, Peggy closed the red curtains, and the little tavern room looked cozy and warm. She banished her feeling that this was an alien place, and a sense of "home" came into her heart.

Several times during supper she looked around the room and then at her husband and exclaimed, "If our sisters were here, if they could but take a peep at us for a single moment ... I wish they could see us now."

The scene, she wrote to her sisters, was "all that my fondest hopes had pictured, all that my heart could require. There was not a thought, a feeling we concealed. We poured out our souls to each other, and if ever there were two human beings completely happy, we were that couple."

After breakfast the next morning, Peggy unpacked her trunk and found everything uninjured by the journey in the jolting coach. She placed her Bible, several volumes of poems, and other books on the mantle, along with a mirror, and then paid a courtesy call on the innkeeper's wife and her new-born baby.

Peggy kissed the baby, and seeing a little boy about the size of her nephew, Littleton Kirkpatrick, she took him into her lap and caressed him. Tears of homesickness rushed into her eyes. "Your little boy is so much the size of a dear little fellow whom I have left, that I cannot help weeping," she explained. When she mentioned that Littleton was a son of Judge Kirkpatrick, Mrs. Stelle said, "I am well acquainted with him, as he lodged a whole winter with us."

"Is it possible?" Peggy cried. "Why, I shall feel as if I met with an old acquaintance in you." Then she and Mrs. Stelle conversed for hours, as if they had known each other all their lives.

After dinner (at three o'clock in the afternoon) the newly-weds went forth like pioneers in the western wilds to walk through the tanglewood of Washington and see for themselves this strange new "city" in the wilderness. Being accustomed to the formal blocks of brick buildings and the neat checkerboard pattern of the paved streets of Philadelphia and New York, they could scarcely realize that this maze of trees, shrubs, vines and briars could be the capital of the United States. The same sight, a few years later, would inspire Tom Moore, the youthful Irish poet, to write the famous lines:

> This embryo capital, where Fancy sees
> Squares in morasses, obelisks in trees;
> Which second-sighted seers even now adorn
> With shrines unbuilt, and heroes yet unborn,
> Though nought but woods and Jefferson they see;
> Where streets should run, and sages ought to be.

Standing amid the mud, bricks and litter of the yard in front of Stelle's tavern and peering through the green jungle, now being tinged lightly with the golden colors of autumn and warmed by the first touch of the Maryland Indian Summer, the Smiths could see only one building that even remotely reminded them that this was a center of government. That building was the square white sandstone box, three stories high, which would become the North Wing of the Capitol.

Congress had allowed ten years for the building of the capital city, in the District of Columbia, and only this one part of Congress Hall had arisen when the government moved to Washington in mid-1800. Now workmen were striving feverishly to have at least this portion ready when Congress would convene in Washington, for the first time, in late November.

From Capitol Hill, the Smiths could get an excellent view of the beautiful wooded countryside sloping downward into the peninsula formed by the junction of the broad Potomac with its smaller eastern branch, which the Indians had named the "Anacostia." The two rivers, and the cultivated fields and the blue hills of Maryland and Virginia on their banks, provided "a prospect of surpassing beauty."

Between the foot of Capitol Hill and the Potomac extended a wide level woodland through which Tiber Creek—known to the natives merely as Goose Creek—wound its way, its banks shaded by tall trees. In Margaret's view, the groves of trees and shrubs gave Washington the most romantic scenery of any American city, and the appearance of a "fine park."

All this scenery was fine enough, but where was the city? To find it, the Smiths had to trudge on foot along muddy roads cut straight through the virgin forest. They learned, through their travels, that there really was no one central city but four little neighborhoods, so widely separated that their total of about three thousand inhabitants seemed even fewer.

The first neighborhood consisted of the Capitol and a few buildings clustering around it—Stelle's tavern, a few other boardinghouses, a grocery and dry goods store (advertising "soft-shelled almonds, china oranges, lemons, figs and raisins") a bookshop, and the homes of a tailor, a shoemaker and a washerwoman. Here, too, was the unfinished row of the Ten Buildings which would eventually include the Smiths' home and the printing shop and office of Samuel's newspaper.

The second settlement covered the waterfront at the point where the two rivers met. Here at the wharves clustered the square-rigged ships of the coastal trade, and here lay the new Navy Yard which was to build and repair the nation's fleet. Here, also, were a lumber yard, a brewery, and several blocks of houses built by speculators; most of the buildings were now abandoned and looked like "the ruins of Palmyra."

The third community, more than a mile to the northwest along the swamp-bordered causeway called Pennsylvania Avenue, huddled around the yet-unfinished white stone palace intended to be the President's House. One of the few homes of distinction here was the Octagon House, the home of Colonel John Tayloe, a rich Virginia planter who chose to live in the capital during the winter social season and race his horses on the oval track at the edge of town.

The fourth neighborhood, still farther west, about three miles from the Capitol, was Georgetown. This thriving port, on the far side of the Rock Creek bridge, had been for many years a settled community, reveling in its prosperity from the tobacco trade of the nearby Maryland plantations, and proud of its fine brick mansions that looked down from the heights on the vessels moving to and fro along the Potomac.

For half a century, sailing ships had taken on tobacco at Georgetown for sale in Europe and had brought back silks and satins for the gentry to wear, wine for them to drink, and gossip from London and Paris for them to talk about. Alexandria, a few miles downstream, had performed a similar function for the planters in northern Virginia. Georgetown considered itself, with some reason, the "court end" of the capital, for it had a society of wealthy and refined merchants and planters.

Washington could claim no such society yet, for most of its three thousand residents were people who worked for a living. Among these were the laborers who dug the foundations, cut the stone and laid the bricks; the carpenters, plasterers and mechanics; the men who felled the trees and grubbed the stumps and cleared the streets and, in their leisure hours, crowded the taverns and cheered the cockfights and got into brawls with the idlers of Georgetown. These workmen usually lived in crude wooden shacks that sometimes had no windows and used only the ground for a floor; the hovels were a dismal contrast to the stately brick and stone buildings which occasionally could be seen amidst the trees.

The city generally was "covered with shrub-oak bushes on the higher grounds and on the marshy soil either trees or some sort of shrubbery," one of the early settlers later recorded. "Pennsylvania Avenue, leading, as laid down on paper, from the Capitol to the presidential mansion, was nearly the whole distance, a deep morass covered with alder bushes. The roads in every direction were muddy and unimproved. . . . In short, it was a new settlement."

In letters to their sisters, Margaret and Samuel Smith painted a graphic picture of their life in the "new settlement" along the Potomac. "Margaret and I have been exploring the variegated rural beauties of this city, now rising to the summit of a commanding hill bounded by one of the handsomest streams of our country, now descending into a cool valley covered with wood and watered by gently flowing rills," Samuel wrote to his sister Susan in Philadelphia. "A walk here is truly a herculean task. So many objects, apparently near but in truth distant by several miles, invite your approach, that step follows step until the rapid declension of the sun or the imperious calls of hunger compel your return.

"We have often set out with a resolution to walk a mile, but never have we finished our walk without extending it to three and sometimes to six miles. . . . Margaret is quite enraptured with the profusion of sweetbriars and magnolias that spring up around you wherever you shape your course. I am a thousand times better pleased with the wildness and romantic situation of this place than with all the regularity and elegance of art. Shady roads, extensive plains and lofty woods are in my eye preferable to wide paved streets and superb palaces."

To her sister Jane in New Brunswick, Margaret sent this description of the scene of her future home in the Ten Buildings on New Jersey Avenue:

"Mr. Smith and myself walked to our house. We continued on the road, which leads from this house down a steep hill where some fine houses are built, but which are surrounded with bushes and trees. We descended the hill, and on the right hand we saw a row of houses, the two first of which are ours. They were perfectly enveloped in large forest trees and shrubs of various kinds.

"The road on Jersey Avenue passes the front of the houses, which is to the east; on the opposite side of the road rises a hill covered with shrub oak and blackberries; behind the houses a fine wood extends to the river, which is about ¾ of a mile distant. Our lot will contain some fine oaks and hickory and plenty of blackberries and other vines and briars.

"We went through the houses. The office was finished sufficiently for use; as for the rest of the buildings, I do not expect they will be done in less than three weeks. One great advantage arises from this: We have the liberty of dividing the house as we please, of having closets, windows, etc., wherever we like them. Mr. S. and I are to draw a plan and give it to the builders. You will learn from this that the walls alone are up and the roofs on. In the cellar and kitchen, shrubs and blackberries grow very plentifully, interspersed with shavings and bricks.

"We left the house and followed the footpaths through the woods. After going a quarter of a mile we found what we mistook for a stream of water; we ascended its high banks, which were covered on each side with a variety of shrubs and vines, among which the grape and the magnolias are most profusely scattered. The bank was flat on top and formed a fine terrace shaded by trees.

"We soon discovered that this was a canal, about 25 feet deep and 40 broad, but which has been dug so long since that the banks have lost their regular form and are overgrown with grass, shrubs, trees and vines. Our walk along here extended about half a mile, frequently so entangled by the thickness of the shrubbery and vines that we could scarcely make our way. The magnolias are higher and more luxuriant than any I have ever seen.

"We found a road, or the Pennsylvania Avenue, which led through the wood up to the Capitol. This we pursued and reached home between six and seven."

Being incorrigible romantics themselves, Margaret and Samuel loved living in Nature's wonderland. This opinion, however, was not universally shared by the government officials who were jammed into the makeshift quarters in the vicinity of the President's house and longing for their Paradise Lost, the comforts of civilized life in Philadelphia.

There were 126 such waifs, making up the entire staff of the Federal government in the new capital—75 in the Treasury, 17 in the War Department, 16 in the Navy Department, 10 in the Post Office Department, and only 8 in the State Department.

Oliver Wolcott, the Secretary of the Treasury, turned up his Connecticut Yankee's nose at the so-called city in the woods. "You may look in almost any direction over an extent of ground nearly as large as the city of New York without seeing a fence or any object except brick kilns and temporary huts for laborers," he wrote his wife. "Most of the inhabitants are low people, whose appearance indicates vice and intemperance, or Negroes. The people are poor, and as far as I can judge, they live like fishes, by eating each other."

Turning his cold gaze to the President's Mansion, next door to his own office, the Secretary said: "I cannot but consider our Presidents as very unfortunate men if they must live in this dwelling. It must be cold and damp in winter, and cannot be kept in tolerable order without a regiment of servants. It was built to be looked at by visitors and strangers, and will render its occupant an object of ridicule with some and pity with others."

Wolcott also pitied the "legislators of the Capitoline Mount" who would be "surrounded with mud to an immeasurable distance" whenever Congress met. He could not perceive how the members of Congress could possibly find lodgings, unless they would crowd ten or twenty to a house and "live like scholars in a college or monks in a monastery."

Most maddening of all, to the thrifty Yankee in charge of guarding the Treasury, was the "folly and infatuation of the people who have directed the settlements." He said "immense sums have been squandered in buildings which are but partly finished, in situations which are not, and never will be, the scenes of business; while the parts near the public buildings are almost wholly unimproved."

Yet, to his amazement, Wolcott found the people apparently shared "a confident expectation that the place will soon exceed any city in the world." One official "spoke of a population of 160,000 people, as a matter of course, in a few years."

"No stranger can be here a day and converse with the proprietors," Wolcott commented acidly, "without conceiving himself in the company of crazy people."

There was some basis for thinking the town was full of "crazy people." The Federal City had been most haphazardly developed in the past decade by a curious conglomeration of speculators, adventurers, idealists, artists, and swindlers. No less a financier than Robert Morris now dwelt in the debtors' prison at Philadelphia after losing his fine ruffled shirt in a Washington land speculation. The new capital, like every other frontier settlement before or since, had been a magnet drawing in young men who sought their fortune and older men who, having failed at their previous ventures, trekked to the new El Dorado in hope of a second chance.

Margaret Bayard Smith could see that "in this place people of the lower order have been induced to settle from being unfortunate in other places." These unfortunate people came from every part of the United States, and from many foreign lands: architects and engineers from France and England and the West Indies; Irish ditch diggers, stonecutters and brick masons; German artisans, machinists and engravers; Italian artists and sculptors. As in every American city, here, too, were Frenchmen who had fled from the Terror of their own country or in Santo Domingo.

Possibly the most versatile man in Washington was Dr. William Thornton, who designed the Capitol in 1792 when he was only 31 years old. Born at Tortola in the Virgin Islands, he had studied medicine in Edinburgh and Paris and had made himself an artist and architect by self-study. "He could have attained perfection in any art or science had he given up his mind solely to one pursuit," said his admiring wife. "But such a mind must sometimes be led away by the meteors of genius to a versatility of pursuits." Another woman described him as "full of information, which he details slowly from a natural impediment in his speech."

As one of his many pursuits, the doctor devised a method of teaching the "surd"—the deaf and dumb—to speak. He also promoted plans for freeing his own slaves in the Virgin Islands and leading them, with free Negroes from America, into a colony at Sierra Leone in Africa. But this scheme proved as visionary as many another abolitionist plan of the times.

Dr. Thornton knew nothing about practical architecture when he entered the contest for the best design for the Capitol. He learned enough from books, however, to win first prize of five hundred dollars. He then let more experienced engineers perform the construction work while he served as one of the three commissioners for the new District of Columbia.

The Georgetown *Weekly Ledger* of March 12, 1791, recorded the arrival of "Major LONGFONT, a French gentleman employed by the President of the United States, to survey the land contiguous to Georgetown where the Federal City is to be built." This was, of course, Pierre Charles L'Enfant, whose controversy with the commissioners over his plans for the magnificent capital led finally to an explosion and his dismissal.

Among the other men from abroad who had a hand in building the Federal City were the Irishman James Hoban, who designed the White House; Captain William Mayne Duncanson, a professional soldier from India, who raised a mansion overlooking the Anacostia; and James Barry, an Irishman, who built a wharf at the Anacostia waterfront and bought a large estate on the other side of the river.

Most amazing of all the early investors in Washington was Thomas Law. Son of the Bishop of Carlisle, brother of a Lord Chief Justice of England, and himself a former district governor in India, Law came to America with a quarter of a million dollars to invest in grand enterprises.

He had acquired his fortune in Bengal, where as a most enlightened administrator, he had exercised the judicial and executive functions of chief magistrate over a district containing "more than two million souls." William Duane, the Philadelphia *Aurora* editor, who had left India by request of the authorities because of his own radicalism, was an eye-witness to Law's reforms. Law persuaded the rulers of Hindustan to give up their old system whereby the tenure of land reverted to the emperor upon the death of the landholder, leaving the wives and children of the landholder destitute. Law proposed the Mocurrery system, which made land personal property, and he finally attained his goal after years of labor. Because of his leadership, he became known in India as "the Father of the People." He was, in fact, the father of three sons, George, John and Edmund, who were called the "Asiatic" Laws because they had the dark features of their mother, a native of India.

Law, a widower, and his three sons arrived in New York in 1794, eager to invest in land in the new Federal City. In all, he purchased more than 1,600,000 square feet of real estate between the waterfront and the Capitol. He believed it would surely increase several times in value.

Law also wooed and won as his second wife, the dark-eyed Elizabeth Parke Custis, granddaughter of Martha Washington. Martha opposed the marriage of "Betcy"—as George Washington fondly called her—who was only nineteen, to the wealthy Englishman of thirty-nine. They were married anyway, and lived luxuriously in an elegant brick mansion on the Potomac bluffs at Sixth and N streets, Southwest.

Here the British traveler, Thomas Twining, found them honeymooning in April, 1796, in their house "only a few yards from the steep bank of the Potomac, on a point of land between the Potomac and the Eastern Branch, thus offering a double waterfront." As they stood one evening before his door, Law told of his grandiose plans for enticing other Englishmen from India to invest in the capital city. "Here I will make a terrace, and we will sit and smoke our hookahs," he said, but Twining privately dismissed the scheme as "a delusion."

Twining could not understand how this man who, "as chief of a large district in Bengal had been accustomed to important official functions and the splendor of a prince," could be content with "clearing ground and building small houses amongst the woods of the Potomac." Law was one of the proprietors who painted word pictures of the glorious Federal City of the future, in talks with Oliver Wolcott, so it is no wonder the Treasury Secretary considered himself surrounded by "crazy people."

Short, lean, and energetic, Law had a mind as keen as Dr. Thornton's, and the same unfortunate stammer. He simply could not talk fast enough for his tongue to keep up with his thoughts. He read and spoke Persian as well as the native dialects of India; he wrote poetry and plays of doubtful merit, and recited his works to captive audiences in a grand and orotund manner. It was Law who built the Ten Buildings on New Jersey Avenue, and therefore he became the landlord of Margaret and Samuel Smith. Never such a kind-hearted landlord could they have imagined in their wildest dreams.

The first time he ever spoke to Margaret, she was sitting at the window of her room in Stelle's Tavern, early in October. "Good morning, Mrs. Smith," he called out, "are there any books or anything else which I can send you for your amusement?"

"Well, Mrs. Smith," he hopped to another topic, "your house will be soon done. I have been pushing Moffet on, and this morning paid him twelve hundred dollars so he need not wait for money."

After a few more abrupt speeches, he bade the bride a good morning and went away, leaving her dumfounded. "He is a most singular man," she mused, "one of the strangest I ever met with, all good nature and benevolence; his ruling passion is to serve everyone, which keeps him perpetually busy."

Law often called upon the Smiths and enjoyed long conversations with the young editor, finding, as Margaret remarked, that he was "of much the same political opinions as Mr. S." Without being asked, he subscribed to Samuel's new paper, which was due to appear shortly, and offered to round up many more readers for him.

The beautiful, generous, dark-eyed Mrs. Law won the hearts of both Margaret and Samuel, who agreed that she was a "lovely woman." "Her soft voice, her benevolent countenance, her affectionate manners must make everyone her friend at first sight," Peggy wrote to her sisters. Margaret also fell in love with Mrs. Law's little daughter, Eliza, and determined to pet her as she had petted her own little niece, Mary Ann Kirkpatrick.

Here is Peggy's account of a visit with the Laws at their mansion:

"She saw us from the windows and came to the door to meet us, took each by the hands and led us into the parlor.

" 'Lay down your hat, Mr. Smith,' she said, 'we have a fine roast turkey for dinner, and you must stay and eat of it.'

"She would take no denial, tho', to be sure, we needed no persuasion.

" 'Come,' said she, 'you are young house-keepers, come and look at my kitchen.' She has a contrivance, more convenient than any I ever heard of. The chimney is six feet in width; in this is placed a thing called the 'Ranger.' In the center is a grate, about two feet wide, on one side a place to boil in . . . on the other side a place . . . for an oven . . . both heated by the fire in the grate, which at the same time can roast anything placed before it, and as many pots as you please can hang over it. . . .

"We left Mr. S. in the parlor and she took me upstairs, where she was putting up curtains; I assisted her, went from room to room, chatted like old acquaintances. Then, while she dressed for dinner, I played with little Eliza and her doll. The sweet creature calls me 'Aunt' and I am to call her my 'Mary Ann.'

"When we went down to dinner, we found four or five gentlemen who had accidentally come in. Mr. Peter and Mr. Lewis, her two brothers-in-law, were of the party. Vivacity and good humor prevailed and our party was fifty times more agreeable than if we had all met by previous invitation. When we parted, I had two sweet kisses from Mrs. Law, with an invitation frequently to repeat my visits. . . . I have never met with anyone so destitute of all form or ceremony as this sweet woman."

Captain Tingey, the commandant of the Navy Yard, and his wife also impressed Peggy with their friendliness and complete absence of formality. Mrs. Tingey, Margaret reported to her family, "is an elderly woman, who gave us a good deal of useful information about family matters. She declared her dislike of form, begged we would observe none, asked me to visit her at any hour, to bring my work and occasionally spend the day, and consider her as a mother and not as a stranger. If I would ride, she would often call for me, as they always had a spare seat in the carriage."

With Mrs. Tingey and her two daughters, Margaret began riding regularly to Georgetown and calling on the Bealls, who were a most unusual couple among the worldly Potomac aristocracy: they were not only rich, but religious. Better still, they were Presbyterians. As Margaret remarked with surprise, "Mr. Beall is a very wealthy and respectable man and what is uncommon here, they are professors of religion." Their clergyman, Mr. Balch, called on the bride, a courtesy certainly due the daughter of the Presbyterian elder and Princeton trustee, Colonel John B. Bayard.

One afternoon, Mrs. Beall came and drank tea with Margaret, bringing a large basket of sweet potatoes and some fine cabbages. On another day, Peggy rode over to Georgetown with the Tingeys, and Mrs. Beall served "fine hot bread, cold ham, butter and cakes." "She gave me directions to make bread and yeast; when I came away, she gave me a bottle of yeast, one of milk, a bundle of hops, and my pockets full of cakes and apples—whispering, as she kissed me, 'When I come to see you, I will bring you a jar of pickles and sweetmeats,' " the bride reported to her family.

Thus did the Smiths make friends at once with some of the most prosperous, most "respectable," and yet most generous persons in the Federal City. Peggy seemed to have the appeal which made older women feel maternal urges and wish to adopt her as their own daughter. Amid this scene of happy rambles among the trees and impromptu dinners with the Laws, the Tingeys and the Bealls, only one small cloud appeared to darken the sky: The ship carrying the Smiths' household goods, presumably including the two bedsteads, as well as the presses, types, paper and all other equipment for Samuel's new paper, failed to arrive on time.

Days went by, days of the violent wind and rain storms of October, and Samuel began to fear the ship had been lost in a gale. Anxiously, he wrote to Brother John in Philadelphia: "My operations are unfortunately delayed by the non-arrival of the vessel in which my materials were sent. The extreme violence of the winds for several days gives me some uneasiness. . . . Not a word is yet heard respecting her. Her name is the Harmony, Capt. Douglas. Should you hear anything respecting her, will you please immediately to write to me?"

Thomas Law attempted to reassure the young couple, and begged them not to worry about the long-delayed ship. "Do not be uneasy about the vessel," he said. "If you lose a little, why, you are young people and everyone will be the more willing to assist you."

On October 18, Samuel received the welcome news that the *Harmony* had ridden out the storm with little damage and had reached Alexandria; within a few more days Captain Douglas had brought her to the wharf in Washington. The Smiths found all their articles had arrived "in perfect safety, not a single thing either lost or injured."

Editor Smith began at once to make up for lost time and rushed preparations for the first edition of his paper. *The National Intelligencer, and Washington Advertiser,* issued Volume One, Number One, on Friday, October 31, 1800.

The masthead of the four-column, four-page paper was date-lined, "Washington City, printed by Samuel Harrison Smith, New Jersey Avenue, near the Capitol." The price of the three-times-a-week paper was "five dolls. per ann.—paid in advance."

Samuel began with an apology for his delay: "The appearance of the National Intelligencer has been protracted to this day by the unavoidable, unanticipated embarrassment attending the removal of a Printing Office. The vessel, which contained the greater part of the materials, sailed from Philadelphia on the 20th of September; but did not arrive in this City till the 25th inst. owing to her having been driven on shore by the violence of the late storm."

The editor then gave his readers fair warning of his policy: "While the Editor classes with our dearest rights the Liberty of the Press, he is decidedly inimical to its licentiousness. As, on the one hand, the conduct of public men and the tendency of public measures will be freely examined, so, on the other, private character will remain inviolable, nor shall indelicate ideas or expressions be admitted, however disguised by satire or enlivened by wit. (If that shoe fit the *Aurora* or *Porcupine's Gazette,* so be it!)

210

"The editor need not caution the public against ascribing to him a belief in all the opinions which may be supported, or a disbelief of those which may be opposed. For, as he meant not to surrender his own sentiments, so he does not expect that those who write for The National Intelligencer will surrender theirs."

To avoid being tagged as either "pro-French" or "pro-British," Samuel declared that his paper would be "PURELY AMERICAN." "It will be his effort to promote the true interests of his own country," he said, "uninfluenced either by foreign attachments or enmities." Editor Smith, who had endured enough trouble in trying to run his *Universal Gazette* on a credit basis, warned his readers that the new paper would operate strictly on the basis of cash in advance. As soon as the subscriptions expire, and are not renewed with cash, "in every such case the transmission of the paper will cease." Furthermore, all letters to the editor must be "post paid."

The Universal Gazette, he announced, would be continued as a weekly, the only difference being that it would come from Washington rather than Philadelphia, "whereby its value would be appreciated rather than impaired." In the three-times-a-week *National Intelligencer,* the editor would print not only the facts but many editorials—needless to add, in support of Jefferson and the Republicans. "The tendency of public measures and the conduct of public men will be examined," he pledged, "with candour and truth."

Samuel promised the public, in brief, a newspaper "which shall communicate the language of truth with accuracy, with dignity, and with spirit." "It is the first paper printed in Washington," he proudly proclaimed, and its design is "to diffuse correct information throughout the whole extent of the union."

When *The National Intelligencer* had been safely launched, Samuel and Margaret Bayard Smith moved into their half-finished honeymoon home next door to the printing office on Capitol Hill. On November 4, Margaret wrote in her diary: "Seated in my own room, beside my own fire, I this evening have realized a picture so often drawn by fancy. After a busy day, I at last got everything neatly arranged in my chamber. I sat by my tea table, on my husband's entrance, he tenderly embraced me and we welcomed each other *home.*"

Speaking of the printers who would live in the house next door, she wrote: "I am still very unsettled, having only one room finished. Three men, three boys, and two young women constitute my family. These, I am not only to render comfortable, but the elder I am to teach by example and the younger by precept. To inform their minds, to correct the vices and cultivate the virtues of their hearts is not to be my only care, but I likewise must attend to give them religious instruction which is the only firm basis for true and pure morality."

A week later, Peggy informed her sisters in New Brunswick: "As yet, we occupy only one room, besides the kitchen; the plaster is quite dry and we are both well, altho' we have lodged here a week. My curtains are up, and a neat carpet is on the floor, which gives the room a snug appearance."

At first Peggy was pleased with the Irishwoman and the maid she engaged as her servants. "My little girl is all I wish and much better than I expected," she wrote. "She is quiet and industrious, willing and intelligent. I need never show or tell her a thing twice. The mildness of her manners and delicacy of her appearance inspire affection and I am afraid I shall spoil her.

"The only praise I can give my Irish woman is that she is good-natured and obedient. Several times when I have been out of an afternoon, on my return home I have found a good fire, the tea-table set and candles lighted. This kind of attention is pleasing. Mr. S. enjoys his tea so much that it gives a double relish to mine. Poor Biddy, notwithstanding her stupidity, makes a nice kind of biscuit. She is always delighted when I ask her to make them and if I give any of them to the young men she says, 'Aw, now, Missess, why you give away w'at I make for yoursel'?'

"Betsy, too, desirous of trying her hand, made me this evening some very good short cakes."

Soon after moving into her home, Margaret entertained several of her new-found friends. "We passed an agreeable evening," she reported to her family, "and they were *treated* with my wedding cake."

As her house expanded gradually from one to several rooms, Peggy went shopping for furniture. She gives this charming account of one such venture:

"I stopped at a cabinet maker's. He was an elderly man, his countenance beaming with goodness and his voice and manners soft and mild.

" 'I like this man, and he shall like me,' thought I.

"I observed he was very busy, inquired when he came to the city, where he came from, and who composed his family. The good man seemed pleased with these questions, answered them freely; told me with tears in his eyes that his wife was dead. He was from Trenton.

" 'Why, then,' said I, 'we must be friends. I, too, am from Jersey, you perhaps knew my father—Colonel John B. Bayard.'

"He said he did. 'Well,' said I, 'we are just settled here and although I wish but few articles at present I shall need more in a little while. If your work pleases me, I will always employ you.'

"He promised to do all I wanted at the very lowest price and, added he very kindly, 'I will always do my very best for you and shall at present pick out some of my most excellent materials. You shall have some good Jersey walnut, which, I promise you, I will make nearly as handsome as mahogany.'

"I told him where I lodged. 'Well,' said he, 'I'll call and see you and we will be better acquainted.' "

As she had done many times in her girlhood when her elders had reproached her for dreaming her life away in idleness and books, Margaret resolved again to set down a strict schedule for every day and stick to it.

"I will rise very early," she promised herself. "Before breakfast I will always dress Mr. Smith's hair and see after his men's breakfast. After breakfast I will spend about an hour in giving out things for dinner and looking after my family; then I will read and write until one o'clock, then attend to dinner. I will dine precisely at three and read again until dark; then brighten my fire, meet my husband

213

and pass the twilight hour with him 'in converse sweet.' After tea I will take my work and he will read to me until bedtime."

"But in vain were my good resolutions!" she lamented a short time later. "We do not rise until eight (indeed, it is not my fault alone), then eat breakfast immediately. The moment afterwards, Mr. S. goes into his office, and after putting aside the things, I am in the kitchen and about the house until near eleven; when the leisure hour for reading arrives I feel no inclination and if I do, my thoughts are perpetually wandering; something every hour of the day is to be done, which interferes with the use of the pen.

"Twilight comes, my dear husband enters with only a few minutes at command; those few minutes are indeed precious and the delightful sensations to which they give birth make them truly valuable.

"Betsy always brings in the tea kettle at six o'clock. The moment tea is over, the table is covered with pen, ink and papers and silence reigns for three or four hours. It seems to me impossible that Mr. S. can continue such unremitting employment; his health, I fear, will suffer. His business every day increases. . . . Every day do I congratulate myself on the choice I have made and the only thing I wish for is more of his society."

Peggy found that a housewife managing a "family" of printers in the frontier town of Washington had to perform many tasks she had never dreamed of when she had lived in the civilized cities of the East. "This week I salted down five hundred pounds of pork, as fine as any I ever saw," she reported to her family, "made some sausages, some head cheese and two pots of fine lard, each containing about three gallons. The water in which the heads and feet were boiled, brew me a fine jelly and I have reserved it for my soups and find them much enriched by it. This lard I shall save for summer, as the fat I gather in various ways is sufficient for all culinary purposes."

Provisions in Washington were scarce and quite expensive: "Pork is six cents per pound, the very finest beef one shilling six pence." Fortunately, Samuel's brother John in Philadelphia sent the young couple a barrel of apples, and a firkin of butter, "impossible to

214

procure" in the new capital, and the Smiths were profusely grateful. "My dear brother," Samuel wrote, "the articles you sent are a great treat. I had a few friends to dine with me today, we considered the butter as a very great luxury. Before a word had been said, one of our guests immediately pronounced it to be Philadelphia butter!"

Margaret even wrote home for "a bundle of old things"—worn-out clothing to be used as household rags. "I have to buy new linen for dish cloths, iron holders," etc. She did not mind "how coarse or old" the cloth might be, "for really I have not an old rag about the house. . . . Pray grant the petition of your poor and humble beggar."

Not long after she had praised her two servants, the bride decided she had to dismiss them. Her Irish biddy, "though very honest, very good-natured," was "so ignorant, so slow and so stupid" that she could not do all the work required for running two houses and serving two tables, the Smiths' and the printers'. "Instead of two white women I have now an old black man and his wife, to whom I pay the same wages as I did the women," Peggy later reported. "Betsy is still with me and I continue well pleased with her; she is active and intelligent, but she is proud and irritable."

Betsy, too, eventually left, and, within a year's time, her mistress had dismissed a total of fourteen servants. Some had to go because they drank; for instance, Peggy wrote, "I am in search of a drunken woman whom I sent away once, but am induced to take again as she is one of the best I have had. It is to all the dram houses in the city that I have directed the man in search of her. Is not this dreadful? It is almost impossible to meet with a poor person here, man or woman, who does not drink." Editor Smith was "very much plagued with his workmen on this account."

Even more shocking than the liquor problem was the "vice" which resulted in the downfall of Margaret's maid, promiscuous Polly: "As for poor Polly," her mistress wrote, "from the first week I have had her, she has been a perpetual source of vexation. I have succeeded in subduing the paroxysms of a violent temper, but she is the most incorrigibly idle and unfaithful servant I ever yet tried. She has never cleaned a knife, or brushed a room, without my watching and seeing it was done.

"The vice, which I feared on her arrival, to belong to her, now obliges me immediately to part with her. Her symptoms created suspicions and, on examination, she with the most unblushing effrontery and most hardened and unfeeling manner, confessed a criminal intercourse to have existed between her and one of the young men in the office.

"You may easily believe how greatly I was shocked. I had taken every precaution on this score (which my experience with my two other girls had taught me was necessary) that I could possibly think of, and suffered scarcely a week to pass without giving her the most affectionate advice and enforcing that advice with an exhibition of all the misery such a sin would bring on her.

"However, all has been in vain and my only consolation is that on my part no attention, no effort has been spared. If I had the least hopes of her reformation I would put up with almost any inconvenience rather than part with her, but the hardness and insensibility she discovers leaves me none.

"While I spoke to her in the most solemn and affectionate manner, and while my own ideas made the tears run down my cheeks, she listened unmoved without a single tear or the least embarrassment and her only answer to all I said was:

" 'Shaw, Mrs. Smith, I don't believe that's the reason I'm sick.'

"I fear nothing can save her from the fate of her mother.... I mean in her stead to get a black girl as ... I cannot again venture on a maid-servant while the office is so near the house."

Such examples of loose living among the working classes made Peggy realize eventually that "the row of houses we live in is the most mean and vulgar of any in the city." It was a scene of poverty, illness, and heartbreak for the mothers and children of the laboring families. Margaret's washerwoman lived in a "wretched hovel" with "her husband and four or five sickly children" and not enough food to save them from disease.

Before her first winter in Washington ended, Margaret sent this touching report to Samuel's sister Mary, in Philadelphia: "I have

216

been sitting beside the corpse of one of the most beautiful, most amiable and sensible children I have ever known. It is the third, and all equally beautiful and lovely, that the parents have this winter lost. Yet the mother and father spoke of the death of this lovely little girl with the most perfect composure.

"This family live within a door or two of us, and when I first came I was attracted by the loveliness and delicacy of the children. On inquiry, I found the parents were wretchedly poor and had known better days. The little girl who is now dead was the size of Mary Ann [her niece], with the same kind of hair, but in every other respect more lovely. She was a fascinating little creature, and I often had her with me. Feeling an affection springing in my heart, I determined every day to send for her and to teach her everything that was necessary. But she was attacked with whooping cough and, after suffering two months, has now gone to rest."

Amid such sad scenes, which reminded her of the uncertainty of life, it was a comfort for Margaret to receive letters of love and faith from her father. Colonel Bayard, the staunch old Presbyterian, wrote to his "dear Peggy" on November 11, 1800, in his huge, round script:

"It gives me great pleasure in hearing, by your letters to your sisters, that you enjoy health and seem so well satisfied with your situation; that you have had attention paid you by several respectable inhabitants and that Mr. Smith is like to succeed in his business.

"May a gracious God continue to bless you both and give you gratefull hearts in the receipt of His manifold favors. May the religion you profess and a firm and unshaken trust and reliance on the Blessed Jesus, our adorable Lord and Saviour, ever be your support and refuge and may the blessed Spirit of God lead you in the ways of truth and righteousness. This will enable you to bear up and act right under all the trials of this life; and fit you for a far better state beyond the grave.

"Your education and your short experience has no doubt frequently led you to contemplate this life as a state of probation and that we are but in the infancy of our existence. There is a glorious prize sett before us, and we are directed by the unerring Word of divine inspiration, by our Blessed Lord, to strive to enter in at the the strait gate, to fight the good fight of Faith, to lay aside every weight and the sin that most easily besets us and to run the race that is sett before us, looking to Jesus, as the *Author* and *Finisher* of our Faith. . . .

"I am happy to hear that you have a church and regular worship on the Sabbath. I trust you will not fail to frequent it. . . .

"Tell Mr. Smith to put me down as a subscriber to his paper, altho' you know I am not a friend to his Politicks."

T*he National Intelligencer* came out in time to chronicle the presidential steeplechase, now in its home stretch, and to cheer lustily for Jefferson. Editor Smith confidently predicted that Jefferson would "undoubtedly be President, without a single vote from South Carolina, and with no more than six votes from North Carolina," two of the last states to choose their electors. The Republicans were pressing an outwardly united campaign (though Burr might be suspected of working secretly to advance his own interests) while the Federalists were split wide open.

As Hamilton and his allies were scheming to bring General Pinckney in first on their ticket, the naturally resentful President Adams vowed he would "rip up" their "British faction." Federalists in each faction declared they would rather see Jefferson President than have those other Federalists triumphant. "We should do as well with Jefferson for President and Mr. Pinckney Vice President as with anything we can now expect," George Cabot confided to Oliver Wolcott. "Such an issue of the election, if fairly produced, is the only one that will keep the Federal Party together."

"If Mr. Adams should be reelected, I fear our constitution would be more injured by his unruly passions, antipathies and jealousy, than by the whimsies of Jefferson," Charles Carroll of Carrollton told McHenry. The ousted Secretary of War agreed. "Almost every well-informed man" in Maryland, McHenry said, considered Adams "utterly unfit" and could make "little or no exertions" for such a candidate.

Because of Adams' attacks on the Hamilton faction, Speaker Sedgwick commented, the Federalist party in Massachusetts was "disorganized, and everywhere thro' the nation its energies are paralyzed." Adams "has palsied the sinews of the party," Representative James A. Bayard, of Delaware, charged. "Mr. A. has contrived to forfeit the affection of most Federal men whom I meet with. If events should justify it, there will be no difficulty in keeping him out of the tickets of this State."

Hamilton sent Bayard a pessimistic summary of the Federalists' prospects in the North. New England apparently would again provide an almost solid bloc of electoral votes for the party, but Adams would try to keep several of the electors' second votes away from General Pinckney, and some might even go to Colonel Burr.

"In New York, all the votes will certainly be for Jefferson and Burr," Hamilton figured. "New Jersey does not stand as well as she used to do. If the electors are Federal, Pinckney will certainly be voted for; and Adams will be or not, as leading friends shall advise;" that is, Adams would not be "cut" if his friends in New England would not knife Pinckney.

Bayard replied by giving Hamilton a summary of the situation in the South. Delaware, his own state, was "safe" but "may hesitate" before giving an electoral vote to Adams. Maryland, voting by districts, probably would divide its ten electoral votes about equally between the two parties, but if the Federalists controlled the new legislature, they might grab all ten.

Virginia, Jefferson's home state, with the biggest bloc of all, 21 electoral votes, was "sold and past salvation." As for North Carolina, its Federalist congressmen predicted seven for Jefferson, five for Adams and Pinckney. "Georgia, Tennessee, and Kentucky may be thrown into the scale for Mr. J."

South Carolina might repeat its 1796 division and cast its eight electoral votes for Jefferson and Pinckney. If so, Pinckney should run ahead of Adams and possibly even defeat Jefferson, "unless the Eastern states play a fool game" again and drop votes from Pinckney. "If they do, they forfeit forever the confidence of their friends to the southward," Bayard warned. "They will beget a system of miserable intrigue between the members of the same party, whose efforts can never be united but thro' mutual confidence, and whose united efforts are absolutely necessary to maintain their ground against their enemies."

Bayard pinned his hopes on these statistics: Jefferson, it was true, would gain the twelve electoral votes he had lost in New York four years ago; but he could not repeat his fourteen-to-one sweep in Pennsylvania. There, the Federalist State Senate refused to let the electors be chosen on joint ballot of the legislature. Bayard expected a compromise to give Jefferson eight and the Federalists seven. Jefferson would thus lose six of the votes he had had in Pennsylvania in 1796, and a deadlock in the legislature might leave the Keystone State with no electoral vote at all.

So the Federalists, in Bayard's opinion, still had a fighting chance —if they fought the Republicans instead of fighting each other. But, as McHenry lamented, the Federalists' conduct in most states was "tremulous, timid, feeble, deceptive and cowardly." "They write private letters," he told Wolcott. "To whom? To each other, but they do nothing to give a proper direction to the public mind. . . . They meditate in private. . . . If the party recover its pristine energy shall I ascribe it to such cunning, paltry, indecisive, back door conduct?" No, he would give the credit to "a kind and watchful Providence."

As the campaign progressed, the Federalists fought harder. They revived all the charges they had hurled at Jefferson four years before —"atheist," "Jacobin," "tool of France," "visionary philosopher"— while the Republicans tossed back their time-worn claim that Adams was a "monarchist," and General Pinckney a "Deist."

Many clergymen, sincerely believing that the Vice-President of the United States was an infidel, warned against Jefferson in sermons and pamphlets that bordered on hysteria. The Reverend John M. Mason, in *The Voice of Warning, to Christians, on the Ensuing Election of a President of the United States,* said Christians should read Jefferson's "Notes on Virginia," his doubts about Adam and Eve and the flood, and "the ten thousand impieties and mischiefs" of

221

the paragraph in which he said, "It does me no injury for my neighbors to say there are twenty Gods or no God."

The Reverend Dr. Linn, in *Serious Considerations on the Election of a President,* relayed an anecdote from a Virginia minister: When Jefferson and Mazzei were riding one day, the Italian expressed surprise at the run-down condition of the churches, and Jefferson replied: "It is good enough for him that was born in a manger." That story rocked the Republicans in Maryland, and probably in other states. Gabriel Duvall, writing from Annapolis to James Madison, said "the charge of irreligion had almost subsided" when "the New York pamphlet" brought out the Mazzei tale. "The probability is that no such conversation ever passed," Duvall wrote. "This we insist on."

Realizing that the "religious issue" could ruin them, the Republicans rushed into print to combat it. John Beckley, erstwhile Clerk of the House, cried in a pamphlet: "Read, ye fanatics, bigots, and religious hypocrites, of whatsoever clime or country ye be—and you, base calumniators, whose efforts to traduce are the involuntary tribute of envy to a character more pure and perfect than your own, read, learn, and practice the *Religion of Jefferson,* as displayed in the sublime truths and inspired language of *his* ever memorable 'Act for establishing religious freedom!' "

Jefferson stubbornly refused to make any public statement answering the attacks on his alleged "irreligion." Instead, he outlined his views privately to Dr. Benjamin Rush, the Philadelphia physician and fellow-member of the American Philosophical Society, "I have a view of the subject which ought to displease neither the rational Christian or Deist; & would reconcile many to a character they have too hastily rejected," though it might never satisfy the ministers "who are all in arms against me." Jefferson thought the Sedition Law, curbing the constitutional guarantee of freedom of the press, had "given to the clergy a very favorite hope of an establishment of a particular form of Christianity thro' the U.S., and as every sect believes its own form the true one, every one perhaps hoped for its own; but especially the Episcopalians & Congregationalists.

"They believe that any portion of power confided to me will be exerted in opposition to their schemes," he declared, and then added this famous line: "And they believe truly, *for I have sworn upon the altar of God eternal hostility against every form of tyranny over the mind of man.*"

Charges of Jefferson's "irreligion, wild philosophy and gimcrackery in politics" ran rampant in New England, and Adams spoke up in defense of his opponent—giving rise to further rumors of an alliance between them. Fisher Ames reported "the great man," Adams, had "affected indignation at the charge of irreligion, asking what has that to do with the public and adding that [Jefferson] is a good patriot, citizen and father. The good lady his wife has been often talkative in a similar strain, and she is as complete a politician as any lady in the old French Court."

Ames heard "Jacobins" plainly saying they preferred Adams to Pinckney, and he suspected Jefferson would "not be sorry" to serve as Vice-President one more term with Adams as President, if he could be "actually the ruler" behind the throne. General Pinckney listened suspiciously, too, to tales of Adams' praise of Jefferson. "He certainly used to speak very slightingly of J.'s political talents and now speaks handsomely of him, as the Man in the United States fittest for President," the South Carolinian remarked, with a note of sarcasm, "excepting always, I presume, *himself.*"

Enraged by Adams' attacks on the "British faction," Hamilton wrote twice to him, demanding an explanation, but received not even the courtesy of an answer. To protect his own "character," then, and to expose the President's lamentable lack of it, Hamilton wrote a pamphlet telling the Federalist party leaders exactly what kind of President they had—and exactly how they ought to get rid of him. To prove his claim that the old man was unfit for office, he collected every tidbit he could get from Pickering, McHenry and Wolcott about Adams' eccentric actions in the private council chambers of the government.

The *Letter from Alexander Hamilton Concerning the Public Conduct and Character of John Adams* came off the press of the *New York Gazette* on October 22, 1800. Its author had intended to distribute it only among Federalist party leaders who, in turn, could

223

privately advise the Federalist electors to choose General Pinckney as President instead of Adams. By hook or by crook (possibly through a Republican spy in the *Gazette* office or a Republican printer's devil) a copy of the pamphlet fell into the hands of Aaron Burr. That master of intrigue called three of his myrmidons—Matthew L. Davis, John and Robert Swartwout—to his house. They copied the juiciest passages and had them published in the Philadelphia *Aurora* and the New London *Bee*. Soon the whole country was reading the amazing Federalist attack upon the Federalist President.

Hamilton flayed the poor President with every whip he could lay his hands on. Ever since the days of the American Revolution, twenty years before, he wrote, he had noticed "great and intrinsic defects" in the character of Adams, and doubts about "the solidity of his understanding." Hamilton admitted having tried to steer Thomas Pinckney into the presidency in 1796 because of the "disgusting egotism, the distempered jealousy, and the ungovernable indiscretion of Mr. Adams's temper, joined to some doubts of the correctness of his maxims of administration." Adams had made a grave mistake in sending the second mission to France, and spurning the advice of his cabinet counsellors, Wolcott, Pickering and McHenry. He had fallen into the clutches of "miserable intriguers" with whom "his self-love was more at ease," and they had led him to disaster.

The dismissals of Pickering and McHenry had arisen from the President's "paroxysms of rage, which deprived him of self-command and produced very outrageous behavior." Hamilton conceded he had "causes of personal dissatisfaction," which made him resent the injuries he had received from the President's hands. The General believed he should have been promoted to commander-in-chief of the army after George Washington's death, but, of course, the jealous Adams would never dream of giving such a post of power to the "Creole" he called "a bastard."

Hamilton granted that Adams had patriotism and integrity and "talents of a certain kind." Since "the body of Federalists, for want of sufficient knowledge of facts, are not convinced of the expediency" of dropping Adams, the author would "not advise the withholding from him of a single vote." This conclusion to the astonishing profile seemed inconsistent on the surface; if Adams really was as silly as Hamilton pictured him, he did not deserve a vote. Hamilton, however, had to maintain the pledge of the Federalist caucus to give equal votes to Adams and Pinckney. Thus, he hoped to keep the New Englanders from withholding any votes from Pinckney; and he relied upon South Carolina to do the job of voting for Pinckney—without Adams. If that ruse failed, then perhaps the two Federalist candidates would tie in electoral votes, and the Federalist House of Representatives would choose Pinckney.

Philemon Dickinson of Trenton, New Jersey, thus warned McHenry, in Maryland: "You must at all events secure to the Genr. a majority in Cong., it may there be done with *safety,* his success depends on the accomplishment of this measure." Dickinson hoped "Hamilton's publication will produce the desired effect."

Hamilton's pamphlet produced an "effect," but not precisely the one "desired." Federalists were flabbergasted; Republicans rocked with glee. Even Robert Troup, Hamilton's close friend, reported that Federalists generally "lamented" the publication as likely to harm the party and "greatly lessen" its author's influence. "Our enemies," Troup sighed, "are universally in triumph."

"All agree that the execution is masterly," George Cabot wrote Hamilton, "but I am bound to tell you that you are accused by respectable men, of egotism; and some very worthy and sensible men say you have exhibited the same vanity in your book which you charge as a dangerous quality and great weakness in Mr. Adams." Charles Carroll of Carrollton found all his friends condemning the pamphlet as "ill-timed," but he defended Hamilton: "The assertions of the pamphlet, I take it for granted, are true; and if true, surely it must be admitted that Mr. Adams is not fit to be president, and his unfitness should be made known to the Electors & the publick; I conceive it a species of treason to conceal from the Publick his incapacity."

Naturally, the Philadelphia *Aurora* hooted with delight: "Alexander Hamilton and the New York Feds have split upon the Adamantine rock; he says that John Adams must not be President, they say that John Adams must—so says the proverb, where thieves fall out honest men may come by their own."

"John Adams, Alexander Hamilton, and the Pinckneys are now fairly before the public," jeered Editor Duane, "not in the partial drawings of their political rivals, the Republicans. Their claims and pretensions to public confidence are exhibited by themselves." If the Federalists are all as bad as they paint each other, crowed the Portsmouth *Ledger,* "can any one hesitate to say that Mr. Jefferson is the most suitable . . . for President?"

Recalling how many of their editors had been fined and jailed for printing far less devastating attacks upon the President, some Republicans wondered whether Hamilton might not also fall afoul of the Sedition Law. Thomas Cooper, an English-born Republican who had served six months in jail for libeling Adams, proposed a similar reward for Hamilton. Cooper wrote to Hamilton a "saucy" letter asking if he were, indeed, the author of the pamphlet; if he had said, "yes," Cooper would have filed charges under the Sedition Law. But Hamilton did not answer the letter; he handed it to the newspapers.

No one, perhaps, chuckled more heartily over the discomfiture of the Federalists than did little James Madison, who had a roguish sense of humor. "Hamilton's attack upon Mr. Adams," Madison wrote his bosom friend Jefferson, "will be a Thunderbolt to both. I rejoice with you that Republicanism is likely to be so *completely* triumphant."

The triumph, however, had not yet been achieved when *The National Intelligencer* appeared October 31 and claimed certain victory for Jefferson. Editor Smith believed the Republicans, having won a majority in the legislatures of Pennsylvania and Maryland in October, could carry those states for Jefferson and assure his success. But the Federalists dropped their plan for having the Maryland legislature name the electors, and kept the district system which would give each party five electoral votes. In Pennsylvania the deadlock persisted, with the possibility of no vote for President at all.

From Wilmington, Delaware, the Republican leader Caesar Rodney sent a gloomy bulletin to Jefferson, who was masterminding his campaign from Monticello. "With much regret," Rodney reported that his personal friend and political foe, Representative James A. Bayard, had been reelected by a majority of about three hundred votes, and the Federalists controlled the legislature. Bayard's father-in-law, Governor Bassett, was "about convening the legislature," which probably would choose three electors pledged to Pinckney but not necessarily to Adams. The "leading men on the Federal side" say "Pinckney is undoubtedly their man."

*　　*　　*　　*　　*

One day in late October, a young man drove slowly up the winding road to Monticello and introduced himself to Jefferson as Joseph Alston, of South Carolina. Alston, the scion of a wealthy Low Country family, had been visiting in New York. He was going home to help the cause of Jefferson's election as a member of the legislature, which would select the South Carolina electors in December. Alston may—or may not—have mentioned that he was engaged to marry Aaron Burr's beautiful and brilliant daughter, Theodosia.

The young man gave Jefferson a letter of introduction signed, "Your friend . . . A. Burr." It read:

"Dear Sir:

"The family of Alston of South Carolina is probably well known to you. The young gentleman who will hand you this, bids fair to do honor to his name and his country. His warmest wishes, and his influence which is already important, are engaged in promoting your election.

"He has passed through the Eastern states and is now on his return to attend the legislature of S.C. of which he is a member. I refer you to him for anything regarding domestic politics."

Alston brought Jefferson a second letter. This one was in the tiny handwriting of James Madison, who had entertained the same visitor at Montpellier a few days before. Madison wrote:

"This will be handed to you by Mr. Alston of S. Carolina, who

227

proposes to call at Monticello on his return from a Northern tour. . . . He appears to be intelligent, sound in his principles, and polished in his manners. Coming fresh from N.Y. through Penna. & Maryland, he will be able to furnish many details in late occurrences.

"The fact of most importance mentioned by him, and which is confirmed by letters I have from Burr & Gelston, is that the vote of Rho. Island will be assuredly on the right side. The latter gentleman expresses much anxiety & betrays some jealousy with respect to the integrity of the Southern states in keeping the former one in view for the secondary station. I hope the event will skreen all the parties, particularly Virginia, from any imputation on this subject; tho' I am not without fear, that the requisite concert may not sufficiently pervade the several states."

In plainer words, David Gelston, one of Burr's "little band" in New York, had written Madison (doubtless with his master's knowledge) that Burr feared some of the southern states would not give him all the electoral votes for Vice-President, despite the Republican caucus pledge. Burr recalled how Virginia and North Carolina had "lurched" him in 1796.

So Burr had sent his future son-in-law to Madison and Jefferson, carrying personal assurances that the northern Republicans would give solid support to Jefferson and probably even award him one more electoral vote than Burr. So Jefferson need not worry about the danger of a tie or of Burr slipping into the presidency ahead of him; but to assure that neither Pinckney nor Adams would win the vice-presidency, Burr insisted, the southern Republicans must not take a vote away from the gentleman from New York.

Gelston, in a letter which Alston delivered to Madison, expressed "extreme anxiety" over reports that Burr might lose some electoral votes in the South. "We depend on the integrity of Virginia and the Southern states, as we shall be faithfull and honest in New York," Burr's agent wrote. "We have strong assurances that Rhode Island will give us three votes. . . . *We shall, we will* succeed without Jersey, Pennsylvania having no vote. . . . Rely upon it, no exertions will be wanting, no pains will be spared by the Republicans in this quarter

228

to save our Constitution, to save our country, or in other words to secure the election of Jefferson and Burr."

Madison, who would have a great influence in casting Virginia's 21 electoral votes—he was an elector, himself—heeded Burr's warnings. Madison told Governor James Monroe that Gelston was "uneasy lest the Southern states should not be true to their duty," so "it seems important that all proper measures should emanate from Richmond for guarding against a division of the Republican votes, by which one of the Republican candidates may be lost." "It would be superfluous," Madison added, "to suggest to you the mischief resulting from the least ground of reproach, and particularly to Virginia, on this head."

Alston left the Virginia sages and went on to South Carolina, carrying assurances that the Virginians would cast all their twenty-one electoral votes for his future father-in-law, and Madison made a similar pledge in a letter to Gelston. "Your very obliging letter," Gelston replied, "has removed many fears and jealousies with which my mind was much agitated." Jefferson, Madison and Monroe all had reason to assume that Burr merely was worrying lest the defection of some southern electors might again keep him out of the vice-presidency.

In early November, however, another young man called at Madison's door. He introduced himself as George W. Erving, of Boston, and he presented letters from Monroe and Jefferson, whom he had visited en route, both describing him as a strong and trustworthy Republican. Erving wished to speak confidentially about alarming reports that Burr was intriguing to run ahead of Jefferson in northern electoral votes, so that, if the Southerners gave equal support to both Republican candidates, then the next President probably would be, not Jefferson but Burr.

"We are sufficiently on our guard against our opponents," Monroe commented, "but Mr. Jefferson's election ought to be secured against accident which might otherwise give us in the first station, a friend we did not intend to place there"—to wit, Aaron Burr.

"I cannot apprehend any danger of a surprise that wd. throw Mr. J. out of the primary station," Madison wrote Monroe on November

229

10. "I cannot believe that any such is intended, or that a single republican vote will abandon him. The worst, therefore, that could possibly happen would be a tie that wd. appeal to the H. of R. where the candidates would certainly, I think, be arranged properly, even on the recommendation of the secondary one." That is, in case of a tie, the House would elect Jefferson, and Burr would even recommend it—or so Madison imagined *then*.

Still, Monroe had cause to feel uneasy. He had warned the Virginians eight years before against supporting Burr for Vice-President, because the smooth New Yorker seesawed between the two parties and no one could be sure of his principles. The Virginians had avoided a commitment to Burr in both 1792 and 1796, but in 1800 their congressmen were bound by the Republican caucus to support him along with Jefferson, to guarantee party unity in both North and South.

One of the Virginia congressmen, John Nicholas, warned Madison in November, 1800, that their original "objections" to Burr were being revived "in some force" by the rumors of his alleged intrigues to seize the presidency. Nicholas admitted that the reports contained "no evidence of design," and "suspicion founded on character" alone would not justify withholding a few southern electoral votes from Burr.

"It would be unjust in me not to declare my impression in favour of the disposition of the gentleman whose conduct is in question," Nicholas added. "I do not believe that he would wish a vote which cd. be considered as in his power to be diverted. If the Federalists were brought to decide between our candidates, and, as has been suspected, some of them should give him the preference, I suppose he would have no objection. That is not likely to happen as they are at present very sanguine and the event of the election turns on the choice in So. Carolina, which cannot be known till it is too late."

Nicholas apparently referred to reports that, if the Federalists saw no chance of electing either Adams or Pinckney, some of their electors might vote for Burr, thereby making him President—on the theory that Burr would be less objectionable than Jefferson. Burr's crony, Senator Jonathan Dayton, openly boasted that his Federalist state, New Jersey, might swing to Burr if Pennsylvania killed all chances of Adams' reelection. The Pennsylvania legislature, however, finally broke its long deadlock with a compromise giving the Republicans eight votes, the Federalists seven. The Federalists, therefore, believed they had a chance to win if they could carry South Carolina. John Marshall told General Pinckney that the Pennsylvania decision would "exclude Mr. Jefferson, provided he gets no vote in South Carolina. But it is now reduced to an absolute certainty that any success in your state elects him."

Burr feared the South Carolinians would repeat their 1796 maneuver of voting for Jefferson and Pinckney. To his uncle, Judge Pierpont Edwards, in Rhode Island, Burr wrote in November: "If we have R.I., Jefferson will have a majority even without Penna. or S.C. But in S.C. there is every reason to believe that *he* will have the whole Eight." Later: "S.C. will probably give an unanimous vote for Pinckney & Jefferson. Maryland 5 & 5—N.C. 8 & 4—... Pray favor me with one line respecting your hopes from the Electors of Connect. & R.I. If your people leave out P. [Pinckney] from two or three votes, J. will be Prest.—otherwise doubtful."

On November 21, two weeks before the electors would cast their votes, David Gelston complained again to Madison about new reports that "one, two or more votes" would be taken away from Burr in the South to insure Jefferson's election. "I am not willing to believe it possible that such measures can be contemplated," Gelston declared. "... We know that the honor of the gentlemen of Virginia and N. Y. was pledged at the adjournment of Congress. We in this state have our attachment for Colo. Burr. We will not, however, *even think* of taking a vote from Mr. J. We should consider it as sacrilege."

Gelston reported—inaccurately—that "three states, two at least, will give Mr. J. 3 or more votes more than Mr. B. will have," and he added, "I trust that it never will be said that either Virginia or N.Y. could be guilty of such a subterfuge." (At the end of Gelston's letter is a footnote in Madison's tiny handwriting: "A confidence that this would be the case induced Virginia to give an unanimous tho' reluctant vote for B. as well as J.")

*   *   *   *   *

In late November the center of political turmoil moved to Washington, where Congress convened for the first time amid the forests and swamps of the new capital. The second session of the Sixth Congress was supposed to begin November 17, but bad weather and abominable roads delayed the arrival of a quorum until November 22.

Representative John Cotton Smith, a new member from Sharon, Connecticut, recorded the most vivid picture of the lawmakers' perilous journey to Washington. At New York City, he joined four fellow-Federalists, who hired a private carriage so that they could "enjoy each other's company without democratick annoyance." In the public stagecoach they would have had to endure the presence of social inferiors, as the passengers generally included "squalling children and Republicans smoking cigars." It was hard enough for a gentleman to rub elbows with such ruffians in the filthy taverns where they tried to rest a few hours each night. Such fellows would talk, talk, talk, even in bed till at last, said one weary wayfarer, "sleep closed their eyes and happily their mouths at the same time, for could they have talked in their sleep, I verily believe they would have prated on until morning."

Instead of such silly prattle, Congressman Smith and his friends would enjoy "the sound learning" of House Speaker Theodore Sedgwick, of Massachusetts; "the polished literature" of Jonas Platt, of Poughkeepsie, New York; the "piety and good sense" of John Davenport, of Stamford, Connecticut; and the "eccentricities" of the gentleman from Schenectady, Henry Glen.

Glen was so afraid of dying in transit that he always carried his "death clothes" along in his trunk, to be sure of being properly dressed for his funeral—an event which might occur, he imagined, ere he would see Schenectady again. He also brought along a rope to be tied to his bedstead, for escape in case of fire.

Throughout the five-day journey from New York to Washington,

Glen sat outside on the box with the driver, so that he might "better espy and escape danger"; and he loudly called for "lamps! lamps!" as the carriage careened through the pitch-black night.

The driver assured him he could proceed more safely without lamps, which would merely "show him danger after falling into it." But Glen "murmured the whole distance," Smith recorded, "and we were diverted to hear the driver sporting with his fears."

There were perils enough to frighten a less nervous man than Glen. Crossing the Schuylkill River on the west side of Philadelphia, the carriage sloshed over a floating bridge of logs, chained together and planked. The horses, driven at great speed, sank nearly to their knees in water.

The coach was constantly threatening to turn over or break an axle or bog down as it bumped along over a road full of ruts, stones, stumps and roots. When it swayed to one side, the passengers would throw their weight over to the other side; and when it raced down a hill, they could do no more than hang onto the leather curtains and pray.

In the dark night, the mile-wide Susquehanna River looked like the river Styx, and the ferryman might have been "old Charon," himself, but the congressmen reached the other side safely at Havre de Grace and found the same comfortable inn where the newly-wed Smiths had dined several weeks before. At Baltimore, the next day, the lawmakers dined in the "ordinary" at the Columbian Hotel with a circle of about a hundred gentlemen, "all respectable characters," and delighted with "the great luxury of the Chesapeake, the canvas back duck, prepared on chafing-dishes, with jellies." The five Yankee congressmen, who had never seen the dish before, unanimously voted it "exquisite."

Arriving in Washington, the lawmakers, like the Smiths, could hardly believe this village amid the shrub oaks and blackberries could be the capital. Two boardinghouses for congressmen stood on opposite sides of New Jersey Avenue, between the Capitol and Samuel Smith's printing office. Republicans lived in the house on the west side, where their hosts were Conrad and McMunn; the Federalists in the east-side house, Robert Peacock, proprietor.

233

Speaker Sedgwick was allowed a room to himself; his companions slept in pairs. Board, lodging, candles, wood, and the attendance of a servant, plus liquor, cost fifteen dollars a week.

To Gouverneur Morris, the worldly-wise Federalist senator from New York, who had reveled in the refinements of boudoirs and salons as envoy to Paris, the plight of the poor congressmen in the woods of Washington seemed a capital joke. With a glance at the piles of rock and rubble around the half-finished Capitol, the cynical Senator observed: "Building stone is plentiful; excellent bricks are baked here; we are not wanting in sites for magnificent mansions. We only need here houses, cellars, kitchens, scholarly men, amiable women, and a few other trifles, to possess a perfect city. In a word, this is the best city in the world to live in—in the future. We can walk over it as we would in the fields or the woods, and, on account of the strong frost, the air is quite pure. I enjoy it all the more since my room fills with smoke as soon as the door is closed."

Gradually, the members of Congress arrived at the capital in the forest. On Thursday evening, November 20, three inches of snow— "very unusual," said Samuel Smith's *National Intelligencer*—blanketed the crude city. On Saturday, John Adams dressed in his best velvet suit, with the silver knee buckles, clapped his hat over his powdered hair, climbed into his coach, and skidded through the slush to Capitol Hill.

Greeting the members of Congress who were squeezed into one room of the Capitol, he said: "I congratulate you, gentlemen, on the prospect of a residence not to be changed. Although there is cause to apprehend that accommodations are not as complete as might be wished, yet there is great reason to believe that this inconvenience will cease with the present session."

Adams announced that the three envoys he had sent to seek peace with France had been received by Napoleon "with the respect due to their character." They had concluded a "convention," settling some of the disputes that had led to the undeclared war at sea. The little U. S. Navy had scored many remarkable triumphs over the ships of the powerful French empire, and had made the world look upon the new nation with sudden respect.

234

Custom required the members of Congress to go to the President's house in a body and present their reply. This had been easy enough in Philadelphia, where the President had lived only a block away. But how could they do it in Washington? They could not swim through the mud. Fortunately, several hackney-coaches from Baltimore splashed into town. They were quickly commandeered, and the congressmen rode to the White House in fine style, preceded by the sergeant-at-arms on horseback, carrying the mace.

John and Abigail Adams gave their guests a reception as warm as the shortage of firewood would permit. When the gentlemen had left, the First Lady wrote to her relatives: "Congress poured in—but shiver, shiver."

*   *   *   *   *

The arrival of Congress signaled the beginning of the winter social season. On Tuesday evening, November 25, about a hundred ladies and gentlemen, including members of Congress, met at Stelle's Tavern for the first Dancing Assembly. "Had you been in our crowded assembly room Tuesday night, you would have thought very well of our city-society," Margaret Bayard Smith wrote to her family. One lightly-clad lady caused "great diversion." "I titled her, 'Madame Eve,' " said the irrepressible Peggy, "and called her dress 'the fig leaf.' "

The beautiful, dark-eyed wife of Thomas Law pinched Margaret and pointed to a tall, stiff gentleman on the dance floor, whose powdered wig, erect attitude, and mincing steps made him look as if he had "taken lessons of some antique dancing gentleman of the Year One."

It was General Philip Van Cortlandt, scion of the Hudson River Dutch aristocracy, a hero of the siege of Yorktown and now a Republican congressman from New York.

"Is that gentleman a relation of yours?" Mrs. Law whispered.

"A relation of mine!" Margaret gasped. "Why, I hope you do not think so, from any likeness?"

"No, I only wanted the liberty of laughing at him."

To Peggy's surprise, her solemn husband blossomed forth as a

235

great conversationalist at such social affairs. "I had no idea that his manners were so accommodating, but he can suit himself to young and old, gay and grave," she wrote proudly to his sisters. "The attentions shown to him give me a thousand times more pleasure than those I receive."

Margaret's letters are sprinkled with accounts of gay dinners, dances, and card parties: "On Wednesday, we dined at Mrs. Law's, with a large company of Congress folks. Our party was much enlivened by the pleasantry and wit of Genl. Smith and Edward Livingston. . . . On Thursday, five or six gentlemen of Congress dined with us. The evening was passed in sprightly conversation and whist. . . . The other evening, Mr. and Miss Tingey, the Captain, Dr. May (our physician, an amiable, handsome young man), Gen. Van Cortlandt, sans ceremonie, passed the evening with us and were very merry over the successive dishes of fine oysters."

Peggy's cousin, Federalist Representative James A. Bayard, arrived in Washington some time after Congress convened, and naturally joined in the card-playing and bottle-tossing, being an authority on both. "As soon as night comes," he wrote to Caesar Rodney, "the tables for cards are introduced and there is a choice of whist, loo and brag." "Loo" was the favorite of the ladies, and when a girl had to say she was "loo'ed," she pronounced the word in "a very mincing manner."

Some of the girls blushing behind their fans were setting their caps for husbands. Peggy advised Samuel's sister Mary, in Philadelphia: "I am sure if our brother John were to spend a month here I should be able to transform him from a solitary bachelor into an affectionate and happy husband."

*   *   *   *   *

On November 27 the Vice-President of the United States slipped into Washington. Editor Smith noted in *The National Intelligencer* the next day that Thomas Jefferson had taken up his lodging in "Messrs. Conrad and McMunn's apartments." The Vice-President came several days late for the opening of Congress, and he did so deliberately. He had avoided being on hand to preside over the

Senate on the opening day, to avert any collision with President Adams or a dispute over the reply to the President's message.

The Republican presidential candidate steered clear of the Federalists in Peacock's hotel and found congenial company across the street with the Republicans who made Conrad and McMunn's a general headquarters of their party. Here were Republican Senators John Langdon, of New Hampshire, Abraham Baldwin, of Georgia, John Brown, of Kentucky, Wilson Cary Nicholas, of Virginia and his brother, John, a Congressman; Rep. Theodorus Bailey, of New York, and General Sam Smith, of Maryland. Except for Mrs. Brown and Mrs. Bailey, the thirty men in the house lived like a "refectory of monks."

Jefferson, although potentially the next President, lived in the same style as the other boarders, except that he had a drawing room in which to receive the visitors who flocked to see him. He sat at the foot of the dinner table in the chair nearest the door and farthest from the fire.

No doubt Editor Smith called at Jefferson's two-room suite, to show his new *National Intelligencer* proudly to the man who had persuaded him to start the Washington newspaper as the voice of the Republicans. No doubt, also, the Vice-President supplied the paper with the latest news of the close election campaign, coming in letter after letter from his disciples throughout the country. While Jefferson boasted that he never wrote a line for the newspapers in his life, he supplied much information for those which followed true Republican principles, and solicited subscriptions for them. To one potential subscriber, he wrote in behalf of *The National Intelligencer:* "The paper which probably will be correct . . . will be Smith's, who is at hand to get his information from the offices."

Samuel looked upon his patron as a demigod. His bride, however, after spending all her 22 years in a fiercely Federalist family before her marriage, still believed Jefferson was "an ambitious and violent demagogue, coarse and vulgar in his manners, awkward and rude in his appearance."

One day in December, 1800, while Peggy sat alone in the parlor of her little house on New Jersey Avenue, her servant showed in a gentleman who wished to see Editor Smith. The visitor was a tall, lanky, loose-limbed man, with sandy hair, a red, freckled skin, and bright hazel eyes. His dignified, reserved air at first chilled Margaret's spirits, but the feeling quickly passed. After taking a chair in a free and easy manner, and throwing his arm on the table, he smiled at her with a benevolent expression and in a voice almost femininely soft and gentle drew her into a conversation on the topics of the day.

Casually, he asked the bride how she liked her new home, and she found herself speaking frankly of her life in the rural city. His interest in every word made her think he must be some intimate friend of her husband's, and so kind and conciliating were his looks and manners that she forgot he was a stranger. Indeed, she had not even asked his name.

Then Editor Smith walked in and introduced "Mr. Jefferson."

"I felt my cheeks burn and my heart throb, and not a word more could I speak," she afterwards confided in her journal. "For several years he had been to me an object of peculiar interest. In fact, my destiny, my condition in life, my union with the man I loved, had depended on his success in the presidential election.

"In addition to this personal interest, I had long participated in my husband's political sentiments and anxieties and on the triumph of the Republican party I devoutly believed the security and welfare of my country depended.

"Notwithstanding those exalted views of Mr. Jefferson as a political character, I retained my previously conceived ideas of the coarseness and vulgarity of his appearance and manners, and was therefore equally awed and surprised on discovering the stranger whose deportment was so dignified and gentlemanly, whose language was so refined, whose voice was so gentle, whose countenance was so benignant, to be no other than Thomas Jefferson.

"How instantaneously were all these preconceived prejudices dissipated! From that moment my heart warmed to him with the most affectionate interest and I implicitly believed all that his friends and my husband believed—yes, not only was he a great, but a truly good man!"

238

The Vice-President had come to arrange for the publication of his own Manual for Congress, now called *Jefferson's Manual*. The original was in his own neat, plain, but elegant handwriting, as legible as printing, and its simplicity reflected his own character. Samuel saved the manuscript as a priceless relic.

"After the business was settled," Peggy recorded, "the conversation became general and Mr. Jefferson several times addressed himself to me; but, although his manner was unchanged, my feelings were, and I could not recover sufficient ease to join the conversation. He shook hands cordially with us both when he departed, and in a manner which said as plain as words could do, 'I am your friend.' "

"And is this the violent democrat, the vulgar demagogue, the bold atheist and profligate man I have so often heard denounced by the Federalists?" Margaret asked herself, after he had left her speechless. "Can this man, so meek and mild ... be that daring leader of a faction, that disturber of the peace, that leveler of all rank and order?"

* * * * *

In early December, Washington and the nation waited for the last of the election bulletins which would tell whether the "violent democrat," Jefferson or one of the three other contenders would become the next President of the United States. Nobody could know precisely at the time, because of the slow communications; but, based on the returns from all the states except South Carolina, the last one to vote, this is how the four candidates stood in electoral votes:

Jefferson, 65.

Burr, 65.

Adams, 65.

Pinckney, 64.

The race could hardly be any closer!

The South Carolina legislature, meeting December 2, would choose electors whose eight votes could determine which of the four candidates would be President and Vice-President. The decision would mark the turning point in the election, and, indeed, in the whole political course of the nation's history.

The Republicans had a small majority in the South Carolina legislature which indicated that Jefferson, at least, would receive the state's eight votes; but would the electors also favor Burr? Or would they, out of pride in a native son, cast their second ballots for General Charles Cotesworth Pinckney?

General Pinckney himself was on the scene, to lend his presence to the Federalist cause. Burr had his future son-in-law, Joseph Alston, in the legislature and had sent Timothy Greene, a New York lawyer, as a special agent to persuade the South Carolina Republicans to keep the congressional caucus pledge of equal votes for Jefferson and Burr.

On December 5, Samuel H. Smith's *National Intelligencer* printed a bulletin stating that "an undoubted Republican majority exists in the legislature" of South Carolina, but the electors had not yet been selected. Four days later, Burr's intimate friend, Congressman Edward Livingston, of New York, received a letter from "a man of understanding" in Columbia saying there was "no question" but that the Republicans in control of the legislature would cast a "unanimous vote" for Jefferson and they "spurned . . . the idea of a compromise . . . for Vice-President"—that is, they would stand firm for Burr instead of Pinckney.

On December 11, Federalist Senator James Gunn, of Georgia, sent this gloomy note to Alexander Hamilton in New York: "I have seen a list of the names of the South Carolina electors—they will all vote for Jefferson and Col. Burr. Gen. Pinckney will not get one vote."

The next day, a letter was thrust into Jefferson's hands. It came from Peter Freneau, a Charleston newspaper editor working feverishly for him at Columbia. The legislature, "at one o'clock this day," December 2, had elected eight Republican electors. "The vote tomorrow, I understand, will be Thomas Jefferson 8, Aaron Burr 7, George Clinton 1," Freneau joyfully announced. "You will easily discover why the one vote is varied." (Obviously, this maneuver was to assure that Burr did not top Jefferson.)

In the same mail came a note from U.S. Senator Charles Pinckney, a Republican who had been lobbying vigorously against his Federalist relative, the General: "The election is just finished and we have, thanks to Heaven's goodness, carried it. We have had a hard and arduous struggle and I found that, as there were no hopes from Philadelphia and it depended upon our state entirely to secure your election and that it would be almost death to our hopes for me to quit Columbia, I have remained until it is over and now permit me to congratulate you, my dear sir. . . . Expect me soon in Washington, but I shall be late."

Jefferson evidently relayed the good news quickly to Samuel H. Smith, for *The National Intelligencer* of December 12 came out with this "Extra":

SPLENDID INTELLIGENCE

We have this moment received information from Columbia that the Republican ticket for electors has been carried intire by a majority of from 13 to 18 votes.

MR. JEFFERSON may, therefore, be considered as our future President.

Smith quoted a letter from an unidentified writer in Columbia to General Thomas Sumter, the only Republican Congressman from South Carolina, listing the electors and saying "they are declaredly in favor of Mr. Jefferson and Col. Burr."

"We deserve more credit on this occasion than can well be supposed," the letter went on, "as every art was made use of and the presence of General Pinckney added; whose influence, you know, was counted on as a host. . . . The task was arduous here, as we had heard two days ago of the deficient vote of Pennsylvania and knew that the burthen lay now upon this state. This news excited the spirits and efforts of the Federalists but it also increased our ardor, and the result proves that your countrymen have *deserved well.*"

It is easy to imagine the joy unconfined which reigned among the Republicans who gathered around Jefferson at Conrad and McMunn's boardinghouse to congratulate the next President. It is easy to imagine, too, how Samuel and Margaret Bayard Smith enjoyed drinking their tea on that evening of victory and rejoicing over the triumph of the man who now was a hero to both of them.

Editor Smith exulted, in his next edition: "The storm, which has so long raged in the political world, has at length subsided. Parties have tried their strength and victory has crowned with success in the presidential election, the efforts of the REPUBLICANS.

"To Republicans it must be a cause of sincere felicitation that their country has surmounted, without any other agitation than that of the public sentiment, the choice of their first magistrate."

To his sister Mary, in Philadelphia, he wrote: "Mr. Jefferson's election is secure. The sensation this event has produced baffles all description. Congress have heretofore been paralyzed by alternate hope and fear, and have been unable to do anything. It is indeed a great event; and never has an occurrence taken place in this country more calculated to excite and to reward patriotic feelings."

Among the Federalists gathered in Peacock's boardinghouse and Stelle's tavern on Capitol Hill, universal gloom prevailed. Their party of "talents," the "friends of government," the party which had founded the Republic on the Constitution, which had built up the quarreling states into a cohesive union, which had supplied the great Washington as the first President and Adams as the second, now must pass the reins of power to the despised Republicans. Now that atheist, that dreamy "moonshine philosopher of Monticello," who collected butterflies and mammoth bones and invented swivel chairs and ate French foods and drank French wines and thought French thoughts, would occupy Washington's chair as President!

The Federalists could console themselves with one satisfaction: General Pinckney had "acted nobly." He could have secured the eight votes of South Carolina for himself, through a deal with the Republican legislators, but he insisted upon keeping the pledge of equal votes for himself and Adams, and because of this, the votes went to Jefferson and Burr. This report was received by Rufus King, the Minister to London, from both of Adams' ousted cabinet members, Pickering and McHenry.

"It may with truth be said that John Adams has damned our cause," Senator Gunn told Hamilton, "for the double chance was lost in South Carolina, owing to General Pinckney refusing to give up Mr. Adams."

At the White House, which he soon must vacate, John Adams received the news of his defeat with a mixture of rage and disbelief. He had believed the "assurances from his friend J." that Jefferson wanted nothing more than to serve another four years as Vice-President with Adams as his chief. Adams had concentrated his fire on Hamilton and the "British faction" and had missed the real targets, Jefferson and Burr.

"The triumph of the Jacobins is immoderate, and the Federalists deserve it," Abigail Adams commented. She knew as well as her husband did how Hamilton's men had been scheming to bring Pinckney in as President with South Carolina votes. "They have gulled one another," she said, "by their Southern promises, which have no more faith, when made to Northern men, than lovers' vows."

The election defeat came hard on the heels of a more poignant, more personal loss. The Adamses' son Charles, the charming but dissipated young New Yorker, was dead. His mother had seen him for the last time when she had passed through New York on her way to Washington. His physician then had told the grieving mother that Charles was past hope of recovery. "A distressing cough, an affection of the liver, and a dropsy" ended his life, "which might have been made valuable to himself and others," Abigail mourned. "... He was no man's enemy but his own. He was beloved, in spite of his errors, and all spoke with grief and sorrow for his habits."

* * * * *

Within a few days after the news from South Carolina had sent them dancing for joy, the Republicans received alarming reports that turned their gayety to gloom: Jefferson had not been decisively elected President after all.

He had confidently expected that one vote would be thrown away from Burr in South Carolina, and possibly one or two more in Georgia or Tennessee, so that the final count would be: Jefferson 73, Burr about 70, Adams 65. But something had gone wrong—terribly wrong. Jefferson and Burr were tied, with 73 votes apiece.

Now the House of Representatives must break the tie; not the newly elected House, with its Republican majority, but the "lame duck" House which the Federalists controlled, 55 to 51.

If allowed to vote by individual members, the Federalists might throw the presidency to Burr, just for spite, but the Constitution required an election by states, one vote per state. The Republicans had eight state delegations, the Federalists six, and two were equally divided. Since the winner must carry nine of the sixteen state delegations, a deadlock could result, and nobody would be elected President. March 4, Inaugural Day, would arrive finding the nation without a head; the result, anarchy.

The Federalists faced this prospect with great cheer; they would gladly have their majority in the Senate elect a President pro tempore, who could act as President until a new election; or Congress might pass a bill conferring the presidential powers upon some other official, possibly the Chief Justice.

"The Federalists," Senator Gunn commented, "will have to choose among rotten apples."

"There will be an absolute parity between the two Republican candidates," Jefferson reported glumly to Madison. "This has produced great dismay and gloom in the Republican gentlemen here, and equal exultation in the Federalists, who openly declare they will prevent an election and will name a President of the Senate pro tem. by what, they say, would be only a *stretch* of the Constitution."

"We are brought into a dilemma by the probable equality of the two Republican candidates," Jefferson told John Breckinridge. "The Federalists in Congress mean to take advantage of this, and either to prevent an election altogether, or reverse what has been understood to have been the wishes of the people as to their President and Vice-President, wishes which the Constitution did not permit them specially to designate. The latter alternate still gives us a Republican administration; the former a suspension of the Federal government for want of a head. This opens upon us an abyss at which every sincere patriot must shudder.

"This tells us," Jefferson said in a fling at his Federalist enemies,

244

"who are entitled to the appellation of anarchists, with which they have so liberally branded others."

John Dawson, a Republican Congressman from Virginia, wailed to Madison that, as long as eight state delegations voted for Burr, they could keep either candidate from becoming President. "How are we to act?" he asked. "Who is to be President? In short, what is to become of our government?"

CHAPTER ELEVEN

THOMAS JEFFERSON counter-attacked at once, in mid-December, 1800, against the Federalists' last desperate scheme to bar him from the presidency. He sent a very carefully worded letter to Aaron Burr for the apparent purpose of making sure his running mate would not cooperate with the Federalists' plan to have the House of Representatives elect Burr, or a President pro tempore of the Senate, or perhaps no President at all.

Jefferson began by saying "it is surmised" that a few electoral votes would be dropped from Burr in South Carolina, Georgia, and Tennessee, but not enough to keep him from being Vice-President. "It was badly managed not to have arranged with certainty what seems to have been left to hazard," Jefferson went on. "It was the more material, because I understand several high-flying Federalists have expressed their hope that the two Republican tickets may be equal, and their determination in that case to prevent a choice by the House of Representatives (which they are strong enough to do) and let the government devolve on a president of the Senate.

"Decency required that I should be so entirely passive during the late contest, that I never once asked whether arrangements had been made to prevent so many from dropping votes intentionally as might frustrate half the Republican wish; nor did I doubt, till lately, that such had been made."

It may be true that Jefferson "never once asked" about the "arrangements" for dropping a vote from Burr, but Peter Freneau had certainly told him of the plan for South Carolina to give eight votes to Jefferson, seven to Burr, and one to George Clinton. Jefferson had also kept in close touch with Madison and Monroe and knew of Burr's repeated warnings that he must not be "cut" by the southern Republicans.

Jefferson must have known of the danger of his 73-73 tie with Burr when he wrote this letter on December 15; otherwise, why did he say "several high-flying Federalists" had expressed the "hope" of such a tie? Still acting as if he expected some elector, somewhere, to drop a vote from Burr, Jefferson congratulated him in advance on his election as Vice-President. "I must congratulate you, my dear sir, on the issue of this contest; because it is more honorable, and doubtless more grateful to you than any station within the competence of the chief magistrate; yet, for myself and for the substantial service of the public, I feel most sensibly the loss we sustain of your aid in our new administration.

"It leaves a chasm in my arrangements which cannot be adequately filled up. I had endeavoured to compose an administration whose talents, integrity, names, and dispositions should at once inspire unbounded confidence in the public mind, and ensure a perfect harmony in the conduct of the public business. I lose you from the list, and am not sure of all the others."

Now, what did Jefferson mean by saying to Burr, "I lose you from the list"? Evidently he meant that, if either Adams or Pinckney had won the vice-presidency, Jefferson would have given Burr, as a consolation prize, some high appointive office, probably in the cabinet. Therefore, Burr should not believe any tales that Jefferson and the Virginians had planned once again to leave him in the "lurch."

In a deft thrust against their common enemy, Hamilton, Jefferson wrote that unless "the gentlemen who possess the public confidence" do their part in the new regime, "the evil genius of this country may realize his avowal that 'he will beat down the administration.'"

With his almost morbid distrust of the prying Federalists in the postal service,—a distrust exceeded only by Burr's—Jefferson sent this letter by "Mr. Van Benthuysen," one of the New York electors, who was going home from Washington. Mr. Van Benthuysen also delivered a letter from the Vice-President to another prominent New York Republican, Robert R. Livingston. After a rambling discourse on "mammoth bones" found near the Chancellor's home, and after asking Livingston to help him buy the bones for his collection, Jefferson moved on to the real purpose of the message: He offered to appoint Livingston as Secretary of the Navy. (Incidentally, the Chancellor's brother Edward, being an intimate of Burr and a member of the New York congressional delegation, might be tempted to swing its vote from Jefferson to Burr when the House finally chose between the two Republican candidates.)

Mr. Van Benthuysen did his duty, and Burr dispatched an equally bland and courteous reply. "I do not apprehend any embarrassment in case the votes should come out alike for us," he wrote to Jefferson. "My personal friends are perfectly informed of my wishes on the subject and can never think of diverting a single vote from you. On the contrary, they will be found among your most zealous adherents. I see no reason to doubt of you having at least nine States if the business shall come before the H. of Rep.

"As far forth as my knowledge extends, it is the unanimous determination of the Republicans of every grade to support your administration with unremitted zeal; indeed, I should distrust the loyalty of any one professing to be a Republican who should refuse his services. . . . As to myself, I will chearfully abandon the office of V.P. if it shall be thought that I can be more useful in any active station. In fact, my whole time and attention shall be unceasingly employed to render your administration grateful and honorable to our Country and to yourself. To this I am impelled, as well by the highest sense of duty as by the most devoted personal attachment."

Burr insisted that he had expected Federalist Rhode Island to give Jefferson one more electoral vote than he himself received, which would have prevented a tie. Previously, Burr and Edward Livingston had predicted an extra vote for Jefferson in Federalist Vermont. "Your friend, Col. Dewey," a Vermont elector, had "declared openly" for Jefferson and Adams, Burr asserted in another letter to Jefferson. But Jefferson branded that tale "impossible," and he was right. Both Rhode Island and Vermont went Federalist, as usual. Rhode Island did take one vote away from General Pinckney, but gave it to John Jay. Hence, the final result of the election stood: Jefferson, 73; Burr, 73; Adams, 65; Pinckney, 64; Jay, 1. If that stray Rhode Island vote had gone to Burr instead of to Jay, it would have made Burr President, with 74 electoral votes.

As Hamilton had observed in the summer, Burr was "intriguing" with all his might in Rhode Island and other eastern states, and there was a danger that he might come in ahead of Jefferson. At least, Burr had managed to contrive a tie.

On December 16, Burr sent a letter to General Sam Smith, a Baltimore Republican Congressman working frantically to keep the Federalists in the House from electing Burr.

"It is highly improbable that I shall have an equal number of votes with Mr. Jefferson," Burr stated, "but, if such should be the result, every man who knows me ought to know that I would utterly disclaim all competition. Be assured that the Federal party can entertain no wish for such an exchange.

"As to my friends, they would dishonour my views and insult my feelings by a suspicion that I would submit to be instrumental in counteracting the wishes and expectations of the United States. And I now constitute you my proxy to declare these sentiments if the occasion should require." General Smith was expected to show this letter to all doubting Thomases, including especially Thomas Jefferson, to dispel any rumors about an intrigue between Burr and the Federalists.

This letter has been interpreted in some accounts of this controversy as a frank, explicit, and voluntary declaration by Burr that he would have no part in the Federalists' machinations. In fact, however, the letter was not volunteered by Burr and it did not satisfy Smith. James McHenry, the former Secretary of War, commented at the time that General Smith, "who is extremely anxious for the election of Mr. Jefferson," had "drawn a letter from Mr. Burr" and published extracts from it in a Baltimore paper. Smith himself later testified that he received the famous letter from Burr "in reply to one which I had just before written him."

Burr became angry because General Smith had forced his hand by publishing parts of the letter. Burr had given the General authority to "declare" his sentiments but not to print them in the newspapers.

The letter was unsatisfactory to General Smith because it did not state that Burr would refuse the presidency if the Federalists gave it to him. Even after it appeared in print, the Federalists sailed right ahead with their plans. Some considered it merely a smoke screen to keep the wily New Yorker officially above suspicion while his agents could negotiate secretly for the winning votes. The sophisticated gentlemen at the head of the "party of talents" did not accept Burr's disclaimer at face value. He might not admit any efforts to gain the presidency, but he had not said he would *refuse* it, had he? No, sir! Nor would he!

As McHenry expressed it, the Federalist leaders "think they understand Burr, and that he will not be very angry at being aided by the Federalists, to outwit the Jeffersonians." Senator Uriah Tracy, the Connecticut High Federalist, observed, "Burr is a cunning man. If he cannot outwit all the Jeffersonians, I do not know the man."

Tracy hailed the official returns, showing the 73-73 tie, with a snicker of malicious glee: "Jefferson & Burr have each 73 votes . . . and the Democrats are in a sweat," he chortled. "They are in the most violent state of apprehension, for fear Burr will be chosen, or at any rate that Jefferson will not. . . . It is really pleasant to see the Democrats in such a rage for having acted with good faith. They swear they will never do it again, & mutually criminate each other for having done so now. Each declaring, if they had not had full confidence in the treachery of the others, they would have been treacherous themselves; and not acted, as they promised to act at Philada. last winter, (viz.) all vote for Jefferson & Burr. The Federalists say they like not either of the candidates, but as the anti's have brought them forward, they will take the least of two evils."

President Adams derived some wry satisfaction from the discomfiture of his enemies, too. He wrote to Elbridge Gerry: "73 for Mr. Jefferson and 73 for Mr. Burr. May the peace and welfare of the country be promoted by this result! But I see not the way as yet.

250

In the case of Mr. Jefferson, there is nothing wonderful; but Mr. Burr's good fortune surpasses all ordinary rules. All the old patriots, all the splendid talents, the long experience, both of Federalists and anti-Federalists, must be subjected to the humiliation of seeing this dexterous gentleman rise, like a balloon, filled with inflammable air, over their heads."

Other Federalists professed to find hitherto unsuspected talents in the "dexterous gentleman" from New York. They recalled that Burr was the son of the president of Princeton, and the grandson of Jonathan Edwards, the great theologian; that he had been a gallant officer in the Revolutionary War and a United States Senator. He was a shrewd politician of great energy and a practical man of affairs, not a "French philosopher." If he had a rather shady reputation as an intriguer constantly promoting schemes to pay his enormous debts, well, even that could be turned into an asset. "His ambition and interest will direct his conduct—and his own state is commercial and largely interested in the funded debt," one Federalist rationalized. "If he will honorably support the government for which he has undoubted talents, he will have the support of the Federalists and some of the Jacobins whom he may detach and his election will disorganize and embarrass the party who have given him their votes."

To the Federalists, this last was the cream of the jest. Burr would bring his eastern followers over to the Federalists and, my, how that would mortify the proud Virginians!

Representative Robert Goodloe Harper, of South Carolina, a Federalist leader in the House, sent Burr a most encouraging holiday greeting on Christmas Eve: "I advise you to take no step whatever by which the choice of the House can be impeded or embarrassed. Keep the game perfectly in your own hands, but do not answer this letter, or any other that may be written to you by a Federal man, nor write to any of that party."

Burr, an old hand at intrigue, obeyed Harper's injunction. He did not answer the letter; nor did he make any statement declaring he would not accept the presidency, or that he would resign if elected, so that Jefferson could move into the White House. Quite the contrary: When a Republican asked him if he would resign, Burr wrote, "I would not."

"What do you think of such a question?" Burr angrily asked General Smith on December 29. "I was made a candidate against my advice and against my will; God knows never contemplating or wishing the result which has appeared—and now I am insulted by those who use my name for suffering it to be used."

Burr was irked because he had "received a great number of letters on the subject of the election," and perceived "a degree of jealousy and distrust, irritation by no means pleasing or flattering," and some suggestions downright "impertinent."

Alarmed by Burr's belligerent attitude, General Smith hurried to Philadelphia for a rendezvous with him on the evening of January 4. The General was determined to meet the slippery Colonel face to face and make him commit himself *not* to accept the presidency.

They met, and had a long conversation. According to General Smith's report to two other congressmen from Maryland, Gabriel Christie and George Dent, this is what occurred:

Burr talked all around the subject of the election deadlock and possible solutions, and the General could not imagine what he meant, for he said nothing confidential, and made no observations that might not as well have been made by letter. At last, the General asked, point-blank, what would be done if the Federalist members of the House "would not give up"?

Burr replied—greatly to Smith's surprise—that "at all events, the House could and ought to make a decision," meaning that if they could not get Jefferson, they could take him.

Smith declared that could not be done, for the Republicans "would not give up on any terms." He "came away much mortified," because he had expected that Colonel Burr would give him "full authority to say that he would not serve if elected." Instead, the General was convinced that Burr was quite willing to accept the presidency as a gift from the House of Representatives.

The story of Burr's remarks at Philadelphia does not depend entirely upon Smith's report to his Maryland colleagues. It is substantiated by a note which Jefferson received, at the time, from Benjamin Hichborn, a Massachusetts Republican, who also attended the meeting.

Hichborn wrote, in apparent alarm, from Philadelphia on January 5: "I could not leave this place without intimating to you a circumstance which gives me some little uneasiness. Col. Burr is in ye house with me and Genl. Smith from Baltimore has been here.

"I am convinced that some of our friends, as they call themselves, are willing to join the other party in case they should unite in favor of Colo. Burr."

Jefferson in a diary entry of 1804 relates a conversation with Hichborn which has a deadly parallel:

> He (Hichborn) was in company at Philadelphia with Col. Burr and General Smith (when the latter took his trip there to meet Burr) . . . In the course of the conversation on the elections, Col. Burr said, "We must have a President & a constitutional one in some way."
>
> "How is it to be done?" says Hichborn. "Mr. Jefferson's friends will not quit him, and his enemies are not strong enough to carry another."
>
> "Why," said Burr, "our friends must join the Federalists, and give the president."
>
> The next morning at breakfast Col. Burr repeated nearly the same, saying, "We cannot be without a president, our friends must join the Federal vote."
>
> "But," says Hichborn, "we shall then be without a vice president; who is to be our vice president?"
>
> Col. Burr answered, "Mr. Jefferson."

Some of the Federalists knew about the Philadelphia parley, too. On January 5, the same day Burr made his startling remarks to Smith and Hichborn over the breakfast table, Timothy Pickering wrote from Philadelphia to Rufus King, the minister to London: "General Samuel Smith of Baltimore . . . and Burr are now in this city—doubtless *by concert*. There are said to be many ingenious reasons why the Federalists at Washington are inclined to prefer Mr. Burr. . . . They probably suppose that the Federal interests will not be so *systematically* opposed under Mr. B. as under Mr. J.

Perhaps this may be *previously understood.* In case of a war with any European power, there can be no doubt which of the two would conduct it with most ability and energy."

Burr's stubborn refusal to turn down the presidency disproves the claims of his later apologists, that he honorably spurned the great temptation to snatch the prize from the chief of his own party, who had won it fairly by the votes of the people. Burr's December 16 letter to General Smith had originally fooled even Jefferson, who wrote to his daughter Maria in early January: "The Federalists were confident at first they could debauch Col. B. from his good faith by offering him their vote to be President, and have seriously proposed it to him. His conduct has been honorable and decisive, and greatly embarrasses them."

However, the reports from General Smith and Hichborn, about the Philadelphia parley, coupled with other rumors of Burr's election maneuvers, made it hard to believe "Col. B." was really acting in "good faith."

If he did not wish to receive the presidency at the hands of the Federalists and a few renegade Republicans in the House, Burr should have made a public announcement that he would not take it. That was all he needed to do. He could have made a dramatic dash to Washington, thrown his arms around Jefferson, and declared, before Heaven, that he would not dream of keeping his dear friend out of the office to which the people of the United States had elected him. That would have nipped the Federalist plot in the bud.

Then Burr would have won the respect and undying gratitude of Jefferson and the Republicans, and they would have been compelled to consider him as the first-ranking prospect to succeed Jefferson in the White House. Instead, Burr wrote letters, complaining that he was "insulted" by suggestions that he should resign the presidency if elected. He did nothing to strengthen the public demand that could have forced the reluctant Federalists to give Jefferson his rightful place.

Why did Burr follow this equivocal course? Because he apparently had an excellent chance of being elected by the House.

Here was the situation:

The House would vote by states, starting February 11; each state, large or small, had only one vote. Nine of the sixteen states, a clear majority, were required to win. Jefferson could muster eight, and Burr six; the two other state delegations were tied, thereby having no vote. As Representative James A. Bayard, of Delaware, told Alexander Hamilton January 7, "It is considered that at least in the first instance, Georgia, North Carolina, Virginia, Tennessee, Kentucky, Pennsylvania, New Jersey and New York will vote for Mr. Jefferson . . . Maryland and Vermont will be divided." Burr would get Massachusetts, New Hampshire, Rhode Island, Connecticut, Delaware, and South Carolina.

Theoretically, it should have been easier for Jefferson to pick up the one state he needed than for Burr to gain three. Actually, however, as Bayard said, "it is calculated, and strongly insisted by some gentlemen, that a persevering opposition to Mr. Jefferson would bring over New York, New Jersey, and Maryland," and thus make Burr the President.

New Jersey, Burr's native state, had a House delegation divided three to two for Jefferson. New York, his present residence, had a six to four majority for Jefferson, and Maryland was tied four to four. If one New Jersey congressman, one from Maryland, and two from New York would abandon Jefferson, Burr could pick up the three states to make the necessary total of nine. Four congressmen, therefore, could give Burr the presidency.

Bayard named two of the four: Dr. James Linn, notorious for wavering between the two parties, appeared to be the potential swing man in New Jersey. It was a common joke in Washington that because of the vacillation of "Jemmy" Linn, each party in New Jersey had "two and a half Congressmen." In Maryland, the Federalists pinned their hopes on George Dent, who was technically a member of their party but lately had been voting with the Republicans. In New York, the six-to-four margin for Jefferson could turn to six-to-four for Burr by the switches of two of Burr's personal friends: Congressmen Edward Livingston and Theodorus Bailey.

Besides New York, New Jersey and Maryland, two other states offered prospects of swinging from Jefferson to Burr. They were

255

Vermont and Tennessee. Vermont was deadlocked between the Federalist Lewis R. Morris and the Republican Matthew Lyon. The "spitting Lyon" obviously was no gentleman. If his morals were no better than his manners, might he not be persuaded to favor Burr? Tennessee's one vote was held by the genial William C. C. Claiborne; and Burr, who had been influential in admitting Tennessee to the Union, claimed many friends in the new state—not the least of whom was Andrew Jackson.

Hamilton reported to Senator Gouverneur Morris, of New York, on January 9: "The anti-Federalists, as a body, prefer Jefferson; but among them are many who will be better suited by the dashing, projecting spirit of Burr; and who, after doing what they will suppose to be saving appearances, then will go over to Burr. Edward Livingston has declared among his friends that his first ballot will be for Jefferson—his second for Burr."

Hamilton also informed Senator Morris:

"I know as a fact that overtures have been made by leading individuals of the Federal party to Mr. Burr, who declines to give any assurances respecting his future intentions and conduct, saying that to do it might injure him with his friends, and prevent their co-operation; that all ought to be inferred from the necessity of his future situation, as it regarded the disappointment and animosity of the anti-Federalists; that the Federalists, relying upon this, might proceed in the certainty that, upon a second ballot, New York and Tennessee would join him. It is likewise ascertained that he perfectly understands himself with Edward Livingston, who will be his agent at the seat of government.

"Thus you see that Mr. Burr is resolved to preserve himself in a situation to adhere to his former friends . . . and to use the Federalists as tools of his aggrandisement. The hope that, by his election he will be separated from the anti-Federalists, is a perfect farce."

Hamilton accurately summed up the line of strategy which Burr would most logically follow to win the presidency. Burr would not bargain with the Federalists, nor make deals with them, nor give them any commitments to adopt their conservative policies. He did not need to do that. They would vote for him anyway, for they had nowhere else to go. Besides, if he openly committed himself to the Federalists, he would drive off his "friends," the Republicans. Only by remaining ostensibly a good Republican could he hope to swing the necessary Republicans away from their first love, Jefferson. Burr needed only to keep his mouth shut and let his agents persuade the Republicans to swing three states to him—on the plausible ground that it would be better to elect Burr than nobody at all.

The Federalists, as Bayard told Hamilton, did not believe Burr's letter to General Smith meant that he would not compete with Jefferson. "It is here understood to have proceeded, either from a false calculation as to the result of the electoral votes, or was intended as a cover to blind his own party," Bayard wrote. "By persons friendly to Mr. Burr, it is distinctly stated that he is willing to consider the Federalists as his friends, and to accept the office of President as their gift. I take it for granted that Mr. Burr would not only gladly accept the office, but will neglect no means in his power to secure it."

Upon returning to Washington from his fruitless conference with Burr in Philadelphia, General Smith learned, to his dismay, that a New York lawyer named David A. Ogden had been in the capital trying to swing the New York and New Jersey Republicans from Jefferson to Burr.

"He said he came to Trenton with you, that you have conversed freely with him on the subject of the tie, from which he meant, I presume, to insinuate that he had your confidence," the General wrote Burr on January 11. "He addressed the York members on your account, directly and boldly represented how much New York would be benefited by having you for the President, urging a variety of other reasons to induce them to join the High Federal party in their *pretended* attempt. He was answered with decision that the Yorkers would continue to act on the principles they had commenced, that nothing could and nothing would induce them to vote otherwise than for Mr. Jefferson; that the other states had acted honorably with them and they would on no consideration desert them."

The New Jersey members likewise stood firm for Jefferson, General Smith insisted, and no other state would switch to Burr, either, no matter how long the balloting might run on. "I found on my return a stand taken by the Democrats from which, *be assured,* that nothing can drive them. The eight states will continue to the end of the session to vote for Mr. J. . . . *Believe me*—those eight states are *immovable*—Maryland has four members that must combine with them. In my own opinion (and I have *good reasons*) Maryland will make the ninth state. Vermont has Matthew Lyon; he will vote for Jefferson and cannot be changed. *Rely on it,* the Feds cannot operate on him."

Thus did General Smith, in his letter filled with scratched-out phrases and ink blots, try to persuade Burr not to believe the widespread reports that New York, New Jersey, Maryland, and/or Vermont would swing over and make him President. The General also sought to smooth the ruffled feathers of the Colonel, who had complained to him at Philadelphia that "the Virginians had been abusing him" for not getting out of Jefferson's way. "I told you that I did not believe it," Smith wrote. "I have enquired everywhere and find the whole a fiction. The *personal abuse* of you by the Feds. cannot be repeated. It has invariably been discredited by the Demos. Mr. Ogden's conduct was considered as one of many attempts practicing by his party to disunite, and treated accordingly."

"Mr. J. has received letters of caution relative to you," Smith further informed the touchy New Yorker, but has ignored them, saying "such letters did not merit an answer."

After brushing off the prospect of Burr's election, Smith went on to warn him of two other Federalist schemes for keeping control of the government: one, to deadlock the presidential voting and have the Senate choose a President pro tempore to act as Chief Executive; the other, to pass a law handing the presidential powers to some other official, possibly the Chief Justice.

"I have asked Mr. J. whether he had ever given reason to believe that he meant to afford an opportunity to the Senate to choose a President pro tem.," Smith wrote. "He said, No, on the contrary, he meant to declare from the chair that he would not."

As to the idea of passing a law to create a President, the Republicans would consider any such act a "usurpation" and "act accordingly." The Federalists had seriously considered it, however; one "high-toned Fed." had asked a federal judge if it would be constitutional, and he had said it would be, but it would *not* be "expedient"; "it would irritate the people." The unidentified judge ruled "the intention of the electors was Mr. J. and that it would be prudent to follow their instructions," Smith told Burr.

As a last resort, he said, Jefferson and Burr might jointly call the new Republican Congress into session to elect Jefferson. "An influential character of Virginia" (apparently James Madison) favored that plan. "However, I do not believe that we shall go that far," Smith wrote. "The firmness and decision now shown, and your cooperation, will place things as we wish. Again, let me intreat you to believe that your friends express the highest confidence in you. Disregard every report to the contrary."

In regard to Smith's report about Ogden's electioneering in Washington, Burr replied, a bit stiffly: "I have said nothing to a Mr. 'O'— nor have I said anything to contravene my letter of the 16th ult., but to enter into details would take reams of paper and years of time."

Bayard later said: "I remember Mr. Ogden's being at Washington, while the election was depending. I spent one or two evenings in his company at Stelle's hotel in small parties. . . . It was reported that he was an agent of Mr. Burr, or it was understood that he was in possession of declarations of Mr. Burr, that he would serve as President if elected." Bayard said Ogden did not make any such "declarations" to him, personally, but that would not contradict the report of his appeals to the New York and New Jersey Republicans in Congress.

Ogden himself later said he just happened to meet Burr "at the stage-office" in New York and rode with him as far as Trenton, where Burr left the coach for his conference with General Smith at Philadelphia. They had a "general" conversation about politics along the way, but the Colonel did not send him to the capital on any "errand." Yes, Ogden did recall that "two or three" Federalist members of Congress asked him to "converse with Colonel Burr" and find out whether he would "enter into terms" with them, and upon returning to New York he did so. However, the answers were so unsatisfactory, Ogden insisted, that he advised the Congressmen "to acquiesce in the election of Mr. Jefferson as the less dangerous man of the two."

(A comparison of Burr's and Ogden's statements will show whether Burr was telling the truth or not when he told Smith: "I have said nothing to a Mr. 'O.' ")

Clearly, General Smith was having trouble convincing Burr that there was no hope of his election by the House; and Jefferson could hardly be blamed for feeling an ever-increasing distrust of his companion on the Republican ticket, who now seemed quite willing to take the presidency away from him. Jefferson's suspicions deepened later when he heard rumors that Burr had planned to have one New York elector drop a vote from Jefferson. If that had been done, Burr would have been elected President with 73 electoral votes, leaving Jefferson as Vice-President with 72.

The rumors held that Burr had arranged with young Anthony Lispenard, a New York City elector, to drop Jefferson's name, but the scheme was frustrated when the electors met and General Van Cortlandt "sportively insisted" upon writing each of his colleagues' ballots. If Burr's ally ever had any intention of dropping the vote, he had no opportunity of doing so.

Although Jefferson listed little, if any, evidence to support his suspicions, the various incidents, real or imaginary, fitted together to make a mental jig-saw puzzle in which he could picture the Machiavellian Burr secretly urging his agents to seduce loyal Republicans to desert their leader and give the presidency to Burr. True or false, fair or unfair, the picture must have persisted in Jefferson's mind, and he never trusted Burr thereafter. Indeed, he later wrote in his private journal that he had never trusted him at all.

"I had never seen Colonel Burr till he came as a member of Senate," Jefferson wrote. "His conduct very soon inspired me with distrust. I habitually cautioned Mr. Madison against trusting him too much. I saw afterwards, that under General Washington's and Mr. Adams's administrations, whenever a great military appointment or a diplomatic one was to be made, he came post to Philadelphia to show himself, and in fact that he was always at market, if they had wanted him. . . . With these impressions of Colonel Burr, there never had been an intimacy between us, and but little association. When I destined him for a high appointment, it was out of respect for the favor he had obtained with the Republican party, by his extraordinary exertions and successes in the New York election in 1800."

*   *   *   *   *

In his under-cover struggle to keep the Federalists from taking the presidency away from him, Jefferson found that his most determined, resourceful and brilliant enemy had now become his friend. Alexander Hamilton, from his law office in New York, poured out a steady stream of letters to his former followers begging, pleading, warning them not to make the fatal mistake of handing Burr the opportunity of seizing "supreme power."

Hamilton, better than any other man, knew the truth about Burr, for they had crossed swords in many a combat in New York politics, in the law courts, and in national affairs. The two men were very much alike in personal appearance; each was a small, elegant man of stiff military bearing, overbearing to the point of arrogance; each was dreaming of martial glory and of southern and western empires; each was irresistible to women and usually unable to resist a conquest. Hamilton had publicly confessed his affair with Mrs. Reynolds; Burr had a notorious reputation as profligate, a "voluptuary by system" who kept a little book on his assignations with women of all social levels, high and low.

Yet there was a bedrock difference between them: Hamilton had complete personal integrity. Although he would scheme to defeat John Adams by juggling presidential electoral votes, he would never stoop to profit himself from serving his government nor would he scheme against his own country. Hamilton could have made himself a millionaire by speculating in government securities while Secretary of the Treasury, but he came out of office a poor man. Burr thought him silly for not enriching himself in office.

While Hamilton aspired to lead American armies in the conquest

261

of Spain's New World colonies, he intended always that the territories would strengthen the American Union and make it perpetual. Burr aspired to the conquest of an empire, too, but only to separate it from the Union and set himself up as its chief. In brief, General Hamilton served his country; Colonel Burr served only himself.

When he looked into the glittering black eyes of his rival, Hamilton thought he saw an insatiable lust for power, luxury and wealth. In his favorite phrase, Hamilton compared Burr to the conspirator of ancient Rome, Catiline: "Every step in his career proves that he has formed himself upon the model of Catiline, and he is too cold-blooded and too determined a conspirator ever to change his plan," Hamilton warned Oliver Wolcott.

"Like Catiline, he is indefatigable in courting young men and profligates," he told James McHenry. "He knows well the weak sides of human nature and takes care to play in with the passions of all with whom he has intercourse. By natural disposition, the haughtiest of men, he is at the same time the most creeping to answer his purposes. . . . He will court and employ able and daring young scoundrels of every party and . . . attempt an usurpation.

"No mortal can tell what his political principles are," Hamilton went on. "He has talked all around the compass. At times, he has dealt in all the jargon of Jacobinism; at other times, he has proclaimed decidedly the total insufficiency of the Federal government and the necessity of changes to one far more energetic. . . . If he has any theory, 'tis that of a simple despotism."

Burr favored the French revolutionaries with a zeal at least equal to Jefferson's and probably greater, Hamilton claimed. At recent dinner parties, at his own table, Burr had offered toasts to "the French republic," to the commissioners who had negotiated the peace pact with France, to Bonaparte, and to Lafayette.

Burr "has no principle, public or private," Hamilton informed Gouverneur Morris. "He is bankrupt beyond redemption except by the resources that grow out of war and disorder, or by a sale to a foreign power. . . . He is sanguine enough to hope every thing, daring enough to attempt every thing, wicked enough to scruple nothing."

"If there be a man in the world I ought to hate, it is Jefferson," Hamilton declared. "With Burr I have always been personally well. But the public good must be paramount to every private consideration."

For a brief time, early in the Jefferson-Burr contest, Hamilton played with the idea of having the Federalists "throw out a lure" for Burr, "to tempt him to start for the plate, and then lay the foundation of dissension between the two chiefs." But he quickly dropped that notion when he found the Federalists were not merely holding a "lure" in front of Burr's eager eyes, but actually plotting to make the "Catiline" president. Except for a few of his most faithful followers, Hamilton soon learned to his dismay that the leaders of his own party were scorning his advice.

Senator Morris, cynically amused by the hectic plotting and counter-plotting all about him in the frontier capital, vowed he would take no part in such "intrigues." He asserted that "since it was evidently the intention of our fellow-citizens to make Mr. Jefferson their President, it seems proper to fulfill that intention." But Morris, a Senator, could not vote in the House. Nor could he influence many of the other Federalists, who seemed "moved by passion only" in their zeal to humiliate the hated Jefferson by elevating Burr. Being brushed aside by the fanatics, Morris sympathized with Hamilton who, he said, was in the "awkward situation" of a man "who continues sober" after everyone else at the party is drunk.

Speaker Sedgwick, a ringleader in the plot to elect Burr, admitted "there is no disagreement as to his character." "He is ambitious— selfish—profligate," Sedgwick told Hamilton. "His ambition is of the worst kind; it is a mere love of power, regardless of fame; his selfishness excludes all social affections; and his profligacy unrestrained by any moral sentiments and defying all decency.

"This agreed, but then it is known that his manners are plausible —that he is dexterous in the acquisition and use of the means necessary to effect his wishes. He holds to no previous theories, but is a mere matter-of-fact man. His very selfishness prevents his entertaining any mischievous predilections for foreign nations. . . .

263

"It is very evident that the Jacobins dislike Mr. Burr as President —that they dread his appointment more than even that of General Pinckney. On his part, he hates them for the preference given his rival. He has expressed his displeasure at the publication of his letter by General Smith. This jealousy, and distrust, and dislike, will every day more and more increase, and more and more widen the breach between them.

"Then, to what evils shall we expose ourselves by the choice of Burr, which we should escape by the election of Jefferson?"

Sedgwick agreed "there is part of the character of Burr more dangerous than that of Jefferson": Given a chance, Burr probably would become a "usurper," while Jefferson would not "dare" to try. They were indeed a fine pair to choose from, and the retiring President was no better, in the opinion of the Speaker, who remarked: "We have at one election placed at the head of our government a semi-maniac (Adams) who, in his soberest senses, is the greatest marplot in nature; and at the next a feeble and false, enthusiastic theorist (Jefferson) and a profligate without character and without property, bankrupt in both (Burr)."

Despite his usual respect for Hamilton's opinions, Sedgwick went straight ahead with the plan to elect Burr, and the large majority of the Federalists in the House of Representatives followed him. Ever since Hamilton had lost control of New York and had issued his embarrassing pamphlet against Adams, some Federalists had shied away from his leadership. They said his appeals against Burr arose from personal hostility, or old grudge fights, which need not sway their votes.

John Marshall, the Secretary of State, who had made a reasonably moderate record in Congress in contrast to the High Federalist fanatics, nevertheless refused Hamilton's plea to help Jefferson. Marshall knew Jefferson; he did not know Burr. Marshall believed Jefferson's "foreign prejudices" in favor of France would "totally unfit him" for the presidency; furthermore, he could never forgive his attacks upon their fellow-Virginian, General Washington. "The morals of the author of the letter to Mazzei cannot be pure," Marshall told Hamilton.

264

"Your representation of Mr. Burr, with whom I am totally un-acquainted, shows that from him still greater danger than even from Mr. Jefferson may be apprehended. Such a man as you describe is more to be feared and may do more immediate if not greater mis-chief . . . but I can take no part in this business. I cannot bring myself to aid Mr. Jefferson."

Obviously, Hamilton was getting nowhere with his pleas to the Federalists to drop their "mad" plan for electing Burr. He turned for help to a Federalist congressman who would hold an ace card in the game, James A. Bayard, the lone Representative from Dela-ware.

Since the balloting in the House, starting February 11, would be by states, Bayard's vote would have as much weight as the one from giant Virginia, with its 19 Representatives; and since the Re-publicans claimed eight states for Jefferson, they needed only one more to make the required majority—nine of the sixteen states. Bayard, therefore, could clinch Jefferson's election singlehanded.

Bayard, however, despised Jefferson, and he had no personal reason for disliking Burr. A fiery Federalist, reared by the stern Colonel John B. Bayard, the young congressman had no use for "Jacobins," least of all the philosopher of Monticello. Still, Bayard considered Hamilton his "father confessor" in politics, and he might listen to advice. So Hamilton sent an impassioned appeal to Bayard, urging him to drop Burr:

"Be assured, my dear sir, that this man has no principle, public or private. As a politician, his sole spring of action is an inordinate ambition; as an individual, he is believed by friends as well as foes to be without probity; and a voluptuary by system.

"Great management and cunning are the predominant features" of Burr's talents, Hamilton went on. "He is yet to give proofs of those solid abilities which characterize the statesman. Daring and energy must be allowed him; but these qualities, under the direction of the worst passions, are certainly strong objections, not recom-mendations. He is of a temper to undertake the most hazardous enterprises, because he is sanguine enough to think nothing imprac-

265

ticable; and of an ambition that will be content with nothing less than *permanent* power in his own hands. . . .

"In debt, vastly beyond his means of payment, with all the habits of excessive expense, he cannot be satisfied with the regular emoluments of any office of our government. Corrupt expedients will be to him a necessary resource. Will any prudent man offer such a President to the temptations of foreign gold? No engagement that can be made with him can be depended upon. . . . He will laugh in his sleeve at the credulity of those with whom he makes it; and the first moment it suits his views to break it, he will do so."

Bayard replied that a majority of the Federalists had "a strong inclination" to vote for Burr and the current was "manifestly increasing." If they should decide upon this course in caucus, Bayard would hesitate to "separate myself from them." Besides, "I should fear as much from the sincerity of Mr. Jefferson (if he is sincere) as from the want of probity in Mr. Burr." Furthermore, it would please the representative of little Delaware if the "Virginia faction" would fail to install its hero, Jefferson, in the White House. Burr's election "would disappoint their views" and "immediately create a schism" in the Republican party.

Bayard fully realized that his vote could "decide the question in favor of Mr. Jefferson," but added, "At present I am by no means decided. . . . Before I resolve on the part I shall take, I shall await the approach of the crisis."

Writing from the House chamber, where some of the conspirators were moving about and whispering of their plans, Bayard predicted the Federalist caucus would soon resolve to favor Burr. "Their determination will not bind me," he added, "for though it might cost me a painful struggle to disappoint the views and wishes of many gentlemen with whom I have been accustomed to act, yet the magnitude of the subject forbids the sacrifice of a strong conviction."

Hamilton read the last section of Bayard's letter with great relief. Here, at last, was one important Federalist congressman who might help him to block Burr. "I was glad to find, my dear sir," Hamilton replied on January 16, "that you had not yet determined to go in

266

support of Mr. Burr; and that you were resolved to hold yourself disengaged till the moment of final decision. Your resolution to separate yourself from the Federal party, if your conviction shall be strong of the unfitness of Mr. Burr, is certainly laudable. . . . If the party shall adopt him for their official chief, I shall be obliged to consider myself as an *isolated* man. It will be impossible for me to reconcile with my motives of *honor* or policy, the continuing to be of a party which, according to my apprehension, will have degraded itself and the country."

As for his old enemy, Jefferson, the General painted this profile which shows how the Federalists generally viewed the author of the Declaration of Independence who also chanced to be the Vice-President of the United States:

"I admit that his politics are tinctured with fanaticism; that he is too much in earnest in his democracy; that he has been a mischievous enemy to the principal measures of our past administration; that he is crafty and persevering in his objects; that he is not scrupulous about the means of success, nor very mindful of truth, and that he is a contemptible hypocrite."

"That Jefferson has manifested a culpable predilection for France is certainly true," Hamilton continued, "but I think it a question, whether it did not proceed quite as much from her *popularity* among us as from sentiment; and in proportion as that popularity is diminished, his zeal will cool.

"Add to this, that there is no fair reason to suppose him capable of being corrupted, which is a security that he will not go beyond certain limits. . . .

"As to Burr, these things are admitted, and indeed cannot be denied, that he is a man of *extreme* and *irregular* ambition; that he is *selfish* to a degree which excludes all social affections; and that he is decidedly *profligate.*"

"But it is said," Hamilton went on, "1st, that he is *artful* and *dexterous* to accomplish his ends; 2nd, that he holds no pernicious theories but is a mere *matter of fact* man; 3rd, that his very selfishness is a guard against mischievous foreign predilections (it is always very dangerous to look at the vices of men for good); 4th, that his *local situation* has enabled him to appreciate the utility of our commercial and fiscal systems; . . . 5th, that he is now disliked by the Jacobins, that his elevation will be a mortal stab to them, breed an invincible hatred to him, and compel him to lean on the Federalists; 6th, that Burr's ambition will be checked by his good sense, by the manifest impossibility of succeeding in any scheme of usurpation. . . . These topics are, in my judgment, more plausible than solid."

Then the great genius of Federalism demolished the arguments for Burr, like a sharpshooter picking off his targets:

"As to the first point, the fact must be admitted"—that Burr is "artful and dexterous." But these qualities are "objections rather than recommendations, when they are under the direction of bad principles.

"As to the second point, too much is taken for granted. . . . I myself have heard him speak with applause of the French system. . . . He has contended against banking systems . . . yet he has lately by a trick established a *bank*—a perfect monster in its principles, but a very convenient instrument of *profit* and *influence*. The truth is, that Burr is a man of a very subtle imagination, and a mind of this make is rarely free from ingenious whimsies. . . .

"As to the third point, it is certain that Burr, generally speaking, has been as warm a partisan of France as Jefferson, in some instances with passion. His selfishness, so far from being an obstacle, may be a prompter. If corrupt as well as selfish, he may be a partisan for gain. . . .

"As to the fourth point, the instance I have cited with respect to banks, proves that the argument is not to be relied upon.

"As to the fifth point, nothing can be more fallacious. It is demonstrated by recent facts that Burr is *solicitous* to keep upon *anti-Federal* ground to avoid compromitting himself by any engagements with the Federalists. (He trusts to their *prejudices,* and *hopes* for support.) He will never choose to lean upon good men, because he knows that they will never support his bad projects. But he will endeavor to disorganize both parties, and to form out of them a third, composed of men fitted by their characters to be conspirators and instruments of such projects.

"As to the last point, the proposition is against the experience of all times. Ambition without principle never was long under the guidance of good sense. Besides that, really, the force of Mr. Burr's understanding is much over-rated. He is far more *cunning* than *wise;* far more *dexterous* than *able.*

"*Very, very confidential*—In my opinion, he is inferior in real ability to Jefferson."

"It is past all doubt," Hamilton said, "that he has blamed me for not having improved the situation I once was in, to change the government"—that is, to use his power as George Washington's right-hand man, to seize control of the country. When Hamilton had said he could not do such a thing "without guilt," Burr had replied, *"Les grands âmes se soucient peu des petits moraux,"* or "Great souls care little for small morals."

"Does this prove that Mr. Burr would consider a scheme of usurpation as visionary?" Hamilton asked Bayard. "The truth is, with great apparent coldness he is the most sanguine man in the world. He thinks every thing possible to adventure and perseverance; and, though I believe he will fail, I think it almost certain he will attempt usurpation, and the attempt will involve great mischief.

"But there is one point of view which seems to me decisive: If the anti-Federalists, who prevailed in the election, are left to take their own man, they remain responsible, and the Federalists remain *free, united,* and without *stain,* in a situation to resist, with effect, pernicious measures. If the Federalists substitute Burr, they adopt him and become answerable for him. Mr. Burr must become *in fact* the man of our party, and if he acts ill, we must share in the blame and disgrace . . . becoming answerable for a man who, on all hands, is acknowledged to be a complete Catiline."

Hamilton's impassioned pleas against the "complete Catiline" did not persuade Bayard to act against the wishes of the vast majority of the Federalist congressmen who decided in caucus to vote for Burr until the bitter end. Even if they could not run their six states up to the nine required for victory, they could keep Jefferson out of the White House as long as he had but eight states and two were tied. Then the Federalists, who controlled both houses of

Congress numerically, could appoint a President from their own party—possibly Secretary of State Marshall—until there could be another election.

Thus Bayard, who loved to while away many a pleasant evening with a bottle or two of wine and a pack of cards, found himself playing a game of political poker for the highest possible stakes—the presidency of the United States. The jovial young aristocrat enjoyed holding the trump cards in this new and exciting game of chance. He boasted to friends that his one vote could hand the election to Jefferson, if he chose.

True, Federalist Representative Lewis Morris could do the same by withdrawing his vote from Burr and letting Representative Matthew Lyon transfer Vermont from its one-one tie into the Jefferson camp. One of the Maryland Federalists, whose delegation was deadlocked four to four, also could move over to Jefferson. But all six of these Federalists—Bayard, Morris, and the four from Maryland, Baer, Craik, Dennis and Thomas—agreed to make Bayard their leader, and took a solemn oath to stand together until the final crisis. Therefore, the gentleman from Delaware, only thirty-three years old, held in his hands the cards that could decide the high-stakes game.

The Republicans in his home town of Wilmington groaned at the prospect of seeing Bayard in this place of power. Caesar Rodney wrote to Jefferson that there might be some hope of swinging Bayard over to their side: "I do not know what intrigues, under various shapes, may be going on at headquarters or what influence a system already concerted by the Federal partizans may have on the mind of my friend Bayard ... but I have lately heard him say repeatedly in company that, in case of an equality of votes between yourself and Col. Burr, he should not hesitate to vote for you, and he has spoken frequently of the dignified impartiality observed by you in your conduct as President of the Senate, with marked approbation.

"As we want but one vote from a Federal State, I do confidently trust that Delaware will act a noble and manly part, that she will rival her former conduct on the great question of independence and shine among the brightest stars in the constellation. What a glorious opportunity will be presented to a man possessed of a spirit of independence, to elevate himself above the low, groveling views of prejudice and party!"

Rodney professed to feel "great confidence" that Bayard would not "bow down to the low machinations" of the Federalists conspiring for Burr.

But John Vaughan, also of Wilmington, was not so sure. "Surely our political destiny is suspended by a slender thread, which is dependant on the integrity of Mr. Bayard," Vaughan informed Jefferson. "The manner in which he has acted, since the result of the election was known, is truly characteristic of the time-serving partizan.

"I lately heard him declare in a large company that he should not hesitate a moment in voting for the voice of the people. . . . He is determined to turn with the current of public sentiment; and if he does cut right, for once, we shall give him credit for the *deed* without scrutinizing the motive of action."

Bayard ensconced himself at Stelle's hotel on Capitol Hill, with about thirty other members of Congress, listened to the pleas from both sides in the fierce contest, and refused to commit himself to anyone. "It is my design to make the most of the occasion by giving the strongest impression of the importance of the State," he informed his Federalist confidants in Delaware. "For this purpose, I shall remain inflexibly silent. Many efforts have already been made to ascertain my intention. In fact, I have not yet determined the part I shall take."

The fare at Stelle's, he considered "indifferent" and the expense "immoderate"; for himself and one servant, he grumbled, "I pay twenty dollars a week. An invitation to dinner costs you a ride of six or eight miles and the state of the roads obliging you to return before night, you just have time to swallow your meat."

Bayard had left his wife in Delaware, reasoning that "a wife and additional servants would have been an enormous expense." The young *bon vivant* complained, "There is a great want of society, especially female." That worried him almost as much as the political crisis.

With outward calm, Bayard observed that the members of Congress were so engrossed by the presidential election that they showed "little disposition to attend to any other business." "The Demos are more uneasy at the prospect of Burr's election than they ever were that of Adams," he gloated. "They declare that they will never concur in the vote for Burr, that they would rather see the union dissolved for want of a head than give up Jefferson. The Federal gentlemen have generally declared in favor of Burr, and if Delaware be added to those who have declared, Jefferson cannot be elected."

Jefferson realized that the Federalists of Delaware, Vermont and Maryland had the power of electing him. "There are 6 individuals, of moderate dispositions, any one of which, coming over to us, will make a 9th vote," he told his son-in-law, Thomas Mann Randolph. But Jefferson felt far from confident that "a single one will come over." He had no faith in Federalists.

The more sanguine of the conspirators confidently believed that the Republicans would crack and some would come over to elect Burr. As Bayard recorded their views, "It was generally said . . . that several Democratic States were more disposed to vote for Mr. Burr than for Mr. Jefferson. That out of complaisance to the known intention of the party they would vote a decent length of time for Mr. Jefferson, and as soon as they could excuse themselves by the imperious situation of affairs, would give their votes to Mr. Burr, the man they really preferred. The states relied upon for this change were New York, New Jersey, Vermont, and Tennessee."

"The question of a President is a subject of division and doubt," Bayard wrote his cousin Andrew, the Philadelphia merchant who usually kept him well supplied with wine. "The Federal party will vote for Burr but it is expected upon the first ballot Mr. Jefferson will have eight states. It is, however, certainly within the compass of possibility that Burr may ultimately obtain nine states."

So the hectic January days went by, and James A. Bayard collected the cards and refused to tip his hand to anyone—not even to Hamilton, or his cousin Andrew, in Philadelphia, or his cousin Margaret Bayard Smith in Washington. He certainly would not confide in Margaret now, for she was a "Jacobin" editor's wife, and a newly converted disciple of the Great Jefferson. The gentleman from Delaware followed the advice which his friend Harper had given to Burr. He kept the game in his own hands, free to award the presidency to Jefferson—or to Burr.

CHAPTER TWELVE

WHILE REPRESENTATIVE James A. Bayard sat calmly in the eye of the hurricane raging over the presidential election, his cousin Samuel Harrison Smith was blown about in another storm raging over an issue dear to Thomas Jefferson's heart—the freedom of the press.

Ever since he had founded *The National Intelligencer* as the Washington mouthpiece of Jefferson's party, Editor Smith had been working like a galley slave to print the whole truth about the Federalist administration of the government. But the Federalists, who did not trust newspapers any more than they trusted the common people, threw every possible stumbling block in his path. They withheld information about the government departments and refused even official documents—most of which were given to a new rival paper, the *Washington Federalist,* which was founded as the organ of the Federalist party.

"Official communications I have not yet obtained," the editor wrote to his sister Mary, in Philadelphia, "but I have done better without them than those who had them. In every article my paper has been ahead of all the others.

"I feel somewhat pleased in owing nothing to Federal support. The President is almost the only officer of the govt. that takes my paper."

Samuel was determined "to distance all competition by . . . industry and energy," and that meant that he had to work practically around the clock, much to the regret of his bride. "As I keep all my accounts, direct the greater part of my papers, report the congressional debates, and edit the paper, I perpetually find myself engaged," he said.

This is how Editor Smith personally supervised the circulation department:

"The name of every subscriber is written on each paper, taken from a book kept for that express purpose. After the papers are so directed, the names on the papers are compared with those in the book by two persons. These papers are then enclosed in strong wrappers, on which the names of the postoffices to which the papers are sent, are written, which are again examined. The large packets are secured by twine."

Despite these precautions, the editor received many complaints about the irregular delivery of papers. The complaints came from subscribers in Connecticut, Massachusetts, New York, Pennsylvania, Delaware, Maryland, Virginia and Kentucky. They were so numerous, and from such a wide area, that the Republican editor—who shared Jefferson's and Burr's distrust of the postal service—suspected dirty work at the crossroads by the Federalists manning the post offices. Samuel wrote a sizzling letter to Federalist Assistant Postmaster General Abraham Bradley, charging that "neglect and misconduct" by postal employees had caused his papers to go astray.

Bradley, in an equally warm reply, defended the postmasters as "gentlemen of the first respectability ... bound by the most sacred obligations not to delay or destroy your papers." "The truth is," he told the editor, "you either omit to put up the papers, or misdirect them; and to justify yourself to your subscribers, charge the postmasters with destroying them. The failure of newspapers is generally to be attributed to the printers. The great numbers of papers which you have to send, the employment of all your hands, apprentices, and journeymen, in packing and directing, and omitting to make a proper arrangement for detecting errors, occasion the failure of yours."

Bradley admitted that "newspapers are sometimes sent in a wrong direction by a postmaster," but he insisted the most frequent causes of delay arose from "unavoidable accidents and obstructions" from bad weather and miserable roads.

"It should seem that many of the editors of newspapers either did not know that there was such a thing as boisterous elements, or else considered them subject to the Postmaster-General's command," Bradley commented with fine sarcasm. "It is hardly necessary to state that violent winds and storms, and ice, will at times render it impossible to ferry across rivers; that inconsiderable runs are sometimes swelled by rains to the size of rivers; that heavy rains or the breaking up of frozen ground render some roads so deep that it is impossible to travel on them with the necessary speed; that the mail is carried either in stages or on horseback; that post stages are as liable to break as those of individuals; that they may break where no other carriage is to be had for a number of miles; that a horse may be overcome by heat; may fall dead with disease; may become lame or unable to travel where no other horse can be procured; that the riders may fall sick, and many other accidents may cause a delay of the mail."

Thus ended the Assistant Postmaster General's complete catalogue of alibis for the failure of his agents to deliver *The National Intelligencer* during the swift completion of their appointed rounds.

Another, and even more serious, controversy soon arose. Smith and another newsman, Thomas Carpenter, sent the House a "memorial" in early December, 1800, asking permission to "occupy a situation within the bar"—that is, on the House floor—so that they could hear the debates distinctly and report them in the newspapers.

The Republican members, who had followed Jefferson's lead in raising a great hue and cry against the Federalists' Sedition Law in the late campaign, naturally favored the proposal for the Republican editor, Smith, to hear and to print everything that went on in the Federalist-controlled House. But the prospect of a "licentious" press exposing the congressmen to public ridicule aroused a shout of protest from the Federalists; and none shouted more loudly than Speaker Sedgwick.

Violating the rules of the House which forbade the Speaker to take part in the debates, the gentleman from Massachusetts time and again interrupted the discussions to declare that "the dignity, the order, the convenience of the House would be destroyed" by admitting the editors to the floor. Sedgwick was willing to let the scribblers sit in a little space "within the window frames," as they had done in Philadelphia; if they did not like the acoustics there, they would have to sit in the public gallery, where they could hear even less. In any case, Sedgwick opposed the Republican editor's plans for printing all the actions of the House in his Jacobin sheet.

As he spoke, Sedgwick looked down from the Speaker's chair as did King George from his throne. He was a living example of the supercilious High Federalist who scorned the people as rabble, the Republicans as Jacobins, and editors generally as a pack of penny-a-line scandalmongers. The Republican members of Congress despised him, and even a few of the Federalists were embarrassed by his petty tyranny.

A Federalist-dominated House committee brought in a motion for the "virtual exclusion" of the newspapermen from the floor. There was a 45–45 deadlock, and Sedgwick broke the tie and carried the motion to accept the report. Editor Smith opened fire on him with both barrels in *The National Intelligencer* of December 19.

A "communication to the editor," which may well have been written by the editor himself, said the House vote against the "stenographers" must be "deprecated by every friend to a diffusion of correct information among the people, and every sincere friend to our republican government." Accusing the Speaker of having broken the House rules "over and over again" by his speeches in debate, the letter raised "the great question whether, in a republican government, those who make laws for the people have a right to conceal from the people the ground on which those laws are made."

"I affirm they have not, and if they exercise such a power it is usurped and not legitimate," the writer declared.

Men wishing to "retreat from public scrutiny" altogether would pursue the very plan that has been followed, he wrote. They would "strive to render the situation of a stenographer so unpleasant as to disgust him with the ineffectual attempt to discharge his duty, hoping in that way to get rid of him." Then, after placing him where he could not hear distinctly, they could "cry down his reports" as inaccurate; they could ultimately bar everybody from hearing the debates and "bid defiance to popular discontent."

The fiery idealist, Samuel H. Smith, soon found out how the Speaker felt about such attacks. When the editor took his place outside the "bar" of the House on Monday, January 12, the sergeant-at-arms brought him a message from the Speaker, which could be summarized in two short words: Get out!

Samuel interpreted this to mean he must leave that part of the chamber only; so he retired to the upper gallery, which was open to the general public. From that place, he announced in his next issue, he would "continue to report the proceedings and debates of the House." He vowed he would not "cease publishing a record of truth, whatever or whomsoever it may affect," and he would maintain "a spirit of dignity and moderation that the frowns of power can never dismay."

More "frowns of power" quickly ensued. On Thursday, January 15, when Samuel took a seat in the public gallery and "was in the act of noting the proceedings of the House," the sergeant-at-arms accosted him again and delivered another message from the Speaker: He must "withdraw from the gallery" and get out of the House.

Samuel had no choice but to obey; but he declared in his paper, "The times are changing, but the Editor remains the same.... Unshaken in his regard to truth, which shall still be spoken 'whatever or whomsoever it may affect,' " he promised he would still print the debates of the House, "without excepting the proceedings and debates of the Speaker."

The next morning, Friday, January 16, the undaunted editor bearded the lion in his den.

Smith called on the Speaker at Sedgwick's lodgings in the Peacock boardinghouse on Capitol Hill, for a man-to-man showdown on the issue of freedom of the press. It turned into a remarkable verbal fencing match between the twenty-eight-year-old editor, usually a mild and amiable fellow, and the domineering politician twice his age. The atmosphere must have been as chilly as the wintry morning.

Smith went straight to the point. He wanted to know the "precise extent" of the Speaker's order to get out of the public gallery. Did the order apply to that day only, or "the whole of the session" of Congress?

"Undoubtedly, to the whole of the session," Sedgwick snapped.

"I would then ask, whether the prohibition applies to me in the character of taking the debates and proceedings of the House; or whether it applies to me in the character of a citizen of the United States?"

"I will inform you of the grounds of my order," Sedgwick replied. "I can have no doubt that either through incompetency, or intentionally, you grossly misrepresented my conduct as well as that of the House."

"With respect to intentional misrepresentation, no such charge can be maintained," Samuel said. "With respect to incompetency, I shall be altogether silent, trusting without fear to the decision of others."

"It must be evident to you," Sedgwick went on, "that ever since I have held the office of Speaker, a certain description of men have done everything in their power, by misrepresentation and abuse, to throw me into contempt, and to disgrace the government."

"In reporting the proceedings and debates of the House, I have invariably stated the truth," Samuel insisted.

Sedgwick sniffed: "In my opinion, your conduct, ever since you have been on the floor, has had no other object than to disgrace me and the government."

Samuel held his temper and only with a great effort was icily polite. "These remarks appear altogether improper to be made by the Speaker," he said. "If such remarks are repeated, I may be drawn into the expression of opinions that may give offense." As Sedgwick simmered down, Samuel continued: "Returning to the question I submitted: I wish to know whether, as a citizen, I am excluded?"

"The object of the order was to prevent you from giving any further statements of the proceedings of the House."

"In all events, I shall continue to publish a statement of the debates and proceedings of the House."

"If that be your object, you *cannot* be admitted."

"I do not say that will be the *object* of my personal attendance. Anything which shall be done by the editor out of the gallery is a distinct thing."

"If the attendance be with any view to give the public the proceedings of the House, you must consider yourself absolutely excluded."

Well, then, Samuel persisted, "may I have access to the clerk's office, and obtain copies of official papers?"

"I have no objection to your obtaining copies of those papers that are proper to be published. But it would be wrong to publish papers that relate to transactions in an incipient state. For instance, a member may make a motion that refers to a particular subject. To publish it in this immature state might produce misconceptions and might essentially injure the respect of the people for the government. Such papers ought not to be published. But in cases in which the House has come to a decision, you may publish what is decided upon."

"Mr. Speaker," the editor said, "my ideas are so completely at war with those you have expressed, that I can entertain no expectation of coming into a harmonious correspondence in sentiment. I have always believed, and do still believe, that the only respect which the government of a republican country ought to receive, is that which flows from a knowledge of its acts and of the manner in which those acts are passed."

"I find that you do not understand me any better than you did before," Sedgwick answered. "I think I have explained myself clearly. There are some papers whose publication can do no manner of harm. With respect to those of national importance, until they are decided upon by the House, they ought not to be published."

"I confess, Mr. Speaker," Samuel sighed, "that to my mind the line as drawn by you is still vague. I do not understand it."

"I have drawn the line as clearly as I can," the Speaker retorted. "I have no objection to your obtaining such papers as the Clerk pleases to let you have."

"May I, then, without violating your rule, publish such papers as the Clerk permits me to copy?"

"You may."

That ended the interview, but it did not end Samuel's running battle with the Speaker. In *The National Intelligencer* the editor fired another fusillade at his favorite target:

"On one day," he charged, "the Speaker three times misapplied the rules, and declared those to be rules which had no existence. In two of those cases, confounded by an exposure of his partiality, he acknowledged his error. *But mark the consequence!* He drove from the lobby and afterwards from the gallery the man who, knowing no duty superior to that of the truth, dared to publish, without even a comment, the unquestioned blunders of the chair."

Sedgwick's actions against the editor of *The National Intelligencer,* the editor declared, "are so atrociously hostile to every principle of truth or respect for the rights of the citizen, and betray a mind so weak, and a temper so inflammable, that justice forbids a suppression of them."

The angry interview at Sedgwick's lodgings "established, beyond the reach of palliation, every preconceived conviction of incompetency," Samuel blazed away. "Never, perhaps did any official agent so completely unmask principles, equally indefensible, and ideas equally puerile."

Then Samuel printed the whole story of the argument at Peacock's boardinghouse, blow by blow. He said "there no longer remained a doubt that the Speaker had assumed powers which he did not of right possess, and that a citizen had been deprived of rights which he did possess"—that is, Samuel had been arbitrarily barred from his right, as a citizen, to occupy a seat in the public gallery of the House.

Samuel had "no regret but for the folly of the Speaker." "Several of his own political friends have assured me that none can despise him more cordially than they do," he wrote to his brother John, in Philadelphia. "Several have had honor enough to declare my statements to have been correct. But at the same time they say he is Speaker and must be supported."

Incensed by the Speaker's "tyranny," some of the more excitable Republicans favored striking back at once, possibly with a motion of censure. But cooler leaders of the party observed that there was already one crisis over the presidential election; and a party battle with the Speaker might drive some of the more moderate Federalists away from any hope of helping to elect Jefferson. These "individuals recommend a temporary forbearance as likely, on the ground of conciliation, to favor the election of Mr. Jefferson," Samuel informed his brother. "On this ground I have declared myself ready to waive all personal considerations, and disposed rather to submit to a present evil in relation to myself, than to hazard the great interests of the country. At all events, my deportment will be moderate and firm. Nor need you be under the least apprehension of the issue being favorable."

So, to help Jefferson in the crucial battle for the presidency, Editor Smith laid aside his own personal quarrel for the moment and submerged it into the greater cause. Surely, this was no time to stir up a partisan row, when some Federalist votes would be needed to keep Burr out of the presidency, and Jefferson's managers still did not have enough to win.

*   *   *   *   *

Albert Gallatin, the Republican floor leader in the House, took command of Jefferson's forces and tried to form a solid front of all Republican congressmen against the temptations of the insidious men who were urging them to cast a few courtesy votes for Jefferson and then break the deadlock by coming over to Burr. Gallatin arrived late from his district in the western Pennsylvania mountains, and it was not until January 15 that he informed his wife that he had reached Washington. He doubled up with Congressman Joseph B. Varnum, of Massachusetts, at Conrad and McMunn's, paying fifteen dollars a week for rent, "wood, candles, and liquors." The Republican politicians filling the boardinghouse talked constantly of the election crisis, and very little else. "A few, indeed, drink, and some gamble," Gallatin commented, "but the majority drink naught but politics."

282

Of course, the floor leader conferred often with the star boarder, Thomas Jefferson, about their strategy. They agreed that "the Feds" would try to do three things: First, to "elect Mr. B."; second, if that failed, "to defeat the present election and order a new one"; third, to "assume executive power" by an act of the Federalist majority in Congress.

"The first may be defeated by our own firmness," Gallatin advised. If the eight states pledged to Jefferson would stand firm, Burr could never get more than eight states, either. True, that might mean that no one would be elected President, and then the Federalists would attempt to "usurp" power by handing the presidential powers to someone of their own party. The Republicans should first seek to block such a bill on the floor and, if outvoted, they should try to persuade President Adams to veto it on the grounds that "Mr. A. can gain nothing by it."

Certainly, the High Federalist leaders of Congress would not try to keep Adams in the White House beyond March 4; they had worked closely with Hamilton in the campaign to put him out. They had at least achieved that part of their objective, though they had failed in the larger aim of electing General Pinckney in his place. Now, neither the Republicans nor the Federalists looked to the lame duck President for leadership or even for advice. "I find him infinitely sunk in the estimation of all parties," Madison informed Jefferson. "The follies of his administration," plus Hamilton's pamphlet, had combined to "overthrow" Adams, "staggering . . . in the public esteem."

Nevertheless, Adams might perform one more service by vetoing a Federalist bill to install a temporary President in case of a continued deadlock in the House balloting, and Jefferson called upon his defeated rival in hopes of obtaining a promise of a veto. Adams greeted him with a blast: "You have turned me out! You have turned me out!"

"I have not turned you out, Mr. Adams," Jefferson replied in his mildest manner, as a father would soothe an angry child. "The late contest was not one of a personal character, between John Adams and Thomas Jefferson, but between the advocates and opponents of certain political opinions and measures and, therefore, should produce no unkind feelings between the two men who happened to be placed at the head of the two parties."

As the presidential temper cooled, the Vice-President brought up the Federalists' "very dangerous experiment" of deadlocking the election in the House and declaring the right of the Senate to name an acting President. "Such a measure would probably produce resistance by force," Jefferson said, painting the horrors of possible civil war, and Adams could prevent such a tragedy by vetoing the bill.

Adams, however, did not agree; he thought such an act "justifiable." As he confided to Elbridge Gerry a few days later, "I know no more danger of a political convulsion, if a President pro tempore or a Secretary of State, or Speaker of the House, should be made President by Congress, than if Mr. Jefferson or Mr. Burr is declared such. The President would be as legal in one case as either of the others, in my opinion, and the people as well satisfied."

Jefferson gloomily concluded that the Federalists would go forward with their plans to "devolve the government" upon one of their own men, until the new Republican Congress could meet next December, which would give them "another year's preponderance and the chances of future events," in a run-off election.

But Gallatin would not think of giving in to the Federalists. "We must consider the election as completed, and under no possible circumstance consent to a new election," he asserted. "I think it a miserable policy, and calculated to break for a length of time the Republican spirit, should we at present yield one inch of ground to the Federal faction, when we are supported by the Constitution and by the people."

Governor Thomas McKean, of Pennsylvania, a red-hot Republican, expected that "envy, malice, despair and a delight of doing mischief will prompt the Anglo-Federalists to keep the states equally divided so that Congress may, in the form of a law, appoint a President for us until a new election shall take place." To prevent that, he advised Jefferson, the two Republican nominees should "agree between themselves . . . in writing" that either Jefferson or Burr would become President, the other Vice-President, and dare the Federalists to "destroy or embarrass our general government."

James Madison also advised his Monticello neighbor not to submit to any "usurpation." He, too, said that Jefferson and Burr should jointly summon the new Republican Congress in special session to settle the issue. Jefferson agreed that "a concert between the two higher candidates" might prevent "anarchy, by an operation bungling indeed and imperfect, but better than letting the legislature take the nomination of the Executive entirely from the people."

Would Burr cooperate in a gentlemen's agreement which almost inevitably would mean the election of Jefferson, instead of himself?

Gallatin, upon arriving in Washington, thought Burr had *"sincerely* opposed" the Federalists' "design" for his election, and would "go *any lengths* to prevent its execution." But General Smith, a fellow-boarder at Conrad and McMunn's, could inform him of Burr's refusal at Philadelphia to say he would spurn the presidency or resign if elected so that Jefferson could have his rightful prize. Thereafter the floor leader made no more confident assertions in the good faith of the Colonel, who declined to say the words which could stop the entire project in its tracks. Burr pretended to be all wrapped up in his work as a member of the legislature, and in preparing for the wedding of his daughter, Theodosia, to the rich young South Carolinian, Joseph Alston.

Hamilton's friend, Robert Troup, spread the rumor that "the marriage was an affair of Burr, and not of his daughter, and that the money in question was the predominating motive." Maria Nicholson informed her sister, Mrs. Gallatin, on the eve of the wedding: "As I know you are interested for Theodosia Burr, I must tell you that Mr. Alston has returned from Carolina, it is said, to be married to her this month. She accompanied her father to Albany, where the legislature are sitting; he followed them the next day. I am sorry to hear these accounts. Report does not speak well of him; it says that he is rich, but he is a great dasher, dissipated, ill-tempered, vain and silly. I know that he is ugly and of unprepossessing manners. Can it be that the father has sacrificed a daughter so lovely to affluence and influential connections? They say that it was Mr. A. who gained him the 8 votes in Carolina at the present election, and that he is not yet relieved from pecuniary embarrassments."

While Burr busied himself with his private affairs and would not come to Washington to help block the Federalists' schemes, a young man from New York, named Montfort, *did* arrive in the capital late in January, representing himself as an intimate of Burr. Montfort went to Conrad and McMunn's and urged many of the Republican congressmen there to switch from Jefferson to Burr. Montfort said he had lived in Burr's house, studied law under him, and had recently published a series of newspaper articles in the New York *Gazette,* advocating Burr's election—essays written "under the eye" of Aaron Burr. The young man also claimed that Burr had seen a letter, in Jefferson's own handwriting, which cast aspersions on the Colonel's character.

Well aware that such tales might encourage some wavering Republicans to vote for Burr as an injured martyr, Jefferson hastened to reassure his esteemed running mate that the alleged letter was a forgery, no doubt concocted by some scheming Federalist. "It was to be expected," Jefferson wrote Burr, "that the enemy would endeavor to sow tares between us that they might divide us and our friends. Every consideration satisfies me you will be on your guard against this, as I assure you I am strongly. I hear of one strategem so imposing and so base that it is proper I should notice it to you. Mr. Munford [*sic*], who is here, says he saw at New York before he left it, an original letter of mine to Judge Breckenridge, in which are sentiments highly injurious to you. He knows my handwriting, and did not doubt that to be genuine.

"I enclose you a copy taken from the press copy of the only letter I ever wrote to Judge Breckenridge in my life. . . . Of consequence, the letter seen by Mr. Munford must be a forgery, and if it contains a sentiment unfriendly or disrespectful to you, I affirm it solemnly to be a forgery. A mutual knowledge of each other furnishes us with the best test of the contrivances which will be practised by the enemies of both."

Burr replied, smoothly: "It was so obvious that the most malignant spirit of slander and intrigue would be busy that, without any inquiry, I set down as calumny every tale calculated to disturb our harmony.

"My friends are often more irritable and credulous; fortunately I am the depositary of all their cares and anxieties; and I invariably pronounce to be a lie, every thing which ought not to be true. My former letter should have assured you of all this by anticipation.

"Montfort never told me what you relate and if he had, it would have made no impression on me. Your solicitude in this occasion, though groundless, is friendly and obliging."

To Gallatin, Burr defended himself for sponsoring Montfort and swore he knew nothing of the young man's electioneering for him: "Mr. Montfort was strongly recommended to me by General Gates and Colonel Griffin. At their request I undertook to direct his studies in the pursuit of the law. He left New York suddenly and apparently in some agitation, without assigning to me any cause and without disclosing to me his intentions or views, or even whither he was going, except that he proposed to pass through Washington. Nor had I any reason to believe that I should ever see him again. You may communicate this to Mr. J., who has also written me something about him."

Montfort was not the only youthful disciple loudly calling for the election of Burr as President. Another, according to Burr's enemy James Cheetham, was Matthew L. Davis, who had lobbied successfully with Gallatin in May for his chief's nomination for Vice-President. Cheetham wrote that Davis, "a young man . . . so remarkable for his chattering that it has always appeared strange that Mr. Burr should trust him with his secrets . . . flew about the streets like a shuttlecock thrown from the hands of his master, declaring that after the first or second vote in the House of Representatives the Republicans ought to give up Mr. Jefferson and join the Federalists to support Mr. Burr."

William Van Ness, one of Burr's shrewdest and closest advisers, went to Albany with him for the legislature and wrote to Congressman Edward Livingston in Washington that it was "the sense of the Republican party of this state that after some trials in the House, Mr. Jefferson should be given up for Mr. Burr." Robert Troup considered Livingston was "doubtless one of Burr's confidential agents to manoeuvre him into the presidency." Hamilton expected Livingston to cast his first vote for Jefferson, his second for Burr.

If Livingston and Congressman Theodorus Bailey switched from Jefferson to Burr, they would change New York's delegation from six to four for Jefferson to six to four for Burr; and the Federalists expected two other congressmen from Vermont, Maryland, Tennessee or New Jersey also to swing over and thus give Burr the required nine states and the presidency. It was no wonder, then, that in late January, Jefferson and his lieutenants were gravely concerned about the result of the voting that would begin in the House on February 11.

While Jefferson's friends in the New York delegation worried about Livingston and Bailey, those in New Jersey wondered about Dr. James Linn. The New Jersey delegation would go three to two for Jefferson or three to two for Burr, depending upon which way the doctor would vote. George Jackson, a Virginia congressman, called Linn "a very suspicious character," and said "both parties have been jealous of his vote."

Obviously, bold moves must be made—possibly coupled with threats of punishments and promises of rewards for good behavior—to hold the wavering Republicans in an unbroken line, so that no one would merely cast a few face-saving courtesy votes for Jefferson and then hop over on the next ballot to help elect Burr.

On Saturday night, January 31, the Republican congressmen from New York and New Jersey had an important caucus. Its announced purpose was to pledge every member to stay with Jefferson on every ballot until the bitter end. After the caucus, Congressman Jackson reported cheerfully to James Madison that "the business is now fixt"—New York and New Jersey would vote for Jefferson without a change. This, Jackson said, assured that Burr, with his six Federalist states, could not pick up these additional two. The only three left, which could give him the nine-state majority, were Maryland, Vermont, and Tennessee.

Jackson did not disclose the methods that whipped the vacillating New York and New Jersey men into line. Others later thought they saw a clue when Edward Livingston became district attorney for New York; his brother, Chancellor Robert Livingston, became minister to France.

Congressman Bailey became postmaster of New York City; and the "very suspicious" Dr. Linn received a federal post as a supervisor of the revenue.

There is one other plausible explanation for Edward Livingston's pro-Jefferson vote. Robert Troup learned "the Chancellor wrote a very peremptory letter to his brother Edward on the subject of an alarm which Hamilton gave the Chancellor for the purpose"— apparently, the report that Edward would cast his first vote for Jefferson, his second for Burr. "Pains were also taken to inform Jefferson of the plots and manoeuvres against him, and hence it is concluded that there is, and can be, no cordiality" between Jefferson and Burr, Troup said.

Burr's supporters kept up their pressure for votes in New York and New Jersey as the day of the balloting neared; they continued maneuvering to swing Representative William C. C. Claiborne, who held the lone vote of Tennessee, and they worked to crack the one-one tie in Vermont and the four-four tie in Maryland. Vermont's Representative Matthew Lyon was pledged to Jefferson; while Representative George Dent was the nominal Federalist who had gone over to Jefferson and changed the Maryland delegation from five to three for Burr to a deadlock. Naturally, the Burr adherents tried hard to convert the "Spitting" Lyon and to pull Dent back into the Federalist camp.

A few days before the voting began, three of Jefferson's backers in the Maryland delegation—Dent, General Smith, and Gabriel Christie—met in a boardinghouse room and pledged themselves to stand with Jefferson. Dent said "perhaps it might be necessary for all the friends of Mr. Jefferson's election to pledge themselves to stick together and never to give him up for any other man whatever," and they "solemnly agreed to give no vote but what should make Mr. Jefferson President, believing that he was the voice of the people of the United States."

Jefferson's fourth supporter in the Maryland delegation, Joseph

Nicholson, fell ill and might not be able to vote. If so, the tie would be broken and Burr would gain Maryland by a four-three margin. So, on the very eve of the voting February 11, no one could be sure of the result.

If the House should deadlock, and elect neither man, then Jefferson expected the Federalists would try to name someone else as an interim president—possibly John Marshall or John Jay. In the case of such an outrageous "usurpation," Jefferson's lieutenants notified Republican Governors McKean, of Pennsylvania, and Monroe, of Virginia, to have militia ready to march on Washington "for the purpose, not of promoting, but of preventing, revolution and the shedding of a single drop of blood." Gallatin advised Republican states to refuse to obey the acts of a "usurper President." They should ignore any call for militia to support him, declaring their intention to "have the usurper punished according to law as soon as regular government shall have been re-established."

Jefferson told Monroe, "We thought it best to declare openly and firmly, one & all, that the day such an act passed, the Middle States would arm, & that no such usurpation, even for a single day, should be submitted to." Furthermore, Jefferson advised, the Republicans were determined not only to resist the "usurpation by arms" but to set aside the Constitution and call "a convention to reorganize and amend" the government—presumably along more "democratic" lines which would surely strike terror into the hearts of the conservative Federalists. "The very word 'convention' gives them the horrors," he added.

Congressman Jackson, of Virginia, warned the Federalists, "Take care of your banks and paper currency. . . . If you will not give us Jefferson for President, . . . suffer an interregnum to take place and see if your small states will ever get so much power in your hands again."

Between Washington and Richmond, a chain of express riders carried messages day and night to keep the Virginians fully informed of events in the capital. Similar messengers raced back and forth between Washington and the capitals of other states where Republicans were threatening to arm against the reported "usurpation."

There were angry mutterings that if any man became acting President by act of Congress, he would be assassinated.

"Pennsy. has her courier here & the report is that she has 22 thousand prepared to take up arms in the event of extremities," John Tyler told Governor Monroe in a bulletin rushed by express riders from Washington to Richmond. Representative John Dawson advised Monroe to "be prepared to meet any emergency," even civil war.

General E. Meade of the Virginia militia begged the governor to call him to fight the Federalists. "The infernals have at last unmasked their batteries against virtue and republicanism," the hot-blooded general declared. "Nothing but an appeal to arms will do. ... I will go whenever there is a call for men. ... I wish for the opportunity of sacrificing the Devils and sending them to Moloch, their King."

Republican threats of marching troops did not frighten the High Federalists. The Boston *Centinel,* openly advocating the election of Burr, said Federalists did not fear fighters from the South and West. "Our General (Burr), if called upon, can assure them that he has seen Southern regiments in former times and knows what they are composed of."

To the Jeffersonians, the *Centinel* offered this advice in rhyme:

> Stop ere your civic feasts begin;
> Wait till the votes are all come in;
> Perchance amidst this mighty stir
> Your monarch may be Colonel Burr.

The *Washington Federalist* sneered at the "bold and impetuous partisans of Mr. Jefferson" who, it said, were threatening Congress: "Dare to place in the presidential chair any other than the philosopher of Monticello and ten thousand republican swords will instantly leap from their scabbards in defense of the violated rights of the people!"

"Can our countrymen be caught by so flimsy a pretext?" the Federalist paper asked. "Are they ripe for civil war?

"If the tumultuous meetings of a set of factious foreigners in Pennsylvania or a few fighting bacchanals of Virginia mean the people, and are to dictate to the Congress of the United States whom to elect as President—if the constitutional rights of this body are so soon to become the prey of anarchy and faction—it would be prudent to prepare for the contest.

"With the militia of Massachusetts consisting of 70,000 in arms—with those of New Hampshire and Connecticut united almost to a man, with half the number at least of the citizens of eleven other States ranged under the Federal banner in support of the Constitution, what could Pennsylvania, aided by Virginia—the militia of the latter untrained and farcically performing the manual exercise with *corn-stalks* instead of muskets—what would be the issue of the struggle?"

The New York *Commercial Advertiser* predicted that Burr would be elected President on the second ballot.

The Washington *National Intelligencer* announced that Jefferson had already been elected president—that is, president of the American Philosophical Society in Philadelphia, for another term. "However faithfully or capriciously, therefore, the genius of Liberty may act," commented Editor Samuel H. Smith, "You see that Science and Philosophy have not deserted him."

Jefferson expressed his "grateful thanks for the honor" which he valued among "the most precious testimonies" of his life, and promised always to be "a faithful and zealous associate of the institution." Four years before he had said he preferred this honor to the presidency of the United States. He did not repeat that claim, for this time he wanted more than a consolation prize; he wanted to win.

On February 10 the House of Representatives adopted a motion by Representative James A. Bayard, of Delaware, to stay in continuous session until it had elected a President. "We have this day locked ourselves up by a rule to proceed to choose a president before we adjourn," Federalist Congressman William Cooper, of Cooperstown, N.Y., informed a friend. "We shall run Burr perseveringly.... *A little good management would have secured our object on the first vote,* but now it is too late for any operations to be gone into, except that of adhering to Burr, and leave the consequences to those who have *heretofore* been his friends. If we succeed, a faithful support must, on our part, be given to his administration, which, I hope, will be wise and energetic."

"We are to be shut up for God knows how long," Federalist Congressman Harrison Gray Otis, of Massachusetts, informed his wife. "Our committee room must be garnished with beefsteaks, and a few Turkey carpets to lie upon would not be amiss. . . . We shall, however, have the use of pen, ink and paper, which is more than all prisoners enjoy."

"Tomorrow we proceed to ballot for President under a resolution not to adjourn till an election be made," Bayard wrote to his father-in-law, Governor Bassett. "But we are not to be without meat and drink, fire and candles. It is extremely doubtful how long we shall be kept together. It is certain that no election will be made upon the first ballot. But the course which will afterwards be taken is not easy to be foreseen. Perhaps no one has been more in the secret of the whole business than myself, but I believe no one person is acquainted with all the transactions which have attended it. You will consider also it is a subject upon which, at present, it would not be safe to write by Post or even to write at all."

In New York City, Jefferson's old enemy, Alexander Hamilton, who had lately emerged in the surprising role of friend, had written the last of his urgent letters begging the Federalists not to elect the "Catiline," Burr. He believed he had failed, that "his influence with the Federal party was wholly gone." His lieutenant, Robert Troup, ventured this eleventh-hour forecast of the voting in the House: "The general opinion here is that Burr will ultimately be chosen. Upon the first ballot it is thought Jefferson will have all the democratical states, but as they are not sufficient to elect him, the conjecture is that a second ballot will be taken and that some of the Demos. will come over to vote for Burr, to prevent the election falling through. . . . Hamilton is profoundly chagrined with this prospect! He has taken infinite pains to defeat Burr's election, but he believes in vain. . . . All the leading Demos. are cut to the quick with the idea of Burr's being President."

* * * * *

The night before the crucial vote, the capital in the woods presented a scene of chaos. Its taverns and boardinghouses were jammed with men who slept—when they slept at all—in any bed they could find, usually two or three to a bed or on the dining tables and even on the floors. Until late at night, the quarreling bands of Republicans and Federalists argued and schemed and relayed wild rumors: Burr would win on the second ballot, for his secret allies among the Republicans would switch from Jefferson; Jefferson would have eight states on the first test and gain the ninth when Bayard would come over from Burr; there would be a deadlock, and the Federalist majority in Congress would appoint Marshall or Jay; no, they would not dare, for the "usurper" would be assassinated; and troops would march in from Virginia, Maryland, and Pennsylvania, to install the rightful Republican President even at the risk of a civil war with the militia of New England.

It was a night of feverish tallying and re-tallying of votes among the Federalist congressmen clustered in Stelle's hotel and in Peacock's boardinghouse on Capitol Hill, and among the Republicans who gathered about Jefferson at Conrad and McMunn's. It is unlikely that anyone slept very much that night, either, at the near-by home of Samuel and Margaret Bayard Smith.

Vice-President Jefferson was not the only distinctive personage drawing attention at Conrad and McMunn's. For fifty cents (children half price), the visitors could take time off from their politicking to gape at the marvelous sight of a "learned pig." Editor Smith's *National Intelligencer* said, in an advertisement:

"The sagacity of this PIG is equal, if not superior, to any animal ever exhibited in this country; the Proprietor will therefore avoid a puffing advertisement and only state what the PIG actually performs, as follows:

"He reads printing or writing, spells, tells the time of day, both the hours and minutes, by any person's watch in the company, the

294

date of the year, the day of the month, distinguishes colours, how many persons there are present, ladies or gentlemen, and, to the astonishment of every spectator, will add, subtract, multiply, and divide.

"To conclude, any person may draw a card from a pack, and keep it concealed, and the Pig, without hesitation, will discover it."

In short, the Learned Pig could do almost anything except predict whether Jefferson or Burr would be the next President.

The amazed spectators at Conrad and McMunn's would have to wait for the House of Representatives to solve that mystery; and they would not have to wait much longer.

CHAPTER THIRTEEN

WEDNESDAY, FEBRUARY 11, 1801:

On the day set by law for Congress to count the presidential electoral votes, a snowstorm whirled across Washington, covering the crude little capital with a blanket of pure, shining white. Snowflakes drifted over the shores of the Potomac and the Anacostia, over the neat brick homes of Georgetown, over the taverns, boardinghouses and shops of Capitol Hill, over the *National Intelligencer* office and the home of Samuel and Margaret Bayard Smith. Snow sifted through the trees that covered the Hill, making even the unfinished wing of the Capitol resemble a classic temple, white against the slate-gray sky.

Senators, representatives, and a crowd of spectators trudged through the snowdrifts to the Capitol. Affecting a calm which he probably did not feel, Jefferson solemnly presided over the joint session of Congress and opened the electors' certificates. The tellers —William H. Wells, of Delaware, for the Senate and John Rutledge, Jr., of South Carolina, and John Nicholas, of Virginia, for the House—announced the result which surprised no one: For Jefferson, 73; for Burr, 73; for John Adams, 65; for Charles Cotesworth Pinckney, 64; for John Jay, 1. Jefferson then declared that, as the electors had failed to choose a President, the decision devolved upon the House. The representatives arose and marched back to their own chamber to vote.

Amid much grumbling from the spectators, Speaker Sedgwick ordered the galleries completely cleared. Samuel Harrison Smith had to get out along with everyone else. Editor Smith retired to his newspaper office on New Jersey Avenue, and his friends arranged for a messenger to plod through the snow and bring him a bulletin on the result of every ballot.

The members of each state delegation sat together, for they would vote as a unit, each state having the same vote—one. The tellers, also allocated at the rate of one per state, included several men holding decisive ballots in their hands: James A. Bayard, the lone member from Delaware; William Charles Cole Claiborne, the only man from Tennessee; Benjamin Taliaferro, who, although technically a Federalist, would cast Georgia's vote for Jefferson. Also among the tellers were several doubtful members, Theodorus Bailey, Burr's friend from New York state; "Jemmy" Linn, the wavering one from New Jersey; Lewis R. Morris, of Vermont; and George Dent, of Maryland.

Rhode Island's teller was Christopher Champlin, who had fought the duel with Bayard; Pennsylvania's was Albert Gallatin, the Republican floor leader, making sure his party's lines held firm; South Carolina's was Thomas Pinckney, the High Federalists' candidate for President four years before, now cheerfully filling a minor role as a member of the House.

In each delegation, the members cast a slip of paper into the teller's box, and on the paper was written a single word: "Jefferson" or "Burr." Whoever received a majority of the ballots in the box would win the vote of the state.

In a little anteroom off the House chamber lay Representative Joseph H. Nicholson, of Maryland, his face burning with fever, his wife beside him to give him medicine and water. He had risen from a sickbed and insisted upon going through the snow to vote for Jefferson, for he knew his vote could be decisive. With it, the Maryland delegation would be tied, 4–4; without it, the state would go to Burr, 4–3. Even the Federalists could not begrudge Nicholson the credit for his fortitude. "It is a chance that this kills him," commented Massachusetts' Representative Harrison Gray Otis. "I would not thus expose myself for any President on earth."

General Thomas Sumter, of South Carolina, stayed away because of illness, but this did not affect the result, since the other five men in his delegation were all for Burr. Representative James Jones, of Georgia, had recently died. So of the 106 House seats, 104 were filled.

On the first ballot, Jefferson had an actual majority of the 104 members, 55 to 49; but that did not matter; only a majority of *states* would count. Speaker Sedgwick announced the result of the first tally:

"The tellers report, and the boxes agree, that eight states have voted for Thomas Jefferson, six states for Aaron Burr, and two states are divided."

Jefferson had New York, New Jersey, Pennsylvania, Virginia, North Carolina, Kentucky, Georgia and Tennessee.

Burr had New Hampshire, Massachusetts, Rhode Island, Connecticut, Delaware and South Carolina.

Maryland and Vermont were deadlocked.

Thus, neither Jefferson nor Burr had won the required nine states, and Speaker Sedgwick called for a second ballot. This was the one on which, according to many rumors, some Republicans might switch from Jefferson to Burr. Representative Henry Lee, a Virginia Federalist, said he was sure that "before the balloting ended, Burr would get the Maryland vote," and the Republican leaders were worried about New Jersey, New York, Vermont, and Tennessee. Hearing Lee's confident predictions, Representative Gabriel Christie, of Maryland, went into the anteroom where Representative Nicholson lay on his bed. Had Nicholson any idea of giving up? The sick man replied that "whoever counted upon that would be disappointed, for he believed Maryland would stick to their first vote as long as any state in the union."

Again, the congressmen wrote "Jefferson" and "Burr" on the slips of paper. Again, the ballots were dropped into the tellers' boxes. Again the Speaker announced: "The tellers report, and the boxes agree, that eight states have voted for Thomas Jefferson, six states for Aaron Burr, and two states are divided."

A third ballot began at once, then a fourth, fifth, sixth, seventh and eighth, without a change. On each ballot, members flocked

298

around the New York box, expecting to see "the secession of that state from Jefferson," but each time New York cast six votes for Jefferson and four for Burr. On each ballot, also, Representative Dent, the Maryland teller, entered the anteroom where Nicholson lay with his head resting on the arm of his wife. She placed a pencil in his fingers and helped him write one word, "Jefferson."

At the end of every ballot, a messenger fought his way through the snow from the Capitol halfway down the hill to the printing shop on New Jersey Avenue, where Editor Smith had his press all set to announce the news of the election. In mid-afternoon, the press began to print *The National Intelligencer* with this front-page headline:

ELECTION OF A PRESIDENT

Smith reported the 73–73 tie between Jefferson and Burr in the joint session, the 8–6–2 deadlock on the first several ballots, and added: "This was the state of the election at 3 o'clock when the National Intelligencer was put to press. Of consequence, at that hour, there had been no election. The House was still in session."

At 4:30 in the afternoon, Representative John Randolph, of Roanoke, scribbled a note to his stepfather, St. George Tucker, giving the result of the seventh and eighth ballots: "Eight states for J.— six for B.—two, Maryland and Vermont, divided. . . . The order against adjourning, made with a view to Mr. Nicholson, who was ill, has not operated. He left his sick bed, came through a snowstorm, brought his bed, and has prevented the vote of Maryland from being given to Burr."

Outside, the snow continued to drift down upon the capital. The early twilight of winter darkened the sky, and then night fell. Still there was no break in the deadlock. Candles were brought into the cold, drafty House chamber, and blankets and pillows were carried in as it seemed certain the members would be there the rest of the night. After the eighteenth ballot, at eleven P.M., a motion was made to adjourn until Thursday, but this was voted down. The nineteenth ballot came at midnight—with no change.

Representative James A. Bayard, of Delaware, the Federalists' floor leader, scrawled this note to his father-in-law, Governor Richard Bassett:

> Washington 12 Feby 1801
> Chamber of the Representatives
> ½ past 12. night.

My dear sir,

We are now engaged in balloting for President. 19 times the ballot has been repeated & produced the same result—8 votes for Jefferson, 6 for Burr, and 2 divided. We do not know how or when the business will end....

Excuse my brevity at this moment.

> J. A. B.

Then a note to his cousin and adopted brother, Andrew Bayard, the Philadelphia merchant:

> Washington 12 Feby 1801

My dear Andrew,

We have been engaged the greater part of the day balloting for President. Nineteen times the votes have been given in and the result the same: 8 for Jefferson, 6 for Burr, and two divided. There is a resolution of the House not to adjourn till an election is made. As to what is to happen we are all ignorant. I am affectionately yours, JAB.

At one o'clock there was another ballot, and another at two.

At the end of each one, throughout the night, the messenger would wade through the snow down New Jersey Avenue, and knock at the door of Editor Smith. The editor's bride would answer the knock, and every time, she could imagine she heard her heart beat. She was so agitated by the suspense that she could hardly open the door to receive the bulletin. It is easy to imagine that Margaret and Samuel Smith drank plenty of tea that night, and never closed their eyes in sleep.

In the House chamber some of the weary members dozed in their chairs; others sneaked off to committee rooms to snatch a little rest. When a ballot was called, it was "ludicrous to see them running from committee rooms with night caps on." On into the small hours, the voting droned in the same monotonous way: Jefferson eight, Burr six, and two states tied. Still the lines of both the opposing forces were unbroken.

After the twenty-seventh ballot at eight A.M. showed no sign of a change, the bone-tired representatives agreed to adjourn until eleven A.M. and resume voting at noon. That would give each member three precious hours to sleep and time to eat a decent meal. Representative Samuel W. Dana, a Connecticut Federalist, did not mind the food shortage. Having been unwell, he had tried "abstinence from food for three days," anyway, and considered himself "seasoned tolerably to the present singular situation."

"Perhaps we shall continue here a week," Representative Otis informed his wife. "No conjecture can be formed how it will terminate, but if we are true to ourselves *we* shall prevail." "We" were the Federalists determined to keep Jefferson out of the presidency, whatever the cost.

Jefferson's friends were equally determined. "*We* have resolved never to yield and sooner hazard everything that would prevent the voice and wishes of the people being carried into effect," Representative John Dawson wrote to James Madison on Thursday. "I have not closed my eyes for 36 hours."

"Fear not . . . for our firmness," Representative Littleton W. Tazewell assured Governor Monroe. "We never more adjourn but to proclaim Jefferson the President."

So, at eight o'clock Thursday morning, February 12, the representatives stumbled out of their chamber, to be greeted by some of the senators and other hardy spectators who had stayed like sentinels in the chilly corridors all through the night. "They looked banged badly, as the night was cold & they had the most of them not slept a wink; and those who had were none the better for it, as it was caught in a chair or on the floor in a cloak," observed the High Federalist senator from Connecticut, Uriah Tracy.

The balloting at noon showed the battle lines still holding firm. The House then adjourned until eleven o'clock the next day, Friday, allowing 23 hours for feverish electioneering attempts to pull the decisive votes across the line to either Jefferson or Burr.

The Republican leaders huddled with Jefferson at Conrad and McMunn's, and he made this notation in his diary for February 12:

"Edward Livingston tells me, that Bayard applied today or last night to General Samuel Smith, and represented to him the expediency of his coming over to the states who vote for Burr, that there was nothing in the way of appointment which he might not command, and particularly mentioned the Secretaryship of the Navy.

"Smith asked him if he was authorized to make the offer. He said he was authorized. Smith told this to Livingston and to W. C. Nicholas, who confirms it to me.

"Bayard in like manner tempted Livingston, not by offering any particular office, but by representing to him his, Livingston's, intimacy and connection with Burr; that from him he had everything to expect, if he would come over to him.

"To Doctor Linn of New Jersey, they have offered the government of New Jersey."

Jefferson also noted, with apparent concern, a paragraph in a Baltimore newspaper "stating an intimacy of views" between Burr and Federalist Congressman Robert G. Harper, who had advised Burr to "keep the game in his own hands."

On another page of his diary, Jefferson said Matthew Lyon, of Vermont, had informed him that Federalist Representative John Brown, of Rhode Island, had bid for his vote for Burr, asking: "What is it you want, Colonel Lyon? Is it office, is it money? Only say what you want, and you shall have it."

Jefferson evidently felt sure the Federalists were offering rich rewards to tempt key Republicans away from him. These were the four states concerned:

Maryland: Tied, four-four. A switch of one vote would move it to Burr.

New York: six-four Jefferson. A switch by Livingston and Theodorus Bailey could make it six-four Burr.

New Jersey: three-two Jefferson. If the wavering "Jemmy" Linn could be swung over by promises to make him governor, that state would be three-two for Burr.

302

Vermont: Tied, one-one. If the "Spitting" Lyon would come over for "office" or "money," that state would go to Burr.

A fifth possible swing man was Representative William C. C. Claiborne, the only member from Tennessee.

If any three of the five states mentioned could be moved into Burr's column, his total would become nine, and he would be elected.

Jefferson's diary notations, listing the Republicans reportedly tempted by the friends of Burr, throw light upon Bayard's later declaration: "The means existed of electing Burr. . . . By deceiving one man (a great blockhead), and tempting two (not incorruptible), he might have secured a majority of the states." Just which of these three might be the "great blockhead," and which two were "not incorruptible," Bayard left for posterity to wonder.

William Cooper, one of the four Federalist representatives from New York, reported in disgust on Friday, February 13: "Had Burr done any thing for himself, he would long ere this have been president. If a majority would answer he would have it on every vote." Cooper meant that on some of the ballots, Burr had received an actual majority of members present. Jefferson had led 55–49 on the first ballot, but only because a few Federalists in Virginia and North Carolina had supported him. They wrote Burr's name on their later ballots, sending him into the lead, 53–51. These transfers made no difference since Jefferson already had Virginia and North Carolina by safe margins.

The Federalists' hopes of picking up Maryland by wearing out the feverish Joseph Nicholson came to naught. Instead of giving up and going home, Nicholson stayed to continue voting for Jefferson and actually improved in health. The Republicans then tried to break the Maryland deadlock by pulling a member over from Burr. Representative John Chew Thomas, the Federalist whose district surrounded Washington, received a "flood" of petitions from "the most respectable Federal gentlemen," claiming that two-thirds of his constituents wanted him to vote for Jefferson. However, the petitions had no effect; Thomas stayed with Burr.

Intense pressure also was applied to two other Maryland Federalists holding out for Burr—Representatives George Baer and William

Craik. One angry Republican called Baer "a traitor" for not switching to Jefferson. Another said, "Mr. C's lady . . . will renounce her husband if he does not vote for Mr. J." "The people in Thomas' district are extremely clamorous & have instructed him to vote *right* & a certain Mr. Craig [Craik] is on the totter," a third Republican told Governor Monroe. "Some of the people of Maryland say, if their representatives will not speak their sentiments they will go themselves and make them."

Friday's voting and three more ballots on Saturday proved just as indecisive, so the House postponed further action until Monday. Jefferson was told on Saturday that Senator Gouverneur Morris, the New York Federalist, had inquired: "How comes it that Burr, who is 400 miles off, has agents here at Washington with great activity, while Mr. Jefferson, who is on the spot, does nothing?" Jefferson suspected that Senator Morris and his nephew, the Vermont Federalist congressman, were "holden themselves free for a price, i.e., some office, either to the uncle or nephew."

Actually, Bayard and others working for Burr became frustrated because he would make no pledges to get the extra votes required to win. Bayard passed the word to men in both parties that the deadlock could not go on forever. Either Jefferson or Burr must be elected soon, or the government would have no head on Inauguration Day, March 4, and civil war might follow an attempt to install a temporary President.

Bayard's own state, the smallest of all in population, could not defend itself against such mighty neighbors as Virginia and Pennsylvania, whose Republican governors were threatening to mobilize the militia for a march on Washington. Little Delaware must cling to the Constitution, which assured her very existence.

"I took pains to disclose this state of things in such a manner that it might be known to the friends of Mr. Burr, and to those gentlemen who were believed to be most disposed to change their votes in his favor," Bayard later recorded, in an evident reference to the wavering ones in New York, New Jersey, Maryland, Vermont and Tennessee. "If there were any latent engines at work in Mr. Burr's

304

favor," Bayard said, it was time to put those "engines" into gear and roll out those three extra states.

Despite all the intrigues and maneuvers and whisperings in the corridors, however, no one came forward and gave Bayard any positive plan for clinching Burr's election. Bayard concluded that Burr was "determined to come in as a Democrat, and in that event would have been the most dangerous man in the community."

"He was determined not to shackle himself with Federal principles and it became evident that if he got in without being absolutely committed," Bayard concluded, then Hamilton was right: President Aaron Burr, the "Catiline," the politician bankrupt in principles and in pocketbook, might indeed have seized complete power as an American Bonaparte.

When it was "acknowledged on all hands that Burr was resolved not to commit himself, and nothing remained but to appoint a President by law, or leave the government without one," Bayard said, he determined to throw in his cards and let Jefferson win the game.

But—Bayard asked himself—why submit to unconditional surrender? True, with only six states, Burr could not be elected, but then Jefferson, with his eight states, could not be elected either, as long as Maryland and Vermont remained tied; and the Burr supporters in those two states had expressly given Bayard the power to control their votes. Jefferson, he knew, did not relish the prospect of a deadlock continuing until Inauguration Day either. Why, then, should Bayard give Jefferson the winning cards? Why not make him pay for them?

As the Delaware Federalist later stated under oath, he and his friends in the Vermont and Maryland delegations decided that "instead of being obliged to surrender at discretion, we might obtain terms of capitulation." Accordingly, Bayard said, "I applied to Mr. John Nicholas, a member of the House from Virginia, who was a particular friend of Mr. Jefferson. I stated to Mr. Nicholas, that if certain points of the future administration could be understood and arranged with Mr. Jefferson, I was authorized to say that three states would withdraw from an opposition to his election."

305

By a coincidence that is not at all strange considering his close ties with Hamilton, Bayard's terms of surrender proposed exactly the same concessions which Hamilton had been urging the Federalists to demand from Jefferson. Rather than make a deal to elect the "Catiline" Burr, Hamilton had advised them to "obtain from Jefferson assurances" on four "cardinal points":

"1. The preservation of the fiscal system.

"2. Adherence to the neutral plan (that is, neutrality between England and France).

"3. The preservation and gradual increase of the navy.

"4. The continuance of our friends in the offices they fill, except in the great departments, in which he ought to be left free."

Gouverneur Morris, of New York, another recipient of Hamilton's diatribes against Burr, had dangled the same bait in front of Jefferson, in person. Meeting the Vice-President on the Capitol steps one day, the peglegged senator had observed that the chief opposition to Jefferson's election arose from a fear that he would abolish the navy, toss all Federalists out of office, and repudiate the debt—which would, of course, bankrupt the holders of government bonds. Jefferson could clinch his election, Morris advised him, if he would promise to do none of these things.

"I must leave the world to judge the course I mean to pursue by that which I have pursued hitherto," Jefferson answered. "I believe it my duty to be passive and silent during the present contest. I shall certainly make no terms, and shall never go into the office of President by capitulation, nor with my hands tied by any conditions which will hinder me from pursuing the measures which I shall deem for the public good."

Bayard presented his proposal to Congressman Nicholas, who replied that he would personally assure that Jefferson, as President, would carry out all four points.

That was not enough for Bayard; he must have an "engagement" directly from Jefferson, otherwise he would not "surrender."

When Nicholas refused to consult Jefferson, Bayard made the

same proposition to General Smith, the Baltimore congressman who had vainly tried to talk Burr out of the presidential contest. This time Bayard specifically named two Federalist collectors who must be kept in their jobs as part of the bargain. One was George Latimer, at Philadelphia, the other was his old friend, Allen McLane, at Wilmington. (Bayard had fought more than one battle for McLane; his duel with Congressman Champlin had arisen from a move to cut the collector's pay.)

General Smith, too, tried to offer his own assurances, but Bayard would not agree to yield until the pledge came directly from Jefferson. The General, living in the same boardinghouse with the Vice-President, conceivably could have discussed the matter with him.

"The next day," Bayard testified, "General Smith informed me that he had seen Mr. Jefferson, and stated to him the points mentioned, and was authorized by him to say that they corresponded with his views and intentions, and that we might confide in him accordingly."

When Bayard's deposition to this effect appeared in 1806, Jefferson wrote in his diary: "This is absolutely false. No proposition of any kind was ever made to me on that occasion by General Smith, nor any answer authorized by me. And this fact General Smith affirms at this moment."

In the next few sentences, however, Jefferson qualified this claim somewhat: "I do not recollect that I ever had any particular conversation with General Samuel Smith on this subject. *Very possibly* I had, as the general subject and all its parts were the constant themes of conversation in the private *tête-a-têtes* with our friends. But certain I am, that neither he nor any other republican ever uttered the most distant hint to me about submitting to any conditions, or giving any assurances to anybody, and still more certainly, was neither he nor any other person ever authorized by me to say what I would or would not do."

General Smith, in a deposition remarkably similar to Bayard's, said he had discussed the surrender terms with the Delaware congressman and, in particular, Bayard had demanded that Latimer and

McLane be retained as the collectors at Philadelphia and Wilmington.

Smith said he talked with Jefferson on the matter that very night, and the next day, Saturday, February 14, told Bayard:

"Mr. Jefferson had said that he did not think that such officers ought to be dismissed on political grounds only, except in cases where they had made improper use of their offices, to force the officers under them to vote contrary to their judgment.

"As to Mr. McLane . . . he considered him a meritorious officer; of course, he would not be displaced, or ought not to be displaced," and that "Mr. Bayard might rest assured (or words to that effect), that Mr. Jefferson would conduct, as to those points, agreeably to the opinions I had stated as his."

Bayard then said, "We will give the vote on Monday."

Apparently, the controversy turns on this point: Did Jefferson *know* why Smith was asking the questions about his policies, and did he *authorize* the answers relayed to Bayard?

Jefferson, as one of the shrewdest politicians in America, surely must have known why General Smith asked specifically whether he would keep McLane as collector at Wilmington. McLane was widely known to be a close friend of Bayard's, and everyone knew that Bayard could assure Jefferson's election at any moment by switching Delaware's vote.

With utmost discretion, Jefferson made no promises in writing, so there is no written evidence to prove the statements of Bayard and General Smith, which are remarkably alike. Albert Gallatin, many years later, claimed that "one of our friends," obviously General Smith, "who was very erroneously and improperly afraid of a defection on the part of some of our members, undertook to act as an intermediary, and confounding his own opinions and wishes with those of Mr. Jefferson, reported the result in such a manner as gave subsequently occasion for very unfounded surmises."

On Sunday, February 15, the day after Bayard received his assurances from General Smith, Jefferson wrote to Monroe: "Many attempts have been made to obtain terms and promises from me. I have declared to them unequivocally that I would not receive the government on capitulation, that I would not go into it with my hands tied."

When the congressmen met again on Monday, February 16, they had to elbow their way through angry crowds at the Capitol. Jefferson's friends among the plain people were becoming impatient with the Federalists' stalling maneuvers for Burr. Margaret Bayard Smith, who could see the throng from her home on Capitol Hill, said "the mob gathered on the hillside hung like a thunder cloud over the Capitol, their indignation ready to burst."

"The people got so clamorous about the city," another observer said, "that some members expected to be shorter by the head."

There was a buzz of rumors that the "conspirators" were quitting; that the game was up. Albert Gallatin, who had kept the Jefferson lines intact against all raids by the friends of Burr, had predicted that Bayard would run up the white flag of surrender on Monday. Editor Smith, in *The National Intelligencer* for Monday, said the Federalists were "convinced" that they had no hope of "gaining over some Republican votes." "It is believed they will yield," Samuel predicted. "The unanimous and firm decision of the people throughout the U.S. in favour of Mr. Jefferson will be irresistible."

When the thirty-fourth ballot was taken Monday, however, the result was exactly the same as all the others before. The House then postponed the showdown until noon Tuesday, and Representative Samuel Cabell, of Virginia, commented: "How it will terminate, God only knows."

The Federalists went into a caucus at the call of James A. Bayard. Let Representative John Cotton Smith, of Connecticut, begin the story of that stormy session:

Bayard "began by inquiring whether any gentlemen present had received any communication from Mr. Burr touching the pending election, or could inform us why he tarried at Baltimore, when his appearance here would undoubtedly secure his elevation to the presidency? But not one of us could give him the information he desired."

Bayard "then observed that, unless Burr made his appearance

309

here, there was no prospect of our prevailing in the present contest; that the opposite party, he was well assured, would persevere to the 4th of March before they would renounce their candidate, undismayed by whatever disasters might result from leaving the nation without a president and, consequently without a government. . . ." Bayard said he would continue the deadlock until some person present, of Burr's personal acquaintance, would write Burr seeking a commitment to the Federalist cause, and that he would wait a reasonable time for an answer; but, "holding as he did, the vote of a state, he could not consent that the 4th of March should arrive without a chief magistrate."

No one could offer any assurance that Burr would thus pledge himself to the Federalists in return for the presidency. On the contrary, he had been sending letters to Jefferson, Gallatin, Livingston, and General Smith, attempting to stay in the good graces of his fellow-Republicans. He had to gain a few Republican votes to win, and he knew the Federalists would vote for him anyway. Burr told Gallatin on February 12 that he was "utterly surprised" by the deadlock, for he had expected Jefferson would win "10 or 11" states on the first ballot. (Nobody else in either party had ever predicted that.) "In case of usurpation, by law, by President of Senate pro tem., or in any other way, my opinion is definitely made up, and is known to S.S. and E.L.," Burr wrote, apparently referring to General Smith and Edward Livingston. "On that opinion I shall act in defiance of all timid, temporizing projects."

Even after they had little hope of electing Burr, the more violent Federalists from New England were determined to keep right on voting for him until March 4, maintaining the deadlock in the hope that the Republicans might give up or that a Federalist might be made the acting President. They "thought it was better to go without a president," Representative George Baer, of Maryland, observed, "than to elect Mr. Jefferson."

The Federalists, however, did not form a solid phalanx, resolved to go down fighting to the last ditch. Within their ranks were several moderates who, like Bayard, preferred to maintain the government—even through a compromise with the despised Jefferson—than to

310

have no government at all. They had, as Baer said, "received assurances from a source" on which they "placed reliance"—obviously, General Smith—that Jefferson would carry out "certain points of Federal policy." They had no such assurances from Burr, so they might feel safer with Jefferson, after all, just as Hamilton had said.

After some passionate disputes between the moderates and the die-hards, the Federalist congressmen generally agreed that Burr could not be elected, certainly not as a Federalist. Bayard then gave them a shock: He declared his intention of voting for Jefferson.

His announcement touched off an explosion. The New England fanatics leaped to their feet, shouting, "Deserter! Deserter!"

"The clamor was prodigious, the reproaches vehement," Bayard recorded. "I told them . . . they might attempt to direct the vengeance of the party against me, but the danger of being a sacrifice could not shake my resolution. Some were appeased; others furious; and we broke up in confusion."

"The declaration of Mr. Bayard rendered it quite unnecessary to address Mr. Burr, or to prolong the conflict," reported Representative John Cotton Smith, one of the disgusted Federalists. "His remarks became a subject of notoriety and of mutual gratulation to the opposite party within one hour."

The dejected Federalists met again Monday night merely to decide upon "the mode of surrendering." Bayard begged them to act together and accept their defeat in good grace. "After great agitation and much heat," they all agreed, except Representative William Edmond, of Connecticut, who vowed he would never, never be a party to the election of Thomas Jefferson.

"We have yet made no president but tomorrow we shall give up the contest," the embattled Bayard informed his father-in-law. "Burr has acted a miserable, paultry part. The election was in his power, but he was determined to come in as a Democrat, and in that event would have been the most dangerous man in the community. We have been counteracted in the whole business by letters he had written to this place."

On Tuesday, February 17, the weary representatives filed into the House chamber once more for the thirty-sixth ballot, while the crowd outside the closed doors waited expectantly for the Federalist surrender. The *coup de grâce* fell quickly.

Lewis Morris, the Vermont Federalist, did not appear in his seat. That enabled Matthew Lyon to cast Vermont's vote for Jefferson and assure his election. The four Maryland members who had formerly voted for Burr dropped blank pieces of paper into the tellers' box. Thus the four others in the delegation were free to cast the state's vote for Jefferson, and that gave him ten states.

Since he had one more state than he needed for victory, there was now no point in any Federalist voting for Jefferson. Representative Bayard cast a blank ballot for Delaware, and so did the Federalists from South Carolina. The Federalists from Massachusetts, Rhode Island, Connecticut, and New Hampshire voted for Burr until the bitter end. The final result: Jefferson ten states; Burr four; two blank.

Speaker Sedgwick, one of the most fanatic of the die-hards, had to swallow the bitter pill and announce that Thomas Jefferson had been elected the third President of the United States. Burr would, of course, become Vice-President.

"Thus has ended," Albert Gallatin told his wife triumphantly, "the most wicked and absurd attempt ever tried by the Federalists..."

Since Bayard was the man who "gave the turn" to the election by announcing his determination to vote for Jefferson, and by persuading his Vermont and Maryland friends to do likewise, Representative Baer recorded: "I always considered Mr. Bayard as the means of Mr. Jefferson's election, and I believed he was so considered by many others."

Gallatin agreed that the credit for Jefferson's victory belonged to Bayard: "Although he was one of the principal and warmest leaders of the Federal party and had a personal dislike for Mr. Jefferson, it was he who took the lead and from pure patriotism directed all those movements of the sounder and wiser part of the Federal party which terminated in the peaceable election of Mr. Jefferson."

Soon after the congressmen had filed out of the House chamber, to the wild cheers of the multitude for Jefferson, Bayard hastened to file news bulletins to his kinsmen and friends. To his father-in-law, he wrote:

Washington 17 Feby 1801

The question of President is settled. Upon the last vote Mr. Jefferson had 10 votes, M. Burr 4 and two blank. The step was not taken till it was admitted on all hands that we must risk the Constitution and a civil war or take Mr. Jefferson. The New England states admitted this, but still voted for Mr. Burr. But they stood on different ground from Delaware, Maryland, S. Carolina & Vermont, who receded.

To Collector McLane for whom he had labored so faithfully, Bayard sent this bulletin:

Washington 17 February 1801

Dear Sir:

Mr. Jefferson is our President.

Our opposition was continued till it was demonstrated that Burr could not be brought in, and even if he could, he meant to come in as a Democrat. In such case, to evidence his sincerity, he must have swept every officer in the U. States. I have direct information that Mr. Jefferson will not pursue that plan. . . .

I have taken good care of you, and think, if prudent, you are safe.

To Alexander Hamilton, Bayard sent a full account of the wild intrigues and desperate maneuverings that led to the final debacle. In disgust, he told how Burr had refused to make terms with the Federalists:

"He will never have another chance of being President of the United States; and the little use he has made of the one which has occurred, gives me but an humble opinion of the talents of an unprincipled man."

On the night of Jefferson's victory, as can well be imagined, there was joy unconfined among the Republicans sharing quarters with him in the boardinghouse of Conrad and McMunn. There was equal

313

hilarity in the row of houses a few steps down New Jersey Avenue, where Samuel and Margaret Bayard Smith hailed their hero's triumph and prepared to tell the nation about it in the next edition of *The National Intelligencer.*

At sunset on the glorious day, candles blazed in the windows of the Smiths' and in many other homes along New Jersey Avenue, as the residents had "unanimously resolved to illuminate their windows" in honor of Jefferson.

At nine o'clock the joyous Republicans gathered and drank at least sixteen toasts—not to mention many additional potations—to celebrate the triumph of democracy. They toasted Washington, Adams, Benjamin Franklin, and Republican Congressmen Gallatin, Livingston, Claiborne, Lyon, Nicholas, Randolph, and General Smith; and the final toast, to the ladies, was this:

"The American fair. May they instruct their offspring to remember the seventeenth of February, 1801."

* * * * *

At Lancaster, Pa., Governor Thomas McKean was preparing a "bold stroke" of action—possibly a plan to march the Pennsylvania militia into Washington—to stop the Federalists from inaugurating a "usurper" on March 4. His Republican friends in the Pennsylvania legislature would stay in session until that day to aid his plan, even if it meant a threat of civil war.

As the Governor sat writing a letter to Jefferson, detailing his battle plans, a horseman galloped in from Washington, bringing the "glorious" news of victory. "In consequence of this news, my long letter has been committed to the flames," the fiery Republican governor wrote. "The bells in this borough have been ringing ever since, until sundown. The two houses of our legislature were electrified. . . . A new era has commenced and I fear not for the future."

Jefferson would have cheerfully remained as Vice-President, if Burr had been legally elected by the House, he replied to McKean, "because, however it might have been variant from the intentions of the voters, yet it would have been agreeable to the Constitution." But he never would have allowed a "usurpation," because "that prece-

314

dent once set, would be artificially reproduced and end soon in a dictator."

"The voice of the people has prevailed," Editor Smith proclaimed in *The National Intelligencer* of February 18. "This memorable example," he exulted, should prove that the "republican system" far surpassed the government of "an hereditary despot or a military usurper."

On the same day, only 24 hours after Speaker Sedgwick had swallowed his pride and announced the election of Jefferson, Smith's friends offered a resolution condemning the Speaker "in terms of undisguised severity" for having ordered the editor out of the House. The Republicans moved that "the Speaker, in directing the Sergeant-at-Arms to order and expel from the gallery of this House, Samuel Harrison Smith, a citizen of the United States, has assumed a power not given him by the rules of this House, and deprived the said Samuel Harrison Smith of a right, which can only be forfeited by disorderly behavior."

In the hot debate that followed, Sedgwick's conduct received (according to Smith's paper) "the keenest animadversion and censure." But the Federalists, although unable to keep Jefferson out of the presidency on a vote by states, still had enough power to control the House on an individual roll call. They defeated the Republican motion 54 to 49, and they dismissed a motion by Albert Gallatin which would have restored the editor to his place in the lobby and barred the Speaker from any future act of exclusion.

Editor Smith thus lost this round of his feud, but he would yet enjoy his day of triumph: The Republicans, on taking control of the new Seventh Congress late in 1801, would give him not only his old rights to cover the debates of both House and Senate but a large part of the government printing as well. This would salve not merely his pride but his pocketbook.

In the dying days of the Federalist regime, the Senate ratified the French Convention, thus quietly bringing an end to the friction which had brought the United States to a shooting war with France on the high seas, and to the verge of a general, declared war. The treaty gave no clear-cut victory to either side, but it ended the gun play between the ships of the two nations, protected American commerce, and allowed merchant ships, henceforth, to sail the seas without interference from Gallican privateers.

Chief Justice Oliver Ellsworth, one of the three envoys who had brought the treaty from Paris, came home broken in health and spirit. He resigned from the Supreme Court and, as his successor, President Adams nominated the easy-going, loose-jointed Virginian, John Marshall. Few suspected then that Marshall would prove the Federalist rock against the Republicanism of his implacable enemy, Thomas Jefferson.

On their way out of power, the Federalists also created a long list of additional federal judgeships, for the circuit and district courts, and Adams spent his expiring days and nights in the White House, handing these trophies to men he regarded as deserving Federalists. With unintentional irony, he gave one to Oliver Wolcott, who, as Secretary of the Treasury, had constantly undermined him and had worked hand-in-glove with Hamilton to defeat him.

Representative James A. Bayard also cultivated the hot-tempered President to win a couple of lucrative judgeships for members of his family. Bayard placed his father-in-law, Governor Bassett, on the circuit court bench, advising him: "Two thousand dollars are better than anything Delaware can give you, and not an unpleasant provision for life."

Bayard thought he had a similar post assured for his cousin and adopted brother, Samuel Bayard, who had prosecuted Americans' claims in the British admiralty courts and later would be a presiding judge of Westchester County, New York. But at the last minute Adams appointed Egbert Benson, the choice of the New York congressional delegation.

Adams gave the Delaware congressman the highest honor accorded anyone in the entire Bayard family—the post of minister to France. The young congressman had to decline, however, lest he be accused of having brought about Jefferson's election merely for the selfish purpose of placing himself in the mission at Paris.

"The delicate situation in which the late presidential election has placed me, forbids my exposing myself to the *suspicion* of having adopted, from impure motives, the line of conduct which I pursued," he wrote Adams, declining the honor. "Representing the smallest state in the union, without resources which could furnish the means of self-protection, I was compelled by the obligation of a sacred duty, so to act, as not to hazard the Constitution upon which the political existence of the state depends.

"The service which I should have to render, by accepting the appointment, would be under the administration of Mr. Jefferson, and having been in the number of those who withdrew themselves from the opposition to his election, it is impossible for me to take an office, the tenure of which would be at his pleasure."

Bayard was determined to let no one place any stain on the famous name of his family, or to say he had failed to live up to the motto of the knight *sans peur et sans reproche.*"

The Delaware congressman thus busily salvaged souvenirs for his family from the wreck of the Federalist ship, but he drew the line at claiming any loot for himself.

CHAPTER FOURTEEN

WEDNESDAY, MARCH 4, 1801:
The thunder of guns broke the stillness of daybreak, and echoed and re-echoed over Washington.

The guns of the Washington artillery presumably awakened the most distinguished lodger in the boardinghouse of Conrad and Mc-Munn near the Capitol—if, indeed, he had slept at all. Despite his outward expression of perfect calm, Thomas Jefferson must have felt some excitement on the day of his inauguration as the third President of the United States.

Certainly, to the thousands of his admirers who had streamed into the muddy little capital in the Maryland woods, this was a day of rejoicing. "At an early hour," said Editor Smith in *The National Intelligencer,* the town "presented a spectacle of uncommon animation, occasioned by the addition to its usual population of a large body of citizens from the adjacent districts." For the Republicans, as Samuel privately informed his sister Mary in Philadelphia, "it was a day of exuberant gaiety. All was animation and motion. Joy sparkled in every eye, praise hung on every tongue."

For the Federalists, who had lost their last desperate gamble to keep a shred of their power in Washington, this was a day of doom. Representative James A. Bayard, who had tossed in the card that assured the victory of Jefferson, felt no exuberance over his part in his enemy's triumph. The Delaware Federalist had merely chosen the lesser of two evils—a bad government under the theorist Jefferson, rather than no government plus a possible civil war. Bayard had stayed in the capital to see the "coronation," as he called it, and he viewed the future with eyes unclouded by rosy optimism.

Some other Federalists, lacking Bayard's ability to face harsh realities, could not stand to see the spectacle of the "fiend incarnate" taking the oath as President. While the artillery was awakening the town with the racket of its guns, a private carriage might have been seen splashing through the mud of the road to the North. It was carrying John Adams back to Quincy, Massachusetts. At four o'clock in the morning, the defeated President had stepped out of the mansion on Pennsylvania Avenue and hastened away from Washington, wishing never to see it again for the rest of his life. He could not bear to endure the humiliation of seeing his hated rival take the presidency away from him.

It had been embarrassing enough for Adams, four years before in Philadelphia, to become a President "by three votes." On that inaugural day, the great Washington had stepped down with gallantry and there had not been a dry eye in the crowd when the General had handed the reins of office to Adams. But Adams could not bring himself to be polite to Jefferson. "You can have no idea of the meanness, indecency, almost insanity, of his conduct, especially of late," Albert Gallatin confided to his wife. "But he is fallen and not dangerous. Let him be forgotten."

So, John Adams crept off the stage of national politics while the theater was dark and the audience could not wound his vanity with hisses and boos.

Theodore Sedgwick could not stomach the spectacle of the inauguration of the first Republican President, either. Like Adams, he slipped out of the capital in a private carriage, bound for Massachusetts, once more to escape "democratick annoyance."

Samuel H. Smith soon began to enjoy the fruits of Jefferson's victory. The President-elect handed him an advance text of his inaugural speech, so that *The National Intelligencer* would have the complete account in its Inaugural Edition, rolling off the press by the time the noontime ceremony ended. Thus Editor Smith, who had made journalistic history with his twice-a-day paper in Philadelphia, could score another scoop by publishing Jefferson's address as fast as it could have been printed more than a century later.

That morning the President-elect conducted himself with the same democratic simplicity that had marked his behavior on every previous day. He entered the dining room at Conrad and McMunn's to take his usual seat at the foot of the table for breakfast. The wife of Senator Brown of Kentucky arose and offered him her seat, but he declined with a smile, and sat down at his old place near the door.

At ten o'clock, the company of riflemen from nearby Alexandria paraded by, along with the Washington artillerists who had greeted the dawn with the thunder of their guns. At noon, the President-elect —dressed as usual like "a plain citizen, without any distinctive badge of office"—left the boardinghouse, attended by several members of Congress and many more citizens streaming along in his wake, and strode the two blocks to the Capitol. As he crossed the threshold, another volley of artillery rent the air. Margaret Bayard Smith describes the scene in the little chamber where Jefferson took the oath:

"The Senate chamber was so crowded that, I believe, not another creature could enter. On one side of the House the Senate sat, the other was assigned by the Representatives to the ladies. The roof is arched, the room half circle; every inch of ground was occupied. It has been conjectured by several gentlemen whom I've asked, that there were near a thousand persons within the walls. . . . I cannot describe the agitation I felt while I looked around on the various multitude."

When Jefferson walked into the Senate chamber, the crowd arose and Aaron Burr, the new Vice-President, left the presiding officer's chair. Then Jefferson sat down in the same place he had filled until only a few days before. That was a scene which should have been painted by Gilbert Stuart, whose portraits soon would be all the rage in fashionable Washington: Jefferson in the center, with Burr on his right hand and Chief Justice John Marshall on his left. Only a few years hence Burr would be arrested for treason, at the insistence of Jefferson, and would be tried for his life at Richmond, Virginia, with Marshall presiding at the trial.

What thoughts must have flashed through the minds of the three

320

men—Jefferson, Burr, and Marshall—as they met on the Senate dais! The smiles of courtesy must have veiled the secret hates of men who never would trust each other, for Marshall had determined to use his powers as Chief Justice to block Jefferson at every turn, and Burr would soon discover that the Jefferson administration had no place for him.

Burr had come to the capital, hailed as a hero by those Republicans who did not know how he had refused to get out of Jefferson's way. At Baltimore, the leading citizens had praised his "patriotism" which had "disclaimed competition for the presidential chair." Suavely, the dark-eyed New Yorker had replied that he felt "great satisfaction" over "the triumph of principle." "As to his stepping between the will and wishes of the people in opposition to that great and good man, Mr. Jefferson," Burr had said, "he should consider himself unworthy of confidence, ungrateful to his own feelings, and to those principles by which he had always been actuated."

Jefferson had marked his running mate as "unworthy of confidence" on this, the first day of the administration. Burr was already starting downward on the path that would lead from the threshold of the presidency, to his fatal duel with Hamilton, to accusations of "murder" and "treason," and eventual exile and ruin.

After sitting a few moments in silence, President Jefferson arose and started to read his address. He spoke in a tone so low that few of the people jammed into the little Senate chamber could hear it. None could mistake, however, the conciliatory tone of the most important lines:

"We are all Republicans; we are all Federalists.

"If there be any among us who would wish to dissolve this Union, or to change its republican form, let them stand undisturbed as monuments to the safety with which error of opinion may be tolerated where reason is left free to combat it."

With infinite tact the leader of the Republicans was carrying out his design of wooing the more moderate Federalists through appeals to reason and national unity. "Let us, then, fellow-citizens, unite with one heart and one mind," he pleaded. "Let us restore to social intercourse that harmony and affection without which liberty and even life itself are but dreary things. And let us reflect that, having banished from our land that religious intolerance under which mankind so long bled and suffered, we have gained little if we countenance a political intolerance as despotic, as wicked, and capable of as bitter and bloody persecution. . . . Every difference of opinion is not a difference of principle."

"Sometimes it is said that man cannot be trusted with the government of himself," Jefferson went on in a fling at the High Federalist faction which desired a stronger central power. "Can he, then, be trusted with the government of others? Or have we found angels in the form of kings to govern him? Let history answer this question."

In a series of dexterous thrusts at the clergy who had been denouncing him as an "atheist," the Philosopher of Monticello said the American people, "enlightened by a benign religion" and "adoring an overruling Providence," had all the blessings to make them "a happy and prosperous people." They needed, he said, but "one thing more: A wise and frugal government, which shall restrain men from injuring one another, shall leave them otherwise free to regulate their own pursuits of industry and improvement, and shall not take from the mouth of labor the bread it has earned."

Next, the first Republican Chief Executive set forth the "essential principles" of his administration:

"Equal and exact justice to all men, of whatever state or persuasion, religious or political. . . .

"Peace, commerce, and honest friendship with all nations, entangling alliances with none. . . .

"The support of the state governments in all their rights. . . .

"The preservation of the General Government in its whole constitutional vigor, as the sheet anchor of our peace at home and safety abroad. . . .

"A jealous care of the right of election by the people. . . .

"Absolute acquiescence in the decisions of the majority. . . .

"A well-disciplined militia. . . .

"The supremacy of the civil over the military authority. . . .

"Economy in the public expense, that labor may be lightly burthened. . . .

"The honest payment of our debts and sacred preservation of the public faith. . . .

"Encouragement of agriculture, and of commerce as its hand-maid. . . .

"The diffusion of information, and the arraignment of all abuses at the bar of the public reason. . . .

"Freedom of religion. . . .

"Freedom of the press. . . .

"Freedom of person under the protection of the habeas corpus, and trial by juries impartially selected."

Concluding his speech, the new President turned to Chief Justice Marshall, who administered the oath. Amid another roar of artillery, Jefferson left the Capitol, strolled back to his lodgings at Conrad and McMunn's, accompanied by Burr, Marshall and the heads of the departments, and "was waited upon by a number of distinguished citizens."

Editor Smith, with his usual enterprise, had his "extra" with the inaugural address all ready to be distributed when the crowd came out of the Capitol. He and Margaret and the printers kept busy, selling newspapers at the shop on New Jersey Avenue, while joining in the general rejoicing of the Republicans on their great day of triumph. "This day a new era commences; the era of principle," Samuel commented in his lead editorial of the day. Margaret wrote her sister that evening, "There has been a constant succession of persons coming for the papers. I have been interrupted several times in this letter by the gentlemen of Congress, who have been to bid their adieus; since three o'clock there has been a constant succession."

"The remainder of the day was devoted to purposes of festivity," Samuel's next edition said, "and at night there was a pretty general illumination."

At sunset candles were brought and the tea table was set for the meal of the day which the editor enjoyed more than any other. Then,

Samuel and Margaret found new proofs that—in the words of the new President—all were Republicans and all Federalists, at least on this happy day. Among their guests at tea were three hard-shelled Federalists, Senator Gouverneur Morris, of New York, Senator Jonathan Dayton, of New Jersey, and Cousin James A. Bayard.

The topic on every tongue was the President's speech. It "has raised him even in the opinion of his friends and from appearances has gone far to diminish his enemies," Samuel commented. "Even Gouverneur Morris and Mr. Dayton, who drank tea with us, spoke of it in terms of general approbation."

Congressman Bayard admitted he had been pleasantly surprised. The speech, in political substance, was better than he expected, he told Alexander Hamilton, "and not answerable to the expectations of the partisans of the other side."

Naturally, Editor Smith viewed the scene of Republican glory more cheerfully than his Federalist cousin did. "Congress has risen, the inauguration is over, the executive arrangements are made, and we have every appearance of a short political calm," he wrote his sister Mary. "This, to me, is a source of indefinable pleasure. No longer obliged to stand in the painful attitude of opposition, I find myself the government printer!

"Strange event! Can you believe it? I scarcely can. It seems a mystery! A Republican, printing the President's speech. Can it be possible? Truly, these are strange times. But they are glorious ones, and they promise perpetuity."

To Samuel's sister Susan, Margaret sent an equally glowing account of the inauguration:

"Let me write you, my dear Susan, ere that glow of enthusiasm has fled, which now animates my feelings. Let me congratulate not only you, but all my fellow citizens, on an event which will have so auspicious an influence on their political welfare. I have this morning witnessed one of the most interesting scenes a free people can ever witness. The changes of administration, which in every government and in every age, have most generally been epochs of confusion, villainy and bloodshed, in this our happy country take place without any species of distraction or disorder.

324

"This day, has one of the most amiable and worthy men taken that seat to which he was called by the voice of his country. I listened to an address, containing principles the most correct and sentiments the most liberal, and wishes the most benevolent, conveyed in the most appropriate and elegant language and in a manner mild as it was firm. If doubts of the integrity and talents of Mr. Jefferson ever existed in the minds of anyone, methinks this address must forever eradicate them."

Certainly, such doubts about Mr. Jefferson had occupied Peggy's own mind before she married Samuel, but they had been removed by meeting the "great and good man" in her own parlor.

"Could you suppose that I could spend three months in the society I have, and yet retain any prejudice against republicanism?" she asked Mary Smith. "We have been visited by many firm and decided Republicans, the measures of government have been openly and candidly discussed, the views of the different parties have been unveiled, and while those of the Federalists have been condemned as inimical to the true interests of our country, the condemnation has applied more to principles than persons and never in a single instance have I heard the whole party branded with those vile and illiberal epithets which I have been so accustomed to hear the Federalists attach to their opponents."

Then she paid her respects to the Federalists who had plotted to sneak Burr into the presidency: "If I had not been before convinced that, instead of being the enemies, the Republicans had been the true supporters and friends of the Constitution, the late conduct of the other party would have opened my eyes. That a few men should attempt to resist the wishes of a people, and the wishes of their constituents, and that without one plausible or generous motive to support them, can be attributed to personal ambition, or self-love, which led them to forget the interests of their country in order to promote their own designs.

"I am surprised not only at my own previous convictions, but at the opinions embraced by so many honest and enlightened men. For my own part, while I have learned to prefer the principles of republicanism, I hope never to forget that the majority of the Federal party are men equally desirous of the welfare of their country, equally zealous in the promotion of that object, and that they have only mistaken the true means of arriving at that end.

"I have no doubt that the next administration will correct this mistake; when the people discover that, instead of French revolutionists and a visionary Philosopher, they are governed by men who are determined to support the Constitution and by a man whose principles are as correct as his heart is benevolent.

"Now, if my Federal friends were to read this, what would they say? No matter. While I honestly endeavour to discover truth, I will never hesitate honestly to own my convictions."

Peggy frankly admitted one reason for her conversion to Republicanism: "I am aware how much I am influenced by affection, and that this influence must increase with my increasing tenderness and regard for my excellent husband. Oh, my dear Mary, scarcely a day passes without affording me some new cause of self-congratulation. I had prepared myself to suffer occasional indifference and irritability, believing a person so immersed in business, often harried and perplexed, could not at all times be equally tranquil and affectionate. I had imagined that the lively emotions of tenderness which I experienced in the first moments of our union would have been blunted by familiarity. But how sweetly have all my hopes been realized and all my fears destroyed! Every day seems to draw closer round my heart the ties by which we are united."

From Boston to Savannah, and far out in the wilds of Kentucky and Tennessee, the joyous Republicans celebrated the inauguration by firing guns, ringing bells, singing songs, drinking toasts, and general merriment. At the German Reformed Church, in Philadelphia, they sang a new anthem written especially for the occasion by Rembrandt Peale, entitled, "The People's Friend." It hailed the new President in these words:

> Devoted to his country's cause,
> The Rights of Men and equal Laws,
> His hallow'd pen was given:

326

And now those Rights and Laws to save,
From sinking to an early grave,
    He comes, employ'd by Heaven.

What joyful prospects rise before!
Peace, Arts and Science hail our shore,
    And thro' the country spread:
Long may these blessings be preserv'd,
And by a virtuous land deserv'd,
    With JEFFERSON our head.

"The joy is general among the farmers and laborers of all classes," an enthusiastic Republican wrote to Madison from the capital. "Some merchants and the monied interest, with the bigots and fanatics in religious matters, may have their fears. But the old Tories and new Gallants of the Whore of England can never be won, even by justice and moderation; their hate will be irreconcilable."

Benjamin Ring, who lived near Chadds Ford on the Brandywine, not far from Philadelphia, took his pen in hand and with quaintly original spelling, thus expressed his congratulations to the new President:

Most Noble Jefferson, at the heering of thy Being appoynted president was cause of greate joy to Mee wich I inwardly felt. I love a tru & faithfull American who is tru to his Cuntry, not baliving his private intrust eqquel to that of his cuntry's prosperytye & Growth. . . . I may inform thee at thy being appoynted president is caus of greate joy in oure part of the cuntry for their is greate confidence reposed in thee wich, i hath no doubt, will be answarred according to expectulatishon.
    From thy assured friend, unknown but real,
                    Benjam. Ring.

With unconscious irony, Benjamin Ring added this postscript:

I wish to be Remembered to our tru friend Curnell Burr. A tru Amerakin in whome their is No Gile.

*   *   *   *   *

EPILOGUE

The full story of the Federalists' scheme to slip Burr into the presidency ahead of Jefferson has remained an intriguing mystery down through the years, leading to many disputes about the motives and maneuvers of the major characters in the drama.

Burr's enemies—a mighty host in both parties—charged that he had plotted directly with the Federalists in their mischievous attempt to thwart the will of the people. There is no written evidence of such a direct negotiation; certainly several men claiming to be Burr's agents lobbied with the members of Congress and wrote letters urging Republicans to switch their votes to him. It is hard to believe these men were all spontaneous volunteers who would pull so many strings for Burr without knowing he would approve of their enterprises.

Representative James A. Bayard was disgusted that Burr had played such a "miserable, paultry part," and had refused to pledge himself to carry out Federalist policies in return for the presidency. This statement has been interpreted by some defenders of Burr as indicating he played a completely honorable role and did not interfere with Jefferson's election.

Actually, however, Burr followed the only strategy which could have given him the prize. He had the six Federalist states anyway, without making any pledges, and, to pick up the three Republican states essential to make a majority, he professed to remain a loyal Republican. Those three states would never have gone over to him if he had declared himself a Federalist. He had good reason to

329

think he could gain the votes of New York, New Jersey, Vermont, Maryland, and Tennessee, and any three of these would have been enough to give him the victory.

Alexander Hamilton expected Burr to win; Jefferson's managers were afraid of the possibility until the very last minute. They knew, too, that Burr would accept the presidency, because he had flatly rejected General Smith's pleas that he resign if elected, so that Jefferson could enter the White House.

Burr revealed his true intentions when he angrily refused to do the one thing that would have killed the whole Federalist plot at the outset. His refusal proved to be his greatest mistake, for Jefferson never trusted him thereafter.

Burr evidently had good reason to think, in January, 1801, that three Republican states would come over and assure his victory. Hamilton's lieutenant, Robert Troup, claimed afterwards that Edward Livingston went to Washington as "one of Burr's confidential agents" with instructions to make the switch, but that Livingston went over to the Jefferson forces instead.

"If Livingston had not betrayed his trust, Burr would certainly have been President," Troup wrote in May, 1801.

Bayard charged publicly in House debate in February, 1802—just one year after the event, when it was fresh in his memory—that Jefferson's lieutenants had held the Republican congressmen in line by promising choice federal offices to those whose votes held the balance of power. Somehow, the Republican line did not break as the Federalists had hoped and no Republican, after thirty-six ballots, dared to cross over and vote for Burr. Bayard charged, in effect, that the Jefferson men had outbid him for the crucial votes.

"Every man on whose vote the event of the election hung has since been distinguished by presidential favor," the Delaware Federalist declared on the House floor. He named names and offices:

Representative William C. C. Claiborne, the lone member from Tennessee, stayed with Jefferson and "has since been raised to the high dignity of governor of the Mississippi Territory."

Representative James Linn held the "doubtful" vote in the New Jersey delegation; "he gave it to Mr. Jefferson and Mr. Linn has since had the profitable office of supervisor of his district conferred upon him."

Representative Matthew Lyon "neutralized the vote of Vermont. His absence alone would have given the vote of a state to Mr. Burr." He stayed and voted for Jefferson; the Federalist, Lewis Morris, went out on the thirty-sixth ballot and let Lyon deliver the state. "Mr. Lyon's son," said Bayard, "has been handsomely provided for in one of the executive offices."

Of Edward Livingston, Bayard said, bitterly: "I knew well, full well I knew the consequence of this gentleman. His means were not limited to his own vote; nay, I always considered more than the vote of New York within his power. Mr. Livingston has been made the attorney for the district of New York; . . . and his brother has been raised to the distinguished place of minister plenipotentiary to the French Republic."

"This catalogue might be swelled to a much greater magnitude," Bayard said, cryptically, "but . . . it might be supposed that I myself harbored the uncharitable suspicions of the integrity of the chief magistrate, and of the purity of the gentlemen whom he thought proper to promote." Bayard said he did not have "the remotest intention to tarnish the fame" of Jefferson or his appointees; he merely wished to note that the President had rewarded every man who "had any distinguished means . . . of deciding the election in his favor."

The charges against Burr increased when he ran for the office of governor of New York in 1804 in an effort to build a solid base for another bid for national power, since he knew he would be dropped as Vice-President that year. Burr denied that he had made any deals with the Federalists, and his defenders charged that the deals had really been made by Jefferson's men.

Burr believed one of Jefferson's "confidential friends" offered the jobs to Livingston, Linn and Claiborne, "and to this alone he attributes his disappointment of the presidency," said James Cheetham, an anti-Burr newspaper editor.

Burr's defeat in the gubernatorial race led directly to the duel in which he killed Hamilton, July 11, 1804.

Jefferson became embarrassed by the publication of charges that he had sent assurances to Bayard, through General Smith, that he would accept the points of Federalist policy laid down by Hamilton, and would keep certain Federalists in office—in particular, Bayard's friend Allen McLane, who stayed on as collector of the port of Wilmington despite Republican efforts to get him out.

In 1830, four years after Jefferson's death, his papers were published; and they contained several diary references intimating that Bayard had offered offices to certain key Republican congressmen if they would switch to Burr. Bayard's sons, James A. and Richard, leaped to the defense of his memory, and collected letters from several of the principal actors in the drama of 1801.

George Baer, one of the four Maryland members who voted for Burr and thereby helped to bring about the deadlock, avowed Bayard was "substantially correct" in saying General Smith had brought him apparent assurances from Jefferson. Both General Smith and Edward Livingston were members of the Senate when the uproar occurred in 1830. Both declared that they remembered no overtures from Bayard, twenty-nine years before.

In 1855, James A. Bayard, Jr., who had followed his father to a seat in the Senate (in fact, the position of senator from Delaware was handed down from one Bayard to another through a century of Delaware history), placed in the Senate record a full story of the 1801 election and published it as a pamphlet entitled, *Vindication of Bayard*.

Yet it does seem that the son, in his effort to protect the good name of his father, did protest too much. Bayard's own letters at the time indicate that he made some sort of offers in hopes of electing Burr, and he surely thought he had a pledge from Jefferson to keep McLane in office. That was why he told McLane, "I have taken good care of you and think, if prudent, you are safe."

The manuscript of Jefferson's private journal, dated March 8, 1801, four days after his inaugural, contains a long list of faithful Republicans favored for federal offices. One paragraph reads: "Jersey—propose to Linn to accept atty's place vice Frelinghuysen, Mr.

Gallatin will write. Turn out the Tory collector, an atrocious appointment."

Another line reads: "Delaware—the collector McLane to be retained. Enquire as to Marshal & collector."

*   *   *   *   *

The presidential election of 1800 was the only one in which two candidates tied in electoral votes. The Twelfth Amendment was added to the Constitution in 1804 specifically to prevent a repetition of the deadlock which nearly led to anarchy and civil war. This amendment ended the system whereby each elector cast two votes for President; it states that the candidates for President and Vice-President must run for a separate office.

The Constitution still requires that a President receive a majority of the electoral votes, and several have been elected without a plurality of the popular votes. In case no presidential candidate wins an electoral majority, the House of Representatives still has the duty to select a President from the leading contenders, and the winner must get a majority of the *state delegations*.

*   *   *   *   *

And what happened to Samuel and Margaret Bayard Smith?

Did they live happily ever after, as lovers are supposed to do?

Well, they did live in Washington for many years after the memorable days of 1801. The first of their four children was born on November 29, 1801—a daughter, named Julia—and Margaret exclaimed, "I can scarcely believe it possible that the thoughtless Margaret Bayard is now a mother."

Julia's arrival strengthened the ties of a love that had already made a happy marriage. "We had loved each other before," Margaret wrote in her private journal, "but ... how greatly were the glow of tenderness and the bonds of affection strengthened!"

The Smiths' friendship with Thomas Jefferson also ripened through the years, and they frequently were his guests at the White House and at Monticello. *The National Intelligencer* prospered mightily with the patronage of the new administration, and the paper once said, in a profile of Editor Smith:

"During the whole administration of Mr. Jefferson, the relations of confidence and friendship, which had for several years existed between Mr. Jefferson and Mr. Smith were extended to the paper . . . which was justly considered as generally representing the views of the administration."

Samuel made so much money that he was able to sell the paper in 1810, to Joseph Gales, Jr., and retire to the country when only thirty-eight. The Smiths enjoyed "rural pursuits and literary and philosophical" studies at their country estate called "Sidney," which now is encompassed by the grounds of Catholic University in Washington. In 1813, President Madison called Samuel back to the city to be Commissioner of the Revenue, with the arduous duty of raising the taxes to fight the unpopular second war with Britain. Later, the former Republican editor, who had so zealously fought the Federalist fiscal policies, became president of the Bank of Washington—a solid citizen, indeed.

Margaret distinguished herself as the author of two books, and for forty years the great figures of the nation gathered in her drawing room.

Margaret died on June 7, 1844, and Samuel on November 1, 1845. They sleep side by side in Rock Creek Church Cemetery in Washington.

The following sketch of the Bayard family tree clarifies the relationship of Margaret Bayard and her cousin, Samuel Harrison Smith, and Margaret's adopted brother, James A. Bayard.

Their great-great-great-grandmother, Anna, widow of Samuel Bayard, an Amsterdam merchant, came to New York in May, 1647. She arrived on the same ship which brought her brother, Peter Stuyvesant, the last Dutch governor of "New Netherlands." With Anna came her daughter, Catherine, and three sons, Peter, Balthazar and Nicholas.

Peter took part in settling the Bohemia Manor lands in Cecil County, Maryland. His son, Samuel, in 1698, built the "Great House" there.

Samuel had a daughter, Mary Ann, and three sons, Peter, Samuel, and James. Peter was the grandfather of Samuel Harrison Smith; James was the grandfather of Margaret and James A. Bayard.

Peter's daughter, Susannah, married Jonathan Smith, who took the middle name, "Bayard," at her father's request. Jonathan Bayard Smith and Susannah Bayard Smith were the parents of Samuel Harrison Smith (1772-1845).

James Bayard married Mary Asheton. They had twin sons, John Bubenheim Bayard (1738-1807) and James A. Bayard, Sr. (1738-1770). Colonel John Bayard was the father of Margaret Bayard. Dr. James A. Bayard, Sr., was the father of James Asheton Bayard, the Delaware Congressman (later Senator), who cast the deciding vote which elected Jefferson President. Since his parents died when he was a child, James Asheton was adopted by his uncle, Colonel John Bayard, and reared as one of the Colonel's own children.

COLONEL JOHN B. BAYARD'S CHILDREN

Colonel John B. Bayard and his wife, Margaret Hodge Bayard, had fourteen children, six of whom died in childhood. These are the eight who lived to maturity:

1. James Asheton (1760-1788), an associate in his father's mercantile business, who died at sea at age 28.
2. Andrew (1762-1833), a Philadelphia merchant-banker.
3. John Murray (1766-1823), who lived on a farm in Monmouth County, New Jersey.
4. Samuel (1767-1840), a lawyer and judge in New York, Philadelphia, and Princeton, New Jersey.
5. Jane (1772-1851), who married Andrew Kirkpatrick, lawyer and judge at New Brunswick, New Jersey.
6. Nicholas (1774-1821), a physician, who spent the last twenty years of his life at Savannah, Georgia.
7. Margaret (1778-1844), who married Samuel Harrison Smith.
8. Anna Maria (1779-1869), who married Samuel Boyd, a New York lawyer, and lived to be ninety years old.

NOTES

CHAPTER ONE

Page 1. George Washington and his Philadelphia house in 1796 are described by Thomas Twining in *Travels in America One Hundred Years Ago* (New York, 1894), pp. 128-33. For Claypoole's version of his conference with Washington, see *Washington's Farewell Address,* by Victor H. Paltsits (New York, 1935), pp. 29-92.

Page 2. Washington's letter to John Jay, May 8, 1796, is in *The Writings of George Washington,* edited by John C. Fitzpatrick (39 vols., Washington, D.C., 1931-44), Vol. 35, p. 37. Hereafter cited as "Fitzpatrick."

Page 4. For Jefferson's description of Washington's wrath see *The Complete Anas of Thomas Jefferson,* edited by Franklin B. Sawvel (New York, 1903), p. 159; *The Writings of Thomas Jefferson,* edited by Paul Leicester Ford (12 vols., New York, 1904), Vol. 1, pp. 307-8. For Washington's "pick-pocket" letter to Jefferson, July 6, 1796, see Fitzpatrick, Vol. 35, pp. 118-20. Washington to Alexander Hamilton, June 26, 1796, Fitzpatrick, Vol. 35, p. 103.

Pages 5-7. For text of Washington's Farewell Address see Fitzpatrick, Vol. 35, pp. 214-38.

Page 7. Fisher Ames to Oliver Wolcott, September 26, 1796, in *Memoirs of the Administrations of Washington and John Adams, Edited from the Papers of Oliver Wolcott,* George Gibbs, editor, cited hereafter as "Wolcott Papers," Vol. 1, pp. 384-85. Jefferson to James Madison, April 27, 1795, Ford, Vol. 8, p. 169. Irving Brant, *James Madison* (6 vols., Indianapolis, 1941-61), Vol. 3, p. 444.

Page 8. For Hamilton's pen-profiles of Aaron Burr, see *The Works of Alexander Hamilton,* edited by John C. Hamilton (6 vols., New York, 1851), Vol. 5, pp. 526-32. James Monroe to Madison, September 18, 1792, in *Writings of James Monroe,* edited by Stanislaus Murray Hamilton (7 vols., New York, 1893-1903), Vol. 1, p. 240. Wolcott to Oliver Wolcott, Sr., October 17, 1796, Wolcott Papers, Vol. 1, p. 387.

Page 9. Adams to his wife, January 20, 1796, in *Letters of John Adams Addressed to His Wife,* edited by Charles Francis Adams (2 vols., Boston, 1841), Vol. 1, p. 191. Madison to Jefferson, December 5, 1796, Madison Papers, Library of Congress, Vol. 19, p. 104.

Page 10. For Congressman Robert Goodloe Harper's opinion of Jefferson see pages 24-27 in the American Historical Association's Annual Report for 1913 (Vol. 2, Washington, 1915), containing letters of Harper and Congressman James A. Bayard, edited by Elizabeth Donnan. Hereafter cited as "Donnan."

Page 11. Timothy Pickering called Jefferson "Long Tom, the Moonshine Philosopher of Monticello," in a letter to James McHenry, January 5, 1811, in *The Life and Correspondence of James McHenry,* by Bernard Steiner (Cleveland, 1907), p. 561. Pamphlet, *The Pretensions of Thomas Jefferson to the Presidency Examined,* by William Smith (Philadelphia, 1796), pp. 57-60.

Page 13. The Papers of Mrs. Samuel Harrison Smith, in the Library of Congress, hereafter cited as "SHS Papers," provide the manuscripts of "SHS" and Margaret Bayard. Margaret described "SHS" in her diary entry of October 5, 1801. "SHS" admitted his ambition in a letter to Margaret, November 26, 1797. Commission to Jonathan Bayard Smith is in the J. Henley Smith Papers, Library of Congress, Vol. 1, p. 1,406.

Pages 14-15. SHS to Margaret Bayard, July 4, 1800, SHS Papers, Vol. 6, p. 66,817. SHS to Mary Smith, June 3, 1794, SHS Papers, Vol. 1, p. 65,867. SHS to Mary Smith, August 26 and September 11, 1796, SHS Papers, Vol. 1, pp. 65,915-17.

Page 16. Benjamin Davies, *Some Account of the City of Philadelphia, the Capital of Pennsylvania and the Seat of the Federal Congress* (Philadelphia, 1794).

Pages 16-17. Advertisements in various issues of the *New World,* September-December, 1796.

Page 18. SHS to Mary Smith, June 18, 1796, SHS Papers, Vol. 1, p. 65,908.

Page 20. Rufus W. Griswold, *The Republican Court: or American Society in the Days of Washington* (New York, 1854), p. 253. *Moreau de Saint-Méry's American Journey,* translated and edited by Kenneth Roberts and Anna M. Roberts (New York, 1947), p. xix.

Page 21. Twining, p. 167. François Alexandre Frédéric, Duc de la Rochefoucauld-Liancourt, *Travels Through the United States of North America* (London, 1799), Vol. 4, pp. 104-5; Isaac Weld, *Travels*

Through the States of North America (London, 1807), Vol. 1, p. 21.
Moreau de Saint-Méry, pp. 282-83.

Page 22. The *New World,* December 19, 1796.

Pages 23-24. The *New World,* October 26, 1796.

Page 25. The *New World,* November 1, 1796.

Pages 26-27. The *New World,* November 3, 1796.

Page 28. Adet's letters in the *New World,* October 31, 1796, *et seq.*

Page 29. George Cabot to Oliver Wolcott, October 11, 1796, Wolcott Papers, Vol. 1, p. 386; Wolcott to his father, November 19, 1796, *ibid.,* Vol. 1, p. 397. John Adams, *Letters Addressed to His Wife,* November 27, 1796, pp. 229-31. The *New World,* November 5, 1796.

Page 30. The *New World,* November 25, 1796. Wolcott to his father, November 27, 1796, Wolcott Papers, Vol. 1, p. 401. Andrew Jackson to John Sevier, January 18, 1797 (original in New York Historical Society), *Correspondence of Andrew Jackson,* edited by John Spencer Bassett (Washington, 1926), Vol. 1, pp. 27-28.

Page 31. SHS to Mary Smith, December 4, 1796, SHS Papers, Vol. 1, pp. 65,922-23. The *New World,* December 22, 1796. Chauncey Goodrich to Oliver Wolcott, Sr., December 17, 1796, Wolcott Papers, Vol. 1, p. 413. Andrew Jackson to Robert Hays, January 8, 1797, Bassett, Vol. 1, p. 25.

Page 32. John Adams, *Works,* edited by Charles Francis Adams (10 vols., Boston, 1850-56), Vol. 8, p. 524. Jefferson to Edward Rutledge, December 17, 1796, Jefferson Papers, L.C., Vol. 101, p. 17,260. Jefferson to Madison, January 1, 1797, *ibid.,* p. 17,272; Jefferson to Benjamin Rush, January 22, 1797, *ibid.,* p. 17,298.

Page 33. Adams to Abigail Adams, December 30, 1796, in *Letters Addressed to His Wife.*

Page 34. Jefferson to Madison, January 1, 1797, Jefferson Papers, L.C., Vol. 101, p. 17,272. Adams to Tristram Dalton, January 19, 1797, New York Public Library. William Paterson to James Iredell, March 7, 1797, Griffith John McRee, *Life and Correspondence of James Iredell* (2 vols., New York, 1857) Vol. 2, p. 495. Hamilton to Rufus King, February 15, 1797, Hamilton, *Works* (J. C. Hamilton, ed.), Vol. 6, p. 206.

Page 36. Twining, pp. 37-38, describes Adams. Adams to Abigail, March 5 and 17, 1797, in *Letters Addressed to His Wife,* pp. 244-45, 251-52.

Page 37. The *New World,* March 4, 1797. Jefferson to Madison, January 8, 1797, Madison Papers, Library of Congress, Vol. 20, p. 7.

Pages 39-40. Margaret Bayard's diary, Library of Congress. SHS to Mrs. Jane Kirkpatrick, March 15, 1797, SHS Papers, Vol. 1, pp. 68,264-67.

Page 41. SHS to Mary Smith, June 29, 1796, SHS Papers, Vol. 1, pp. 65,910-11.

Page 42. Margaret Bayard's diary.

Pages 42-44. The story of Colonel John B. Bayard and his family is derived from the J. Henley Smith Papers, SHS Papers, and James A. Bayard Papers, L. C.; James Grant Wilson, *Memorials of Andrew Kirkpatrick and His Wife Jane Bayard* (New York, 1870); James Grant Wilson, *Colonel John Bayard and the Bayard Family of America* (New York, 1885); Morton Borden, *The Federalism of James A. Bayard* (New York, 1955); Walter R. Fee, *The Transition from Aristocracy to Democracy in New Jersey, 1789-1829* (Somerville, N.J., 1933); and Mrs. Jane Kirkpatrick, *Light of Other Days* (New Brunswick, N.J., 1856).

Page 44. John B. Bayard to John Nicholson, March 11, 1786, Gratz Papers, Historical Society of Pennsylvania.

Pages 44-45. Theophile Cazenove's *Journal,* 1794, edited by Rayner W. Kelsey (Haverford, Pa., 1922).

Pages 45-47. Margaret Bayard's accounts of her youthful escapades are in her diary and a letter to SHS, July 26, 1798, SHS Papers, Vol. 4, p. 66,383.

Pages 47-48. James Grant Wilson, *Memorials of Andrew Kirkpatrick and His Wife, Jane Bayard. Letters of Benjamin Rush,* edited by L. H. Butterfield (2 vols. Philadelphia, 1951), Vol. 1, p. 602.

Page 48. Margaret Bayard's diary.

Page 49. Margaret Bayard to Mary Smith, December 26, 1795, SHS Papers, Vol. 1, pp. 65,900-901.

Pages 50-58. Letters of Margaret Bayard and SHS about his courtship, January through April, 1797, are in the SHS Papers, Vol. 1, pp. 65,936-70; also a few undated letters, Vols. 14, 15, and 16.

Pages 60-61. Wilson, *Memorials,* p. 42; Wilson, *Colonel John Bayard.*

Pages 61-68. Love letters of Margaret Bayard and SHS in April and May, 1797, are in SHS Papers, Vol. 1, pp. 65,970-66,031.

CHAPTER THREE

Page 69. Fisher Ames to Wolcott, March 24, 1797, Wolcott Papers, Vol. 1, p. 477. Hamilton to Timothy Pickering, March 22, 1797, Hamilton, *Works* (Hamilton), Vol. 6, p. 213. Washington to Hamilton, January

22, 1797, *ibid.*, Vol. 6, p. 197. Cabot to Wolcott, May 15, 1797, Wolcott Papers, Vol. 1, p. 533. Harper to his constituents, March 13, 1797, Donnan, p. 38.

Page 70. James D. Richardson, ed., *A Compilation of the Messages and Public Papers of the Presidents, 1789-1927* (20 vols., Washington, 1896-1927), Vol. 1, pp. 233-39. Hamilton's pamphlet, *The Warning,* 1797.

Page 71. Wolcott Papers, Vol. 1, pp. 486-87. Jefferson to Elbridge Gerry, June 21, 1797, Jefferson Papers, L.C., Vol. 102, p. 17,436.

Page 72. Hamilton to Wolcott, June 6, 1797, Hamilton, *Works* (Lodge), Vol. 10, p. 268.

Page 73. James A. Bayard is described by Senator William Plumer in Plumer Papers, L.C.; by Benjamin Henry Latrobe in *Impressions Respecting New Orleans,* edited by Samuel Wilson, Jr., New York, 1951.

Page 74. Otis is described in *Life and Letters of Harrison Gray Otis, Federalist,* by Samuel Eliot Morison (2 vols., Boston and New York, 1913), Vol. 1, p. 219.

Page 75. Albert Gallatin is described by Twining, pp. 51-52. For Bayard's maiden speech, see Borden, *The Federalism of James A. Bayard,* p. 26.

Page 76. Jefferson to Madison, June 15, 1797, Madison Papers, L.C., Vol. 20, p. 50. Gallatin to his wife, June 26, 1797, Henry Adams, *Life of Albert Gallatin,* p. 185.

Page 77. Jefferson to Burr, June 17, 1797, Jefferson Papers, L.C., Vol. 102, pp. 17,429-31.

Page 78. Burr to Jefferson, June 21, 1797, Jefferson Papers, L.C., Vol. 102, p. 17,438.

Page 79. Adams, *Gallatin,* p. 187; *Porcupine's Gazette,* July 3, 1797.

Page 80. Jefferson to Mazzei, April 24, 1796, Jefferson Papers, L.C., Vol. 100, pp. 17,129-31.

Page 81. Jefferson to Rutledge, June 24, 1797, *ibid.,* Vol. 102, pp. 17,444-46. Jefferson to Peregrine Fitzhugh, June 4, 1797, *ibid.,* Vol. 101, p. 17,414. Jefferson to Madison, June 15, 1797, Madison Papers, L.C., Vol. 20, p. 50. The *New World,* April 12, 1797.

Pages 82-83. Margaret Bayard to SHS, July 1, 1797, SHS Papers, Vol. 2, p. 66,058.

Page 85. Wolcott to his wife, September 15, 1797, Wolcott Papers, Vol. 1, p. 561.

Pages 86-88. Margaret Bayard's letters to Samuel and Mary Smith, July, 1797, are in SHS Papers, Vol. 2, pp. 66,060-78.

CHAPTER FOUR

Pages 89-101. Letters of SHS and Margaret Bayard, July to December, 1797, are in SHS Papers, Vol. 2, pp. 66,060-178.

Pages 92-93. Margaret Bayard's anecdotes of the Kirkpatrick children are in SHS Papers, Vol. 2, pp. 66,151-52 and in her diary.

Page 95. *Porcupine's Gazette,* February 11, 1799.

Page 96. Jefferson to John Taylor, October 8, 1797, Jefferson, *Writings* (Monticello edition 1905), Vol. 18, pp. 202-3. James T. Callender to Jefferson, September 28, 1797, and March 21, 1798, Jefferson Papers, L.C., Vol. 102, p. 17,492; Vol. 103, p. 17,651.

Pages 97-99. SHS' *Remarks on Education* appeared as a pamphlet in Philadelphia in 1798. SHS to Margaret Bayard, May 30, 1798, SHS Papers, Vol. 3, pp. 66,328-29.

Pages 99-100. Margaret Bayard to SHS, December 31, 1797, and January 11, 1798, SHS Papers, Vol. 2, pp. 66,177-78 and 66,185-86.

Pages 102-4. James A. Bayard to Gov. Richard Bassett, February 7, 1798, Donnan, pp. 48-50. Abigail Adams to Mary Cranch, February 15, 1798, Stewart Mitchell (ed.), *New Letters of Abigail Adams* (Boston, 1947), pp. 132-33.

Page 104. Donnan, p. 51. Jefferson to Madison and to Monroe, March 21, 1798, Jefferson Papers, L.C., Vol. 103, pp. 17,648-50.

Page 105. *Annals of Congress,* Fifth Congress, p. 1,380.

Pages 105-6. The "XYZ Affair" is recounted in *The Life of John Marshall,* by Albert J. Beveridge (4 vols., Boston and New York, 1916), Vol. 2, pp. 214-373. Jefferson to Madison, April 6, 1798, Madison Papers, L.C., Vol. 20, p. 101. Madison to Jefferson, April 15, 1798, *ibid.,* Vol. 20, p. 104. Washington to Pickering, April 16, 1798, Fitzpatrick, Vol. 36, pp. 248-49.

Pages 107-9. SHS to Margaret Bayard, March 23 and 25 and April 16, 1798, and Margaret Bayard to SHS, March 28, 1798, SHS Papers, Vol. 3, pp. 66,263-72.

Pages 109-10. James A. Bayard to John E. Howard, August 30, 1798, Donnan, pp. 71-73. *Porcupine's Gazette,* May 7, 1798. Adams, *Works,* Vol. 9, p. 279.

Page 111. Abigail Adams to Mary Cranch, April 26, 1798, Mitchell (ed.), *New Letters of Abigail Adams,* p. 165. Jefferson to Madison, June 21, 1798, Jefferson Papers, L.C., Vol. 104, pp. 17,810-12.

Page 113. Henry Tazewell to Andrew Jackson, July 20, 1798, Bassett (ed.), *Correspondence of Andrew Jackson,* Vol. 1, pp. 50-54. Washington to Adams, July 4, 1798, Fitzpatrick, Vol. 36, p. 313.

Pages 116-17. Margaret Bayard to SHS, March 17 and June 23, 1798, SHS to Margaret Bayard, June 25, 1798, SHS Papers, Vol. 3, pp. 66,255-56 and 66,352-55.

CHAPTER FIVE

Pages 118-23. Letters of Margaret Bayard and SHS in the yellow fever epidemic of August and September, 1798, are in SHS Papers, Vol. 4, pp. 66,397-445.

Pages 123-25. J. Fairfax McLaughlin, *Matthew Lyon: The Hampden of Congress* (New York, 1900). *Porcupine's Gazette*, February 21, 1799. Callender to Jefferson, October 26, 1798, Jefferson Papers, L.C., Vol. 104, pp. 17,887-88.

Page 126. *Greenleaf's New Daily Advertiser*, New York, October 15, 1799.

Pages 127-29. Jefferson to General Samuel Smith, August 22, 1798, Jefferson Papers, L.C., Vol. 104, pp. 17,844-47. Jefferson to John Taylor, November 26, 1798, *ibid.*, pp. 17,895-97. Washington to McHenry, September 30, 1798, Fitzpatrick, Vol. 36, p. 474.

Page 129. Adams, *Works,* Vol. 10, p. 124.

Pages 130-31. Hamilton to King, August 22, 1798, Hamilton, *Works* (Lodge), Vol. 10, pp. 314-15. Randall, *Jefferson*, Vol. 2, pp. 457, 464. Hamilton to Otis, January 26, 1799, Hamilton, *Works* (Hamilton), Vol. 6, pp. 390-92.

Pages 132-35. For scenes of the SHS-Margaret Bayard courtship in the winter of 1798-99, see her letters to him and to Jane Kirkpatrick in SHS Papers, Vol. 4, pp. 66,487-510, and her 1799 diary.

CHAPTER SIX

Page 136. Steiner, *McHenry,* p. 568.

Page 137. Pickering to Hamilton, February 25, 1799, Hamilton, *Works* (Hamilton), Vol. 6, p. 398. George Cabot to Rufus King, *King,* Vol. 3, p. 249. Steiner, *McHenry,* p. 606. Harper to the Secretary of War, August 2, 1799, Harper Papers, L.C. Jefferson to Madison, February 19, 1799, Madison Papers, L.C., Vol. 21, p. 32.

Pages 139-40. *Aurora,* April 27, 1799. Morison, *Otis,* Vol. 1, pp. 174-75.

Pages 142-44. The *Universal Gazette,* April 25, 1799. Justice James Iredell to his wife, April 18, 1799, McRee, *Iredell,* Vol. 2, pp. 571-72.

Pages 144-45. SHS-Margaret Bayard letters of the summer and autumn of 1799 are in the SHS Papers, Vol. 5, pp. 66,573-654.

Page 146. A concise account of the Cobbett-Rush feud is in *The Letters of Benjamin Rush*, edited by L. H. Butterfield, Vol. 2, pp. 1,213-18.

Page 147. Beveridge, *Marshall*, Vol. 2, p. 444.

Pages 147-53. Margaret Bayard's accounts of Gouverneur Morris' funeral oration for George Washington, and other New York events of 1799-1800, are in the SHS Papers, Vol. 5, pp. 66,687-818. Detailed descriptions of Dr. Samuel Latham Mitchill and other New Yorkers are in her journal and in *Old New York: Or, Reminiscences of the Past Sixty Years*, by John W. Francis (New York, 1860).

CHAPTER SEVEN

Page 154. Jefferson to Madison, March 4, 1800, Madison Papers, L.C., Vol. 21, p. 72. Jefferson, *Writings* (Ford), Vol. 9, pp. 118-23.

Pages 155-56. Troup to King, March 9, 1800, *King*, Vol. 3, p. 208; King to Troup, May 8, *ibid.*, p. 235. Sedgwick to King, December 12, 1799, *ibid.*, pp. 154-56.

Page 157. Jefferson's shrewd summary of his own prospects in 1800 is in his letter to Madison, March 4, 1800, cited above.

Page 158. Bingham to King, March 5, 1800, *King*, Vol. 3, p. 205.

Page 160. Troup to King, March 9, 1800. *Ibid.*, p. 208. New York *Advertiser*, April 3, 1800. *Albany Centinel*, May 6, 1800.

Page 161. Adams, *Gallatin*, pp. 234-41.

Pages 161-62. John Dawson to Madison, May 4, 1800, Madison Papers, L.C., Vol. 21, p. 84. Hamilton to Jay, May 7, 1800, Hamilton, *Works* (Lodge), Vol. 10, pp. 371-74. Dawson to Madison, December 12, 1799, Madison Papers, L.C., Vol. 21, p. 53.

Pages 163-65. Adams, *Gallatin*, pp. 239-43.

Page 166. Steiner, *McHenry*, pp. 454, 458. Pickering to King, June 26, 1800, *King*, Vol. 3, p. 261.

Page 167. Benjamin Goodhue to Pickering, June 2, 1800, *King*, Vol. 3, p. 263. Pickering to McHenry, May 7, 1810, *McHenry*, p. 558; Cabot to King, May 29, 1800, *King*, Vol. 3, p. 249.

Pages 167-69. C. C. Pinckney to McHenry, June 10, 1800, *McHenry*, p. 459. Sedgwick to King, May 11, 1800, *King*, Vol. 3, p. 238. Hamilton to Sedgwick, May 10, 1800, Hamilton, *Works* (Hamilton), Vol. 6, pp. 441-42. McHenry to Hamilton, November 19, 1800, *ibid.*, pp. 479-80. James A. Bayard to Hamilton, August 18, 1800, *ibid.*, p. 467.

Pages 169-71. Comments by Margaret Bayard and SHS on the New York election of 1800 are in SHS Papers, Vol. 6, pp. 66,795-800.

Pages 171-73. Bayard-Champlin duel is recorded in Donnan, pp.

110-11; also see Sedgwick to King, May 11, 1800, and Gore to King, May 14, 1800, in *King,* Vol. 3, pp. 239, 242.

CHAPTER EIGHT

Page 174. Stephen G. Kurtz, *The Presidency of John Adams* (Philadelphia, 1957), pp. 397-99.

Page 175. Sedgwick to King, September 26, 1800, *King,* Vol. 3, pp. 307-10.

Page 176. Hamilton to McHenry, August 27, 1800, Hamilton, *Works* (Lodge), Vol. 10, pp. 388-89. Cabot to King, July 19, 1800, *King,* Vol. 3, pp. 278-79. Ames to King, July 15, 1800, *ibid.,* p. 277.

Page 177. Hamilton to Bayard, August 6, 1800, Hamilton, *Works* (Hamilton), Vol. 3, pp. 45-53; Hamilton, *Works* (Lodge), Vol. 10, pp. 384-88. James Cheetham, *A View of the Political Conduct of Aaron Burr* (New York, 1802), pp. 42-46.

Page 178. Troup to King, June 24, August 9 and September 14, 1800, *King,* Vol. 3, pp. 250, 290, 300; Cabot to Hamilton, August 10, 1800, Hamilton, *Works* (Lodge), Vol. 6, p. 454; Charles Carroll to Hamilton, August 27, 1800, Hamilton, *Works* (Hamilton), Vol. 6, pp. 467-68.

Pages 179-83. Letters of Margaret Bayard and SHS about his newspaper offers of 1800 are in SHS Papers, Vol. 6, pp. 66,754-82; pp. 66,811-16.

Page 183. SHS to Madison, August 27, 1800, Madison Papers, L.C., Vol. 21, p. 99.

Pages 184-93. Letters of Margaret Bayard and SHS about their wedding preparations are in SHS Papers, Vol. 6, pp. 66,842-80.

CHAPTER NINE

Pages 194-203. Details of the Smiths' wedding journey to Washington and descriptions of the frontier capital appear in Margaret's letters to her sister Jane and Samuel's letters to his family in Philadelphia, October 5 and 6, 1800, SHS Papers, Vol. 6, pp. 66,881-85; also Vol. 16, p. 68,556, and Margaret's diary, October 6, 1800.

Page 198. Margaret's conversation with Mrs. Stelle appears in SHS Papers, Vol. 15, p. 68,461.

Page 203. Wolcott to his wife, July 4, 1800, Wolcott Papers, Vol. 2, pp. 376-78.

Pages 204-5. Allen C. Clark, "Dr. and Mrs. William Thornton," in Columbia Historical Society *Records* (Washington, 1915), Vol. 18, pp. 144-208. See also Mrs. Thornton's diary, L.C.

Pages 205-7. Allen C. Clark, *Greenleaf and Law in the Federal City* (Washington, 1901); Allen C. Clark, *Thomas Law, a Biographical Sketch* (Washington, 1900).

Page 207. Margaret Bayard Smith to Jane Kirkpatrick, October 19, 1800, SHS Papers, Vol. 6, p. 66,839.

Page 208. Margaret's description of dinner with the Laws appears in two letters to her sisters, November 12 and 16, 1800, in SHS Papers, Vol. 6, pp. 66,899-902.

Page 209. Mrs. Smith to Mrs. Kirkpatrick, October 19 and November 16, 1800, SHS Papers, Vol. 6, pp. 66,892, 66,902.

Pages 209-10. SHS to John Smith, October 6, 1800, SHS Papers, Vol. 6, pp. 66,885-86.

Pages 210-11. *The National Intelligencer,* October 31, 1800.

Pages 211-17. Scenes of the Smiths' life in Washington in late 1800 are in the SHS Papers, Vol. 6, pp. 66,881-914, and in Margaret's diary.

Pages 217-18. John Bayard to Margaret Bayard Smith, November 11, 1800, SHS Papers, Vol. 6, pp. 66,897-98.

CHAPTER TEN

Page 219. Cabot to Wolcott, October 5, 1800, Wolcott Papers, Vol. 2, p. 433. Carroll to McHenry, November 4, 1800, *McHenry,* p. 473.

Page 220. Sedgwick to King, September 26, 1800, *King,* Vol. 3, p. 308. Bayard to Rutledge, June 8, 1800, Donnan, pp. 111-12. Hamilton to Bayard, August 6, 1800, Hamilton, *Works* (Hamilton), Vol. 6, pp. 451-53. Bayard to Hamilton, August 18, 1800, *ibid.,* pp. 455-58.

Page 221. McHenry to Wolcott, July 22, 1800, *McHenry,* p. 462; Wolcott Papers, Vol. 2, pp. 384-86. *The Voice of Warning, to Christians, on the Ensuing Election of a President of the United States,* by John M. Mason, D.D. (New York, 1800).

Page 222. *Serious Considerations on the Election of a President,* by the Rev. William Linn (New York, 1800). Gabriel Duvall to Madison, October 17, 1800, Madison Papers, L.C., Vol. 21, p. 110. *Address to the People of the United States,* by John Beckley (Philadelphia, 1800). Jefferson to Rush, September 23, 1800, Jefferson Papers, American Philosophical Society (italics added); also in Jefferson's *Writings* (Ford), Vol. 9, pp. 146-49.

Page 223. Ames to King, September 24, 1800, *King,* Vol. 3, p. 304. C. C. Pinckney to McHenry, June 19, 1800, *McHenry,* p. 461.

Page 224. *Letter from Alexander Hamilton Concerning the Public Conduct and Character of John Adams* (New York, 1800).

Page 225. Philemon Dickinson to McHenry, October 7 and 31, *McHenry*, pp. 471-72. Troup to King, November 9, 1800, *King*, Vol. 3, p. 331. Cabot to Hamilton, November 29, 1800, Lodge, *Cabot*, pp. 298-300. Carroll to McHenry, November 4, 1800, *McHenry*, p. 473. *Aurora*, October 29, 1800.

Page 226. Madison to Jefferson, November 1, 1800, Jefferson Papers, L.C., Vol. 107, p. 18,431.

Page 227. Rodney to Jefferson, October 13, 1800, *ibid.*, p. 18,413. Burr to Jefferson, October 9, 1800, *ibid.*, p. 18,407.

Page 228. Madison to Jefferson, October 21, 1800, Madison Papers, L.C., Vol. 21, p. 111. David Gelston to Madison, October 8, 1800, Madison Papers (Rives Collection), L.C., Vol. 2, p. 313.

Page 229. Monroe to Madison, November 6, 1800, *ibid.*, p. 314. Madison to Monroe, November 10, 1800, Monroe Papers, L.C.

Page 230. John Nicholas to Madison, November 28, 1800, Madison Papers (Rives Collection), L.C., Vol. 2, p. 318.

Page 231. For Jonathan Dayton's boasts, see Cheetham, *View*, pp. 43-45. Burr to Edwards, November 26 and 29, 1800, Burr Papers, New York Public Library. Gelston to Madison, November 21, 1800, Madison Papers (Rives Collection), L.C., Vol. 2, p. 317.

Page 232-33. *Correspondence and Miscellanies of John Cotton Smith*, by William W. Andrews (New York, 1847), pp. 199-221.

Page 234. Morris, *Diary*, Vol. 2, pp. 394-95. Richardson, *Messages and Papers of the Presidents*, Vol. 1, pp. 305-8.

Page 235. Margaret Bayard Smith to Jane Kirkpatrick, November 27, 1800, SHS Papers, Vol. 6, pp. 66,905-6.

Page 236. MBS to Susan Smith, January 1, 1801, *ibid.*, p. 66,913. James A. Bayard to Caesar Rodney, January 9, 1801, Donnan, pp. 119-20. Augustus John Foster, "Notes on the United States," *William and Mary Quarterly*, January, 1951, p. 84. *The National Intelligencer*, November 28, 1800.

Page 237. Jefferson to William Findley, March 24, 1801, Jefferson Papers, L.C., Vol. 111, p. 19,048.

Pages 238-39. Margaret Bayard Smith's account of her first encounter with Jefferson is in her commonplace book, SHS Papers, L.C.

Page 240. Edward Livingston to Jefferson, December 9, 1800, Jefferson Papers, L.C., Vol. 108, p. 18,480. Peter Freneau to Jefferson, December 8, 1800, *ibid.*, p. 18,461. Gunn to Hamilton, December 11, 1800, Hamilton, *Works* (Hamilton), Vol. 6, p. 483.

Page 241. Charles Pinckney to Jefferson, December 2, 1800, Jefferson Papers, L.C., Vol. 108, p. 18,450. *The National Intelligencer*, December 12, 1800.

Page 242. Pickering to King, December 27, 1800, *King,* Vol. 3, pp. 352-53. McHenry to King, January 2, 1801, *ibid.,* pp. 362-64. Gunn to Hamilton, December 13, 1800, Hamilton, *Works* (Hamilton), Vol. 6, p. 483.

Page 243. Abigail Adams to Thomas B. Adams, November 13, 1800, *Letters of Mrs. Adams,* p. 239. Charles Adams, age thirty, died in New York, November 30, 1800. See *New Letters of Abigail Adams* (Mitchell, ed.), pp. 255, 261-62, for her letter to her sister, Mrs. Mary Cranch, December 8, 1800.

Page 244. Gunn to Hamilton, December 18, 1800, Hamilton, *Works* (Hamilton), Vol. 6, p. 492. Jefferson to Madison, December 19, 1800, Madison Papers (Rives Collection), L.C., Vol. 2, p. 321. Jefferson to John Breckinridge, December 18, 1800, Jefferson Papers, L.C., Vol. 108, p. 18,504.

Page 245. John Dawson to Madison, December 18, 1800, Madison Papers, L.C., Vol. 21, p. 123.

CHAPTER ELEVEN

Pages 246-47. Jefferson to Burr, December 15, 1800, Jefferson Papers, L.C., Vol. 108, pp. 18,494-95.

Page 248. Jefferson to Robert R. Livingston, December 14, 1800, *ibid.,* pp. 18,490-92. Burr to Jefferson, December 23, 1800, *ibid.,* p. 18,525. Edward Livingston to Jefferson, December 9, 1800, *ibid.,* p. 18,480. Burr to Jefferson, December 26, 1800, *ibid.,* p. 18,540. Jefferson to Madison, December 19, 1800, *ibid.,* pp. 18,507-8.

Page 249. Burr to General Samuel Smith, December 16, 1800. Letter printed in *The National Intelligencer,* January 1, 1801. McHenry to King, January 2, 1801, *King,* Vol. 3, pp. 362-64.

Page 250. Uriah Tracy to McHenry, December 30, 1800, *McHenry,* p. 483. Adams to Gerry, December 30, 1800, Adams, *Works,* Vol. 9, p. 577.

Page 251. Theophilus Parsons to Harrison Gray Otis, January 23, 1801, Morison, *Otis,* Vol. 1, p. 213. Harper to Burr, December 24, 1800, McLaughlin, *Lyon,* p. 386.

Page 252. Burr's most significant letter to General Smith, December 29, 1800, saying "I would not" resign the presidency if elected, is in the Smith-Carter Papers, Alderman Library, University of Virginia. Cited by John S. Pancake in the *William and Mary Quarterly,* April, 1951, Vol. 8, No. 2. Gabriel Christie's written account of General Smith's report of the fruitless talk with Burr at Philadelphia is in General Smith's Papers, L.C.

Page 253. Benjamin Hichborn to Jefferson, January 5, 1801. The original of this important letter is in the Jefferson Papers, L.C., Vol. 108, p. 18,589. Jefferson's *Anas*, January 2, 1804, *Complete Anas* (Sawvel), p. 223. Pickering to King, January 5, 1801, *King,* Vol. 3, p. 366.

Page 254. Jefferson to Maria Jefferson Eppes, January 4, 1801, Randall, *Jefferson,* Vol. 2, p. 594.

Page 255. Bayard to Hamilton, January 7, 1801, Hamilton, *Works* (Hamilton), Vol. 6, pp. 505-7.

Page 256. Hamilton to Gouverneur Morris, January 9 and 13, *ibid.,* pp. 508, 520.

Pages 257-58. Bayard to Hamilton, January 7, 1801, *ibid.,* p. 506. General Smith to Burr, January 11, 1801, General Samuel Smith Papers, L.C.

Page 259. Burr to General Smith, January 16, 1801, *ibid.* For Bayard's deposition in *Gillespie vs. Smith,* see Davis, *Burr,* Vol. 2, pp. 129-33. For David Ogden's deposition, *ibid.,* p. 120.

Page 260. McMaster, *A History of the People of the United States,* Vol. 2, p. 509; Cheetham, *View,* p. 49; Randall, *Jefferson,* Vol. 2, p. 574; Hammond, *Political History of New York,* Vol. 1, p. 141. Cheetham, *Reply to Aristides,* p. 127, mentions Anthony Lispenard as "the particular friend of Mr. Burr," tempted to throw an electoral vote away from Jefferson. Jefferson, *Complete Anas* (Sawvel), p. 227.

Pages 263-69. Hamilton's diatribes against Burr, and other Federalists' replies, are in Hamilton, *Works* (Hamilton), Vol. 6, pp. 487-522.

Pages 270-71. Rodney to Jefferson, December 28, 1800, Jefferson Papers, L.C., Vol. 108, pp. 18,545-48. John Vaughan to Jefferson, January 10, 1801, *ibid.,* p. 18,605.

Pages 272-73. Jefferson to T. M. Randolph, January 9, 1801, Jefferson Papers, L.C., Vol. 108, p. 18,599. Bayard's deposition, Davis, *Burr,* Vol. 2, pp. 129-33.

CHAPTER TWELVE

Pages 275-76. Editor Smith's squabble with Bradley appears in *The National Intelligencer,* February 2 and 9, 1801.

Pages 276-81. Smith reported his battle with Speaker Sedgwick in *The National Intelligencer,* December 5, 10 and 12, 1800, and January 16 and 19, 1801. SHS to John Smith, January 18, 1801 (incorrectly dated "1800"), SHS Papers, L.C., Vol. 5, pp. 66,700-701.

Page 282. Gallatin to his wife, January 15, 1801, Adams, *Gallatin,* pp. 253-55.

Page 283. Adams, *Writings of Albert Gallatin*, Vol. 1, pp. 18-23. Madison to Jefferson, January 10, 1801, Madison Papers, L.C., Vol. 22, p. 3. Randall, *Jefferson*, Vol. 3, p. 639 and Vol. 2, p. 599.

Page 284. Adams to Gerry, February 7, 1801, Adams, *Works*, Vol. 9, p. 98. Randall, *Jefferson*, Vol. 2, p. 578. Gallatin to his wife, January 22, 1801, Adams, *Gallatin*, p. 256. Governor Thomas McKean to Jefferson, January 10, 1801, Jefferson Papers, L.C., Vol. 108, pp. 18,606-7.

Page 285. Madison to Jefferson, January 10, 1801, Madison Papers, L.C., Vol. 22, p. 3. Gallatin to his wife, January 15, 1801, Adams, *Gallatin*, p. 254. Troup to King, May 27, 1801, *King*, Vol. 3, p. 459. Maria Nicholson to Mrs. Gallatin, February 5, 1801, Adams, *Gallatin*, pp. 244-45.

Page 286. Cheetham, *View*, p. 69. Jefferson to Burr, February 1, 1801, Jefferson Papers, L.C., Vol. 109, p. 18,688. Jefferson, *Writings* (Lipscomb, ed.), Vol. 10, pp. 103-4. Burr to Jefferson, February 12, 1801, Jefferson Papers, L.C., Vol. 109, p. 18,726.

Page 287. Burr to Gallatin, February 12, 1801, Adams, *Gallatin*, p. 246. Cheetham, *View*, p. 64. Hammond, *Political History of New York*, Vol. 1, pp. 141-42.

Page 288. George Jackson to Madison, February 5, 1801, Madison Papers, L.C., Vol. 22, p. 7.

Page 289. Troup to King, May 27, 1801, *King*, Vol. 3, pp. 458-61. General Samuel Smith Papers, L.C.

Page 290. Jefferson to Monroe, February 15, 1801, Monroe Papers, L.C., Vol. 6, p. 1,057. George Jackson to Madison, February 5, 1801, Madison Papers, L.C., Vol. 22, p. 7.

Page 291. John Tyler to Monroe, February 11, 1801, Monroe Papers, L.C., Vol. 6, p. 1,036. John Dawson to Monroe, February 13, 1801, *ibid.*, p. 1,051. General E. Meade to Monroe, February 17, 1801, *ibid.*, p. 1,067. Boston *Centinel*, January 7, 1801. *Washington Federalist*, February 12, 1801.

Page 292. Jefferson to Robert Patterson, December 10, 1800, Jefferson Papers, L.C., Vol. 108, p. 18,481. William Cooper to Thomas Morris, February 10, 1801, Davis, *Burr*, Vol. 2, pp. 112-13.

Page 293. Otis to his wife, February 9, 1801, Morison, *Otis*, Vol. 1, p. 207. James A. Bayard to Governor Bassett, February 10, 1801, Donnan, pp. 124-25. Troup to King, February 12, 1801, *King*, Vol. 3, pp. 390-91.

Page 294. *The National Intelligencer*, February 11, 1801.

Page 296. *Annals of Congress*, Vol. 10, p. 1,023, names the tellers.

Page 297. Otis to his wife, February 11, 1801, Morison, *Otis*, Vol. 1, p. 207-8.

Page 298. Gabriel Christie to General Samuel Smith, December 19, 1802, General Samuel Smith Papers, L.C.

Page 299. *The National Intelligencer*, February 11, 1801. Randall, *Jefferson*, Vol. 2, p. 596.

Page 300. James A. Bayard to Governor Bassett and to Andrew Bayard, February 12, 1801, Donnan, pp. 125-26. Margaret Bayard Smith's journal, L.C. New York *Commercial Advertiser*, February 16, 1801.

Page 301. Samuel W. Dana to Wolcott, quoted in Randall, *Jefferson*, Vol. 2, pp. 596-97. Otis to his wife, February 11, 1801, Morison, *Otis*, Vol. 1, p. 208. John Dawson to Madison, February 12, 1801, Madison Papers, L.C., Vol. 22, p. 10. Littleton W. Tazewell to Monroe, February 12, 1801, Monroe Papers, L.C., Vol. 6, p. 1,043. Uriah Tracy to Mr. Gould, February 16, 1801, Historical Society of Pennsylvania.

Page 302. Jefferson, *Complete Anas* (Sawvel, ed.), pp. 209-10, 223.

Page 303. Bayard to Hamilton, March 8, 1801, Hamilton, *Works* (Hamilton), Vol. 6, pp. 522-24. William Cooper to Thomas Morris, February 13, 1801, Davis, *Burr*, Vol. 2, p. 113.

Pages 304-5. George W. Erving to Monroe, February 9, 1801, Monroe Papers, L.C., Vol. 6, p. 1,030. John Tyler to Monroe, February 9, 1801, *ibid.*, p. 1,034. John Hoomes to Monroe, February 16, 1801, *ibid.*, p. 1,062. Jefferson, diary, February 14, 1801, *Complete Anas* (Sawvel, ed.), p. 210. Davis, *Burr*, Vol. 2, pp. 129-33.

Page 307. Jefferson, diary, April 15, 1806, *Complete Anas* (Sawvel, ed.), pp. 238-41.

Page 308. Deposition, General Samuel Smith Papers, L.C. Gallatin to Henry Muhlenberg, May 8, 1848, Adams, *Gallatin*, p. 250. Jefferson to Monroe, February 15, 1801, Monroe Papers, L.C., Vol. 6, p. 1,057.

Page 309. MBS Journal, SHS Papers, L. C. John Hoomes to Monroe, February 19, 1801, Monroe Papers, L.C., Vol. 6, p. 1,075. *The National Intelligencer*, February 16, 1801. Andrews, *Correspondence and Miscellanies of John Cotton Smith*, pp. 216-20.

Page 310. Burr to Gallatin, February 12, 1801, Adams, *Gallatin*, p. 246. George Baer's recollections are in the pamphlet, *Vindication of James A. Bayard*, pp. 24-26.

Page 311. James A. Bayard's reports of the stormy Federalist caucus are in letters to Governor Bassett, February 17, 1801, and Samuel Bayard, February 22, 1801, in Donnan, pp. 127, 131, 132; and to Hamilton, March 8, 1801, Hamilton, *Works* (Hamilton), Vol. 6, pp. 522-24.

Page 312. Gallatin to his wife, February 17, 1801, Adams, *Gallatin*, p. 262.

Page 313. Bayard to Bassett, February 17, 1801, Donnan, p. 127. Bayard to McLane, February 17, 1801, copy in Jefferson Papers, L.C., Vol. 109, p. 18,739. Bayard to Hamilton, March 8, 1801, Hamilton, *Works* (Hamilton), Vol. 6, pp. 522-24.

Page 314. *The National Intelligencer*, February 18, 1801. Thomas McKean to Jefferson, February 20, 1801, Jefferson Papers, L.C., Vol. 109, p. 18,758. Jefferson to McKean, March 9, 1801, *ibid.*, Vol. 110, p. 18,904.

Page 315. *The National Intelligencer*, February 18, 1801.

Pages 316-17. Bayard to Bassett, February 10, 1801, Donnan, p. 124. Bayard to Adams, February 19, 1801, *ibid.*, pp. 129-30, Randall, *Jefferson*, Vol. 2, p. 622; *Vindication of Bayard*, p. 23.

Page 319. Gallatin to his wife, March 5, 1801, Adams, *Gallatin*, p. 265. In Adams, *Works*, Vol. 9, p. 581, the ex-President said a storm had tossed a hundred loads of seaweed into his barnyard. "I thought I had made a good exchange," he said, "of honors and virtues for manure."

Page 320. MBS commonplace book, SHS Papers, L.C. MBS describes Jefferson's inauguration in a letter to Susan Smith, March 4, 1801, SHS Papers, L.C., Vol. 6, pp. 66,921-22.

Pages 321-23. Jefferson's first inaugural address appeared in *The National Intelligencer*, March 4, 1801, and in Richardson, *Messages and Papers of the Presidents*, Vol. 1, pp. 321-24. Drafts in Jefferson's own handwriting are in the Jefferson Papers, L.C., Vol. 110, pp. 18,836-38.

Page 324. Bayard to Hamilton, March 8, 1801, Hamilton, *Works* (Hamilton), Vol. 6, pp. 522-24. Robert Troup told Rufus King, "Jefferson's inaugural speech has had a wonderful lullaby effect." Troup to King, May 27, 1801, *King*, Vol. 3, p. 461. SHS to Mary Smith, March 7, 1801, SHS Papers, L.C., Vol. 6, p. 66,923.

Pages 325-26. MBS to Mary Smith, February 27, 1801, SHS Papers, L.C., Vol. 6, p. 66,919. Text of "The People's Friend" in Jefferson Papers, L.C., Vol. 110, pp. 18,848 and 18,896-98.

Page 327. Arthur Campbell to Madison, March 23, 1801, Madison Papers, L.C., Vol. 22, p. 25. Benjamin Ring to Jefferson, March 8, 1801, Jefferson Papers, L.C., Vol. 110, p. 18,900.

Pages 329-31. Troup to King, May 27, 1801, *King*, Vol. 3, p. 461. *Annals of Congress*, 7th Congress, 1st session, Vol. 11, pp. 640-41.

Page 332. Jefferson's diary, March 8, 1801, Jefferson Papers, L.C., Vol. 110, p. 18,892.

Page 333. MBS diary, SHS Papers, L.C.

Page 334. *The National Intelligencer*, obituary notices of MBS and SHS, June 8, 1844, and November 2, 1845.

BIBLIOGRAPHY

I. UNPUBLISHED MANUSCRIPTS

The love story of Margaret Bayard and Samuel Harrison Smith is told for the first time from the original sources, their love letters and her diaries and commonplace books. These are a treasure trove, called "The Papers of Mrs. Samuel Harrison Smith," in the Manuscript Division of the Library of Congress. The "SHS Papers," as they are cited below and in the chapter notes, also contain much firsthand material about the political turmoil of the 1796-1801 era, most of it never published before.

Other manuscripts consulted in writing this account of Thomas Jefferson's battle for the Presidency were the following in the Library of Congress:

James A. Bayard Papers
Thomas F. Bayard Papers
Aaron Burr Misc. Folder
Robert Goodloe Harper Papers
Alexander Hamilton Papers
Thomas Jefferson Papers
James McHenry Papers
James Madison Papers
James Monroe Papers
Joseph Nicholson Papers
William Plumer Manuscript Autobiography and Letters
William C. Rives Papers
J. Henley Smith Papers, including those of Jonathan Bayard Smith
General Samuel Smith Papers
George Washington Papers

II. PUBLISHED MANUSCRIPTS

Adams, Abigail. *Letters of Mrs. Adams, the Wife of John Adams,* ed. Charles Francis Adams. Boston, 1841.

————. *New Letters of Abigail Adams, 1788-1801,* ed. Stewart Mitchell. Boston, 1947.

Adams, John. *Letters of John Adams Addressed to His Wife,* ed. Charles Francis Adams. 2 vols. Boston, 1841.

————. *The Works of John Adams,* ed. Charles Francis Adams. 10 vols. Boston, 1850-56.

Adams, John Quincy. *Memoirs of John Quincy Adams, 1795-1848,* ed. Charles Francis Adams. 12 vols. Philadelphia, 1874-77.

Ames, Fisher. *Works of Fisher Ames,* ed. Seth Ames. 2 vols. Boston, 1854.

Bayard, James. "Papers of James A. Bayard," ed. Elizabeth Donnan. (American Historical Association *Report* for the Year 1913, Vol. II). Washington, D.C., 1915.

Biddle, Alexander. *Old Family Letters.* Philadelphia, 1892.

Boudinot, Elias. *The Life, Public Services, Addresses and Letters of Elias Boudinot,* ed. Jane J. Boudinot. Boston, 1896.

Burr, Aaron. *Correspondence of Aaron Burr with His Daughter, Theodosia,* ed. Mark Van Doren. New York, 1929.

————. *Memoirs of Aaron Burr,* ed. Matthew L. Davis. 2 vols. New York, 1858.

Gallatin, Albert. *Writings of Albert Gallatin,* ed. Henry Adams. 3 vols. Philadelphia, 1879.

Hamilton, Alexander. *Works of Alexander Hamilton,* ed. J. C. Hamilton. 7 vols. New York, 1851.

————. *Works of Alexander Hamilton,* ed. Henry Cabot Lodge. 12 vols. New York, 1904.

————. *The Papers of Alexander Hamilton,* ed. Harold C. Syrett. Vol. I, 1768-1778. New York, 1961.

Harper, Robert Goodloe. *Letters to Constituents,* AHA *Report,* 1913. Washington, D.C., 1915.

Jackson, Andrew. *Correspondence of Andrew Jackson,* ed. John Spencer Bassett. 7 vols. Washington, D.C., 1926-35.

Jefferson, Thomas. *The Papers of Thomas Jefferson,* ed. Julian P. Boyd. 52 vols in preparation. Princeton, N.J., 1950-.

————. *Writings of Thomas Jefferson,* ed. Paul Leicester Ford. 10 vols. New York, 1892-99.

————. *Writings of Thomas Jefferson,* ed. A. A. Lipscomb. 20 vols. Washington, D. C., 1903.

————. *The Complete Anas of Thomas Jefferson,* ed. Franklin B. Sawvel. New York, 1903.

King, Rufus. *The Life and Correspondence of Rufus King,* ed. Charles R. King. 6 vols. New York, 1894-1900.

Madison, James. *Writings of James Madison,* ed. Gaillard Hunt. 9 vols. New York, 1900-10.

Monroe, James. *Writings of James Monroe,* ed. Stanislaus Murray Hamilton. 7 vols. New York, 1898-1903.

Morris, Gouverneur. *Diary and Letters of Gouverneur Morris,* ed. Anne C. Morris. 2 vols. New York, 1888.

Rush, Benjamin. *The Letters of Benjamin Rush,* ed. L. H. Butterfield. 2 vols. American Philosophical Society, Philadelphia, 1951.

Smith, John Cotton. *The Correspondence and Miscellanies of John Cotton Smith,* by William W. Andrews. New York, 1847.

Smith, Mrs. Samuel Harrison. *The First Forty Years of Washington Society,* ed. Gaillard Hunt. New York, 1906.

Sullivan, William. *Familiar Letters on Public Characters and Public Events.* Boston, 1834.

Washington, George. *The Writings of George Washington,* ed. John C. Fitzpatrick. 39 vols. Washington, D.C., 1931-44.

Wolcott, Oliver. *Memoirs of the Administrations of Washington and John Adams,* edited from the Papers of Oliver Wolcott by George Gibbs. 2 vols. New York, 1846.

III. NEWSPAPERS

Albany, N.Y.:
  Albany Centinel
  Albany Register
Alexandria, Va.:
  Alexandria Advertiser
  Alexandria Times
Baltimore:
  Federal Gazette

Boston:
  Columbian Centinel
  Independent Chronicle
Georgetown, D.C.:
  Cabinet
  Centinel of Liberty
  Museum and Washington and George-town Daily Advertiser
  Washington Federalist
  Weekly Ledger
New Brunswick, N.J.:
  Guardian
New London, Conn.:
  Bee
New York:
  American Citizen
  American Minerva
  Argus
  Commercial Advertiser
  Daily Advertiser
  Evening Post
  Gazette
  Greenleaf's New Daily Advertiser
  Greenleaf's New York Journal
  Mercantile Advertiser
  Minerva
  Republican Watch-Tower
  Spectator
  Time Piece
  Times
Philadelphia:
  Aurora
  Claypoole's American Daily Advertiser
  Gales's Independent Gazetteer
  Gazette of the United States
  National Gazette
  New World
  Pennsylvania Gazette
  Philadelphia Gazette

Porcupine's Gazette
True American
Universal Gazette
Richmond, Va.:
  Examiner
Washington, D.C.:
  The National Intelligencer
  Universal Gazette

IV. CONTEMPORARY PAMPHLETS

Bayard, James A. *Documents Relating to the Presidential Election in the Year 1801.* Philadelphia, 1831.

Beckley, John James. *Address to the People of the United States.* Philadelphia, 1800.

Callender, James T. *The History of the United States for 1796.* Philadelphia, 1797.

Clinton, De Witt (Pseud. "Grotius"). *A Vindication of Thomas Jefferson.* New York, 1800.

Cheetham, James. *A View of the Political Conduct of Aaron Burr.* New York, 1802.

————. *Nine Letters on the Subject of Aaron Burr.* New York, 1802.

————. *A Reply to Aristides.* New York, 1804.

Hamilton, Alexander. *Letter from Alexander Hamilton Concerning the Public Conduct and Character of John Adams.* New York, 1800.

———— (anonymous), *The Alarm.* New York, 1799.

Linn, Rev. William. *Serious Considerations on the Election of a President.* New York, 1800.

Mason, Rev. John M. *The Voice of Warning.* New York, 1800.

Smith, Samuel Harrison. *Remarks on Education.* Philadelphia, 1798.

Smith, William. *The Pretensions of Thomas Jefferson to the Presidency Examined.* Philadelphia, 1796.

Van Ness, William P. (Pseud. "Aristides"). *An Examination of the Various Charges Exhibited Against Aaron Burr, Esq., Vice President of the United States; and a Development of the Characters and Views of His Political Opponents.* New York, 1803.

V. MAGAZINES

American Heritage
American Historical Review
Delaware History
Maryland Historical Magazine
Pennsylvania Magazine of History and Biography
William and Mary Quarterly

VI. PRINTED COLLECTIONS OF DOCUMENTS

American Historical Association. *Reports.*

Annals of Congress: The Debates and Proceedings of the Congress of the United States, Gales and Seaton, eds. Washington, D.C., 1834-56.

Morris, Richard B., ed. *Alexander Hamilton and the Founding of the Nation.* New York, 1957.

VII. UNITED STATES GOVERNMENT PUBLICATIONS

Biographical Directory of the American Congress. House Doc. 607, Eighty-first Congress, Second Session. Washington, D.C., Government Printing Office, 1949.

Caemmerer, H. Paul. *A Manual on the Origin and Development of Washington.* Senate Doc. 178, Seventy-fifth Congress, Third Session. Washington, D.C., Government Printing Office, 1939.

————. *Washington, the National Capital.* Senate Doc. 332, Seventy-first Congress, Third Session. Washington, D.C., Government Printing Office, 1932.

Richardson, James D., ed. *A Compilation of the Messages and Papers of the Presidents.* 20 vols. Washington, D.C., 1896-1927.

VIII. BIOGRAPHIES

Adams, Henry. *The Life of Albert Gallatin.* Philadelphia, 1879.
Adams, James Truslow. *The Adams Family.* Boston, 1930.
Alexander, Holmes. *Aaron Burr, the Proud Pretender.* New York, 1937.

Beveridge, Albert J. *The Life of John Marshall*. 4 vols. Boston and New York, 1926.

Biddle, Charles. *Autobiography*. Philadelphia, 1883.

Borden, Morton. *The Federalism of James A. Bayard*. New York, 1955.

Bowers, Claude G. *Jefferson and Hamilton*. Boston, 1925.

Brant, Irving. *James Madison*. 6 vols. Indianapolis, 1941-61.

Carroll, John Alexander, and Ashworth, Mary Wells. *George Washington*. Vol. 7, completing the biography by Douglas Southall Freeman. New York, 1957.

Chinard, Gilbert. *Honest John Adams*. Boston, 1933.

Cresson, William Penn. *James Monroe*. Chapel Hill, N.C., 1946.

Francis, John Wakefield. *Reminiscences of Samuel Latham Mitchill*. New York, 1859.

Hamilton, Allan McLane. *The Intimate Life of Alexander Hamilton*. New York, 1910.

Hamilton, John C. *Life of Alexander Hamilton*. New York, 1911.

Hatcher, William B. *Edward Livingston*. Baton Rouge, La., 1940.

Kirkpatrick, Jane, *Light of Other Days*. New Brunswick, N.J., 1856.

Lodge, Henry Cabot. *Life and Letters of George Cabot*. Boston, 1877.

Logan, Deborah N. *Memoir of Dr. George Logan of Stenton*. Philadelphia, 1899.

McLaughlin, J. Fairfax. *Matthew Lyon, the Hampden of Congress*. New York, 1900.

McRee, Griffith John. *The Life and Correspondence of James Iredell*. 2 vols. New York, 1857.

Miller, John C. *Alexander Hamilton, Portrait in Paradox*. New York, 1959.

Miller, Samuel. *The Life of Samuel Miller*. New York, 1869.

Mitchell, Broadus. *Alexander Hamilton, Youth to Maturity, 1755-1788*. New York, 1957.

Morison, Samuel Eliot. *The Life and Letters of Harrison Gray Otis, Federalist*. 2 vols. Boston and New York, 1913.

Parton, James. *The Life and Times of Aaron Burr*. 2 vols. Boston and New York, 1892.

―――. *The Life of Thomas Jefferson*. 2 vols. Boston, 1874.

359

Pickering, Octavius, and Upham, Charles W. *Life of Timothy Pickering.* 4 vols. Boston, 1867-73.

Pinckney, C. C. *Life of General Thomas Pinckney.* Boston, 1895.

Plumer, William, Jr. *Life of William Plumer.* Boston, 1857.

Randall, Henry S. *The Life of Thomas Jefferson.* 3 vols. New York, 1858.

Schachner, Nathan. *Aaron Burr.* New York, 1937.

———. *The Founding Fathers.* New York, 1954.

———. *Alexander Hamilton.* New York, 1946.

———. *Thomas Jefferson.* New York, 1951.

Steiner, Bernard C. *Life and Correspondence of James McHenry.* Cleveland, 1907.

Wandell, Samuel H., and Minnigerode, Meade. *Aaron Burr.* New York, 1925.

Wilson, James Grant. *Colonel John Bayard and the Bayard Family of America.* New York, 1885.

———. *Memorials of Andrew Kirkpatrick and His Wife, Jane Bayard.* New York, 1870.

IX. HISTORIES

Adams, Henry. *History of the United States During the Administrations of Thomas Jefferson and James Madison.* 4 vols. New York, 1909.

Channing, Edward. *History of the United States.* 6 vols. New York, 1928.

Hildreth, Richard. *History of the United States.* 6 vols. New York, 1871.

McMaster, John B. *A History of the People of the United States from the Revolution to the Civil War.* 8 vols. New York, 1883-1913.

X. SPECIALIZED WORKS

Abernethy, Thomas Perkins. *The Burr Conspiracy.* New York, 1954.

Allen, Gardner W. *Our Naval War with France.* Boston, 1909.

Beirne, Francis F. *Shout Treason: The Trial of Aaron Burr.* New York, 1959.

Bemis, Samuel F., ed. *American Secretaries of State*. 10 vols. New York, 1927-29.

————. *Jay's Treaty, a Study in Commerce and Diplomacy*. New York, 1923.

Brigham, Clarence S. *History and Bibliography of American Newspapers, 1690-1820*. 2 vols. Worcester, Mass., 1947.

Bryan, Wilhelmus Bogart. *A History of the National Capital*. 2 vols. New York, 1914.

Charles, Joseph. *The Origins of the American Party System*. Williamsburg, 1956.

Channing, Edward. *The Jeffersonian System*. New York, 1906.

Columbia Historical Society. *Records*. 52 vols. Washington, D.C., 1895-1955.

Clark, Allen Culling. *Greenleaf and Law in the Federal City*. Washington, D.C., 1901.

————. *Thomas Law, a Biographical Sketch*. Washington, D.C., 1900.

Darling, Arthur B. *Our Rising Empire, 1763-1803*. New Haven, 1940.

Dauer, Manning J. *The Adams Federalists*. Baltimore, 1953.

Dos Passos, John. *The Men Who Made the Nation*. New York, 1957.

Emery, Edwin, and Smith, Henry Ladd. *The Press and America*. New York, 1954.

Fee, Walter R. *The Transition from Aristocracy to Democracy in New Jersey, 1789-1829*. Somerville, N.J., 1933.

Francis, John W. *Old New York: or, Reminiscences of the Past Sixty Years*. New York, 1860.

Griswold, Rufus W. *The Republican Court, or American Society in the Days of Washington*. New York, 1854.

Hammond, J. D. *The History of Political Parties in the State of New York*. New York, 1852.

Kull, Irving S. *New Jersey, a History*. New York, 1931.

Kurtz, Stephen G. *The Presidency of John Adams*. Philadelphia, 1957.

Lee, Francis B. *New Jersey, Colony and State*. New York, 1902.

Mallery, Charles Payson. "Ancient Families of Bohemia Manor." Papers of the Historical Society of Delaware, VII. Wilmington, 1888.

Miller, John C. *Crisis in Freedom*. Boston, 1951.

Mott, Frank Luther. *American Journalism*. New York, 1950.

Parsons, Jacob Cox, ed. *Extracts from the Diary of Jacob Hiltz-heimer of Philadelphia, 1765-1798*. Philadelphia, 1893.

Paltsits, Victor H. *Washington's Farewell Address*. New York, 1935.

Pollard, James E. *The Presidents and the Press*. New York, 1947.

Powell, John. *Bring Out Your Dead*. Philadelphia, 1952.

Roseboom, Eugene H. *A History of Presidential Elections*. New York, 1957.

Scharf, John Thomas, and Westcott, Thompson. *History of Phila-delphia, 1609-1884*. 3 vols. Philadelphia, 1884.

Scharf, John Thomas. *History of Delaware*. 2 vols. Philadelphia, 1888.

Smith, James Morton. *Freedom's Fetters*. Ithaca, N.Y., 1956.

Stanwood, Edward. *A History of the Presidency*. Boston, 1898.

Syrett, Harold C., and Cooke, Jean G., eds. *Interview in Wee-hawken, the Burr-Hamilton Duel*. Middletown, Conn., 1960.

Westcott, Allen, ed. *American Sea Power Since 1775*. Phila-delphia, 1952.

White, Leonard. *The Federalists, a Study in Administrative History*. New York, 1948.

Wilson, James Grant. *The Memorial History of the City of New York*. 4 vols. New York, 1892.

XI. TRAVELERS' ACCOUNTS AND CONTEMPORARY GUIDEBOOKS

Davies, Benjamin. *Some Account of the City of Philadelphia, the Capital of Pennsylvania and the Seat of the Federal Congress*. Philadelphia, 1794.

Davis, John. *Travels of Four Years and a Half in the United States of America during 1798, 1799, 1800, 1801 and 1802*. Bristol, England, 1803.

Roberts, Kenneth and Anna M., eds. *Moreau de Saint-Méry's American Journey*. New York, 1947.

Rochefoucault-Liancourt, Duc de la. *Travels Through the United States of North America*. 2 vols. London, 1799.

Stephens, Thomas. *A Short Account of Philadelphia, 1796.* Philadelphia, 1796.

Twining, Thomas. *Travels in America One Hundred Years Ago.* New York, 1893.

Wansey, Henry. *An Excursion to the United States of North America in 1794.* Salisbury, England, 1798.

Weld, Isaac, Jr. *Travels Through the States of North America.* 2 vols. London, 1807.

Liston (British minister), 29
Livingston, Edward, 75, 236, 240, 248, 255, 256, 288, 289, 302, 310, 314, 330, 331, 332
Livingston, Robert, 159, 163, 248, 289
Lloyd, James, 115
Logan, George, 112, 131-32
Logan Act, 132
Louis XVI, King of France, 76
Louis Philippe, King, 20
Louisiana, 130, 131, 138, 146
Lyon, Matthew, 75, 101-3, 105, 123-25, 256, 258, 270, 289, 302, 303, 312, 314, 331

Macon, Nathaniel, 75
MacPherson, William, 142
Madison, James, 7, 156
    and election of 1800, 227-30, 231, 285
    on Hamilton's attack on John Adams, 226
    as President, 334
    refusal to go on special mission to France, 71
    and "XYZ affair," 106
Marshall, John
    Chief Justice, 316, 320
    Congressman from Virginia, 147, 158
    and election of 1800, 231, 264, 290, 294
    and Jefferson's inauguration, 320-21, 323
    Secretary of State, 167, 264, 270
    and special mission to France, 71, 106, 109, 112
Mason, Rev. John M., 221
Mason, Stevens T., 124, 125
May, Dr., 236
Mazzei, Philip, 80, 222, 264
McHenry, James, 72, 129, 139, 166, 168, 170, 219, 221, 223, 224, 242, 249, 250
McKean, Thomas, 25, 79, 112, 146, 157, 172, 284, 290, 314
McLane, Allen, 103, 171-72, 307, 308, 332, 333
Meade, E., 291

Mifflin, Thomas, 30, 37, 79
Miller, Edward, 150
Miller, Samuel, 49, 150, 171
Miranda, Francisco, 130, 131
Mitchill, Samuel Latham, 150, 151
Monroe, James
    and election of 1800, 229, 230, 290
    quoted on Burr, 8
    U. S. minister to France, 70, 79
Monticello, 7, 11, 80, 156, 174, 227, 228, 242, 333
Moore, Tom, 198
Moreau de Saint-Méry, Médéric-Louis-Eli, 20-21, 22, 59, 126
Morgan, Daniel, 103
Morris, Gouverneur, 139, 147, 234, 263, 304, 306, 324
Morris, Lewis R., 172, 256, 270, 297, 312, 331
Morris, Robert, 18, 204
Mount Vernon, 2, 129
Murray, William Vans, 136, 137, 140

National Intelligencer, The, 210-11, 219, 226, 234, 236, 237, 240, 241, 274-77, 281, 292, 294, 296, 299, 309, 314, 315, 318, 319, 333
Naturalization Act (1798), 114
New London Bee, 125, 224
New Orleans, 130
New World, 12, 14-18, 20, 23-31, 35, 37, 39, 49, 53, 56, 81, 91, 94, 119, 134
New York Commercial Advertiser, 292
"New York Friendly Club," 150
New York Gazette, 223, 286
New York Magazine, 152
New York Minerva, 80
Nicholas, John, 75, 230, 237, 296, 305, 306, 314
Nicholas, Wilson Cary, 237, 302
Nicholson, James, 161, 163-64
Nicholson, Joseph, 289-90, 297, 298, 299, 303
Nicholson, Mrs. Joseph, 299
Nicholson, Maria, 150, 285

369